Variorum Revised Editions:

M.-M. ALEXANDRESCU-DERSCA
La campagne de Timur en Anatolie (1402)

DENIS A. ZAKYTHINOS
Le Despotat grec de Morée. Histoire politique
Le Despotat grec de Morée. Vie et institutions

KENNETH M. SETTON
Catalan Domination of Athens, 1311-1388

Variorum Reprints:

NICOLAS IORGA
Philippe de Mézières et la croisade au XIVe siècle
Paris 1896 edition

In the Collected Studies series:

ANTHONY LUTTRELL
The Hospitallers in Cyprus, Rhodes, Greece and the West (1291-1440)

GEORGE T. DENNIS
Byzantium and the Franks, 1350-1420

PAUL WITTEK
La formation de l'empire ottoman

DAVID AYALON
The Mamluk Military Society

DAVID JACOBY
Recherches sur la Méditerranée orientale du XIIe au XVe siècle

DAVID JACOBY
Société et démographie à Byzance et en Romanie latine

FREDDY THIRIET
Etudes sur la Romanie gréco-vénitienne (Xe-XVe s.)

PETER TOPPING
Studies on Latin Greece, 1205-1715

BARIŠA KREKIĆ
Dubrovnik, Italy and the Balkans in the Late Middle Ages

NICOARA BELDICEANU
Le monde ottoman des Balkans (1402-1566)

Latin Greece, the Hospitallers and the Crusades 1291-1440

Dr Anthony Luttrell

Anthony Luttrell

Latin Greece, the Hospitallers and the Crusades 1291-1440

VARIORUM REPRINTS
London 1982

British Library CIP data Luttrell, Anthony
Latin Greece, the Hospitallers and the Crusades, 1291-1440. – (Collected studies series; CS158)
1. Knights of Malta – History
I. Title
271′.79 CR4723

ISBN 0-86078-106-2

Published in Great Britain by Variorum Reprints
20 Pembridge Mews London W11 3EQ

Printed in Great Britain by Galliard (Printers) Ltd
Great Yarmouth Norfolk

VARIORUM REPRINT CS158

CONTENTS

This volume contains a total of 322 pages

PREFACE

The studies reprinted below all derive in one way or another from a programme of research on the Hospitallers in the period from 1291 onwards. The only complete history of the Hospitallers at Rhodes from 1306 to 1522 which is firmly based on the archives is still that of Giacomo Bosio who died in 1629. The work of Joseph Delaville le Roulx was interrupted by his death and reached only to 1421; it was published as *Les Hospitaliers à Rhodes jusqu'à la mort de Philibert de Naillac: 1310-1421* (Paris, 1913), and was reprinted by Variorum Reprints in 1974. As what is, in effect, a supplement to it Variorum Reprints republished twenty-four articles of mine in my earlier volume in their Collected Studies series, *The Hospitallers in Cyprus, Rhodes, Greece and the West: 1291-1440* (London, 1978). The present collection adds to these publications a further sixteen studies which widen the theme in three particular directions: the historiography of the Order of the Hospital; Latin intervention and settlement in mainland Greece in which the Hospital was involved; and the changing nature of Western attitudes to the crusade, which was the major concern of the Hospital as a military order and which was increasingly directed towards the defence of Latin Greece.

The first six studies are directly concerned with the Hospital, Item I containing a summary of the state of the question, outlining problems and possibilities for future research, and presenting a survey of contemporary Hospitaller historiography. The next four pieces discuss the earlier historians of the Hospital and their sources, Item V providing a specific detailed example of their methods. A significant element in Hospitaller policy favoured the occupation of some part of mainland Greece, and the consequent need to understand Latin settlement, exploitation and colonization there, subjects for which documentation is notably scanty, led to the studies of Latin rulers in Greece and of Western policies towards Greece which are reprinted as Items VII-XIII. These items require some amendment in the light of more recent work by David Jacoby, Kenneth Setton, Peter Topping and others, much of it republished by Variorum Reprints. These articles also lead towards another project now well under way, an edition and study of the Aragonese version of the Chronicle of the Morea which was compiled for the Hospitaller Juan Fernández de Heredia. As the Turks advanced into the Balkans, the question of the defence of Latin Greece became fused with that of the crusade. Item XV is a detailed examination of one pope's reaction to this problem and of his military dependence on the Hospital. Item XVI republishes an essay written twenty years ago, before the publication of two major standard works: *A History of the Crusades*, ed. K. Setton, iii (Madison, Wisconsin, 1975), and K. Setton, *The Papacy and the Levant: 1204-1571*, i (Philadelphia, 1976).

Though the articles reprinted contain points demanding correction or additions, no alterations have been made to the text, a few errors being noted in the Corrigenda et Addenda. The original pagination of each item is retained throughout in order to avoid possible confusions when reference is made to individual studies. In such a collection an element of repetition is inevitable; many footnote references will now refer to articles elsewhere in this volume or to the collected studies published in 1978. The Royal Malta Library has become the National Library of Malta, but that presents no problems since references are always given in the form "Malta, Cod."

I am most grateful for the generosity of the editors and publishers of the items listed in the table of contents for their kind permission to reprint the materials in this volume, while my thanks go to Variorum Reprints for including this work in their series. Margaret and Cecilia Luttrell have contributed wholeheartedly to the production of the texts and index respectively. I wish also to express my gratitude for their help and encouragement across the years to Giuseppe Billanovich, Giorgio Fedalto, Jean Glénisson, David Jacoby, Anne-Marie Legras, Donald Nicol, Emilio Sáez, Kenneth Setton, Peter Topping and Elizabeth Zachariadou. Most sadly two notable mentors, both historians of the Hospital, died at the end of 1981. Sir Hannibal Scicluna, who had reached the age of a hundred and one, was outstanding both for his work in safeguarding and developing the Hospitallers' archives as also for many acts of personal kindness. The loss of Professor Lionel Butler leaves unfinished his projected history of the Hospital at Rhodes, which would have been of especial value for the period from 1421 to 1522. It was Lionel Butler who introduced me to the Order at Rhodes, who supervised my doctoral thesis at Oxford, who encouraged me to work beside him in the archives at Malta, and who in many ways promoted the study of the Hospitallers with such knowledge, understanding, care and charm. This book is a by-product of his enthusiasms for the subject and it is dedicated to his memory.

ANTHONY LUTTRELL

Mosta, Malta

January 1982

I

The Hospitallers of Rhodes: Prospectives, Problems, Possibilities[1)]

The Order of the Hospital of St. John of Jerusalem, Rhodes and Malta has almost always lacked effective historiographical machinery[2)]. There is only one complete history of the Hospital which is seriously founded on the main archive sources in Malta and Rome, that of Giacomo Bosio who died more than 350 years ago in 1627.[3)] Individual scholars have produced works on particular topics, periods or regions, but many of them are limited in scope or largely repetitive; often they fail to utilize significant materials, published or unpublished. The Hospital has survived as a chivalric or hospitaller institution; but it has been separated from its own archives on Malta since 1798 and it does not naturally produce historians of its own, while Maltese scholars have ignored the history of the Hospital during the centuries before it reached their own island in 1530.[4)] The Military Orders do attract a fringe of writers interested in bogus modern foundations or esoteric revivals, some of which are inspired by a scarcely scientific attraction for the glamours of titles,

1) The standard work is J. DELAVILLE LE ROULX, Les Hospitaliers à Rhodes jusqu'à la mort de Philibert de Naillac: 1310–1421 (Paris, 1913; reprinted with preface by A. LUTTRELL: London, 1974), supplemented by the survey in A. LUTTRELL, "The Hospitallers at Rhodes: 1306–1421," in A History of the Crusades, gen. ed. K. SETTON, iii (Madison, Wisc., 1975). This item and 23 other articles are reprinted in A. LUTTRELL, The Hospitallers in Cyprus, Rhodes, Greece and the West, 1291–1440: Collected Studies (London, 1978). The present paper looks to future problems and possibilities rather than the repetition of what has recently been published; it concentrates on the years before 1421.

2) A. LUTTRELL, "The Hospitallers' Historical Activities: [1291–1630]," Annales de l'Ordre Souverain Militaire de Malte, xxiv–xxvi (1966–1968); this work requires revision, which is under way. See also R. HIESTAND, Papsturkunden für Templer und Johanniter (Göttingen, 1972), 12–38.

3) G. BOSIO, Dell'Istoria della sacra religione et ill.ma militia di San Giovanni Gierosolimitano, 3 vols. (2nd ed. of vols. i–ii: Rome, 1622–1629; vol. iii one ed. only: Rome, 1602, reprinted Naples, 1684).

4) The Malta period offers numerous opportunities for study; even the 1565 siege awaits proper analysis. Historians tend at present to show more interest in the indigenous Maltese than in the Hospital, but R. CAVALIERO, The Last of the Crusaders: The Knights of St. John and Malta in the Eighteenth Century (London, 1960), partly fills a serious gap. Studies on the modern period have concentrated in particular on the juridical status of the Order in international law, and on emphasizing the continuities of Hospitaller achievement, the work of the Malteser-Hilfsdienst in Vietnam and other contemporary activities elsewhere.

genealogies, medals and uniforms, but serious Hospitaller history before 1530 is no one's history, devoid of effective support, of a scholarly journal, of any coherent programme. The archives are widely scattered and sometimes difficult of access. Some individual priories and commanderies have been the subject of studies which are excellent within their limitations, but the problems in the largely unexplored central archive are almost overwhelming.

The centuries before 1310, the year by which the conquest of Rhodes had definitively been concluded, are comparatively well covered for they form part of the general history of the crusades, and it was possible for Joseph Delaville le Roulx, who had a team of assistants, to collect and print the bulk of the major sources in the four mammoth volumes of his Cartulaire.[5] Delaville himself wrote a book and numerous studies on the period[6], and in 1967 Jonathan Riley-Smith published an admirable synthesis of the materials available, incorporating valuable topographical studies into new interpretations which are placed within a broad understanding of the whole crusading movement; this is the outstanding recent contribution to Hospitaller studies, especially because it provides so clear a picture of the Order's institutions.[7] Extensions or improvements are conceivable, but they would probably have made the book unmanageable and perhaps have prevented its completion. Riley-Smith makes little use of unpublished sources, although these are quite plentiful for the late thirteenth century and not insignificant for the twelfth century.[8] The lack of detailed treatment of Western affairs, though largely excusable for a period when the Hospital held extensive Eastern estates, leaves certain aspects of the Order's history untouched. Attitudes and spiritual impulses, as well as men and money, originated in the Latin West where, in Spain for example, the Hospitallers played a major role in local affairs. Much can be done with the archives of the priories, though they are probably better studied on a topographical basis across a span of centuries rather than within narrow chronological divisions. Riley-Smith's treatment of the Cypriot interlude which followed the fall of Acre in 1291 is inevitably incomplete, for at that point the papal registers, the Aragonese and other archives, the chronicles and the crusading treatises all begin to provide a mass of material, much of it not fully published.

There would be advantages in a periodization of Hospitaller history which emphasized admittedly arbitrary turning points such as 1271, with the fall of Krac des Chevaliers, or 1334, with the renewal of active Hospitaller crusading, rather than the habitual 1291 or

5) Cartulaire général de l'Ordre des Hospitaliers de S. Jean de Jérusalem, ed. J. DELAVILLE LE ROULX, 4 vols. (Paris, 1894–1906).

6) IDEM, Les Hospitaliers en Terre Sainte et à Chypre: 1100–1310 (Paris, 1904); IDEM, Mélanges sur l'Ordre de S. Jean de Jérusalem (Paris, 1910).

7) J. RILEY-SMITH, The Knights of St. John in Jerusalem and Cyprus: c. 1050–1310 (London, 1967).

8) Cf. HIESTAND, 43–200 et passim. Archaeological evidence naturally continues to emerge in Acre and other towns, in castles and villages: M. BENVENISTI, The Crusaders in the Holy Land (trans: New York, 1972).

1310, just as it was in many ways the great siege of Malta in 1565 rather the loss of Rhodes in 1522 or the acquisition of Malta in 1530 which truly marked the beginning of a new epoch.[9] The problems of the period from 1310 to 1522, for which the second edition of Bosio of 1629 is still the only overall coverage, lie not merely in the quantity of unpublished sources but also in their inequalities, since the fifteenth-century material is more considerable and consistent than that for the fourteenth century, particularly after 1459 when many texts illustrating the decision-making processes become available in the *Libri Conciliorum.* In some ways the Rhodes period needs to be studied and interpreted as a whole; in fact, given the lack of fourteenth-century documents, certain institutional themes can be treated only in that way. Delaville le Roulx' volume on the years 1310 to 1421 appeared posthumously and was never continued to 1522 as its author had intended, and most subsequent studies have been concerned primarily with the pre-1421 period. The massive documentation at Malta, in the prioral archives, and in other published and unpublished sources very largely remains to be exploited. The Greek and Turkish materials, together with a daunting and almost inexhaustible range of printed items of astonishing diversity in topic and quality, are still to be studied, as are a wide variety of problems stretching right across Mediterranean and Western history. The history of the Hospital from 1421 to 1565 awaits its historians.

Delaville le Roulx' final work contains much information for the period down to 1421 and it outlines the broad political developments, but his book is awkwardly arranged in such a way that chapters correspond chronologically to successive Masters of the Hospital which impedes any coherent treatment of institutional arrangements. Delaville failed, furthermore, to overcome the difficult problem of integrating two major complications into his account. One of these was the continued disturbance caused in the Order's affairs by that extraordinary personality the Aragonese Hospitaller Fr. Juan Fernández de Heredia; the other was the papal schism which from 1378 onwards impinged heavily, though not in the end disastrously, on numerous aspects of the Hospital's activities. For the rest, Delaville's genealogical hypotheses occupy space which would now be devoted to social and economic realities, while Hospitaller attitudes and motivations demand interpretation. Financial and manpower resources, royal and papal policies require investigation, and the whole context of developments throughout the East and West, and especially in the priories, remains to be elaborated and related to the Hospital's central problems at Rhodes.[10]

9) L. Butler, "The Maltese People and the Order of St. John in the Sixteenth Century," Annales de l'Ordre Souverain Militaire de Malte, xxiii–xxiv (1963–1964).
10) Cf. A. Luttrell's introduction to the 1974 reprint of Delaville (1913).

Apart from difficulties with bibliographies[11] and with finding books,[12] there can be little immediate hope of cataloguing or absorbing the narrative sources or the contents of the greater and lesser archival repositories which should eventually produce major contributions to the Hospital's history. The archives of priories and commanderies contain a mass of valuable local information and occasional items of direct central importance.[13] The Malta documents are incompletely, but none the less usefully, catalogued.[14] The earliest surviving portion of a Master's annual register dates to 1346, and there are registers for the years 1347/8, 1351/2, 1358/9, 1365/6 and 1374, but the rest of the period from 1310 to 1380 has to be studied from original papal and Magistral bulls, from the acts of the Chapters-General and from other miscellaneous materials; these must be supplemented from the prioral archives, from the Vatican registers and from sundry information gathered here and there. The Magistral registers from 1381 to 1396 were mostly kept in Avignon where the Master was then residing, and only in 1399 does a regular series of Rhodian registers commence. Hospitaller studies therefore require a combination of scattered archival sources, and the need to work in Malta and Rome as well as in Madrid, Marseilles, Venice, London or elsewhere is one of the factors which make Hospitaller research so complex and slow.

11) The compilation of a satisfactorily complete bibliography presents almost totally insuperable problems. Much important material is contained in works with a title which has no connection with the Order; other items which do deal directly with the Hospital are valueless or trivial. The standard work is F. de HELLWALD, Bibliographie méthodique de l'Ordre de S. Jean de Jérusalem (Rome, 1885), which omits many works, and the *aggiunta* to it in E. ROSSI, Riassunto storico del S. M. Ordine di San Giovanni Gerosolimitano (Rome, 1924); these two works were reprinted in one volume in 1968. ROSSI published further *aggiunte* in revised editions of his Riassunto (Rome, 1929, 1934). Many recent works are listed in J. MIZZI, "A Bibliography of the Order of St. John of Jerusalem: 1925–1969", in The Order of St. John in Malta, ed. for the Council of Europe (Malta, 1970), which records 1507 titles. See also G. FUMAGALLI, Bibliografia rodia (Florence, 1937), and the "Aggiunte e correzioni" to it published by E. ARMAO, in La Bibliofilia, xlvi (1944). Other bibliographies are listed in MIZZI, 108–117, and P. XUEREB, A Bibliography of Maltese Bibliographies (Malta, 1978). Also useful are H. MAYER, Bibliographie zur Geschichte der Kreuzzüge (Hanover, 1960), and IDEM, "Literaturbericht über die Geschichte der Kreuzzüge: Veröffentlichungen 1958–1967," Historische Zeitschrift, ccvii (1969).

12) Some relevant works are expensive, rare or unobtainable even in major national libraries, but many books, together with invaluable collections of offprints and other opuscula, can be found in special collections, notably the Order's own library at Palazzo Malta, Via Condotti, Rome; the "Melitensia" collection at the University of Malta; the library at St. John's Gate, Clerkenwell, London; the Scicluna Collection at Rhodes House, Oxford; and the Foster Stearns Collection at the Catholic University of America, Washington, DC, catalogued in O. KAPSNER, A Catalog of the Foster Stearns Collection . . . (Washington, 1955).

13) Eg. text in LUTTRELL (1978), III 771–773. On the prioral archives, see DELAVILLE, Cartulaire, i. pp. XXVII–CCXXX; HIESTAND, 47–168.

14) A. ZAMMIT GABARRETTA et al., Catalogue of the Records of the Order of St. John of Jerusalem in the Royal Malta Library, i- (Malta, 1964–).

Delaville's Cartulaire closes in 1310 and, despite the many losses in the archives, there can be no question of continuing it to include the voluminous and almost entirely unpublished body of later documents. However, in addition to the major publication of the papal inquests of 1373,[15] other editions are under way. The statutes for 1330 have been printed[16] and those for 1311 and 1315 are in preparation, while the statutes subsequent to 1330 also await publication, a matter much complicated by their survival in variant manuscripts and languages.[17] Two versions of the brief but informative obituaries known as the *Cronica Magistrorum Defunctorum* are in print,[18] but the wide variety of redactions, translations and local variants of this short chronicle is being collated. A fascinating, but seriously mutilated, roll of proposals for the reform of the Hospital made between 1334 and 1342 by an anonymous Hospitaller is also being prepared for publication,[19] as are various detailed financial accounts, mostly those of the Receiver-General in the West, which date from 1365 onwards.[20] These are some of the major *desiderata.* Other materials migth more usefully be calendared; for example, a list of all surviving Magistral bulls from 1310 to 1346 would not only be of general utility but would facilitate the study of Hospitaller chancery practice. The poor handwriting of many scribes at Rhodes, some of them possibly Greeks, creates real difficulties, but it seems important that scholars should have at least some published specimen texts to give an idea of the form and phrasing of Hospitaller documents.[21]

Turning from texts to topics, many subjects await research: the colonization and defence of the Rhodian islands; the condition of their Greek inhabitants; the background of crusading and trading affairs, of Byzantine collapse and Turkish expansion; and relations with the popes and princes, bankers and sea-captains on whom the Hospital depended. Hospitaller studies can provide new insights into relatively unexplored areas; they also possess a certain topical relevance in that they illuminate a late-medieval "NATO-cum-Red Cross" type of organization operating on the front line of an ideologi-

15) Infra, 257–258, 260.

16) Text in C. TIPTON, "The 1330 Chapter General of the Knights Hospitallers at Montpellier", Traditio, xxiv (1968).

17) There was no Chapter-General in 1370, a confusion deriving from errors in the contemporary sources and found in BOSIO, ii. 117, and in DELAVILLE (1913), 166–169. There was an unnoticed Hospitaller assembly at Montpellier in 1325: Archivio Vaticano, Reg. Vat. 81, f. 397–401v.

18) In W. DUGDALE, Monasticon Anglicanum, vi part 2 (London, 1830), 796–798, and in L. DE MAS LATRIE, "Notice sur les Archives de Malte à Cité-la-Valette," Archives des missions scientifiques et littéraires, 1 ser., vi (1857), 26–30.

19) Toulouse, Archives départementales de la Haute-Garonne: H. Malte 237.

20) Specimen text and details in J. NISBET, "Treasury Records of the Knights of St. John in Rhodes," Melita Historica, ii no. 2 (1957); cf. LUTTRELL (1978), VII, VIII. Some general accounts from the West dating ca. 1319/1325 are printed in J. MIRET Y SANS, Les cases de Templers y Hospitalers en Catalunya (Barcelona, 1910), 317–402.

21) As eg. in LUTTRELL (1978), III 771–775, IX 382–383, XIV 511; on the chancery ibid., XV.

cal "cold war" between two very different societies. The Hospitallers were defending the frontiers of Christendom in general and not those of their own homelands, while they differed from other Military Orders in their "multi-national" composition, with brethren of many tongues or *langues* residing together inside their *collachium* or convent walls yet living in daily confrontation with Greeks, Turks and others.

To what extent a body of such diverse social, educational and geographical origins possessed a collective ethos or mentality is hard to determine from the type of documentation available concerning so largely illiterate a group. As Philippe de Mézières alleged, many became Hospitallers and made a brief visit to Rhodes merely in order to secure a comfortable livelihood on a European commandery,[22] possibly doing a term of garrison duty without any active fighting against the infidel in order to secure promotion and a safe career in the West with a routine devoted to the liturgy, to estate management and to participation in local affairs. Some never went to the Levant; in point of fact, the majority of brethren were priests. Most Hospitallers were essentially normal men who had chosen a marginally unusual life. They were not the *pauperes* or flagellants, the husbands escaping from wives or other types of hysterical pilgrim so convincingly studied by sociologically-minded crusading historians. Nor had their activity much to do with chivalry. The Hospital provided a permanent, disciplined, experienced, even brutal corps of trained military men whose value in action went far beyond their restricted numbers. There was a mystique of martyrdom for the Cross of the type which Catherine of Siena propounded to the Prior of Pisa before the Hospital's *passagium* of 1378 – "bathe yourself in the blood of Christ crucified";[23] yet few men can have been drawn to the Order by such sententious ideals. There may have been families with a tradition of entry into the Order, but it is doubtful how far one can positively identify a Hospitaller mentality, a residue of military-monastic sentiment supposedly preserved in a life of poverty, chastity and obedience spent apart from family, women and children. Despite a degree of laxity in observing the rules, this renunciation constituted a genuine problem. Even that profound idealist Philippe de Mézières in drawing up the rules for his model Military Order provided for his *chevaliers* to live in conjugal chastity with wives, since complete chastity was difficult to achieve and he considered that its demands were seriously restricting recruitment to other existing Orders;[24] the Spanish Order of Santiago did in fact allow marriage for its brethren and a conventual life for their families. There must have been established traditions and an *esprit de corps* at Rhodes, but convincing generalizations demand a great gathering of biographi-

22) Cited in LUTTRELL (1978), I 300.

23) Epistole devotissime de sancta Catharina da Siena . . . (Venice, 1500), no. xlvi, to Niccolò, Prior of Pisa, who had gone to Venice to prepare the *passagium.* This was presumably the prior's mission of April 1377: LUTTRELL (1978) V 207. The Prior of Pisa, Fr. Niccolò de Strozzi of Florence, was at Vonitza with the *passagium* on 24 April 1378: Malta, cod. 48, f. 168v–169.

24) Text in A. HAMDY, "Philippe de Mézières and the New Order of the Passion," Bulletin of the Faculty of Arts [Alexandria], xviii (1964), 81; cf. PHILIPPE DE MÉZIÈRES, Letter to King Richard II, ed. G. COOPLAND (Liverpool, 1975).

cal details on the careers of individual brethren, with literary texts and informal non-chancery documents perhaps offering the clearest insights into Hospitaller attitudes.

*

The Hospital of St. John was founded at the beginning of the twelfth century as a charitable and medical body, but it gradually acquired a predominantly military character. Like the Temple, the Teutonic Order and the Hispanic Orders of Santiago, Calatrava and Alcántara, the Hospital had its own rule which in the Hospitallers' case was a variation on that of the Augustinians; it had its Master and governing officers, dependent ultimately on the pope; its priories and commanderies with their *milites,* sergeants-at-arms and priests, together with the lay brethren and female members; its privileges, exemptions, estates and incomes; and its military and colonizing functions. In addition to the lesser Orders and the predominantly local confraternities, there were numerous exclusively hospitaller Orders as well as the select chivalric groups such as the Orders of the Garter and the Golden Fleece, but these lacked any genuinely military character.[25] The Hospital and the Temple developed above all in Latin Syria where both Orders played a leading role in the kingdom's political and military affairs, acquiring great estates, building castles, shaping policies and increasing their own importance as the Latin domain dwindled to a slim seaboard strip which was finally extinguished with the fall of Acre in 1291, when the two Orders withdrew to Cyprus. There ensued an epoch of crises and confusions which set new patterns for decades to come. The papacy came under lay attack and moved to France; while the affairs of Greeks, Turks and Armenians, Mongols and Mamluks, were all in upheaval. The crusade changed its character and, directly or indirectly, the whole context in which the Hospital operated was reshuffled so that the Order was forced to alter many of its modes of existence. Cyprus proved an unsatisfactory base. The Temple was attacked in 1307 and suppressed in 1312; the Teutonic Order, which had retreated from Syria to Venice, transferred its headquarters to Prussia in 1309; and between 1306 and 1310 the Hospital conquered Rhodes. This conquest and the settlement of the island, together with the lengthy process of absorbing the Templars' goods into the Hospital, form two principal early fourteenth-century themes.

Turning from this mélange of problems and prospectives to matters more securely established, an understanding of the Hospitallers' difficulties during the years after 1291 is essential. The hostile attitudes and perennial instabilities of the Cypriot Crown, the mirage of Mongol collaboration, and the impracticability of old-style anti-Mamluk crusading directed towards Egypt and Syria, all constituted serious drawbacks. The Latins' strength was in their sea-power but the Military Orders, though now established on an island, continued to lack effective fleets. The Templars defended the island of Ruad off Tortosa until 1302. The Hospitallers seriously considered a major commitment in Christian

25) No comprehensive bibliography covers these lesser orders, but note A. FOREY, "The Military Order of St. Thomas of Acre," English Historical Review, xciii (1977).

Cilicia[26] but eventually they opted for the acquisition of Rhodes which ultimately did provide a defensible, independent base for crusading activity. However, important questions remain concerning the conquest of Rhodes. It is not yet clear to what extent it had previously been under Turkish control; what were the motives of the Hospital's Genoese allies; whether the conquest was really completed in 1308, 1309, or 1310; or whereabouts the mainland acquisitions which came with the islands were situated. The affairs of the Emirate of Menteshe and the identity of the Turks with whom the Hospitallers made an alliance remain obscure, though their leader may have been the Emir's son-in-law Sasa.[27] Equally obscure are the machinations of the Master Fr. Foulques de Villaret who spent much of the time from 1307 to 1309 at the papal *curia* negotiating for the money and shipping which sailed eastwards in 1310 apparently to accomplish little more than the final subjection of the Rhodian islands which had already been largely subdued.

A complete muster of all the evidence – Turkish, Greek, Catalan, papal and so forth – might well reveal ambiguities amounting to fraud in the Hospitallers' declarations of intent, as the Aragonese party at Avignon and others indeed alleged. The papal bulls and the *Vitae Paparum* were possibly inspired by deceptions engineered by Fr. Foulques de Villaret, who may have misled the pope not only about events at Rhodes but also about his own intentions; possibly he was manoeuvring to grab Greek islands by securing troops and credits in the West on false pretences while treating with the Turks in the East and thus ensuring the Hospital's acquisition of Rhodes and, indirectly, the Order's very survival. After Boniface VIII's quarrel with the French Crown the papacy moved to France and the Templars were attacked. This created a psychological climate in which it was essential for the Hospital to succeed, where the Temple had partly failed, in projecting a defensible image before pope, council and public opinion. The sources for the final decades of the Templars' history are more numerous than has generally been recognized,[28] and much

26) A. LUTTRELL, "The Hospitallers' Interventions in Cilician Armenia: 1291–1375," in The Cilician Kingdom of Armenia, ed. T. BOASE (Edinburgh, 1978).

27) LUTTRELL (1978), I 287, states that Villaret "curbed the power of Orkhan, Emir of Menteshe, and incited the other emirs . . ." However, Marino Sanudo actually wrote that Villaret supported Orkhan *e suo fratello Strumbachi* against Orkhan's father, the emir. Possibly *Strumbachi* was Sasa (described by Pachymeres as the emir's "son-in-law") who captured Ephesus in 1304 but then went over to the Christians and was slain: the sources, listed in P. LEMERLE, L'Émirat d'Aydin, Byzance et l'Occident (Paris, 1957), 16, 20–24, may require detailed reinterpretation. A late source suggests that Nisyros was taken from the Turks before mid-1316: LUTTRELL (1978), III 759 n. 2. Villaret himself was accused of treating with the Turks: DELAVILLE (1913), 16. Turkish disruption on Rhodes may be reflected by the discovery in a grotto just above a frescoed chapel of 34 gold Byzantine coins, the latest datable 1282–1328, and 39 silver Muslim coins, the latest datable 1290: C. BRANDI, "La Cappella rupestre del Monte Paradiso", Memorie: Istituto Storico-Archeologico di Rodi, iii (1938), 10, mistakenly giving Hegira 689 as 1311 rather than 1290.

28) Apart from the detailed analysis of a great deal of prosopographical material in the sources already published and the reworking of the Aragonese materials used by HEINRICH FINKE, there is the possibility of using computer techniques to restore passages in largely illegible documents such as the

remains to be explained not merely about their dissolution but about the reasons why the Hospital, though it was criticized, was seldom accused in the same way as the Temple, and why the Hospitallers not only escaped unscathed but even received the bulk of the Templars' goods. There had long been a strong current of criticism in the West directed against all the Military Orders in general and especially against their privileges, but opinion looked to the union or reform of the two great Orders rather than for their abolition. It was probably true, though it would be difficult to demonstrate with precision, that the Hospitallers were more subtle than the Templars in avoiding provocation and that they had less wealth and were less involved in financial operations, though these do not seem entirely adequate explanations for an extremely complex problem.

In one sense the pope, unintentionally perhaps, sacrificed the Temple to save the Hospital, at the same time securing in practice that union of the two Orders which had so frequently been advocated. Certain cardinals were anxious that the Temple's goods should continue to be devoted to the crusade, while the French king, having secured the destruction of the Templars who had opposed his plans for a single unified Order, perhaps hoped to gain control of the Hospital. In the great struggle between popes, kings, cardinals, counsellors and propagandists for the very considerable wealth still theoretically devoted to the crusade, only one party could claim a victory; the triumph of Foulques de Villaret and the Hospital was as spectacular as the failure of Jacques de Molay and the Temple. This extraordinary achievement has seldom been appreciated, and its explanation awaits a major study devoted to that single extremely complex point, for the collapse of the Temple cannot be understood without a clarification of the Hospital's role, while the history of the Hospital is explicable only in the light of the Temple *affaire*.[29] The Hospitallers realized that they had profitted, and their Lieutenant in the West even told the pope on 30 March 1313 that he had made them a greater gift than the Donation of

Templar inquest in the Papal States: A. GILMOUR-BRYSON, in Manuscripta, xxi no. 1 (1977), 14; xxii no. 1 (1978), 7–8. See also M. BARBER, The Trial of the Templars (Cambridge, 1978), which had not appeared at the time of writing.

29) The details of Villaret's itinerary and the chronology and background of the conquest in France and Aragon are still confused: see especially J. HILLGARTH, Ramon Lull and Lullism in Fourteenth-Century France (Oxford, 1971), 64–107; L. THIER, Kreuzzugsbemühungen unter Papst Clemens V.: 1305–1314 (Werl, 1973), 82–89; M. BULSTE-THIELE, Sacrae Domus Militiae Templi Hierosolymitani Magistri: Untersuchungen zur Geschichte des Templerordens 1118/9–1314 (Göttingen, 1975), 313–316, 344–346. BULSTE-THIELE, 350, misinterprets a passage now in LUTTRELL (1978), XI 2, which does not indicate acceptance of the French king's charges against the Temple. J. FAVIER, Philippe le Bel (Paris, 1978), 425–480, restates the case for the king, emphasizing the deficiencies of the French Templars. J. FAVIER, Un Conseiller de Philippe le Bel: Enguerran de Marigny (Paris, 1963), 123–124, 143–148, 185–188, shows how Marigny worked to secure the Temple goods for the Hospital because this was in the king's interest; his reiterated assertion that the Hospitallers influenced, or even bribed, Marigny is not supported by the documents.

Constantine,[30] but the experience of the brutal tortures used to destroy the Temple and the memory of the burning of the Master and many other brethren must have haunted the Hospitallers for many decades.

The move to Rhodes almost suggests that the Hospitallers, having acknowledged the general renunciation of Jerusalem as a practical goal, had shrewdly anticipated the transformation of the crusade into a defensive struggle against the Turks.[31] Latin society, in which an *esprit laïque* was increasingly strong, was turning not only against the papacy but also against the crusade which too often seemed to be a papal instrument exploited largely for political ends. The Hospital was an integral part of the Church and as such dependent on the papacy, and all the more obviously and inescapably so after the dissolution of the Temple; yet if it could not abandon the crusade which was its *raison d'être* it could in its own ways divert, or even pervert, it. Idealistic theorists such as Ramon Llull and Philippe de Mézières were not without their practical influence, but more decisive considerations were those of money. Western governments exercized a measure of control over ecclesiastical wealth and nominations. They could prevent Hospitallers and their monies leaving for the East and could convert the Order's resources for their own temporal ends, while by influencing appointments they were able to secure the effective "nationalization" of the Military Orders. Rulers who asserted the Templars' innocence none the less seized, and often retained, their goods while the flow of endowments and donations to the Hospital diminished to a sporadic trickle. Behind these secularizing trends lay unavoidable determinations of finance. The Templars' financial activities had something to do with their downfall; the Hospitallers' crusade of 1310 augmented the debts which dominated their policies until about 1334. Crusading activities and inactivities, constitutional disputes, promotions and indiscipline, royal and papal policies, in fact almost every aspect of Hospitaller affairs, turned on the availability of funds or on schemes to appropriate or misappropriate crusading and Hospitaller incomes, so that the genuinely ideological content in the Order's policies was often largely obscured.

In the absence of detailed accounts before about 1365[32] the very real financial obstacles to crusading action can be estimated only indirectly. The number of brethren who could be supported in Cyprus had to be limited in 1295,[33] and eleven years later only two galleys were available for the invasion of Rhodes.[34] In 1320 the enormous debts which had been

30) ... *et quod mayorem donacionem fecerat inde Hospitali, quam fuisset facta per aliquem citra donationem, quam fecit Constantinus imperator ecclesie Romanie:* text in H. FINKE, Papsttum und Untergang des Templerordens, ii (Münster, 1907), 219–221.

31) Cf. F. CARDINI, "La Crociata nel Duecento: L'Avatara di una ideale," Archivio Storico Italiano, cxxxv (1977).

32) While incomes are not generally available, there are totals of *responsiones* theoretically due; for the dues fixed in 1330, see the text in TIPTON, 301–304.

33) Unpublished magistral bull dated Nicosia, 31 March 1295, in Malta, cod. 16 no. 8, summarized in DELAVILLE, Cartulaire, iii, no. 4276.

34) LUTTRELL (1978), II 163 n. 3.

incurred to finance the acquisition of the Temple's lands stood at more than 580,000 florins, more than twice the ordinary annual income of the papacy, and they could not be extinguished until about 1334, despite extraordinary impositions and the large-scale alienation of Templar properties.[35] A credit then accumulated and in 1334 and 1335 the Hospital was actively pursuing an aggressive crusading programme around Smyrna.[36] The new pope, Benedict XII, seems deliberately to have obstructed these initiatives, partly to avoid the papal declaration of a crusade which would have involved the assignation of clerical crusading tenths to the French king who would almost certainly have employed the incomes for his English war.[37] Benedict must furthermore have realized that a Hospitaller crusade would mean the withdrawal of funds from the pope's own banks, which were in serious difficulties. He may, therefore, have discouraged Hospitaller activity and, when the Bardi, Peruzzi and Acciaiuoli went bankrupt soon after, the Hospital lost the very large reserve of some 360,000 florins which it had deposited with them; by 1351 the number of brethren at Rhodes had to be restricted.[38] Nevertheless, the Hospital continued to participate in crusading initiatives, most spectacularly in the Latin recapture of the castle in Smyrna harbour in 1344, in the sack of Alexandria in 1365, and in the Nicopolis crusade of 1396.

The Hospital also resisted in other ways of its own, defending the seas around Rhodes, defeating the Turks of Miletus in 1312 and those of Ephesus in 1319, and to some extent bottling them up so that the Emir of Aydin moved his naval operations northwards to Smyrna.[39] After the Christians recaptured Smyrna in 1344, the Hospitallers became

35) LUTTRELL (1978), VIII 317–318.
36) The account of the attack on Lesbos, in which the Hospital at first participated, given in LUTTRELL (1978), I 293, is too condensed. Lesbos seems to have been invaded late in 1334: P. SCHREINER, "Zur Geschichte Philadelpheias im 14. Jahrhundert: 1293–1390," Orientalia Christiana Periodica, xxxv (1969), 398, 418. Difficulties remain, but this invasion may have followed the unsuccessful Byzantine-Cypriot-Hospitaller attack on Smyrna in or after September 1334: LEMERLE, 100–101. The Hospitallers withdrew either because Cattaneo cheated them or in the face of a Byzantine counter-attack; LEMERLE, 108, is scarcely justified in saying that Cattaneo evicted them. The chronology of this period will be further revised in forthcoming publications by Dr. Elisabeth Zachariadou.
37) A. LUTTRELL, "The Crusade in the Fourteenth Century," in J. HALE et al., Europe in the Late Middle Ages (London, 1965), 133–134; LUTTRELL (1978), I 293–294 et passim. Other objectives were Lesbos, and, possibly, Armenian Cilicia.
38) LUTTRELL (1978), I 294–296; VIII 318–319.
39) LUTTRELL (1978), I 288–289, 293, describes three battles, reduced to two in ibid., XXV 1. L. GATTO, "Per la storia di Martino Zaccaria signore di Chio," Bulletino dell'Archivio Paleografico Italiano, ns. ii–iii (1956–1957), publishes further documents but is probably incorrect in dating that of 1 September to 1318. Distressingly little is known about the Emirate of Menteshe in classical Caria. P. WITTEK, Das Fürstentum Mentesche: Studie zur Geschichte Westkleinasiens im 13.–15. Jh. (Istanbul, 1934), now requires amendment; the present author plans to publish a study of Hospitaller relations with the Turks between 1306 and 1344.

increasingly responsible for the castle's defence and between 1343 and 1349 they had charge of the papal payments for the Genoese galleys serving the Latin league in the Aegean; in 1359 Fr. Niccolò Benedetti became papal Captain of Smyrna, receiving various pecuniary and commercial rewards.[40)] In 1374, following scandals over the accounts of the Genoese captains who were supposed to pay the garrison, Smyrna castle was entrusted entirely to the Hospital,[41)] and in 1391, as Turkish pressure grew, Pope Clement VII granted a special indulgence which raised considerable sums for its defence.[42)] In 1402 Smyrna castle was brutally destroyed by the Mongol leader Timur. The Hospitallers began to rebuild the castle and when their new work was dismantled by the Ottoman Mehmed, the Master reportedly protested to the Turks that the pope would send a great force to destroy Mehmed's realms.[43)] The Hospitallers clearly felt the need of a substitute for Smyrna, and they soon constructed a new castle on the mainland opposite Kos on the site – though they did not know it – of the ancient Halikarnassos, securing a new, and presumably lucrative, papal indulgence for it in 1409.[44)] The Hospital defended its own territories while presenting the West with a show of crusading action which had across the years after 1306 gone at least some way towards containing the Turks of the Anatolian seaboard.

A particular current of Hospitaller opinion looked, chiefly to Greece, for a less routine, more active field of action or at least for wider, richer lands to dominate. In 1351 the Hospital briefly acquired the castle of Karystos on Negroponte; in 1356 and 1357 an obscure and secret *negotium Achaye* concerned the Morea, possibly Corinth; in 1376 the Hospitallers leased the Principality of Achaea for five years, but were eventually driven out by the mercenaries of the Navarrese Companies; in 1378 the Hospitallers, having secured rights to the Principality of Achaea and to the port of Vonitza, invaded Epirus with a small expedition which was ignominiously ambushed by the Albanians of Arta, who captured and ransomed the Master Fr. Juan Fernández de Heredia; from 1384 that Master made repeated attempts to acquire claims and launch interventions in the Morea; and between 1397 and 1404, at a crucial moment of danger from the Turks, the Hospital defended the Castellany of Corinth and the Despotate of the Morea, which it had purchased from the Byzantine Despot Theodore. Then, in 1405, the Hospitallers proposed to refortify the

40) Details in K. SETTON, The Papacy and the Levant: 1204–1571, i (Philadelphia, 1976), 186–187, 191, 194 n. 165, 202–203, 208–210, 218, 222–223, 234–236.

41) Cf. SETTON, i. 328.

42) DELAVILLE (1913), 231.

43) DUCAS, translated in Decline and Fall of Byzantium to the Ottoman Turks, ed. H. MAGOULIAS (Detroit, 1975), 117–118; the chronology of this episode is obscure.

44) DELAVILLE (1913), 318. The present author is preparing a study of these fortifications between 1407 and 1421 in collaboration with Professor Kristian Jeppesen and the Danish mission excavating the nearby Mausoleum.

island of Tenedos at the mouth of the Dardanelles. This whole complicated trend of interest in Greece requires detailed elucidation.[45)]

*

Many aspects of Hospitaller rule await investigation in the Malta archives, and researches there should be supplemented by survey and excavation work in the Rhodian islands. The massive sixteenth-century gunpowder fortifications at Rhodes largely obliterated the earlier defences which require a theoretical reconstruction built up through a topographical approach.[46)] Place-names, patterns of agrarian settlement and the castles defending Rhodes and the other islands all need further study. A considerable emporium, a naval base and a banking centre developed at Rhodes, where the Hospitallers and other Latins protected corsairs, trafficked in slaves and imported foodstuffs, horses, war materials and Western cloth. The registers at Malta document militiamen and galley-crews, Greek and Latin colonists, taxation and justice, land-holding, the pilgrim trade, the Order's great hospital, the position of the Greek church, and the Jewish and Armenian minorities. The Hospitallers evolved a system of relations between rulers and ruled which is difficult to parallel elsewhere, and its study should take account of developments on Chios, Cyprus, Crete and other islands. Rhodes was a colonial society in so far as a Latin class governed a Greek population, but it was not a typical colony exploited by a foreign metropolis; in fact, in Hospitaller terminology *outremer* meant Western Europe. Feudal contracts were rare, and the land was not held by foreign dynasties established on it as a perpetual nobility. Though they certainly disrupted Greek ways of life, the Latins somehow established a paternalistic relationship, perhaps evolved in Syria, with their subjects who were reasonably secure and well treated. There were no uprisings of indigenous Greeks or Latin colonists such as occurred, for example, on nearby Crete.[47)]

The government of the Order involved very much more than the limited problems of the Rhodian islands, which were managed by the Master and a group of senior brethren. Periodical Chapters-General met at Rhodes or sometimes in Southern France to promulgate new statutes and to deal with promotions, discipline and taxation. The Hospital was

45) LUTTRELL (1978), I 296–297, 302–303, 306–310, V 208–210; A. LUTTRELL, "La Corona de Aragón y la Grecia Catalana: 1379–1394," Anuario de Estudios Medievales, vi (1969), 242–248. Concerning Tenedos, see SETTON, i. 326. These matters will be covered in a forthcoming biography of Juan Fernández de Heredia; an edition and study of the Aragonese version of the Chronicle of the Morea compiled for Fernández de Heredia is also in preparation.

46) References in LUTTRELL (1978), I 292 n. 22, 311 n. 65. The well-preserved medieval Latin town, now dramatically threatened by plaster-wash, concrete, tourists and new "medieval" building, urgently requires, at the very least, an emergency campaign of photographic record. Recent archaeological activity is recorded in the journal Archaeologikon Deltion; on the Byzantine church beneath Santa Maria del Castello, ibid., xxv (1970), 518–527.

47) Cf. LUTTRELL (1978), passim, and A. LUTTRELL, "Slavery at Rhodes: 1306–1440", Bulletin de l'Institut Historique Belge de Rome, xlvi–xlvii (1976–1977).

largely dominated by a majority of French-speaking brethren, some of whom had predominantly Levantine careers at Rhodes while others controlled the French priories; until 1377 the Master was always a Frenchman. This quasi-monopoly of power was periodically resisted by brethren of other *langues*, and occasionally it was seriously threatened. Fr. Foulques de Villaret, the over-mighty Master who conquered Rhodes, was forcibly deposed in 1317. The ensuing squabble was settled by Pope John XXII who chose his successor, reflecting the universal trend towards papal interference and papal provisions throughout the Roman Church. This danger was enhanced by the pope's power to threaten disestablishment Temple-style, and it became more real when the Aragonese Hospitaller Fr. Juan Fernández de Heredia obtained the patronage of a succession of popes who encouraged his insubordinations and his self-aggrandizement in the Western priories, of which at one point he controlled no less than three, and who in 1377 invoked papal prerogatives to provide him, against the protests of the French oligarchy at Rhodes, to the Mastership itself. Such developments can be studied in various ways. The Vatican archives naturally reflect the changing nature of papal interference; thus Fernández de Heredia's election, previously misunderstood and explained in various misleading ways, has now been documented from Gregory XI's registers.[48)] Papal relations can also be illustrated iconographically. A Hospitaller *cubicularius* guards a sleeping pope in a fresco at Assisi.[49)] Fr. Juan Fernández de Heredia stands in a papal group in what may be to some extent a crusading scene painted in the great *ecclesia* fresco at Santa Maria Novella in Florence.[50)] Ulrich Richental's Konzilschronik shows the Master, Fr. Philibert de Naillac, holding the key to the conclave and crowning Pope Martin V at the Council of Constance in 1417.[51)]

As with every administration, there were perennial acts of indiscipline which included the non-payment of the *responsiones*, the monies owed to Rhodes. The extent and seriousness of such troubles, which varied greatly from one priory to another, are difficult to gauge. The statutes emphasized the brethren's liturgical life which had to be maintained, but in the West their charitable and medical obligations seem to have been much neglected. Some preceptors and priors, notably those in France, continued to pay their dues and to travel to give service at Rhodes, at least as far as wars and economic conditions permitted.

48) LUTTRELL (1978), VIII 323.

49) LUTTRELL (1978), X 104–105, and a manuscript of 1343 which shows Benedict XI holding court in Perugia with three Hospitaller attendants sitting on the ground: G. LADNER, Die Papstbildnisse des Altertums und des Mittelalters, ii (Vatican, 1970), 347–349; Taf. lxxxiii: (information kindly provided by Miss Joanna Cannon). These scenes support Professor Hans Belting's thesis that the Assisi programme was papally-inspired.

50) A. LUTTRELL, "A Hospitaller in a Florentine Fresco: 1366/8" Burlington Magazine, cxiv (1972). S. ROMANO, "Due affreschi del Cappellone degli Spagnoli: Problemi iconologici", Storia dell'Arte, xxviii (1976), correctly casts some doubt on this interpretation, especially as Urban V, unlike the pope in the fresco, was not bearded; the present author will publish further considerations on this problem.

51) Reproduced in A. HAIDACHER, Geschichte der Päpste in Bildern (Heidelberg, 1965), 115; sources collected in The Council of Constance: the Unification of the Church, ed. J. MUNDY – K. WOODY (New York, 1961), 92, 102, 110, 162–164, 170–171, 385, 422–423, 429, 467.

Others, the Portuguese were an extreme example, did neither. Sometimes priors played a leading role in national politics. Juan Fernández de Heredia was the outstanding instance, but there were others such as Fr. Robert Hales, Prior of England and royal Treasurer, who was beheaded during the Peasants' Revolt of 1381. The ruling body of the Order at Rhodes could summon brethren to the East, manage the *responsiones,* send visitors to the priories and threaten depositions, and it had a Lieutenant in the West, procurators and cardinal-protectors in the *curia* at Avignon, and a Receiver-General in Languedoc who accounted for incoming monies and sent them to Rhodes, often using Florentine and other bankers to transfer funds. An unofficial law school was set up at Paris to train brethren in law so that they could play their part in this Hospitaller bureaucracy.

The real problems of government were more political than bureaucratic. Local interference and secular resistance could be decisive when rulers determined appointments, imposed taxes or prevented the departure for Rhodes of men and money. Relations, generally friendly, with the Genoese were important but await detailed research. Venice was particularly hostile, and other Latin powers ignored Hospitaller demands and protests. The pope could commandeer individual brethren for his own service or secure favours for others, and he exercized an overall surveillance of policies. Popes could summon assemblies to Avignon, seek to impose reforms or changes, and divert Hospitaller resources to papally-oriented crusading schemes. By 1373 the Hospital was the only power on which Pope Gregory XI could rely for even a semblance of military action in the East, for the defence of Smyrna, for diplomatic interventions in Cyprus, for a fact-finding mission to Constantinople, and ultimately in 1378 for a minor crusading *passagium* against the Turks. It was presumably Gregory XI's realization of this state of affairs which led him to initiate the episcopal inquests of 1373 which were designed to provide statistics regarding the extent of the Hospital's wealth and manpower and the way in which they were employed, even if the pope subsequently ignored the results of his own inquiry when he issued summonses for many more brethren than existed to serve on the *passagium* which eventually invaded Greece in 1378.[52] Papal interventions were not, however, always disadvantageous; quarrels among the brethren had to be settled and monies to be raised, while protection was needed against both secular and ecclesiastical interferences.

The impact of the great plague, of innumerable European conflicts, of general economic recession and other such universal afflictions was inescapable. As conservative landholders, the Hospitallers' incomes suffered dramatically from devaluation, depopulation and destructive wars to which they often had to contribute taxes and manpower. The inquest of

52) On Gregory XI, the crusade, and the general situation in the priories, A. LUTTRELL, "The Papal Inquest into the Hospital of 1373 and its Historical Background" (forthcoming). See also IDEM, "Popes and Crusades: 1362–1394", in Genèse et débuts du Grand Schisme d'Occident: 1362–1394 (Avignon, 1978). If Urban VI failed to support the Hospitaller *passagium* in 1378, he forcefully rejected a suggestion from the cardinals that he should seize all the Hospital's lands: text in O. RINALDI, Annales Ecclesiastici, vii (Lucca, 1752), 315.

1373 showed the Hospital reluctant to give up the administration of its own estates. The demand for an estimate of the incomes which would result from each commandery being farmed out to a secular agent raised issues which were unlikely to be resolved in purely economic terms. Individual witnesses were obviously incapable of analyzing such a problem with any precision, though they may have reacted with sound management instincts.[53] By 1373 recruitment and incomes had fallen; lands lay uncultivated and buildings in ruin; the brethren had become astonishingly aged and non-military. The Priory of France in north-western France supported some 250 or 300 *fratres* including 20 or 30 serving at Rhodes or elsewhere, a decline of about one-third with respect to 1319. 124 out of 178 named *fratres,* roughly 70 percent, were *presbiteri* or priests, 49 were *sergentes* or sergeants-at-arms, and no more than 4 or 5 were *milites.* Of the 54 who were theoretically fighting men, 81 percent were more than forty years of age and roughly 60 percent were over fifty.[54] In many dioceses the inquests were never conducted or have not survived, but in general they revealed an alarming crisis in the West, and if Rhodes was reasonably safe difficulties were increasing there as well. Eventually the inquests and, where they are lacking, the painstaking accumulation of other information should produce an almost complete prosopography of the brethren in 1373, with precious details on backgrounds, ages, incomes, length of service and promotions. It will probably emerge that the few *milites* came from the petty nobility, from royal service or from the urban patriciate.

The study of Hospitaller finances would not produce a full picture – that was not really available even to contemporaries – but it would assist in interpreting policies by providing details of monies received in Southern France and either expended there or forwarded to Rhodes in cash, credit, cloth or silver. Complications with currencies and exchange rates, the partial nature of the statistics and non-payment by some priories all obscure the picture, but reasonably reliable overall figures could be secured. Extraordinary imposts, mortgages and, after 1391, the profits from the special indulgences granted to the Hospital by the pope permitted an astonishing and as yet unexplained growth in incomes, even allowing for inflation. The average receipts of the Receiver-General in the West between 1367 and 1373 probably stood around 22,700 florins annually; those for 1378 to 1399 around 38,500 florins, an increase of about 70 percent which was all the more remarkable in that it was achieved in a period of schism during which some priories paid little or

53) W. KULA, An Economic Theory of the Feudal System: Towards a Model of the Polish Economy: 1500–1800 (trans: London, 1976), considers such difficulties. It may have been felt that the *milites* should be serving in the East and not engaged in rural administration, and Philippe de Mézières made this a rule for his proposed Order: text in HAMDY (1964), 82.

54) These surprising statistics are supplied from detailed work in A.-M. LEGRAS, L'Enquête pontificale de 1373 sur l'Ordre des Hospitaliers de Saint-Jean-de-Jérusalem: édition et commentaire des documents relatifs au Grand Prieuré de France (unpublished thesis: Paris, 1976).

nothing.[55] In December 1398 the commanders of the Priory of Catalunya refused to provide a subsidy for Pope Benedict XIII on the grounds that only nine out of twenty-one priories were sending their *responsiones* to Rhodes, that the pope was no longer paying for the defence of Smyrna so that the burden fell on the Hospital, that the Priory of Catalunya had to pay 3600 of the 25,000 florins which, they claimed, had to be spent each year on defence against the Turks, and that the whole priory was in financial straits.[56]

The schism in the papacy, which lasted nearly forty years from 1378 until 1417, revealed surprising strengths in the Hospital. Fr. Juan Fernández de Heredia was undoubtedly the legally-elected Master but, together with the majority of the brethren, he supported the Avignonese "anti-popes" though a number of Italian, German and other Hospitallers followed an "anti-Master" nominated by the Roman pope in 1383.[57] A plot to win Rhodes over to the Roman obedience failed miserably; overall incomes were actually increased; and the English Hospitallers, whose government recognized the Roman pope, continued with explicit royal support to travel to Rhodes and to send considerable sums there.[58] For a brief period between 1394, when Pedro de Luna was elected pope as Benedict XIII, and 1396, when Fr. Juan Fernández de Heredia died, both the Avignonese pope and the Master of the Hospital were natives of *Aragón* proper. Meanwhile when the Romanist "anti-Master" died in 1395 the Roman pope decided not to replace him. Fr. Philibert de Naillac, the Master elected at Rhodes in 1396, spent many years in the West struggling with the problems of the schism. In 1409 he was at the Council of Pisa, where he guarded the conclave, and the Hospitallers recognized the pope, Alexander V, elected there. In 1410 a compromise arrangement ended the schism in the Hospital, seven years before that in the papacy. Fr. Philibert de Naillac worked hard to end the schism in both Church and Hospital, and the Prior of the Convent at Rhodes, Fr. Gautier le Gras, was one of the electors who chose Martin V as pope at Constance in 1417.[59] At a local level the schism was often disruptive and damaging. It was not so much that the Hospital split into two clearly-aligned diplomatic camps, but rather that brethren tried to secure the confir-

55) Approximate figures calculated from NISBETT, 102–104. In 1448 the Commander of Torrente and Valencia claimed that out of a total income of 411 libras, he had expenses of 312, paid 60 to Rhodes and kept a balance of 39 for himself: MA. D. CABANES PECOURT, "Las Órdenes Militares en el reino de Valencia: notas sobre su economía", Hispania, cxiii (1969), 515–516.
56) Text in MIRET, 456–458.
57) LUTTRELL (1978), XXIII; on the "anti-Master" and the "anti-Lieutenant" who succeeded him, see A. STRNAD, "Caracciolo, Riccardo", and A. ESCH, "Carafa, Bartolomeo", both in Dizionario Biografico degli Italiani, xix (Rome, 1976), 443–446, and 494–496.
58) C. TIPTON, "The English Hospitallers during the Great Schism", Studies in Medieval and Renaissance History, iv (1967); the important "revisionist" points advanced result from the combination of material from the English and the Malta archives; note also P. FIELD, "Sir Robert Malory, Prior of the Hospital of St. John of Jerusalem in England: 1432–1439/40", Journal of Ecclesiastical History, xxviii (1977).
59) DELAVILLE (1913), 262, 305–306, 311–318, 329-335; supra, 256.

mation of their positions from both popes and both Masters while at the same time giving obedience and *responsiones* to neither. Yet the Hospital did retain its lands and incomes, thus conserving the strength to defend Rhodes against major Mamluk and Ottoman assaults later in the fifteenth century.

*

The foundations of Hospitaller power, that is the uninterrupted flow of funds and brethren and the continued will to resist, largely derived from the extensive European hinterland. The Western priories have received some study, but they have too often been left out of the Hospital's general history, too often been studied without reference to its central archives. The large-scale investigation into the inquests of 1373, of which the first volume is nearing completion, should gradually fill many gaps. It involves the compilation of a complete bibliography for every priory and every commandery, the identification of properties and toponyms, their incomes and methods of exploitation, and the *curriculum vitae* of every *frater* mentioned in 1373. The information from each of the surviving inquests is roughly comparable, since the same six questions were to be asked in every diocese, but there are many technical difficulties, especially as diocesan boundaries did not correspond to Hospitaller commanderies. The inquests have to be supplemented from the Maltese archives and from other sources, and even where the inquests are not available it is possible to assemble bibliographies and data to complete the picture.[60)]

The surveying of material remains has become dramatically urgent as roads and other modern developments destroy buildings and mechanized agriculture eliminates chapels, barns, hedges, paths and other landmarks. Hospitaller structures have on occasion been excavated scientifically, notably in Poland and England,[61)] and a collection of photographs is being built up in France; twenty minutes with a camera and a measuring tape can save precious information about a building. Much topographical data is contained in the archives where the early-modern estate-books, the *terriers* or *cabrei,* are especially valuable. Local histories, prints and other antiquarian materials can be used in conjunction with old maps, aerial photographs and inspections *in situ.* The extent of Hospitaller estates, the disposition of churches, hospices, cemeteries, stables, mills and fields can be re-created. Frescoes and paintings, liturgical manuscripts and tombstones can provide iconographical clues concerning the Hospitallers' cults and mentalities or their dress, equipment and material culture.[62)]

The information in print relating to the priories is most unequal, and it indicates great diversities between one region and another. The French priories, together with those of

60) The inquests are now being published; cf. J. GLÉNISSON, "L'Enquête pontificale de 1373 sur les possessions des Hospitaliers de Saint-Jean-de-Jérusalem", Bibliothèque de l'École des Chartes, cxxix (1971), and A. LUTTRELL – A.-M. LEGRAS, "Les Hospitaliers autour de Gap: une enquête de 1330", Mélanges de l'École française de Rome: Moyen Age – Temps Modernes, xc (1978).
61) Cf. LUTTRELL (1978), X 90 n. 2.
62) Cf. LUTTRELL (1978), X et passim.

Spain and Italy, were, statistically speaking, the most important. Others, such as Portugal, Ireland or Poland, were scarcely in touch with Rhodes, owing partly to distance and partly to local preoccupations. There were usually a few German brethren in the East,[63)] yet the German Hospitallers were not fully integrated into the Order. In the first half of the fourteenth century certain brethren and certain districts sided with Lewis of Bavaria in his disputes with the pope.[64)] The Hospitallers of Brandenburg achieved an astonishing, and officially recognized, quasi-independence while there were difficulties in Bohemia even before the papal schism and the Hussite movement.[65)] The bulk of the German commanderies were situated further west in the lands along the Rhine where they did not come directly in contact with Poles or Slavs or in open competition with the Hospital's ancient rivals of the Teutonic Order. There was evidently an active liturgical life, with a highly developed emphasis on the cult of the dead.[66)] The extensive bibliography on the *lingua* of *Alamania* is predominantly local in orientation and seldom uses Maltese materials,[67)] though the very detailed work of Walter Rödel is based on visitations of 1494/5 and 1540/1 preserved in Malta, and his book includes a good deal of much earlier information concerning commanderies and incomes;[68)] the 1494/5 visitation itself contains important documents and details referring to earlier periods.[69)] Rödel did not utilize the Magistral registers in which the German materials are always grouped together into the same section so that their rapid consultation is relatively easy. Inquests of 1373 survive only for Prague, Minden, Osnabruck and some marginal dioceses,[70)] but topographical work, the gathering of prosopographical and other detail at Malta and the rearrangement of Rödel's materials would permit the construction of a general picture of the German Hospital.

*

63) Eg. LUTTRELL (1978), I 288–289, 303–304, 311; XXII 35, 39–40.

64) J. VON PFLUGK-HARTTUNG, Der Johanniter und der Deutsche Orden im Kampfe Ludwigs des Bayern mit der Kurie (Leipzig, 1900).

(65) DELAVILLE (1913), 72–75, 217–219 et passim. E. OPGENOORTH, Die Ballei Brandenburg des Johanniterordens im Zeitalter der Reformation und Gegenreformation (Würzburg, 1963), 29–47, is useful though brief and based mainly on German sources. No attempt at a bibliography on the German Hospital is attempted here, but see infra notes 67–68.

66) B. WALSTEIN-WARTENBERG, "Beiträge zur mittelalterlichen Liturgie des Johanniterordens, I: Der Festkalender; II: Das Totengedächtnis", Annales de l'Ordre Souverain Militaire de Malte, xxx (1972); cf. IDEM,"Die kulturellen Leistungen des Grosspriorates Böhmen–Österreich im Mittelalter", ibid., xxxiii (1975).

67) Cf. Der Johanniterorden – Der Malteserorden: Der Ritterliche Orden des hl. Johannes vom Spital zu Jerusalem. Seine Aufgaben, seine Geschichte, ed. A. WIENAND (Cologne, 1970), with end-map of commanderies. Note particularly B. WALDSTEIN-WARTENBURG, "Donaten-Confratres-Pfründner: Die Bruderschaften des Ordens", Annales de l'Ordre Souverain Militaire de Malte, xxxi (1973).

68) W. RÖDEL, Das Grosspriorat Deutschland des Johanniter-Ordens im Übergang vom Mittelalter zur Reformation (Cologne, 1972), with useful bibliography.

69) Malta, cod. 45.

70) GLÉNISSON, 110.

Although the Military Orders of Santiago, Calatrava and Alcántara evidently exercized a profound influence on the evolution of Castilian society, there is no detailed historical vision of their overall development as an institution; old clichés still await new interpretations.[71] It is claimed that the Military Orders replaced the primitive rural communities of Castile, which were supposedly characterized by their free *concejos* or councils, by their Muslim agrarian traditions, and by a system of *latifundios*; and furthermore that

> the pure warriors of the Military Orders deformed the original nature of the Castilian resettlement and raised a barrier of social prejudices between the north and south of the country, creating a new Castilian character – anti-economic, anarchic, domineering.[72]

Such affirmations, debatable even for Southern Castile, derive from a conception of the Orders in post-medieval times when they had indeed become largely a source of wealth and of honours for those concerned with nobility or *hidalguía* and purity of blood or *limpieza de sangre.* Historians of early modern Spain may well judge that the Orders became "venerable archaisms, shocking or comic", neither religious nor military, "ossified forms" dissociated from reality;[73] the problem is to analyze this process and to establish how far it had advanced by 1300 or 1400. The evidence for a preoccupation with nobility, however defined, among the medieval Orders is partial and inconclusive, though the Knights of Santiago were raising the barriers in the late thirteenth century;[74] in 1338 King Alfonso founded the *Real Cofradía del Santísmo y Santiago* at Burgos, apparently as a substitute for Santiago intended to satisfy the *caballeros villanos,* the non-noble knights who constituted the town's élite.[75]

An important turning-point came when the fall of Granada in 1492 concluded the

71) Extensive bibliographies in E. BENITO RUANO, "La investigacíon reciente sobre las Órdenes Militares Hispánicas", A Cidade de Évora, lix (1976); D. LOMAX, "Las Órdenes Militares en la Península Ibérica durante la Edad Media", in Repertorio de Historia de las Ciencias Eclesiasticas en España, vi (Salamanca, 1976). Note especially E. BENITO RUANO, Estudios Santiaguistas (León, 1978), and the works of A. FOREY, A. JAVIERRE MUR, D. LOMAX and J. O'CALLAGHAN. What follows is based on A. LUTTRELL, "Las Órdenes Militares en la Sociedad Hispánica – los Hospitalarios Aragoneses: 1340–1360", communicated to the unpublished Congreso International Hispano-Portugués sobre las Órdenes Militares en la Península durante la Edad Media: 1971. Work by the present author on the Hospital in Castile and Portugal awaits publication.

72) J. VICENS VIVES, Aproximación a la Historia de España (revised ed: Barcelona, 1960), 91, 232; more balanced views in C. BISHKO, "The Castilian as Plainsman: the Medieval Ranching Frontier in La Mancha and Extremadura", in The New World Looks at its History, ed. A. LEWIS – T. MCGANN (Austin, Texas, 1963).

73) A. DOMÍNGUEZ ORTIZ, La Sociedad Española en el siglo XVII, i (Madrid, 1963), 198.

74) D. LOMAX, La Orden de Santiago: 1170–1275 (Madrid, 1965), 87–88. Calatrava restricted entry to the sons of *caballeros* or *escuderos* in 1325, but Montesa did not exclude non-nobles until 1468: J. O'CALLAGHAN, The Spanish Military Order of Calatrava and its Affiliates (London, 1975), I 11–12, X 225.

75) T. RUIZ; "The Transformation of the Castilian Municipalities: the Case of Burgos, 1248–1350", Past and Present, lxxvii (1977), 17–18.

Orders' military mission within the peninsula, provoking a great debate over their functions and leading to the incorporation of the national Orders into the Crown through the *Consejo de las Órdenes Militares,* which completed their reduction to a source of royal wealth and patronage.[76] Yet the earlier changes which followed the attack on the Temple were probably even more decisive. The Aragonese Templars defended themselves against the Crown for months in their castles, demonstrating a military capacity which worried the king who had probably well over 150 Templars within his realms.[77] Their downfall precipitated protracted negotiations concerning the activities and justifications of all the Orders in the Iberian kingdoms where the Templars' lands were specially exempted by the papal bull of 1312 from passing automatically to the Hospital; eventually the Hospital did secure most of the Templar possessions in *Aragón* and Catalunya and some of those in Castile. Though they played some part in campaigns against the Muslims of Granada, the Spanish Hospitallers were supposedly concerned with the Eastern Mediterranean, and they were subject to foreign control; the Templar lands would have made them immensely powerful. The Iberian kings therefore insisted on a form of quasi-secularization through the creation, from the Templars' possessions, of the Orders of Christ in Portugal and of Montesa in Valencia, and they partially subordinated all the Orders through their influence over nominations to the Masterships; long before 1492 this control led to the domination of the Castilian Orders by the Crown, which secured the Masterships and extensive incomes for its own royal cadets or favourites, with resultant quarrels and abuses within the Orders.[78] In 1331 the Castilian king did seek to create a new Order with the Temple goods, a proposal rejected by the pope on the grounds that the Hospital could make more satisfactory use of those goods and that internal dissensions within the new Orders of Christ and Montesa cast doubts on their utility.[79] Decades later, on 28 January 1388, Pope Clement VII authorized King Juan of Castile to found a new Order in Tarifa to fight the Muslims of Africa[80] yet it was the Portuguese who captured the African town of Ceuta in 1415 and the Order of Christ which subsequently fought in Morocco. The Hospitallers scarcely participated in the conquest of Africa and the Atlantic islands, a process which raised awkward questions concerning the justification of crusading action against pagans as opposed to *infideles.* This problem also arose in Poland where Paulus Wladimiri and other jurists developed paradoxical notions of a »just war« directed against the Teutonic

76) L. WRIGHT, "The Military Orders in Sixteenth and Seventeenth Century Spanish Society: the Institutional Embodiment of a Historical Tradition", Past and Present, xliii (1969), 37 et passim.
77) A. FOREY, The Templars in the "Corona de Aragón" (London, 1973), 27–28, 276–278 et passim.
78) O'CALLAGHAN, I, VIII, X; LUTTRELL (1978), XI–XII; A. JAVIERRE MUR, "Pedro IV el Cerimonioso y la Orden de Montesa", in Martínez Ferrando, Archivero: Miscelánea de estudios dedicados a su memoria (Madrid, 1968). The Hospitallers' lands in Valencia passed to Montesa, as did those of the Temple.
79) Archivio Vaticano, Reg. Vat. 116, f. 84v–85 (16 April 1331).
80) Archivio Vaticano, Reg. Vat. 299, f. 49v.

Order.[81] Early in the sixteenth century the Military Orders were finally secularized in the Protestant lands of England and Prussia but they had not altogether outlived their utility; the new maritime Order of Santo Stefano was founded in Tuscany in 1562, and the Hospitallers fought the Turks and defended Malta until 1798.

These are preliminary and uncertain conclusions, demanding much further research. The Hospitallers' Priory of *Aragón,* known as the *Castellanía de Amposta,* provides an excellent opportunity for a case-study in depth of a segment of an Order in Spain. There are no 1373 inquests for Spain but the *Registros de Amposta* contain a mass of information from 1340 onwards,[82] and this can be supplemented with numerous other documents from that priory and from the archives of the Priory of Catalunya, of the Aragonese Crown, of the papacy and of the Masters of Rhodes. Existing works seldom go beyond 1300,[83] yet brethren and incomes could be counted, the origins and careers of Hospitallers established, and general Aragonese problems, such as urban topography or the status of the Muslim population, elucidated.[84] After its separation from the Priory of Catalunya in 1319 the *Castellanía* had some thirty commanderies. Forty-two brethren attended the prioral chapter of 1351[85] while others remained on their commanderies and a few were at Rhodes, making a total, perhaps, of more than a hundred. Many brethren came from the lesser nobility or the bourgeoisie though Magistral documents stipulated that the *fratres milites,* whose numbers await calculation, should be legitimately born *ex utroque parente nobili.*[86] More serious discrimination came after 1420.[87] In Catalunya the *consellers* of Barcelona were resisting attempts from Rhodes to exclude non-military citizens from the Order in

81) J. Woś, "Sul concetto della guerra giusta e l'intervento degli *infideles* alla battaglia di Grunwald: 1410", Annali della Scuola Normale Superiore di Pisa: classe di lettere e filosofia, III ser., ii (1972).

82) Registros de Amposta, I–IV = Madrid, Archivo Histórico Nacional, Sección de Códices, 599–B a 602–B.

83) S. García Larragueta, El gran priorado de Navarra de la Orden de San Juan de Jerusalén: siglos XII–XIII, 2 vols. (Pamplona, 1957); A. Ubieto Arteta, El real monasterio de Sigena: 1188–1300 (Valencia, 1966); Ma. L. Ledesma Rubió, La Encomienda de Zaragoza de la Orden de San Juan de Jerusalén en los siglos XII–XIII (Zaragoza, 1967).

84) Preliminary studies in Luttrell (1978), XI–XIV; Ma. L. Ledesma Rubió, "La Zuda de Zaragoza y la Orden de San Juan de Jerusalén", Cuadernos de Historia Jerónimo Zurita, xvi-xviii (1963–1965); Idem, "La población mudéjar en la vega baja de Jalón", in Miscelánea ofrecida al Ilmo. Sr. D. José Maria Lacarra y de Miguel (Zaragoza, 1968).

85) Madrid, Registro de Amposta, III, f. 17–20.

86) Text of 1351 in Luttrell (1978), XIV 511.

87) Statutes of 1262 and 1270 established that a *miles* had to be legitimately born of noble or knightly lineage or, if illegitimate, a *filius principis aut domini maioris:* Delaville, Cartulaire, iii, docs. 3039, 3396. In 1420, because the rule had been badly observed during the papal schism, it was reaffirmed that a *miles* had to be of *lignage.* A statute of 1428 added that a *miles* was to be *gentil homme de nom et darmes Et de leal marriage,* and another of 1433 that he was to be of *lignage* or, if illegitimate, the son of a count or greater lord, and that he was to be admitted only after an inquiry into his birth: Paris, Bibliothèque Nationale, Ms. français 17,255, f. 92v, 100, 111–111v.

1437[88] and in 1447 the burgesses claimed to belong to the military class and therefore be eligible.[89] The great plague of 1347 produced a manpower crisis in *Aragón*; prices rose and rents had to be lowered in order to keep fields under cultivation. Some land was farmed indirectly, sometimes through contracts for improvements *ad plantandum*. At moments of trouble the Priory of *Aragón* produced large sums of money for the king, who also summoned it to provide military forces, seventy horsemen in 1342 for example. For such reasons the Crown sought to establish a degree of control over the Order. Successive kings insisted on retaining their overall *dominium* and on occasion they effectively vetoed certain Magistral appointments by refusing to accept homage from the Master's nominees. The result was a compromise, a sharing of resources between the Aragonese Crown and the Hospital at Rhodes.[90]

Though the Temple *affaire* changed the whole climate within which the Orders operated in Spain, the Hospital continued to play a positive role in Aragonese life. Nepotism and concubinage, the preoccupation with nobility and the corruption of benefices were probably no more widespread than in other branches of the Church. The *reconquista* was largely at a halt after the failure to take Gibraltar in 1350, but the Hospitallers had repopulated and continued to cultivate extensive areas, supervising estates, collecting rents and administering justice. They constituted a stable, conservative element in society, and they continued furthermore to send at least some men and money to Rhodes. All the Hispanic Orders were progressively »nationalized« but the Aragonese Crown established only a partial control over the Hospitallers, who retained a significant function and the lands and privileges which enabled them to fulfill it.

⁂

88) *Item sien membrants los Consellers esdevenidors de proseguir ab nostre sant pare la revocacio del stament odios fet per lo Mestre e capitol de Rodes, per lo qual, en gran destruccio e prejudici del stament dels honorables ciutedans e honorables homens de ciudats, viles e lochs de la senyoria del senyor rey, han statuit que algu no sie admes a religio del dit orde si no es militar de paratge.* Text partially edited in C. CARRÉRE, Barcelone, centre économique à l'époque des difficultés: 1380–1462, ii (Paris, 1967), 642 n. 3.

89) *A 7, de Agost 1447, y a 27, y 28 de Febrer 1448, scriuen al Rey querellantse del Mestre de Rodes, y son Convent, que havian fet un Statut, que aquells sols qui devallaran de Linatge militar sien admesos en la Religió de St. Joan, per que en Cathalunya lo Stat militar, e dels Ciutadans Burgesos, y homens honrats de Viles, axí per Constitucions, com altrament son reputats en un mateix grau, e stament, e axí en guerres en qualsevols parts, com en tots actes, y armes ques pertanyen a Cavallería.* Text in Rúbriques de Bruniquer: Cerimonial dels Magnífichs Consellers y Regiment de la Ciutat de Barcelona, ed. F. CARRERAS I CANDI – B. GUNYALONS I BOU, v (Barcelona, 1916), 153, misleadingly cited in LUTTRELL (1978), XI 3. Note that a notable *mercader* of Barcelona was received in 1438 after an investigation into his *linatge, custumes e vida* had shown him to be related, through his mother, to several families of *gentils homens:* text in MIRET, 430–431.

90) Details in LUTTRELL (1978), XI–XIV. Apart from the un-typical Commanderies of Zaragoza and Sigena studied by LEDESMA and UBIETO, the question of agrarian exploitation awaits research. FOREY (1973), 189, concludes that the Temple "normally sought to retain direct control over its lordships and estates."

The Hospital should be studied within the context of the Military Orders considered as a category. The only reasonably modern general consideration of the Orders was published in 1908 and halts at 1312,[91)] but new work covering many aspects of different Orders now provides considerable scope for comparisons and generalizations. Thus the German Hospital, theoretically concerned with distant Rhodes, could be contrasted with the Teutonic Knights who became a compact »national« Order of great efficiency and with a rather special ideology of its own, expansionist, colonizing, militaristic.[92)] The Hispanic Orders provide the obvious points of comparison. Their non-Christian opponents were cultural equals or superiors whom they seldom converted by force, so that the conflict lacked the ferocity of that in Germany. Losing much of their conquering and colonizing role during the thirteenth century, the Hispanic Orders never achieved the power or independence of the Teutonic »state«. As for the Hospital, only in the seventeenth or eighteenth century at Malta can it be described as a »state«. At Rhodes the Hospital, unlike Orders such as Calatrava which depended juridically on the Order of Cîteaux and was visited by its abbots, was largely independent politically and, saving the powers of the pope, jurisdictionally. Yet its relations with its subjects were conceived much as they had been in Cyprus or Syria; legislation in the statutes might affect the Rhodians very directly[93)] but it was intended primarily for the Order. In considering such varied questions the need is not for a facile »sociology« of the Orders but for the collection and interpretation of information about each of them, their relations with each other, with the Church and with society as a whole. The Hospitallers lived within the community and were in fact subject to a multiplicity of allegiances, some of which conflicted with each other. Most standard surveys of medieval Europe or of the medieval Church devote little or no space to what Bernard of Clairvaux had recognized as »a new type of *militia*«, the warrior-monks who did not fit neatly into conventional divisions of society, yet the Military Orders deserve appreciation as a distinctive, individual element in Western life, its expansion, its evolution and its defence.

91) H. PRUTZ, Die geistlichen Ritterorden: Ihre Stellung zur kirchlichen, politischen, gesellschaftlichen und wirtschaftlichen Entwicklung des Mittelalters (Berlin, 1908). The semi-popular work by D. SEWARD, The Monks of War: the Military Religious Orders (London, 1972), is much wider in scope.
92) The bibliography is most extensive. For a Polish view, K. GÓRSKI, L'Ordine Teutonico alle Origini dello Stato Prussiano (Turin, 1971); reply in U. ARNOLD, "L'Ordine Teutonico alle Origini dello Stato Prussiano", Römische Historische Mitteilungen, xvi (1974); countered in K. GÓRSKI, "Polemica ad Udo Arnold", ibid., xix (1977). Note the curious Danish-Polish proposal of 1418 to transfer the Teutonic Order to Novgorod, Jerusalem, Cyprus or Rhodes: E. JOACHIM – W. HUBATSCH, Regesta Historico-Diplomatica Ordinis S. Mariae Theutonicorum: 1198–1528, i (Göttingen, 1948), 176.
93) Eg. LUTTRELL (1978), IV; the juridical bases of Hospitaller statutes and edicts require investigation.

II
The Hospitallers' Historical Activities: 1400-1530

The Hospitallers apparently produced only one general history of their Order during their period at Rhodes from 1306 to 1523; furthermore that single work remained in manuscript, and was lost or forgotten long before the end of the sixteenth century. During the fourteenth century the standard of education and literacy among the brethren, especially the *fratres presbiteri*, had improved considerably; a few developed interest in theology or the classics, while after 1356 the Hospital regularly trained some of its chaplains in Canon Law at Paris and other universities. Yet, with a few exceptions, there was no serious interest in history, though the brethren preserved their records and registers, and they continued to extend their crude lists of the deceased Masters, which contained a few remarks about each Master. The Hospitallers' general failure to publicize their own achievements was partly responsible for their bad reputation in Europe, where unjustified criticism of the Order was readily accepted. (1) The public had to rely largely on the accounts of travellers and pilgrims, which often included interesting scraps of historical information but scarcely provided a history of Rhodes. (2)

Historical activity at Rhodes naturally centred in the Chancery and it depended on the quality of men employed there. Though a Chancellor of the Hospital was recorded in 1126, (3) the institution apparently lapsed. The office was revived early in the fourteenth century when Fr. Pietro de Imola acted as chancellor in authenticating documents of the Order. (4) A Professor of both Canon and Civil Law who came to be venerated in Italy for his saintliness, he served as the Master's Secretary and as a procurator for the Order, and in 1327 he became Prior of Rome. (5) In 1360 Fr. Pierre de Meyronnes, Preceptor of Avignon, was *socius et cancellarius* of the Master. (6) The *canceller de moss. le maistre* at Rhodes in 1381 was Fr. Mathieu de Saint George, a Hospitaller who was a *licentiatus* in Canon Law and who was still Chancellor of the Master in 1401. (7) In 1420 *Michelus Paquanti,* the Master's Secretary who acted as Chancellor, was sent on a mission to the papal *curia* and to France. (8) Thereafter the Chancellor came to be used quite frequently on such

(1) A. LUTTRELL, "*The Hospitallers' Historical Activities: 1291-1400,*" *ANTE,* xxiv (1966).

(2) Incomplete lists in G. FUMAGALLI, *Bibliografia rodia* (Florence, 1937), 77-83; R. MITCHELL, *The Spring Voyage* (London, 1964).

(3) J. DELAVILLE LE ROULX, *Cartulaire général de l'Ordre des Hospitaliers de S. Jean de Jérusalem: 1100-1310,* i (Paris, 1894), nos. 77, 399.

(4) Eg. Royal Malta Library, Archives of the Order of St. John, cod. 16, nos. 16 (28 August 1325), 19 (19 March 1327).

(5) G. BOSIO, *Dell'Istoria della Sacra Religione ... di San Giovanni Gierosolimitano,* i-ii (2nd ed: Rome, 1621-1629), i. 476; J. DELAVILLE LE ROULX, *Les Hospitaliers à Rhodes jusqu'à la mort de Philibert de Naillac: 1310-1421* (Paris, 1913), 60, n. 6, 77.

(6) Archivo de la Corona de Aragón, Barcelona, Reg. 1173, f. 6v-7.

(7) Malta, cod. 48, f. 65 (1381); A. LUTTRELL, "Fourteenth-Century Hospitaller Lawyers," *Traditio,* xxi (1965), 453; this article overlooked Fr. Pietro de Imola.

(8) BOSIO, ii. 191-192; A. ZAMMIT - J. MIZZI, *Catalogue of the Records of the Order of St. John of Jerusalem in the Royal Malta Library,* i- (Malta, 1964-), i. 95.

embassies; at the same time he became less a personal secretary to the Master and more the head of a department in control of the Chancery.

Fr. Melchiore Bandini, Preceptor of Brindisi, Mugnano and Camerino, was already Chancellor by 1445 when he was sent to Rome; and in 1446 he was appointed Visitor in France. (9) When Bandini was called from Rhodes to the *curia* in 1448 he was replaced by a Vice-Chancellor, presumably by *Heliseus della Mana* who was described as *magni magistri Rhodi cancellarius* in 1449, and who was Chancellor of the Convent and Secretary to the Master in 1454. (10) By 1457 Guillaume Caoursin of Douai was both Secretary to the Master and Vice-Chancellor, and in 1459 when Bandini again went to Rome, this time more permanently as Procurator-General at the *curia,* Caoursin remained in Rhodes to act for him. Bandini was the principal mediator in the great dispute between the French and other Hospitallers in 1459; in 1464 he delivered an oration on the election of Pope Paul II; and in 1467 he voted for Fr. Giovan Battista Orsini when he was elected Master by one vote. By 1469 he was so ill that he had to resign his Procuratorship at Rome, and by 1471 he was no longer Chancellor; probably he was dead. (11) He built a chapel in the church of Sant'Agostino at Camerino in the Marche, where there was also a crucifix with his portrait and a silver cross inscribed:

Melchior Illustris Bandinae gloriae gentis
Hanc fieri magno iussit honore Crucem. (12)

Clearly a cultured man, (13) Fr. Melchiore Bandini apparently produced a history of the Hospital down to his own times, written during the Mastership of Fr. Jean de Lastic who ruled from 1437 to 1454. (14) Probably this was the first continuous history of the Order, but whether it was based on investigations in the archives or had much historical value is doubtful.

The office of Chancellor acquired a more formal character after 1462 when, in order to create a *baiulivum* for the new *langue* of Castile, it was agreed that the senior of the Castilian and Portuguese brethren at Rhodes was to hold the office as a *baiulivum.* (15) This produced a curious situation at the Chapter-General held at Rome in 1466. On leaving Rhodes for Italy, the Master had ordered that since Bandini was indisposed, Caoursin was to travel to Rome taking the necessary books from the Chancery. At Rome Bandini acted as Vice-Chancellor; the Castilian Fr. Arias Gonçalez del Rio as Lieutenant of the Chancellor; and Caoursin as Secretary to the Master and Lieutenant of the Vice-Chancellor. By 1471 Bandini was presumably dead; Fr. Arias became Chancellor; and Caoursin, who had been sent on an important mission to Rome in 1470, was confirmed in the position of Vice-Chancellor, although he was never a member of the Order. An oration delivered in Rome by Caoursin in 1485 so pleased Pope Innocent VIII that he made him an Apostolic Secretary and Count Palatine. This oration was published, as was a similar speech made in 1493 by Marcus Montanus, Latin Archbishop of Rhodes. Montanus dedicated his oration to Caoursin, who had been his teacher and on whose advice he had gone to study in the university at Paris. On Caoursin's death in 1501, Bartolomeo Poliziano, Secretary to the Master and Lieutenant of the Vice-Chancellor, succeeded Caoursin and was made a *miles* of the Hospital. After the fall of Rhodes, however, Poliziano decided to stay there. The Order then resolved

(9) Bosio, ii. 223-225, 227-228.

(10) N. Iorga, *Notes et extraits pour servir à l'histoire des croisades au XVe siècle,* ii (Paris, 1899), 429, 434; B. Krekić, *Dubrovnik (Raguse) et le Levant au moyen âge* (Paris, 1961), 358; Malta, cod. 282, f. 5v (1454).

(11) Bosio, ii. 254, 262-263, 265-266, 292, 310, 316, 329.

(12) C. Lilii, *Dell'Historia di Camerino,* part 2 (Macerata, 1652), 208.

(13) P. Savini, *Storia della Città di Camerino* (2nd ed: Camerino, 1895), 241, states, but without reference: "versato nella lingua greca tradusse in essa, ed annotò l'opera *de Civitate Dei* di S. Agostino".

(14) Bosio, i (1st ed: 1594), proemio.

(15) Texts in S. Pauli, *Codice diplomatico del sacro militare ordine Gerosolimitano,* 2 vols. (Lucca, 1733-1737), ii. 140-141.

not to choose another secular, and on 20 January 1523 Fr. Thomas Guichard, who held a university doctorate, was elected Vice-Chancellor. After Guichard's death in 1526 he was succeeded by another Hospitaller, Fr. Tommaso Bosio, a chaplain who in 1517 had been sent by the Master at the Order's expense to study at Paris where he secured his doctorate in law. (16)

The Chancery had to draw up letters and decrees in the correct florid style, to register sentences, and to issue and seal bulls and other documents. It was laid down that the Chancellor should be able to read and write, while the Vice-Chancellor, to whom the real control of the Chancery passed, was to be learned and competent. (17) In fact, from about the middle of the fifteenth century a certain humanist rhetoric, with classical references and even quotations from Virgil, appeared in Chancery documents, though in the anxious years following the fall of Constantinople in 1453 the Order's appeals for aid often reverted to the factual tone of a military despatch. (18) In 1471 Guillaume Caoursin, who had some knowledge of the classics and almost certainly introduced this humanist trend, was commissioned to reform the style of the bulls, and on his marriage in 1480 he was granted 1000 ducats for having revised the statutes. (19) The statutes of the Hospital had grown increasingly complex and had been translated into various languages. (20) Caoursin's complete recodification, in which the confusing chronological arrangement was abandoned in favour of a classification by subjects, was approved by the Chapter-General of 1489 and published with his *proemium* in 1493. New editions and translations followed rapidly. (21)

The organization of the Chancery and archives was periodically improved. Many old papal privileges and even title-deeds referring to the Order's former Syrian possessions were preserved. The Hospitallers also continued to record the statutes adopted at each Chapter-General. Sentences, decrees and other documents of the Master and Council were copied into the *libri bullarum* and other registers, and from 1459 the decisions taken in Council were minuted in the *libri conciliorum*. The old provisions for the sealing and preservation of documents, such as the decree of 1262 that each priory should keep two copies of its property registers, were repeated and new regulations brought in. In 1420 the overseas priors were instructed to keep their archives in a strong and secret place; in 1466 they were ordered to classify their documents and to maintain an up-to-date inventory of them. The Chapter-General of 1428 legislated for a chest with compartments in which the archives at Rhodes could be kept in an orderly way: papal and royal privileges; documents relating to the Hospital's estates; the Master's registers; Treasury accounts; documents concerning the overseas priories. In 1466 it was agreed to build a suitable place for the Chancery within the Master's palace. The archives were to be kept there, with separate labelled cupboards for the documents of each *langue,* and there was to be a special room in which the Chancellor could conduct secret business. (22)

In 1461 the Chapter-General declared that its chaplains should be instructed in Latin and singing. (23) At this time a new interest in education and learning was developing among the classes from which many of the brethren were recruited. A humble example of this trend was Fr. Otte Lamelin, Preceptor of Catillon in the Priory of France, who in 1457

(16) Bosio, ii. 300-303, 320, 329, 331, 489-491, 540-541, 619; iii (1st ed: 1602), 4, 46, 50.

(17) A. Mifsud, "Appunti sugli archivi di Malta", *Archivum Melitense*, ii, no. 13 (1914), 10-11; *Stabilimenta Rhodiorum militum ...* (Venice, 1495), *de baiuliuis*, xxxv-xxxviii, xl.

(18) As noted in R. Valentini, "L'Egeo dopo la caduta di Costantinopoli nelle relazioni dei Gran Maestri di Rodi", *Bulletino dell'Istituto storico italiano per il medio evo,* li (1936), with documents.

(19) Bosio, ii. 331, 431.

(20) R. Valentini, "Redazioni italiane quattrocentesche di Statuti della religione Gioannita", *Archivum Melitense,* ix (1933).

(21) E. Nasalli Rocca di Corneliano, "Origine et évolution de la Règle et des Statuts ...," *ANTE*, xix (1961), 121-125.

(22) Details in Mifsud, 9-12.

(23) Bosio, ii (1st ed: 1594), 215.

transcribed a French translation of Boethius' *consolatio*; (24) in 1438 he had become the Order's Procurator-General and in 1449 he was nominated Receiver-General at Avignon, an important post he still held in 1468. (25) Fr. Jean de Fransières, who served at Rhodes and died as Prior of Aquitaine in 1488, was responsible for a compilation on falconry, in which he included a treatise composed much earlier in the century by *Ayme Cassien*, a Rhodian Greek who was falconer to several Masters. In fact, the Hospitallers apparently played a significant rôle in spreading to Europe some knowledge of Oriental falconery and vetinerary art. (26) A different type of activity was that of Fr. Laudivio Zacchia, "poeta laureatus clarissimus et philosophus ornatissimus," who was the author of the *Epistolae Magni Turci*. In 1471 he was received into the Hospital at the command of the Master, who agreed that the Order would finance his study at Bologna or some other university for four years, provided he returned to Rhodes thereafter. (27) Away from Rhodes, and especially in Italy, there was a type of learned Hospitaller who often had little genuine connection with the Order. Such were the distinguished physician Michele Savonarola of Padua who was a *miles* of the Hospital, (28) and Fr. Pietro Bembo of Venice, Prior of Hungary in 1513 and later a cardinal, whose many works included a history of Venice but who probably never visited Rhodes. (29)

There were learned Greeks at Rhodes and a few Hospitallers who could speak Greek. The cultural level of the brethren presumably improved as the island became a minor centre for Greek studies to which Westerners, like William Lily the first headmaster of Saint Paul's School in London, came to learn Greek. Among the more scholarly of the brethren who fought in the great siege of 1480 were Fr. Benvenuto de Sangiorgio, who was considered learned in his time and wrote the history of the Marqueses of Monferrato, and Fr. Pietro Borromei, author of a history of the families of Padua. It was said of the Portuguese Fr. Andres d'Almaral, the last Chancellor at Rhodes, that he knew Pliny as well as other men knew their own names. (30) Outstanding among the intellectuals at Rhodes was Fr. Sabba da Castiglione, cousin of the famous Baldassare Castiglione and a lover of letters and the arts, who entered the Order at Rhodes in 1505 and spent three years there. He disliked life among the brethren many of whom considered his classical interests heretical and idolatrous, and he found that his military duties interrupted his classical studies. He saw many ancient sites and statues, which he said the Hospitallers ignored while he himself wrote sonnets among the ruins. Later, on his return to Italy, he interested himself in education and the poor; his well-known *Ricordi* were published in 1546. (31) Cristoforo Bondelmonti, writing in 1422, reported the frequent discovery of classical vases and statuettes at Rhodes. A decade earlier the Hospitallers had erected the castle of Saint Peter on the mainland at Bodrum, plundering the Mausoleum at Halikarnassos for stone and building pieces of ancient sculpture into the castle walls. The site was, apparently, only identified as the classical Halikarnassos early in the sixteenth century. By that time various Italian patrons were interested and a number of Hospitallers, including Fr. Sabba da Castiglione who acted as an agent for Isabella Gonzaga, became antique dealers and hunted the Aegean for fragments of classical sculpture which they sent back to Italy. (32)

The successful defence of Rhodes against the Egyptians between 1440 and 1444, various

(24) National Library of Wales, Aberystwyth, Ms. 5031 D.

(25) ZAMMIT - MIZZI, i. 97-99; BOSIO, ii. 314.

(26) J. RICHARD, "La fauconnerie de Jean de Francières et ses sources", *Le moyen âge*, lxix (1963); R. WISTEDT, *Le livre de fauconnerie de Jean de Fransières: l'auteur et ses sources* (Lund, 1967).

(27) Texts in J. GALEA, *ANTE*, xx (1962), 67-68.

(28) A. SEGARIZZI, *Della vita e delle opere di Michele Savonarola* (Padua, 1900), 12.

(29) BOSIO, ii. 607-608.

(30) V. FLYNN, "The Intellectual Life of Fifteenth-Century Rhodes," *Traditio*, ii (1944).

(31) A. LUZIO, "Lettere inedite di Fra Sabba da Castiglione", *Archivio storico lombardo*, xiii (1886).

(32) F. HASLUCK, in *Annual of the British School at Athens*, xviii (1911-1912), 211-216.

accounts of which reached Europe, (33) did something to improve the Hospitallers' reputation. In Fr. Melchiore Bandini's time the Chancellor was instructed to chronicle the lives of the Masters while they were alive, though without allowing them to see their own obituaries, and after Bandini's death the task passed to Guillaume Caoursin. (34) This presumably represented an elaboration of the traditional practice of adding to the official chronologies of the deceased Masters, for these lists were still being continued during the fifteenth century. (35) The Vice-Chancellor also composed reports which were almost historical works in their own right. Thus the Master's despatches of September 1480 to the Emperor and the Pope were included almost verbatim in Guillaume Caoursin's history of the 1480 siege. (36)

An increased awareness of the importance of propaganda, which would help raise the men and money to defend Rhodes, seems to have followed the introduction of printing. Only four months after the siege of 1480 was over, Guillaume Caoursin's *Obsidionis Rhodie Urbis Descriptio* was in print. The *liber conciliorum,* which was not kept up during the siege, contained the following entry:

> *Quia Civitas Rhodi obsidebatur per Turcos, et summo conatu oppugnabatur, in tanta rerum perturbatione ac formidine peracta in scriptis non sunt redacta; sed habita victoria historia est edita per Guillelmum Caoursin Rhodiorum Vicecancellarium, quae per orbem impressorum arte est divulgata, qua propter in hoc spatio nihil est registratum. Ita est: G. Caoursin Rhodiorum Vicecancellarius.* (37)

Another early work printed for the Order, at Cologne apparently in 1481, was a papal indulgence designed to help the Hospitallers raise money for the defence of Rhodes. (38) A volume of papal privileges conceded to the Hospital was printed, also at Cologne, in 1495. (39) Meanwhile translations, adaptions and new editions of Caoursin's history had been appearing. In 1496 Caoursin added various treatises on aspects of the Order's history in his own times, such as the earthquake at Rhodes, the affair of the Ottoman prince Djem, and the arrival of the right hand of Saint John the Baptist. Among those who were present at the siège of 1522 and published accounts of it were the Hospitaller Fr. Jacques, *bâtard* de Bourbon, whose history, which was published in French, included extracts from his own siege diary, and Jacques Fontaine of Bruges, a judge in the court of appeal at Rhodes, whose Latin history appeared in 1524 and became very popular. There were accounts in Greek, popular laments in Italian and, once again, numerous translations. (40)

Caoursin seems not to have attempted a general history, perhaps because of the existence of Bandini's work, but in the introduction to his new codification of the statutes, published in Latin in 1493, he included a brief treatise on the origins of the Hospital. This was placed before the statutes in the position formerly occupied either by the old legends and *miracles* or by the version of the Order's foundation written by Fr. Guglielmo di San Stefano at the end of the thirteenth century. Caoursin sought to establish a mid-term between the *miracles* and Fr. Guglielmo's dissertation; he had no new sources concerning the Order's origins. His treatise concluded with a reference to the second Master of the Hospital Fr. Raymond du Puy:

(33) L. Nicolau d'Olwer, "Un témoignage catalan du siège de Rhodes en 1444", *Estudis universitaris catalans,* xii (1927); C. Marinesco, "Du nouveau sur *Tirant lo Blanch*", *Estudis romànics,* iv (1953-1954), 139-156, 197-203. These two articles contain important information on the 1444 siege.

(34) Mifsud, 11, 33, n. 112 (the exact date of these instructions is not made clear).

(35) Eg. Biblioteca Nazionale, Florence; Ms. cl. xxxii. 37, f. 347-349v.

(36) C. Torr, *Rhodes in Modern Times* (Cambridge, 1887), 21, n. 1, 98.

(37) Text in E. Leopardi, *ANTE,* xiv, no. 1 (1950), 15.

(38) *Catalogue of Books Printed in the XVth Century now in the British Museum,* i (rev. ed: London, 1963), 311.

(39) Zammit-Mizzi, vii. 167-168.

(40) Fumagalli and F. de Hellwald, *Bibliographie méthodique de l'Ordre souverain de Saint Jean de Jérusalem* (Rome, 1885); cf. E. Mizzi, *Le guerre di Rodi; Relazioni di diversi autori sui due grandi assedi di Rodi: 1480-1522* (Turin, 1934).

> *Cuius magistri vestigiis plerique successores inherentes; egregia facinora in Rhodiorum gestorum commentariis diffusius enarrata perpetrarunt: que hoc loco recensere necessarium non videtur. Nam in presentia historiam texere propositum non est. Sat quidem fuit ordinis primordia et originem demonstrasse. Quomodo autem: et quo tempore militia Hierosolymitana hospitalitas et hec sancta observatio ad Rhodios transmigraverit dilucide declarant commentaria.*

An ordinance of 5 August 1493 provided for the translation of the new statutes into "various vulgar tongues", and in the French edition, published within a decade, the phrase *Rhodiorum gestorum commentariis* wrongly appeared as *Histoires des gestes de Rhodes* while the final *commentaria* became *Histoires Rhodiennes.* In fact, the *commentaria* were either the *miracles,* or Fr. Guglielmo di San Stefano's treatise, or the lists of deceased Masters, or — just conceivably — Bandini's history. There was no other general work for Caoursin to use. (41)

(41) Texts and discussion in *Recueil des historiens des croisades: historiens occidentaux,* v (Paris, 1895), cxxvi-cxxviii, 402-435. The text is here quoted from *Stabilimenta, primordium.* TORR, 96, deduces from the Latin text that, in addition to Caoursin's works, there were lost "commentaries" containing the Order's history. He also cites a reference of 10 October 1489 to the *commentarij,* but it is clear from the text (*Stabilimenta, de ecclesia,* xxxix) that the reference was to Caoursin's works on the 1480 siege. TORR added that the preface to PAULI (*op. cit.*) suggests that these "commentaries" were extant at Malta in 1737; yet it is difficult to find any passage in the preface to either volume to justify that. In fact PAULI, i. 299-300, omitted the final sentence *Quomodo . . . commentaria* in transcribing this passage.

The sources, the scholars, the public interest were not lacking; yet, except for Fr. Melchiore Bandini's work, the history of the Hospital continued — apparently — to be neglected during the fifteenth century, as it had been in the fourteenth. Only in the second half of the sixteenth century was a proper general history of the Order produced, and by then much material for such a work had been lost. When Giacomo Bosio came to write the Hospitallers' history he noted, in the *proemio* to the first edition published in 1594, that some authors had treated "certain particular events and actions"; that others had begun the whole story but died without completing it; and that Caoursin's treatises were too brief. Above all he lamented the loss of Bandini's history of the Hospital:

> *Affaticossi prima d'ogni'altro intorno à ciò, il Cavaliere Fra Melchionne Bandino, il quale essendo Cancelliero di quest'Ordine, in tempo del Gran Maestro Fra Giovanni di Lastic, scrisse l'Istoria della detta Religione fin a tempi suoi. Però di quanto egli scrisse, poco, o nulla si trova; essendosi quell'Istoria con danno incomparabile de gli Studiosi perduta.* (42)

(42) The present study is based almost exclusively on printed sources; it should be emphasized that it does little more than raise questions which demand detailed research in the archives, above all at Malta. Professor Lionel Butler most kindly gave his help over a number of problems connected with this study.

III
The Hospitallers' Historical Activities: 1530 - 1630

When the Hospitallers occupied Malta in 1530 there was still no proper general history of the Hospital from the time of its foundation onwards (1). In the mid-fifteenth century the Chancellor, Fr. Melchiore Bandini, had — apparently — written some sort of account of the Order down to his own times, but it was never published and seems to have been lost (2). During their early years at Malta the brethren were primarily occupied with the practical problems of government and defence, and their historical activities remained in neglect. Descriptions of the sieges of Rhodes in 1480 and 1522, together with papal privileges and indulgences, speeches by the Order's orators and editions of the statutes, continued to be printed and reprinted, while the great vogue for matters concerning the Turks brought the Hospitallers increasingly to the public notice(3). Fr. Jean Quintin's report on Malta, the *Insulae Melitae Descriptio*, appeared in 1536. Translations of Jacques Fontaine's history of the final siege of Rhodes and of Theodorico Adameo's *Commentario dell'Isola di Rhodi e dell'ordine di Cavalieri di Quella* were published at Venice in 1544 by Francesco Sansovino, who himself wrote a work on the military orders. In 1524 the adventurous Fr. Antonio Pigafetta dedicated his account of Magellan's circumnavigation of the world, in which he had participated, to the Master of the Hospital. Then in 1542 and 1553 Fr. Nicolas Durand de Villegaignon, who had studied at Orleans University, published accounts of the North African campaigns in which he had served; subsequently Villegaignon became a Protestant, attempted to colonize Brazil, and wrote theological works. More conventional Hospitallers like Fr. Bernardo Salviati, Fr. Giulio Cesare Falcone and Fr. Lodovico Melzo produced manuals on fortifications and other military and naval topics (4).

There were always a number of scholarly brethren, such as the Vice-Chancellor Fr. Thomas Guichard, and Fr. Tommaso Bosio who, after studying law at Paris, succeeded Guichard as Vice-Chancellor in 1527 and became Bishop of Malta in 1538. Fr. Tommaso and his brother Fr. Antonio Bosio, another distinguished Hospitaller, were uncles to Giacomo Bosio, who between 1594 and 1602 finally published the first complete history of the Hospital (5). Among various French Hospitallers with historical interests was Fr. Jean Quintin, known as *Haeduus*. Born at Autun in 1500, he travelled in the Levant, visited Rhodes and joined the

(1) A. Luttrell, « The Hospitallers' Historical Activities: (i) 1291-1400: (ii) 1400-1530 », *ANTE*, xxiv (1966); xxv (1967).

(2) *Infra,* 146.

(3) See F. De Hellwald, *Bibliographie méthodique de l'Ordre souverain de Saint Jean de Jérusalem* (Rome, 1885); E. Rossi, *Aggiunta alla Bibliographie... Hellwald* (Rome, 1924); T. Guarnaschelli - E. Valenziani, « Saggio di una bibliografia di Malta... », *Archivio storico di Malta,* ix (1938); and the standard modern catalogues.

(4) Cf. A. Gilbert, « Fr. Lodovico Melzo's 'Rules for Cavalry' », *Studies in the Renaissance,* i (1954).

(5) G. Bosio, *Dell'Istoria della Sacra Religione... di San Giovanni Gierosolimitano,* 3 vols. (1st ed: 1594-1602), ii. 514; iii. 4, 46, 50 *et passim.* (The 1602 edition of vol. iii is that cited below).

Order, serving in the Master's household. He was a member of the commission which inspected Malta before the Hospital accepted it in 1530, after which he wrote his *Insulae Melitae Descriptio*. Later he became a Professor of Canon Law at Paris where he died in 1561, having published various scholarly works on law, theology and history (6). Quintin was a regent in the Chancery at Malta in 1535, and became Secretary to the new Master, Fr. Didier de Saint-Jaille. He may have explored the archives at Malta, for apparently he wrote what Giacomo Bosio later described as "brevi Epitome, o siano Annotationi", of the Masters. Bosio consulted it and noted that while Quintin stated that Fr. Odo de Pins was corruptly elected Master in 1294, this was not mentioned in the "antiche Annotationi de' Maestri" then preserved in the Chancery at Malta, which was presumably a version of the old chronologies of the deceased Masters (7).

Among the Hospitallers in Quintin's circle was Fr. Antoine Geoffroi who, having travelled in Syria and the Levant, was able to publish an account of the Ottoman state based on his own experiences as well as on various Italian works. While naturally biased against the Turks, his description of their customs, religion, government and history was the most trustworthy and realistic then available in French; it even contained the Paternoster in Turkish and attempted to reproduce Turkish words in Latin script. Geoffroi stated that his book was written for his old friend Fr. Jean Quintin, who composed a Latin preface for it which he addressed to another Hospitaller who had given help and encouragement, Fr. Guillaume Quignon who was Preceptor of Saint-Jean-du-Lateran at Paris, Prior of the Order's Convent of Corbeil, and *Stamparum generalis Hospitalis Militiae per Galliam Procurator*. The original French version, published at Paris and Antwerp in 1542, was reprinted in 1543 and 1546, and appeared in Latin editions of 1573 and 1577 (8).

Geoffroi may not have visited the Chancery at Malta before he wrote his book, in which he devoted only a few pages to Rhodes and the Hospitallers there. Nothing in his work, which was largely based on first-hand knowledge, suggested that he was familiar with the Order's archives at that time. However, he was at Malta in 1547 when he was received into the English *langue* and given seniority in the Scottish Preceptory of Torphichen. In 1555, acting as Lieutenant of the Turcopolier, he presided at a meeting of the English *langue* at Malta (9). In 1548 Geoffroi, by then Preceptor of Vinadières, went on a mission from Malta to the papal *curia*. In 1551 he accompanied Fr. Claude de la Sengle to Rome and delivered a Latin oration before the pope; this was printed and later received praise from Giacomo Bosio, who said that "considering it was the work of a Knight of the Order it was truly very ornate and honorable in style". When de la Sengle was elected Master in 1553 Geoffroi, who was in Rome at the time, became his secretary, and he once again made a speech announcing the election to the pope and cardinals. In 1555 Geoffroi was officially charged by the Chapter-General at Malta with the task of writing the history of the Hospital, but he died in the following year. He had worked both at Malta and in the Vatican archives, and had begun his history, but it remained unfinished and in 1594 Giacomo Bosio wrote that this incomplete part of Geoffroi's history was not to be found (10). Fr. Antoine Geoffroi did little more than collect material, yet while others had written about the Order in their own times, he was one of the first, perhaps the very first, to search systematically in the archives, thus pointing the way

(6) P. Papillon, *Bibliothèque des auteurs de Bourgogne*, i (Dijon, 1742), 175-177.

(7) Bosio, ii (1594), 5; iii. 155, 158.

(8) Antoine Gueffroy, *Estat de la court du Grand Turc...* (Paris, 1542), preface; cf. C. Rouillard, *The Turk in French History, Thought and Literature: 1520-1600* (Paris, 1938), 185-189.

(9) H. Scicluna, *The Book of Deliberations of the Venerable Tongue of England: 1523-1567* (Malta, 1949), 31, 48, 74-75, 77.

(10) Bosio, i (1594), proemio: iii, 254, 281, 343, 359, 375.

ahead at Malta and in Rome where so much important material survived.

Scholarly activities continued at Malta. Throughout the century there was a good deal of copying of documents and composing of treatises, both in the Chancery and in the archives of the priories, while the great siege of 1565 brought a new swell of public interest in the Hospital. The Chapter-General of 1569 ordered the transcription of the original documents in the archives; in the case of the Chapters-General, however, the earliest records copied were those of 1526 (11). In addition to the French associates of Fr. Antoine Geoffroi and a group of German-speaking brethren at Strassbourg, the Order contained scholars like the English Hospitaller Fr. Oliver Starkey Latin Secretary to the Master, who also had both an Italian and a Spanish Secretary. Giacomo Bosio mentioned the Genoese Fr. Raffaele Silvago and Fr. Nicolas de Blancheline of France, both of whom spent time at Malta and were there in 1565, as being among those who wanted to write the history of the *attioni* of the Hospital but who were impeded by death and the difficulties of the task, so that "they did not leave any writings" (12). A more exclusively literary member of the Order was the distinguished scholar Annibale Caro, whose chief interest in the Hospital lay in the benefices it provided him in Italy, and who was quick to excuse himself from service in Malta. However he kept some of the brethren in touch with learned circles, corresponding with Fr. Antoine Geoffroi, with Giacomo Bosio's uncle Giannotto Bosio, and with Fr. Raffaele Silvago, to whom he wrote in 1565: "I wish that you too may become an antiquarian and connoisseur of medallions" (13).

One member of this group was the Piemontese Fr. Giuseppe Cambiano, who was the Order's Receiver-General in Rome in 1558 (14). He was Procurator-General in 1561, and Ambassador in Rome in 1562. When he visited Malta in 1567 he left Giannotto Bosio in charge at Rome, and later he returned from Malta with the young Fr. Giovanni Ottone Bosio (15). Cambiano's only published work was a brief thirty-five page edition, dated 1568, of a papal confirmation of the Hospital's privileges (16), but in about 1555 he composed a dialogue in which he discoursed with two Venetian Hospitallers on the contemporary organization of the Order, and expounded his conviction that the Hospital should abandon Malta for Tripoli. This dialogue, which Bosio knew, was accompanied by a short description of Malta (17). Cambiano touched briefly on the foundation and early history of the Hospital, but most of the several pages he devoted to the period at Rhodes were concerned with the great siege; his information was mainly derived from the well-known legends about the origins of the Order and from the commentaries of the fifteenth-century Vice-Chancellor, Guillaume Caoursin, whom Cambiano specifically mentioned (18). Like many people, Cambiano and his friends were concerned at the lack of a proper general history of the Order which, they complained, forced them to rely on old chronicles or a few fragments which were mostly in manuscript and dealt chiefly with more modern affairs. Cambiano mentioned that the talented Fr. Antoine Geoffroi was working in the Vatican archives and library, and one of his interlocutors declared enthusiastically that if he ever secured Geoffroi's history, he would possibly have it printed (19).

Interest was high not only among the Italian, French and German brethren, but also among the Spaniards, at a time when the Vice-Chancellors included Fr. Martín Royas de Por-

(11) A. Zammit - J. Mizzi, *Catalogue of the Records of the Order of St. John of Jerusalem in the Royal Malta Library*, i- (Malta, 1964-), iv. 3.

(12) Bosio, i (1594), proemio; iii. 332, 342-343, 513, 542-543, 659, 697 *et passim*.

(13) Annibale Caro, *Lettere familiari*, ed. A. Greco, 3 vols. (Florence, 1957-1961), nos. 410, 419, 427-429, 512-518, 608, 700, 760-762, 766 *et passim*. Greco fails to identify *Vinadera Turcopiliero* and confuses Gianotto with Ottone Bosio.

(14) Caro, no. 514.

(15) Bosio, iii. 453, 455, 796-797.

(16) Hellwald, 226.

(17) Excerpt and date *infra*, 146; Bosio, iii. 317.

(18) Archivio Vaticano, Misc. Arm. II 81, f. 220-233 (Caoursin: f. 230v; *nostri annali*: f. 232v).

(19) Text *infra*, 146.

talrubio and the Catalan Fr. Tomás Gargallo. A version of the statutes had appeared at Salamanca in 1534; the 1556 edition of the rule was the work of Fr. Díaz Rodriguez; the first two editions of Francesco Balbi di Correggio's history of the siege of 1565 appeared in Spain in Castilian; and the new statutes of 1577 were published from Madrid. The international character of the interest in the Hospital's history was emphasized by the appointment of a Catalan Hospitaller, Fr. Joan Antoni Foxa, to continue Geoffroi's work. Foxa's history of the Hospital from the earliest times onwards was originally completed in 1563. One version, carrying the story to 1553 and dated Barcelona, 25 June 1563, was entitled *Primera parte dela ystoria dela sacra Religion y milicia de sant Joan bautista de hierusalem en la qual se contenien los Echos de los grandes maestres y Religiosos desde su principio y fundacion Asta el año de mill y quinientos y cinquenta y tres, la qual Recogio y compuso fr Joan Antonio de foja cavallero dela mesma Horden* (20). This work was sufficiently popular for four other copies, at the very least, to be made (21). Foxa became the "fiel coronista" of the Hospital; he wrote at the express command of the Master Fr. Jean de La Valette, continuing his work though complaining of various head and stomach aches (22). One version was continued down to 1565, and concluded with an account of the siege (23).

Foxa was at Malta in 1556 when he went on a mission to Sicily (24), and probably he knew Fr. Antoine Geoffroi. He wrote the history Geoffroi had planned, using the notes Geoffroi had made at Malta: "un somario de las cosas antiguas de nuestra religion que yo tengo escrito de mano de Fray Antonio Jofre", who had used "unos quadros viejos de nuestra cancilleria" (25). Foxa was not quite accurate in complaining that all his own material for the period down to 1350 had to be drawn from the chronicles, many of which, he added, paid scant attention to the Order's affairs (26). Among the 105 items Foxa listed as his sources were documents in the archives at Malta which included "algunas cartas y breves apostolicas y de la cancilleria de nuestra Orden... juntamente con las breves y registros de cancilleria"; certain papal bulls; the statutes, "dictarios", and an "institucion" of the Order (27). Foxa also cited documents from the archives of the Order's Priory of Catalunya in Barcelona, where he worked (28). In addition, Foxa found fourteenth-century material in an extended version in French of the chronology of the deceased Masters which had been continued down to the Mastership of Fr. Philippe Villiers de l'Isle Adam; this was given him by Fr. Pierre Gozon de Melac, Prior of Saint-Gilles de Provence (29). Gozon had fought at Rhodes in 1522, later serving at Malta and fighting the Turks at sea; he became Prior of Saint-Gilles in 1558 and General of the Galleys in 1561, dying at sea in 1562. He was the sort of person who could have provided first-hand information on sixteenth-century events, but he may also have retailed to Foxa, who accepted it, the old story of how his ancestor Fr. Deodon de Gozon, Master of the Hospital from 1346 to 1353, had slain a dragon at Rhodes and how the family still possessed a relic of the dragon which had miraculous properties (30).

While Foxa's work remained in manuscript

(20) Biblioteca Nacional, Madrid, Ms. 3027 (the version cited here). Foxa's work awaits thorough study.

(21) Royal Malta Library, Biblioteca Ms. 314, in 2 vols. (to 1523 only; copied in 1574); British Museum, London, Egerton Ms. 1877 (to 1565); Archivio Histórico Nacional, Madrid, Ordenes militares, cod. 674-B (to 1391 only); Biblioteca Nacional, Madrid, Ms. 18236 (title says *Hasta 1553* but it closes in 1523; copied September 1576).

(22) Malta and London Mss., dedication.

(23) London Ms: the account of the siege at f. 734-808 may not have been by Foxa, for a marginal note at the foot of f. 733 reads: "No llegoâmos el Coronista". The date of Foxa's death is unknown.

(24) Bosio, iii. 372.

(25) Foxa, f. 180, 185.

(26) Foxa (London Ms.), f. 11-12.

(27) Foxa, f. 6-8v. The lists of books in the London and Malta Mss. make no mention of Pantaleon, but Madrid, Ms. 3027, f. 7v (presumably copied after 1581), included: "Henrrique pantaleon de los Hechos De los cavalleros de san Juan y de germania Historia de los Turcos".

(28) Foxa, f. 171v, 176v.

(29) Foxa, f. 163v (London Ms., f. 213); cf. Ante, xxiv. 128-129; xxv. 149.

(30) Bosio, iii. 245, 392, 395, 445, 454; F. Hasluck, « Dieudonné de Gozon and the Dragon of Rhodes », *Annual of the British School at Athens,* xx (1913-14).

it was, strangely enough, a Swiss Protestant who became the first writer to publish a history of the Hospital from its foundation onwards. A number of scholars at Protestant universities such as Basel and Strassbourg were interested in ecclesiastical history, and Heinrich Pantaleon, born in 1522, grew up in a bookish, hard-working, evangelical atmosphere at Basel. He reveived his baccalaureate at Heidelberg in 1541, became Professor of Latin at Basel in 1544, and Professor of Rhetoric there in 1548; his *Chronographia Ecclesiae Christianae* appeared at Basel in 1550. Pantaleon then abandoned theology for medicine. His fellow-citizen Felix Platter, whom he visited in Montpellier in 1553, described him as a jovial, noisy German: "he had little taste for preaching; he preferred the bottle, good company and amusements". Pantaleon received his doctorate in medicine at Valence and then returned to Basel in 1554. At this time he developed his interest in history. In 1557 he became Professor of Physics, but he was also occupied with editions of the New Testament and of Aristotle; his version of the *Martyrum Historia* appeared in 1559, and in 1564 he published an edition of Guillaume of Tyre's history of the crusades, to which he wrote a preface. In many ways Pantaleon was a typical Northern patriotic historian and perhaps his greatest work was his three-volume *Prosopographiae,* a collection of lives of eminent Germans published in 1565 and 1566. In 1566 the Emperor created him Count Palatine and Poet Laureate; he was Rector of Basel University in 1585; and he died in 1595 (31).

Heinrich Pantaleon was friendly with a group of literary-minded Swiss-German Hospitallers. Two of these were Fr. Martin Schmid, Preceptor of Strassbourg, and Fr. Johannes Hol who was with Schmid at Strassbourg from 1534 onwards and succeeded him as preceptor in 1562. In 1565 Pantaleon visited Hol and gathered from him some learned information on the Order's history. He also met Fr. Georg Bombast von Hohenheim. Born of a noble Swabian family in 1500, Fr. Georg was educated at the imperial court and served in various European wars; he became a Hospitaller and went with the Master in 1530 to Malta. On his return to Germany he administered various preceptories including that at Basel, but he was again in Malta in 1549 when he became Grand Baillif of Germany; in 1551 he served in Tripoli, and in 1552 was appointed to command Fort San Elmo at Malta. In 1554 he became Prior of Germany, and from then until his death in 1566 Bombast, who patronized various literary men, aided and encouraged Pantaleon in his work on the Hospital and provided him with information on its history (32).

Pantaleon probably began to take notes for his history of the Hospital, in which Fr. Georg Bombast at first cooperated, in the years after Bombast's return to Basel in 1554; the work was continued, improved and finally published at Basel in 1581 (33). In his *Prosopographiae,* which appeared in 1565 and 1566, Pantaleon paid considerable attention to various German Hospitallers and even gave brief outlines of the Order's history. In his history of the Hospital Pantaleon again emphasized the deeds of the German brethren, probably for patriotic reasons but perhaps also because information on them was more readily available to him. By contrast with the bulk of his writings, which followed a well-established pattern of editions, translations and patriotic history, Pantaleon's work on the Hospital was rather original. In his preface Pantaleon, like others, noted the absence of a complete history of the Hospital from its origins to modern times, and he wrote

(31) H. Buscher, *Heinrich Pantaleon und sein Heldenbuch* (Basel, 1946), listing surviving letters and Mss; *IDEM, Der Basler Arzt Heinrich Pantaleon: 1522-1595* (Aarau, 1947). Neither work discusses the problems studied here.

(32) H. Pantaleon, *Prosopographiae Heroum atque Illustrum Virorum Totius Germaniae,* 3 vols. (Basel, 1565-1566), iii. 165, 333, 335, 423-425, 532; Bosio, iii. 262, 286-287, 323-325, 751.

(33) H. Pantaleon, *Militaris ordinis Joannitarum, Rhodiorum aut Melitensium equitum ... Historia Nova* (Basel, 1581), preface. R. Thommen, *Geschichte der Universität Basel: 1532-1632* (Basel, 1889), 275, mentioned Pantaleon's "Historia Johannitarum equitum Basil. 1559"; no such work is known, and the 1581 edition preface itself referred to "prima hac editione".

of the inadequacies of his own studies and of the difficulties, which had deterred other scholars, of research among so many books. In fact, he worked mainly from printed books, mostly chronicles. His list of sources included "Ioannitarum annales", possibly the works of Guillaume Caoursin, and the "Statuta Ioannitarum" which were also in print, and he mentioned that the materials supplied by Fr. Georg Bombast included "aliquot Ordinis annales" and certain "peregrinae epistolae". Considerably over half of the history was given to the period between 1500 and 1580; only eleven pages out of 387 were devoted to the years from 1319 to 1398, and part of those eleven pages was taken up with pictures and with disquisitions on Rhodes in classical times, on the doings of the Genoese, and so on. Pantaleon apparently saw little or no original material on that period, and the "annales" and "epistolae" probably related mainly to the period after about 1480; he did not know Foxa's manuscript history completed in 1563, which was based on documents from Malta and the Vatican. Heinrich Pantaleon's work was of strictly limited value, yet it did provide the first continuous history of the Hospital to be published.

The need for a more scholarly work remained, however, and Foxa's successor was Giacomo Bosio who had close connections with the Order through his uncles Fr. Antonio, Fr. Tommaso the Vice-Chancellor, and Giannotto who was the Master's agent at the papal *curia*; Giacomo, in fact, replaced Giannotto in that office in 1571. Giannotto Bosio had accompanied Geoffroi to Rome in 1553, and Giacomo may have met Geoffroi then. In 1577 Giacomo visited Malta briefly. His elder brother Fr. Giovanni Ottone Bosio became a secretary to the Master Fr. Jean de La Valette, lost an eye in the siege of Malta in 1565, and wrote a treatise on the Hospitallers' vow of poverty. Giacomo Bosio moved in a literary world in Rome and kept a fine library in his *palazzo* in Via Condotti. He wrote *La Corona del Cavalier Gierosolimitano*, an unctuous allegorical mélange of classical history, theological moralization and precepts for the good Hospitaller which was published in 1588, while his translations of the statutes into Italian received the approbation of the Order and appeared in print in 1589 (34).

On 11 March 1589 Giacomo Bosio was created *historiographus* of the Order and granted a pension for three years in which he was to revise, extend and complete the history of the Hospital begun by Foxa and others; the work was to be in Italian, and Bosio was given permission to secure copies of documents at Malta and in the archives of the priories. Two volumes appeared in 1594, and on 28 January 1598 Bosio's pension was extended to him for life, as Foxa's had been, in order to avoid a change in authorship for the third volume, which finally appeared in 1602; Bosio was also encharged to publish all the Order's privileges in a single volume. Then in 1604 Bosio, declaring that he was old, feeble and ill, and that he wished to retire, secured the confirmation of his pension together with powers to delegate his duties as agent in the *curia* and as historian, and to nominate as his successor either his nephew and adoptive son, the famous archaeologist Antonio Bosio, or some other kinsman (35). Though not a member of the Order, Giacomo Bosio was familiar through his family, his career and his own writings with the Order's past. He had worked so quickly that the first two volumes of his history were published in 1594; the third, which he discreetly closed in 1571, appeared in 1602. He seems never to have begun the fourth part which he mentioned in his 1594 preface. He published a revised and extensively amplified edition of volume one in 1621; he died in 1627, and the second volume of the revised edition appeared posthumously in 1630,

(34) Details in P. FALCONE, « Il valore documentario della storia dell'Ordine Gerosolimitano di Giacomo Bosio », and « La patria di Giacomo Bosio », both in *Archivio storico di Malta*, x (1938-1939), correcting numerous errors. FALCONE, 100, wrongly places Cambiano's Maltese visit of 1567 to 1561.

(35) Royal Malta Library, Archives of the Order of St. John, cod. 445, f. 257-257v; cod. 450, f. 241v-243v; cod. 454, f. 243v-245.

being edited by Fr. Carlo Aldobrandini. There followed a second impression of the third part published at Naples in 1684, and a third impression of part one at Venice in 1695 (36).

Bosio repeated Foxa's claim that there was little material for the period before 1350 except in the chronicles. On the death of Antonio Bosio in 1629 the works relating to the Hospital from the Bosio library in Via Condotti were sent to Malta by Fr. Carlo Aldobrandini. These apparently included three manuscript histories of the Hospital: one, presumably in Italian, "in fogl. scritt. a penna con coperte di corame rosso dorate"; one in French; and one in two volumes in Spanish, which was possibly Foxa's history (37). It is clear from Bosio's own writings that, in addition to Foxa's manuscript, which he realized was in need of revision, and all the work published on the later history of the Order from about 1480 onwards, he had a single manuscript notebook in which Geoffroi had noted material discovered in the Vatican. Bosio may have had this from his uncle Giannotto, a friend of Geoffroi; he considered Geoffroi's other notebooks lost. Bosio himself conducted considerable researches in the Vatican, claiming to have gone through all the registers available there. He was also fortunate in having access to a large amount of material from the registers and other documents in the archives at Malta, for his brother Fr. Giovanni Ottone, who was at Malta and in 1593 became Vice-Chancellor, worked hard to supply him with copies and to collect information from the more senior Hospitallers. In particular, his brother provided him with sixteenth-century material collected by Agostino Santa Maura, a scribe in the Treasury. As a result Bosio was able to contradict Foxa, who — he said — had never worked "diligently" in the archives, on points of detail. Bosio made use of histories and chronicles already published but often he failed to extract important information from them. For example, he cited Zurita's history of Aragon on a relatively unimportant episode of 1336, but ignored other more significant details in the same work. He sensibly followed Geoffroi's history of the Ottomans in relying on the Armenian Hayton over a disputed point of Armenian history, arguing that an Armenian would know the history of his own country best, but on other occasions he accepted clearly unreliable chronicle evidence. He was prepared to include the story of Fr. Deodon de Gozon and the dragon in his history, but in doing so he did carefully refer readers to Foxa's text (38).

An example of the unreliability of both Foxa and Bosio is provided by their treatment of the obscure expedition of Hospitallers which reached Greece under the command of the Master Fr. Juan Fernández de Heredia in 1378. The relevant registers are missing both at Malta and in the Vatican, and Foxa was aware of the poverty of his sources with regard to this affair. Concerning Fernández de Heredia, he spoke of "lo poco del se halla escrito con aver tenido el magisterio 22 años", and he stated "no ai ystoria que buelba por el"; he also wrote of "el descuido que tuvo de mandar escrevir la coronica de su tiempo". Foxa said that Fernández de Heredia left Italy for Rhodes, but at the suggestion of the Venetians turned aside and captured Patras from the Turks, only to be taken prisoner by the Turks (39). In fact, the Master went neither to Rhodes nor to Patras, which was not in Turkish hands; nor was it the Turks who captured him. Fr. Giuseppe Cambiano, writing in about 1555, had also stated, though without reference to the Venetians, that Fernández de Heredia captured Patras from the Turks (40). Bosio, presumably referring to Foxa, said "alcuni scrivono" that the Venetians persuaded the Master to attack Patras and that he did so at once. Bosio also re-

(36) To FALCONE, add details in A. MIFSUD, « Appunti sugli archivi di Malta », *Archivum Melitense,* ii no. 13 (1914), 33, n. 112, (but note that his references are often inaccurate).

(37) A. VALERI, *Cenni biografici di Antonio Bosio* (Rome, 1900), 57-59.

(38) BOSIO, i (1594), proemio; i (2nd ed.: 1621), 758-759; ii (2nd ed.: 1630), 63, 71-74, 90, 220; iii. 359, 513-514.

(39) FOXA, f. 192v-193, 199.

(40) Archivio Vaticano, Misc. Arm. II 81, f. 232v.

ported that a "vita" of Fernández de Heredia, a manuscript copy of which had been sent to him on the orders of the Master Fr. Hugues de Loubenx Verdalle by Fernández de Heredia's descendants in Aragon, stated that Fernández de Heredia did sail first to Rhodes, and that he was finally captured not at Patras but at Corinth. Bosio contradicted Foxa at other points, citing both the registers and the statutes at Malta, and certain documents of which he wrote "tengo in casa molte"; probably these last were copies sent from Malta. In any case both Foxa and Bosio were wildly inaccurate in their accounts of the 1378 expedition. Bosio did note his sources and their contradictions, but nonetheless he reproduced material which was patently unreliable (41).

Bosio worked at the first edition of his history very quickly. The second edition, in part posthumous, was greatly enlarged and considerably improved, especially as the result of much more work done in the Vatican (42), and perhaps also at Malta, for Giacomo's brother the Vice-Chancellor was in Rome from 1603 until 1608, when he returned to Malta to find the Chancery in great disorder (43). Bosio's work was certainly in a different class from that of Pantaleon and a distinct advance on that of Foxa; it was a great achievement which has remained the most acceptable general history of the Hospital. It can not, however, be considered as reliable in the modern sense. Bosio's judgement was often at fault. He tended to reproduce documents word for word, but with serious errors. Even for the sixteenth century he is not an accurate authority but rather a *compilator* (44). Bosio's history was soon being adapted and diffused. Pierre de Boissat's French history of the Order, which appeared in 1612, and Geronimo Funes' history in Spanish, published in 1626 and 1639, were little more than translations of Bosio. Such works did include additional material, but usually it was drawn from local sources and added little to the story of the Hospital in Syria or at Rhodes; in any case, such information was often of doubtful value. By far the most popular of these histories was that of the unscrupulous popularizer, the Abbé Vertôt, which first appeared in 1726, and was subsequently augmented, translated and reprinted. As an historian Vertôt was far less reliable than Bosio on whose work he leaned heavily, repeating, compounding and embroidering Bosio's errors and introducing completely new ones (45). That there was soon dissatisfaction with this state of affairs was shown by a twenty-eight page pamphlet by Fr. François-Zacharie Pourroy de Quisonnas de Lauberivière, entitled *Prospectus d'une nouvelle histoire de l'Ordre de Malte dégagée de la prolixité de Bosio des écarts de Vertot et continuée depuis l'année* 1567 *d'après le dernier siège ou ils l'avaient abandonnée jusqu'à la presente* 1754 (46).

By 1642 there was a printing press in Malta (47), and in 1647 it issued the *Descrittione di Malta* by the Vice-Chancellor, Fr. Gian Francesco Abella, a most distinguished scholar who was not however primarily interested in the history of the Order (48). Fr. Salvatore Imbroll, Prior of the Conventual Church, was awarded a pension in 1633 to continue Bosio's history for the period after 1571, but his unfinished work remained in manuscript, for in 1634 he was replaced as official historiographer by Fr. Cesare Magalotti. The new historian of the Hospital apparently remained in Italy, and he had to bring a lawsuit against Imbroll in an attempt to secure both the pension and various papers which were thought to include

(41) Compare Bosio, ii (1630), 126-128, with A. Luttrell, « Intrigue, Schism, and Violence among the Hospitallers of Rhodes: 1377-1384 », *Speculum*, xli (1966), and the works there cited.

(42) Examples in Falcone, 123-128.

(43) B. Dal Pozzo, *Historia della Sacra Religione Militare di S. Giovanni Gerosolimitano Detta di Malta*, i (Verona, 1703), 489, 542.

(44) Falcone emphasizes Bosio's unreliability; his examples could easily be multiplied.

(45) Eg. R. Aubert de Vertôt, *Histoire des chevaliers hospitaliers de S. Jean de Jérusalem*, 4 vols. (1st ed.: Paris, 1726), ii. 94-98, on the 1378 incident.

(46) Cited in *Archivio storico di Malta*, ix (1938), 474.

(47) A. Gauci, « Origine e sviluppo della stampa in Malta... », *Archivio storico di Malta*, viii (1937).

(48) *G.F. Abella: Essays in his Honour by Members of the Malta Historical Society* (Malta, 1961).

some of Bosio's documents (49). Ultimately it was Fr. Bartolomeo dal Pozzo whose two volumes, published in 1703 and 1715, carried Bosio's history from 1571 to 1668. Thereafter there was no proper continuator, though the official historians included the Abbé Vertôt; Sebastiano Pauli, author of the *Codice Diplomatico* which appeared in 1733 and 1737; and Paolo Paciaudi, whose *Memorie de gran maestri* were published in 1780 (50). Except for Pauli's *Codice*, these works contained very little of real value for the period before 1523. The publication of chronicles and of works based on archives other than those of Malta naturally made an accurate assessment of the history of the Order at Rhodes ever more possible, but in effect there was little, apart from Pauli's documents, to add to the revised 1630 edition of Bosio's second volume. For the pre-Malta period there has been only a limited amount of subsequent work based firmly on the documents. J. Delaville le Roulx produced his great four-volume *Cartulaire* containing documents down to 1310, and he revised Bosio's history for the period until 1421, while in 1967 Jonathan Riley-Smith published a new history of the Hospital from its origins to 1310 (51); but for the fifteenth century Bosio remains the only standard work.

A NOTE ON THE MALTA ARCHIVES

When they were expelled from Rhodes the Hospitallers were forced to leave many of their documents there, according to the papal bull of 2 January 1524 which confirmed their ancient privileges, jurisdictions and exemptions:

> relinquere coacti fuerint, ac sub huiusmodi eventu litterae, libri et munimenta seu documenta antiqua privilegiorum et indultorum eis ab Apostolica sede concessorum perierint, et deperdita fuerint (52).

The documents abandoned included almost all the records of the Conventual Church of St. John at Rhodes (53). On 1 May 1527 the surviving *libri dela cancellaria* were placed in the castle at Viterbo to save them from the French, at the orders of the Vice-Chancellor Fr. Tommaso Bosio, who noted:

> furono tutti portati in la Roca che sono in tutto registri cento e quindeze cioe registri de bulle et diverse scripture novanta sete et libri de consegli desdoto e questo per un ricordo (54).

Subsequently the archives were transported to Malta where, according to his nephew Giacomo Bosio, Fr. Tommaso Bosio "ridusse le cose di quella cancellaria al bell'ordine e forma, c'hoggidì si ritrovano" (55).

Foxa's history, originally completed in 1563, mentioned the loss of documents at the fall of Jerusalem, Acre and Rhodes, "demas que algunas pocas que fueron reservadas en estas desgracias, y las que despues se havian escrito se quemaron un dia desastradamente" (56). Foxa was apparently claiming that it was documents written after 1523 rather than those surviving from before 1523 which were burnt. He also mentioned various notes from the Chancery which passed into private hands: "que en algunas notas de Canceleria que se preservaron en manos de algunos particulares en las pressuras que nuestro Convento ha padecido despues de dos desastradas quemas de las Escrip-

(49) V. Borg, *Fabio Chigi, Apostolic Delegate in Malta: 1634-1639* (Vatican, 1967), 129, 135-136, 162, 164-165; cf. A. Neri, « Cesare Magalotti istoriografo della Religione di Malta », *Archivio storico italiano*, 5 ser., ii (1888).

(50) Details in Mifsud, 33, n. 112; cf. E. Nasalli Rocca di Corneliano, « Il P. Paolo Paciaudi *storiografo* dell'Ordine di Malta », Ante, xxii (1964).

(51) J. Riley-Smith, *The Knights of St. John in Jerusalem and Cyprus: c. 1050-1310* (London, 1967).

(52) Text in F. Descluseaulx, *Privillèges des Papes, Empereurs, Roys et Princes de la Chrestienté en faveur de l'Ordre de S. Iean de Hierusalem* (2nd ed.: Paris, 1649), part i. 133.

(53) Malta, cod. 411, f. 5.

(54) Malta, cod. 412, f. 9.

(55) G. Bosio, *La Corona del Cavalier Gierosolimitano* (Rome, 1588), 55.

(56) Foxa, Malta Ms., introduction; London Ms., f. 8.

turas que en nuestra Religion acontecieron hallo mill argumentos..." (57). In one manuscript a marginal note added "dos veces se quemo el archivo de la religion" (58). Bosio mentioned a fire in the Chancery at Rhodes (59). It may be that Foxa was referring to one fire at Rhodes and to another at Malta in which no pre-1530 records were destroyed; this would be consistent with the disappearance of material for the period following 1530 and the apparent survival of all or almost all the pre-1530 material which reached Malta. For a long time the archives seem to have been moved from place to place, to the house of whoever was acting as Vice-Chancellor. The second fire may have caused the Chapter-General's decree of 1565 that a house be erected to serve as a Chancery, a decision repeated in 1588 and 1595, and put into effect after 1603 (60).

The documents removed from Rhodes, which subsequently survived the siege of 1565 and other hazards at Malta, included charters concerning the Order's privileges and possessions in Syria, a good many of the magistral registers of *libri bullarum* from 1346 onwards and of the *libri conciliorum* from 1459 onwards, six or seven volumes of the proceedings of Chapters-General, some *bullaria* containing papal bulls, and various miscellaneous documents. Almost all this material is still at Malta. The Hospital's diplomatic correspondence, its accounts, many administrative records, and possibly the archives of the Templars, were lost. Some records from before 1530, such as the deliberations of the Italian *langue* from 1435 to 1462, have entered the Malta archives, while there has been a small drain, an early but typical migration being the *liber bullarum* for 1516 to 1520 which was apparently borrowed by Giacomo Bosio. At least three *bullaria* of papal bulls and two other volumes of medieval documents have been lost since the early eighteenth century though certain of the gaps can partly be filled from surviving copies, including those made by Sebastiano Pauli. All but one or two of the 97 *libri bullarum* and all but five of the 18 *libri conciliorum* surviving in 1527 still exist at Malta. In all probability there can have been very little pre-Malta material at Malta in the sixteenth century that is not still there now (61). Much the same is also true of the Vatican records.

The bulk of the information on the fourteenth century in Foxa's and Bosio's histories derives from documents still existing in the Malta and Vatican archives (62). Foxa may have made slight use of documents at Barcelona which have since been lost (63), and a few items may have come from the other writers whose historical notes they used. Thus Foxa, in citing Giovanni Villani's chronicle to the effect that in 1334 the Latins captured 5000 Turks and burnt 250 of their ships, added "y en esto concuerda con un somario de las cosas antiguas de nuestra religion que yo tengo escrito de mano de Fray Antonio Jofre"; Foxa added that Geoffroi stated that he took his information "de un quaderno de nuestra cancellaria que el tenia en el qual estaron notadas con esta muchas otras cosas del año de 1303 hasta el de 1336" (64). This "quaderno" seems to be lost. Possibly someone before Geoffroi had been collecting material for a history of the Hospital, but since the evidence of the "quaderno" agreed with that of Villani it probably derived from Villani's chronicle rather than from fourteenth-century documents in the Order's archives which had already been lost

(57) Foxa, Malta Ms., ii. 25; London Ms., f. 212-213.
(58) Foxa, f. 163v.
(59) Bosio, i (1594), proemio.
(60) Details in Mifsud, 13-14.

(61) J. Delaville Le Roulx, *Les archives... de l'Ordre de Saint-Jean de Jérusalem à Malte* (Paris, 1883), 6-8; Mifsud, 16-30; Zammit-Mizzi, *passim*. On more recent changes and certain deficiencies in Delaville's works, A. Scufflaire, « Documents concernant l'histoire de la Belgique conservés ... à la Royal Malta Library, la Valette », *Bulletin de la Commission Royale d'Histoire*, cxxix (1963), 335-336 *et passim*.

(62) This point is immediately clear to anyone working in both archives.

(63) The documents of the Catalan priory, now in the Archivo de la Corona de Aragón at Barcelona where they are being reorganized, suffered disruption and partial destruction in 1936.

(64) Foxa, f. 180, 185; but Madrid, cod. 674-B, f. 165, London, f. 236, and Malta, ii. 66, give "1333 hasta el de 1336".

in Geoffroi's time (65). There is nothing to suggest that Geoffroi had seen any fourteenth-century material at Malta which is not available there now.

Giacomo Bosio and his predecessors obviously had more access to reliable information on the events of their own century than for the period before about 1480, and Bosio may have seen some or all of the five *libri conciliorum* for the period after 1459 which survived in 1527 but were subsequently lost. Yet for the fourteenth century there are very few points in Foxa's and Bosio's histories which cannot be traced either to some obvious printed source, usually a chronicle, or to a document still extant in the Maltese or Vatican archives. Furthermore, when Bosio's text is compared with these sources it can often be seen to be inaccurate. Yet much has been written about the Hospital which derives, directly or indirectly, from Bosio's history; in fact, many historians still use the plainly inferior first edition. This is even to some extent true of J. Delaville le Roulx' standard history of the Hospital in the fourteenth century which, despite extensive work in the archives, contains some unfortunate errors derived from Bosio (66). Ideally, historians of the earlier period should not rely on Bosio's history or on information derived from it, but should work directly from the contemporary records. For the period before about 1450, the sixteenth-century historians who worked on the history of the Hospital can have made only slight use of material not still available today, and where they did such material was likely to be unreliable; for these centuries the earliest histories, including that of Bosio, are therefore best ignored (67).

(65) The chroniclers' treatment of the 1334 incident is analysed in P. LEMERLE, *L'émirat d'Aydin, Byzance et l'Occident* (Paris, 1957), 96-100.

(66) Eg. on the extremely important affair of 1378-1381 discussed *supra,* 145, cf. J. DELAVILLE LE ROULX, *Les Hospitaliers à Rhodes jusqu'à la mort de Philibert de Naillac: 1310-1421* (Paris, 1913), 202-206.

(67) This, of course, is an ideal, and Bosio is frequently cited in the present work which is far from exhaustive, even of the printed material. The archives and manuscripts at Malta and elsewhere could provide more information about the sixteenth-century historians of the Hospital, though it is doubtful whether further research would seriously modify the conclusions contained in this paragraph.

Fr. Melchiore Bandini. Detail from a 15th-century painting by Girolamo di Giovanni, originally in the church of Sant'Agostino and now in the Pinacoteca Comunale, Camerino

FR. MELCHIORE BANDINI'S HISTORY

The assertion that Fr. Melchiore Bandini, who was already *cancellarius conventus Rhodi* on 1 April 1438 (68), wrote a history of the Hospital which was subsequently lost, depends on the passage published by Giacomo Bosio in 1594 (69). More recently A. Mifsud, citing Royal Malta Library, Biblioteca Ms. 339 part iii, Chapter- General of 1447 (*sic*), stated that in 1466(!) the Chancellor was charged with

(68) Royal Malta Library, Biblioteca Ms. 728, f. 1.

(69) Text reproduced ANTE, xxv. 150.

the task of writing a biography of each Master while he was still alive. Mifsud also wrote that Bandini was the first Chancellor to receive the "incarico di tessere gli elogi dei Gran Maestri", citing the register of the Chapter-General of 1469(!) which he said was Biblioteca Ms. 239(!) (70). He was presumably referring, carelessly, to a provision of the Chapter-General of 1446 found in Malta, cod. 1698, f. 87, of which Biblioteca Ms. 339 part iii, f. 73, contains a late copy:

De Annalibus et historiis magistrorum et cronicis

Ad nostre religionis famam perpetuam preteritorum mortuorum gloriam, viventium disciplinam decernimus, ut de singulis magistris hactenus defunctis vitam, mores, et gesta modernus cancellarius describat, quidquid eorum temporibus boni vel mali acciderit, suis locis designando. Item ceteri qui pro tempore futuro erunt cancellarij viventis magistri nobilitatem, genus, mores, vitia virtutes, et gesta, singula describant, sed viventi magistro aut alteri ea que de ipso scripserunt, nullatenus aperiant. Cum autem vita decesserit electo prius quam aliis defuncti predecessoris mores vitam et gesta manifestet, sitque aliis deinde inspiciendi facultas quod si viventi magistro cancellarius aut alter ea que de vivente pro tempore describet demonstraverit, sui officij ipso facto privationis penam incurrat.

Cod. 1689 contains the revision of the statutes passed at the revolutionary Chapter-General held in Rome in 1446, which was confirmed by the pope but never accepted by the Order (71). Bandini was present at the Chapter as Chancellor, but this is scarcely evidence of a specific *incarico;* in any case the official chronologies of the deceased Masters had been maintained since the thirteenth century, and Bandini may have done no more than continue the series. Cod. 1689 at one point belonged to Fr. Carlo Aldobrandini, who acquired and sent part of Bosio's library to Malta (72), but Bosio's account of the Chapter in Rome suggests that even if he knew the manuscript, he paid little attention to the lapsed statutes of 1446 (73); he may have had other information about a lost history by Bandini.

FR. GIUSEPPE CAMBIANO'S DIALOGUE (74)

Dialogo del R. Sig. Commen.re Hierosolimitano Fra Josef Cambiano Piemontese, Imbas.re a Roma: *dove si ragiona d'alcune cose degne di memoria della Religione dell Hospitale di S. Giovanni di Hierusalem, et de' Cavalieri di essa. Interlocutori*: *Mons. Bernardo Giustiniani. Il Commendator Cambiano. M. Hieronimo Quirini*:

" *Giu*: Ho sempre havuto desiderio grande di intendere chi sia stato il fondatore di questa nostra Religione di San Giovanni, et qual sia stato il suo principio, e mezo, col quale è divenuta si grande, et si honorata; che per esser' io Cavaliere, et membro di essa, parmi sia conveniente di saperlo; et però, se si trovasse alcun libro, ò memoria, che ne ragionasse, piglierei gran piacere, et diletto di vederlo. *Cam*: Signore, io non ho visto libro, nè memoria, che precisamente discorra, ò ragioni di questa materia, ò, se pure se ne trova, sono fragmenti scritti a mano, et piu presto si possono chiamar moderni, che antichi; come la descrittione de gli assedi fatti dal Soldano di Egitto, dal Turco alla Città di Rodi, massime nel tempo del Gran Maestro Fra Piero da Busson, nel quale la Religione acquistò gran reputatione,

(70) Mifsud, 11, 33, n. 112.
(71) R. Valentini, « Un capitolo generale degli Ospitalieri di S. Giovanni tenuto in Vaticano nel 1446 », *Archivio storico di Malta,* vii (1935-1936).

(72) Falcone, 133.
(73) Bosio, ii (1630), 224-228.
(74) Archivio Vaticano, Misc. Arm. II 81, f. 220-262 (*olim* f. 202-244); Biblioteca Vaticana, Ms. Urbin. 849, f. 1-62, contains a variant, Venetianized version. Date between 1553 (de la Sengle is mentioned as Master: f. 254v) and 1556 (death of Geoffroi, alive at time of writing: f. 220v); Cambiano, in fact, only became ambassador after 1561 (*supra,* 57).

et credito: Vi è ancora la fuga di Zizimi, fratello del Gran Turco, che si salvò in Rodi, per la ritentione del quale il Gran Turco pagava ogn'anno quarantacinquemila Ducati alla Religione. Sono ancora diversi Autori, che scrivono delle Guerre fatte da Christiani in Levante, che honoratamente parlano de la nostra Religione, et di quelle di Templarij, et di Theutonici, et massime delle Guerre, che si feciono in Hierusalem, et in quelle parti di Soria, et però fino al presente havemo ritenuto il nome di Cavalieri Hierosolimitani. Ci è ancora alcuna notitia del primo fondatore del nostro esercitio di Hospitalarij, a imitatione del quale il Gran Maestro nostro si chiama Maestro dell'Hospitale di Hierusalem; le quali memorie se fussero poste in un volume, credo, che sarebbe opera dilettevole, massime a noi Cavalieri, che siamo professi in essa Religione et che ci dilettiamo di vedere l'opere virtuose de' nostri antecessori, fatte in Hierusalem, et in altri luoghi di terra santa. *Giu*: Mi maraviglio, che fra tanti honorati Cavalieri, non ci sia stato alcuno, che habbia preso assunto di scrivere, ò di far scrivere, i progressi, che si erano fatti, et facevano; perche le virtù, che non restano in luce, et in memoria, in breve tempo si spengono, ne se ne può cavar frutto; et quelle, che si descrivono, danno animo, et esempio, alli successori di seguirle. *Cam*: Voi dite il vero, ma li nostri antecessori sono stati più pronti a far le buone opere, che a descriverle; pure al presente ci è un Cavaliere Fra Antonio Giofre, detto la Vinandiera, che usa gran diligenza di trovare le antichità et memorie delli fatti de' nostri antecessori, et pensa di farne una Cronaca, laquale sarà fruttuosa, et dilettevole, et per tal'effetto ha ricercati quanti registri, e scritture antiche si trovano nelli Archivij di Roma, et la libreria del Papa, et ha ritrovate molte cose, che sono a suo proposito, massime de' molti Privilegij, che ne concedeva la Sede Apostolica et confermatione di terre, e Città, che si guadagnavano in quelle parti di Soria, e d'Armenia, nel tempo, che i Christiani erono Signori di terra santa, et la nostra Religione si trovava in tanta prosperità, che metteva in campagna, cinque, ò seimila fanti, et piu di mille Cavalli. *Giu*: Mi saria molto grata il veder questa opera finita, perche intendo che questo Cavaliere, oltre alle buone lettere, è ancora dotato di buon giuditio, et di eccellente ingegno, et esperientia, et che da lui non potria venire se non cosa buona; et quando quest'opera mi venisse alle mani, potria essere, ch'io la facessi imprimere. Ma, lasciando queste antichità, . . ."

IV

Introduction to
J. Delaville le Roulx,
Les Hospitaliers à Rhodes jusqu'à la mort de Philibert de Naillac 1310-1421

Les Hospitaliers à Rhodes stands unchallenged as the standard treatment of its subject. Its author, Joseph Delaville le Roulx *alias* Le Roulx de la Ville, was born in Paris in 1855. He followed the conventional curriculum of the French medievalist: the École des Chartes, the École des Hautes Études, the École de Rome and the *mission aux archives.* The archives were those of the Hospitallers of the Order of St. John preserved at Malta, where he went in 1878 as a young student. Delaville thus associated himself with the French school of crusading historiography created by Paul Riant, Louis de Mas-Latrie and the aristocratic group of scholars belonging to the Societé de l'Orient latin. These historians were concerned with the evocation of French achievements in the Levant, the *Gesta Dei per Francos*, and they saw their noble crusading ancestors as the forerunners of the founders of the nineteenth-century colonial *France d'Outremer.*

Delaville's studies at Malta were followed by researches in the largely unknown archives of Spain and in many other parts of Europe. A preliminary account of the Malta documents was published in 1883, and a thesis on the origins of the Hospital appeared in 1885. The next year saw the publication of a major work not devoted to the Hospitallers, the two large volumes of *La France en Orient au XIVe siècle: expeditions du Maréchal Boucicault.* In 1893 came a long study of the Hospitaller archives in Spain and Portugal followed, between 1894 and 1906, by a truly stupendous achievement, the four colossal volumes of the *Cartulaire général de l'Ordre des Hospitaliers de St. Jean de Jérusalem*, publishing thousands of documents down to 1310 with an introduction on the Hospitallers' archives across the whole of Latin Europe. 1904 saw a history of the Order in Syria and Cyprus: *Les Hospitaliers en Terre Sainte et à Chypre:*

1100–1310, and if that volume has in many ways been superceded by J. Riley-Smith's *The Knights of St. John in Jerusalem and Cyprus: c. 1050–1310* published in 1967, Riley-Smith's work was made possible, as its author was the first to recognize, by Delaville's monumental *Cartulaire.* In 1910 Delaville reprinted eighteen studies dealing with priors, commanderies, seals, statutes and other Hospitaller topics, in a volume of *Mélanges sur l'Ordre de S. Jean de Jérusalem.*

Delaville died on 4 November 1911, having corrected the proofs of a new work, *Les Hospitaliers à Rhodes jusqu'à la mort de Philibert de Naillac: 1310–1421*, which was published posthumously in 1913 with a somewhat over-rhetorical and francophile preface by the Marquis de Vogüé. This work was no mere postscript to its author's career. If it took him chronologically beyond the Syrian period of the *Cartulaire*, it was a return to the deeds of Marshal Boucicault and *La France en Orient au XIVe siècle*; and it formed part of a project to continue the history of the Hospital at least to the end of its Rhodian era in 1522. For this later period there remains a mass of unused notes and transcripts gathered at Malta and in other archives by Delaville and the researchers who worked for him (1).

As a result of Delaville's premature death, the only major work based on the Hospital's archives and covering the whole medieval period is still that of Giacomo Bosio, published and revised between 1594 and 1629 (2). However *Les Hospitaliers à Rhodes* almost entirely superceded Bosio for the years it covered. Delaville's works had always been closely connected to the publication of documents, but the continuation of the *Cartulaire* beyond 1310 was scarcely a practical possibility; fragmentary as the Hospital's records are for the fourteenth century, it would certainly not be possible to print them in full. Delaville's *Rhodes* book contains merely a brief documentary appendix, but it is very firmly based on numerous references to the unpublished sources, so much so that many footnotes amount to miniature biographies of individual Hospitallers.

Sixty years after its publication, parts of *Les Hospitaliers à Rhodes* naturally require revision in the light of subsequent research, while the modern reader will be less interested than were Delaville's contemporaries in the aristocratic genealogies of the restricted group of French knights who controlled the Order. *Les Hospitaliers en Terre Sainte* had begun with a series of chapters proceeding chronologically from Master to Master, but these were followed by analyses of the Hospital's constitution, and of its central and regional organization; they were also buttressed by many studies printed elsewhere. The Rhodes book consists of a succession of chapters each devoted to a Master; however, this device was upset by the need to insert a chapter on the Hospitallers' absorption of the possessions of the suppressed Templars, and it was confused by the schism in the Roman church which led to the simultaneous existence of two conflicting Masters of the Hospital.

Furthermore the organization of the book could not cope altogether satisfactorily with a situation in which for several decades the dominating figure in the Order was not the Master but a rebellious lieutenant; this, however, is an almost insuperable problem which faces any historian seeking to interpret the development of the Hospital in the fourteenth century. This subordinate, Fr. Juan Fernández de Heredia, did eventually become Master in 1377 and he ruled the Order until his death in 1396. Delaville recognized the grandeur of Fernández de Heredia; indeed he exaggerated absurdly when he described him as "the arbiter of the destinies of Europe, the real head of the church and the true sovereign of Aragon" (3). The French scholar was constitutionally incapable of comprehending the foreign character and background of this Aragonese who broke the monopoly of French power in the Hospital. Fernández de Heredia was not another Albornoz, and Delaville misunderstood and misjudged the motivations of his admittedly obscure ambitions and interventions in mainland Greece, where he apparently hoped to establish Hospitaller rule. In this respect Delaville, though he worked in the Hospitallers' Spanish archives, simply ignored both the rich documentation of the Aragonese archives in Barcelona and the published works of his own Catalan contemporaries (4).

Les Hospitaliers à Rhodes sometimes treated matters at Rhodes rather too much in isolation, and external considerations such as the policies of the Western powers or developments in the Balkans were mentioned rather than explained. In Delaville's time the crusades of the period down to 1291 had already been studied extensively, but the later crusades of the fourteenth century largely awaited clear outlines and background detail, though Nicolai Iorga's *Philippe de Mézières (1327–1405) et la croisade au XIVe siècle* appeared in 1896 to supplement Delaville's own work on *La France en Orient au XIVe siècle.* Affairs at Rhodes had to be fitted into a complicated context. The Byzantine world was in full disintegration, while the

Ottoman state was at an early and unpredictable stage in its evolution. The interventions of the various Latin powers in this confusing situation are difficult to follow, even now that much more is known about papal finances, Venetian trade, the politics of Latin Greece and other subjects which determined Hospitaller policies, but one point seems clear: during the fourteenth century the Hospitallers played a consistent and continuous role in the whole process of Latin crusading, a movement which increasingly turned away from the holy lands in Syria and from attacks on Mamluk Egypt to the defence of Greek and Latin positions in the Aegean and the Balkans against truly spectacular Turkish advances (5). Despite significant progress in many aspects of Levantine history in the fourteenth century, *Les Hospitaliers à Rhodes* remains the fundamental study of its subject. An intelligent article by the Roumanian historian Iorga touched the central themes in a revisionary if idiosyncratic way (6) and a brief and synthetic summary of the Hospitallers' fourteenth-century activities is now due to appear (7), but Delaville's book has yet to be replaced by a major work.

Since Delaville's time there has developed a thoroughly daunting Hospitaller bibliography of astonishing diversity in topic, quality and language. Many of these publications contain little that is new. Much of the work is concerned with special subjects such as the architecture of Rhodes, the Hospitallers' medical activities, or their constitution and statutes. Numerous books and articles concern particular priories, preceptories or churches from Portugal to Denmark, Ireland to Bohemia. Thousands of relevant documents are now available in print (8). It is true that it is difficult to understand developments at Rhodes without a detailed study of the European priories which provided the men and money essential to sustain crusading activity in the Levant, and without an appreciation of the Hospital's relationships with princes and powers; in particular, the interventions of the Avignonese popes were often decisive. Delaville's work could scarcely have been exhaustive in these respects, but the defect of much local work is that it often bears no connection to events at Rhodes; it is purely local history almost all of which, unlike *Les Hospitaliers à Rhodes*, makes no use of the documents at Malta. All these new materials, and many documents still unpublished or unused, await integration into a new synthesis, accompanied by more up-to-date interpretations of Hospitaller policies.

Inevitably, Delaville's book left whole areas of its subject largely untouched. The finances of the Hospital call for much more detailed investigation. The colonization and exploitation of Rhodes and the other islands require a historian who will study their history and institutions, the topography, fortifications, economy and society of Rhodes, with its Greek population and Latin settler class. In the archives of the European priories, individual brethren and preceptories demand further research, and this should extend to topographical and archaeological work. The Hospital's personnel, education and culture need organized study, though it is difficult to re-create the attitudes of so largely illiterate a group; the Hospitallers' social origins and crusading motives, their daily life of estate management in the West or garrison duty in the Levant all await analysis. Especially important will be the publication of a series of inquests into the European preceptories carried out in 1373, which provide valuable statistics on the brethren, their numbers, status, age, activities and incomes (9). These particular problems should also be seen in terms of a general comparative history of the military orders, and of public attitudes to them. The new history should reinterpret the major incident of the trial and suppression of the Templars, and the great crisis which faced all the military orders at the beginning of the fourteenth century.

Whoever attacks these themes will need to lean heavily on *Les Hospitaliers à Rhodes.* Giacomo Bosio had no effective predecessor and few successors (10). Only Delaville le Roulx has faced the problems of the fourteenth-century Hospital on the grand scale necessary for success. The bibliography is vast and unmanageable; Rhodes has to be studied from Malta; largely unexplored archives must be searched in numerous countries; and the whole topic is distorted by the extraordinary figure of Juan Fernández de Heredia, whose motives and influence cannot be ignored but who is not to be appreciated without a proper investigation of the Spanish background. Given the fragmentary state of the surviving documentation in the Malta archives, much of the history of fourteenth-century Rhodes requires illumination from the considerably richer fifteenth-century records, and these await even preliminary published investigation. The Order of St. John, now established at Rome, is cut off from its archives in Malta, and it has seldom produced historians of its own in the way that many of the religious orders have. Bosio, Delaville, and Delaville's few successors all worked single-handed, and progress is slow. Delaville's chronological *histoire événementielle* doubtless requires revision in an age accustomed to social and economic analyses of a statistical nature, and to historical writing organized around topics, but it is certain that future work must be based on Delaville's *Les Hospitaliers à Rhodes* which, though not without defects, is securely founded on a mass of documentary references; this, and the scarceness of this rare book, make its republication an important event in the history of Hospitaller historiography.

(1) Biography and bibliography in A. Dezarrois, 'Un cinquantenaire: Joseph de la Ville Le Roulx, Historien des Chevaliers de St. Jean de Jérusalem 1855–1911', *Annales de l'Ordre Souverain Militaire de Malte*, xix (1961).

(2) It is important to use the 2nd edition: G. Bosio, *Dell'Istoria della Sacra Religione di San Giovanni Gerosolimitano*, ii (Rome, 1629).

(3) *Infra*, pp. 246–247.

(4) See A. Rubió i Lluch, reviewing *Les Hospitaliers à Rhodes*, in *Anuari de l'Institut d'Estudis Catalans,* v part 2 (1913/4), 787–790; cf. A. Luttrell, *Juan Fernández de Heredia, Castellan of Amposta (1346–1377), Master of the Knights of St. John at Rhodes (1377–1396)* (D. Phil. thesis: Oxford, 1959), which will eventually be published in heavily revised form.

(5) For a survey of the later crusade and an assessment of the Hospital's contribution to it, see A. Luttrell, 'The Crusade in the Fourteenth Century', in *Europe in the Late Middle Ages*, ed. J. Hale *et al.* (London, 1965).

(6) N. Iorga, 'Rhodes sous les Hospitaliers', *Revue historique du Sud-est européen,* viii (1931).

(7) A. Luttrell, 'The Knights Hospitallers at Rhodes: 1306–1421', in *A History of the Crusades*, ed. K. Setton, iii (Madison, Wisc., [in press]); this synthesis is largely based on some 30 articles by the same author mostly being reprinted in A. Luttrell, *Hospitaller Studies: 1291–1440* [forthcoming].

(8) The formation of a satisfactory bibliography seems likely to remain a *desideratum*; see F. de Hellwald, *Bibliographie méthodique de l'Ordre Souverain de St. Jean de Jérusalem* (Rome, 1885), reprinted (London, 1968) with an *aggiunta* by E. Rossi; H. Mayer, *Bibliographie zur Geschichte der Kreuzzüge* (Hanover, 1960), and his 'Literaturbericht über die Geschichte der Kreuzzüge: Veröffentlichungen 1958–1967', *Historische Zeitschrift*, ccvii (1969); J. Mizzi, 'A Bibliography of the Order of St. John of Jerusalem: 1925–1969', in *The Order of St. John in Malta*, ed. for the Council of Europe (Malta, 1970).

(9) Cf. J. Glénisson, 'L'enquête pontificale de 1373 sur les possessions des Hospitaliers de Saint-Jean-de-Jérusalem', *Bibliothèque de l'Ecole des Chartes,* cxxix (1971).

(10) See A. Luttrell, 'The Hospitallers' Historical Activities: 1291–1630', *Annales de l'Ordre Souverain Militaire de Malte*, xxiv-xxvi (1966–1968).

V

THE HOSPITALLERS' INTERVENTIONS IN CILICIAN ARMENIA: 1291–1375

Western attitudes towards the Armenians varied during the period after the last of the Christian possessions in Syria fell to the Mamluks in 1291. The Latins had a general obligation to defend their fellow Christians, and after the loss of their Syrian ports Western traders were increasingly drawn to Ayas, or Laiazzo as it was then known, an important harbour and market in the Gulf of Iskenderum where they could secure the profitable luxury goods of Asia. On the other hand, the Latins mistrusted the Armenians, whose Church was in a state of schism with Rome and whose ruling dynasty seemed perpetually unstable. At a time of troubles and preoccupations in the West, the papacy and the Latin powers showed only mild enthusiasm for a new crusade. Mongol and Armenian envoys visited the West in search of alliances and aid against the Mamluks in Egypt and Syria, but the Latins made no effective response and did little to secure the conversion of the Mongols to Christianity. Western rulers were prepared to undertake limited amphibious operations in which they could exploit their sea-power to temporary advantage, but they were reluctant to involve themselves in major continental warfare which offered little prospect of success against a great land-power such as the Mamluks.[1] James II of Aragon, for example, was typical in that he maintained diplomatic relations with the Armenians and spoke of a crusade, but was in reality concerned above all to secure favourable conditions for his subjects to trade in Cilicia.[2]

[1] There is no satisfactory recent study of Latin interests in Cilicia. For a survey to 1307, with useful bibliography, S. der Nersessian, 'The Kingdom of Cilician Armenia', in *A History of the Crusades*, ed. K. Setton, II (2nd ed. Madison, Wisc., 1969); see also G. Hill, *A History of Cyprus* II (Cambridge, 1948). For recent publications, H. Mayer, 'Literaturbericht über die Geschichte der Kreuzzüge: Veröffentlichungen 1958–1967', *Historische Zeitschrift* CCVII (1969).

[2] F. Giunta, *Aragonesi e Catalani nel Mediterraneo* II (Palermo, 1959), pp. 137–9.

N.B. Pp. 120 and 136 have been omitted in this reprint, as the plates to which they refer do not illustrate this article.

The position of the Hospital of St John of Jerusalem was rather different, for its very existence depended on its being able to maintain a semblance of warfare against Islam. After 1291 the Hospital established its new headquarters in Cyprus, where the brethren of the Order sought to employ the resources which they drew from their European estates in the continuation of crusading activity. The Hospital did take part in various ineffectual campaigns against the Mamluks in Egypt and Syria. It was only after 1306, when they began their conquest of Rhodes, that the Hospitallers shifted the focus of their activities away from Cyprus and the Southern Levant towards *Romania* and those Aegean lands disputed between Byzantines and Turks.[3]

Before 1306 there had however been an alternative to intervention in *Romania*, that of assisting the Armenians of Cilicia in the defence of what was almost the last major Christian foothold on the mainland of Asia. The Hospitallers had long been established in the western part of Cilicia, where the Armenian crown intended that they should defend the country against the Selchukid Turks. Early in the thirteenth century the Hospitallers increased their Cilician holdings through their intervention in succession disputes; they secured considerable estates at important points, such as Silifke, but they soon lost control of many of these possessions, being compelled to retreat, like the Armenians themselves, under continual pressure from Turks, Mongols and Mamluks. In 1252 the Hospitallers helped to arrange the marriage of an Armenian princess, and in 1281 the prior of England and other brethren fought with the Armenian king alongside the Mongols at Homs in the battle against the Mamluks. The Hospital's Cilician possessions were organised as the preceptory of Armenia, and towards the end of the thirteenth century the preceptor of Armenia had his own seal and was assisted by a treasurer. In fact the brethren in Syria valued their Cilician estates, depending to a considerable extent on their resources.[4] But their estates continued to dwindle; the Mamluks took

[3] The standard works are J. Riley-Smith, *The Knights of St. John in Jerusalem and Cyprus: c. 1050–1310* (London, 1967), and J. Delaville le Roulx, *Les Hospitaliers à Rhodes jusqu'à la mort de Philibert de Naillac: 1310–1421* (Paris, 1913); the latter is somewhat outdated. For a general assessment of Hospitaller policy, A. Luttrell, 'The Crusade in the Fourteenth Century', *Europe in the Late Middle Ages*, ed. J. Hale *et al.* (London, 1965); on the Templars' involvement, M. Barber, 'James of Molay, the last Grand Master of the Order of the Temple,' *Studia Monastica*, XIV (1972).

[4] Riley-Smith, pp. 132, 152–63, 432, 442, 495–505 *et passim*; C. Cahen, *La Syrie du Nord à l'époque des croisades et la principauté franque d'Antioche* (Paris, 1940), pp. 510–526 *et passim*. These authors use the documents in J. Delaville le Roulx, *Cartulaire général de l'Ordre des Hospitaliers de S. Jean de Jérusalem: 1100–1310*, 4 vols. (Paris,

(N.B. p. 120 omitted)

Arsuf from the Hospitallers in 1265, and Safad and *Arassous* from the Templars in 1266. These places were described by an Armenian chronicler as the fortresses of the brethren 'who wear the garments marked with the cross'.[5] Yet as late as 1282 the Hospital sent a hundred armed horsemen, 50 Hospitallers and 50 turcopoles, to aid the Armenians at their king's request.[6]

After the loss of Syria the Hospital continued to hold certain estates in Armenia and to maintain an interest in that country. During the years that they were based in Cyprus the Hospitallers, having lost their original mission of the defence of Jerusalem and Syria, needed to justify their continued possession of vast estates in the West by some show of crusading activity in the East. On 23 January 1292 Pope Nicholas IV was already instructing the Hospital and the Temple to use their galleys in defence of the Armenians.[7] Certainly there were still Hospitallers with a knowledge of the country such as Boniface de Calamandracen, grand preceptor of the Hospital and one of the most important brethren of his time.[8] He was probably at Ayas in March 1279[9] and he possessed a translation of Albertus Magnus' *Libellus de Alchimia* given to him by one of the Armenian kings.[10] In 1294 the masters of the Hospital and Temple were present at the coronation, probably at Sis, of King Hetoum of Armenia.[11] Hetoum's reign was a troubled one, but his pro-Latin leanings resulted in closer contacts with Cyprus; he was a convert to the Roman Church who became a Franciscan, and he married his sister to Aimery of Lusignan, lord of

1894–1906), but it is difficult to decide which properties were granted to the Hospital, where they were, and for how long the Hospital held them; a detailed analysis of these questions was made in J. Riley-Smith, *The Knights Hospitallers in Latin Syria* (unpublished Ph.D thesis: Cambridge, 1964). Little or nothing can be said on the basis of surviving buildings or inscriptions. On the Latin military orders in Armenia, see also V. Langlois, *Le Trésor des chartes d'Arménie: ou Cartulaire de la Chancellerie royale des Roupéniens* (Paris, 1863), pp. 72–82, and now Riley-Smith, *supra*. For Silifke, see J. Langendorf and G. Zimmermann, in *Genava* n.s. XII (1964), pp. 155–65.

[5] S. der Nersessian, 'The Armenian Chronicle of the Constable Sempad or of the "Royal Historian" ', *DOP*. XIII (1959), p. 164 and n. 1; *Arassous* remains unidentified.

[6] Text in *Cartulaire* III, no. 3782.

[7] Text in *Cartulaire* III, no. 4183.

[8] Cf. Riley-Smith, pp. 205–6, 370–1; Boniface was dead by 1298.

[9] Text in C. Desimoni, 'Actes passés en 1271, 1274 et 1279 à l'Aïas (Petite Arménie) et à Beyrouth par devant des notaires génois', *AOL*. I (1881), pp. 511–12. In 1288 the king of Aragon complained that because Fr. Boniface was his kinsman he had been sent to die of the bad climate in Armenia: *Cartulaire* III, no. 4007.

[10] J. Morelli, *I codici manoscritti volgari della Libreria Naniana* (Venice, 1776), p. 48.

[11] Hetoum of Gorighos, *Flos Historiarum Terre Orientis*, in *RHC.Arm.* II, p. 330.

Tyre, the brother of King Henry II of Cyprus. From Cyprus the Hospitallers kept in contact with Armenia, and when in 1299 Hetoum overthrew his brothers Sempad and Constantine, who had seized power a few years earlier, the Hospitallers in particular apparently gave him a measure of assistance.[12]

In 1299 Ghazan, the Mongol Il-Khan of Persia, invaded Syria, accompanied by Armenian forces which assisted in the rout of the Mamluks near Homs in December. Ghazan twice invited Henry II of Cyprus and the masters of the Temple, the Hospital and the Teutonic Order to join in his campaign. In November the king of Cyprus, the master of the Temple and the grand preceptor of the Hospital conferred together, but inconclusively; the traditional rivalries between the orders probably came into play.[13] The Hospitallers were involved in an acute constitutional crisis during 1299 and 1300, and their master reached Cyprus from the West only late in 1300,[14] while at the same time the Templars were openly quarrelling with King Henry.[15] The Templar castle of *Rocca Guillelmi*, where there was a *domus* and a preceptor of Armenia in about 1288,[16] was taken by the Muslims in 1299,[17] and it is possible that certain brethren of the Hospital and Temple who were stationed in Cilicia may have fought with the Armenian king alongside the Mongols. There were even rumours in the West that Ghazan had temporarily restored to the two orders their former Syrian estates;[18] in fact, Ghazan did offer to return to the Latins their possessions in Syria, but the envoys who took back a reply to Ghazan arrived from Cyprus only after the battle at Homs.[19] In 1300 however the Latins

[12] *Infra*, pp. 123, 129 and 130.

[13] Amadi wrote: *Et fatto conseglio el re con li maestri del Tempio, et commandator del Hospital, che teniva el loco del maestro, non se accordavano troppo tra loro*: in *Chroniques de Chypre d'Amadi et de Strambaldi*, ed. R. de Mas-Latrie, I (Paris, 1891), pp. 234–5. Bustron wrote that the envoy *parlò con li maestri dell'Hospital e del Tempio, quali non furono d'accordo tra loro*: in *Chronique de l'île de Chypre*, ed. *idem* (Paris, 1886), pp. 129–30.

[14] Riley-Smith, pp. 207–8.

[15] Hill, II, pp. 198–9, 202–3; Barber, pp. 97–8.

[16] Text in K. Schottmüller, *Der Untergang des Templer-Ordens* II (Berlin, 1887), p. 206. The Templar Preceptor of Armenia was entrusted in 1285 with the negotiation of a peace between the Armenian and Egyptian rulers (*RHC.Arm.* I, p. lxxxii).

[17] *Les Gestes des Chiprois*, ed. G. Raynaud (Geneva, 1887), p. 292, which does not, however, state whether the Temple still held the castle in 1299.

[18] References in R. Röhricht, 'Les Batailles de Hims (1281 et 1299)', *AOL.* I (1881), p. 649, n. 76.

[19] See Hetoum, II, pp. 319–20, and three letters of 1300: texts in L. Muratori, *Rerum Italicarum Scriptores* XII, part 1 (revised ed.: Bologna, 1938), pp. 396–8; H. Finke, *Acta Aragonensia*, 3 vols. (Berlin-Leipzig, 1908–22), III, pp. 90–1.

responded to Ghazan's invitations, and in July Cypriot, Templar and Hospitaller forces sailed to attack the Egyptian and Syrian coasts; they had some success at Tortosa, but the Hospitallers' troops were routed in a small engagement at Maraclea. Subsequently the Templars and the Hospitallers, who were now led by their master Fr William of Villaret, briefly occupied the island of Ruad off Tortosa.[20]

Statutes of the Hospital passed in 1300[21] and 1301[22] showed that brethren still went fairly regularly to Cilicia, while between 1300 and 1305 the master Fr William of Villaret led two considerable expeditions to Armenia and stayed there some time.[23] But if there was a moment when the Hospitallers considered some more serious involvement in Cilicia, it passed. The country continued to suffer from Mamluk attacks, while Hetoum abdicated in 1305 and was killed in 1307. The Hospitallers were in an unsatisfactory position on an island from which it was difficult to prosecute an effective semblance of crusading activity and where they were at the mercy of the Crown. The political situation in Cyprus deteriorated in 1306, and in that year the Hospitallers initiated the conquest of Rhodes, which provided them with an independent base from which they could oppose the Turks.[24]

A few crusading propagandists still advocated intervention in Armenia. One theorist, possibly Otto of Grandson, had argued at the end of the thirteenth century for a landing at Ayas, where the Armenian king would give assistance and a junction could be made with the Mongols.[25] Others, such as Fidenzio of Padua and the Armenian historian Prince Hetoum, also favoured an overland attack on Syria using Cilicia as a base; they emphasised the advantages of good harbours in Christian hands, of deflecting trade through Ayas, and of the

[20] Hill, II, pp. 212–16; Riley-Smith, pp. 198–9.

[21] *illis exceptis qui ibunt ad ultramarinas partes seu Erminie, aut de hinc ad Suriam* (*Cartulaire* III, no. 4515, para. 16).

[22] The statutes spoke of brethren *qui sera par le mareschal en Ermenie*, and *quant freres partent dou covent pour aner en Ermenie* (*Cartulaire* IV, no. 4549, paras. 8–9).

[23] . . . *eundo bis in Armeniam cum magna comitiva equitum et peditum et ibidem morando aliquo tempore*: text in Finke, III, p. 146.

[24] A. Luttrell, 'The Hospitallers in Cyprus after 1291', *First International Congress of Cypriot Studies* II (Nicosia, 1972), pp. 163–5; contrary to the accepted view, it is clear that the initiative for the conquest actually came from the Hospital.

[25] C. Kohler, 'Deux Projets de croisade en Terre-Sainte composés à la fin du XIIIe siècle et au début du XIVe', *ROL.* X (1903–4). One text (pre-April 1289) suggested that the Hospitallers and Templars should assist the crusade when it reached Armenia; the other (probably post-1312) mentioned only the Hospitallers (ibid., pp. 413, 430, 453).

availability in Armenia of horses and supplies. The majority considered the overland route too difficult and expensive, and judged that victuals would be in short supply. Most of the Latins never overcame their suspicions of the Armenians, especially over the religious issue. James of Molay, master of the Temple, reported to the pope in 1305 that the Armenians were suspicious of Latin intentions and would refuse to co-operate or would flee to the mountains, and that the country and climate were so unhealthy that within a year a force of 4,000 Latin knights would be reduced to 500. A more balanced judgment was that of the Venetian Marino Sanudo who knew Cilicia well; he opposed the use of Armenia as a base for an attack on Syria, but saw the economic advantages of maintaining Christian rule there, and he repeatedly called for an expedition to assist the Armenian Christians against the infidel.[26] In 1309 a crusading *passagium* did sail to the East under Fr Fulk of Villaret, master of the Hospital, but it went to Rhodes and there was no hint in the various crusade projects drawn up by Fr Fulk, nephew of Fr William of Villaret, that he had any particular intention of fighting in Armenia.[27]

Their implication in Cypriot politics created difficulties for the Hospitallers in Armenia. In 1306 Henry II of Cyprus was forced into retirement by his brother Aimery, whose wife Isabella was a sister of King Oshin of Armenia; in the ensuing struggle Aimery was encouraged by the Templars, while the Hospitallers at first remained neutral and then supported Henry. When Aimery was assassinated on 5 June 1310 his Armenian supporters accused the Hospitallers, who were active in the subsequent restoration of Henry. Aimery had previously moved Henry into custody in Armenia, where the grand preceptor of the Hospital, Fr Guy of Séverac, was sent by the master to see him; Oshin prevented the grand preceptor from seeing the king, but Séverac was able to return to Cyprus with a sealed letter by which Henry appointed the master of the Hospital, Fr Fulk of Villaret, to rule for him in Cyprus. Séverac reached Famagusta with this letter on the very day of Aimery's death; he at once returned

[26] Survey in A. S. Atiya, *The Crusade in the Later Middle Ages* (London, 1938), pp. 41–3, 55–6, 59, 62–4, 79–80, 105–6, 122–6, *et passim.*

[27] Text by a Master of the Hospital in *Cartulaire* IV, no. 4681, where it is assigned to Fulk of Villaret and probably to 1305; text of Villaret's letter of 1309, ibid., IV, no. 4841; text in Paris, Bibliothèque Nationale, MS. Lat. 7470, ff. 172–8, which was probably composed after 1306 but during Villaret's Mastership, possibly *c.* 1309. J. Delaville le Roulx, *La France en Orient au XIVe siècle* I (Paris, 1886), pp. 79–81, summarised this last document, dating it to 1323/28; the present author plans to publish this text, which deserves further study.

to Cilicia in an unsuccessful attempt to secure Henry's release, but was compelled to sail back to Famagusta, having narrowly escaped capture.[28] The Hospitallers were clearly in conflict with Oshin; Armenian exiles were finding refuge at Rhodes, and it was rumoured that the master planned to remove Henry from Armenia to Rhodes.[29] It was probably at this time that Oshin sequestrated the Hospital's Armenian estates, and effective participation by the Hospital in the defence of Armenia was scarcely possible, though it was still discussed. In March 1309 James II of Aragon reported to the pope that his advisers considered that the Hospital's coming expedition could deter the Mamluks from attacking Cyprus or Cilicia, but the Aragonese king correctly foresaw that the Hospitallers would concentrate on the conquest of Rhodes and he discounted their empty boast that in five years they would be in Jerusalem.[30]

Once the subjugation of Rhodes was complete the Hospitallers were occupied with the fortification, colonisation and defence of their new territories, which included certain conquests on the mainland,[31] but they retained at least some of their Armenian possessions. The fate of the Cilician estates of the Templars after their dissolution in 1312 is obscure; it is unlikely that any of their lands passed to the Hospital, as they should have done according to the pope's instructions. The possessions of the Teutonic Order were united with those in Sicily and administered by a *magnus preceptor* of Sicily and Armenia.[32] The Hospitallers' Armenian estates still constituted a preceptory which in 1319 was granted for life to Fr Maurice of Pagnac, who became *generalis preceptor Hospitalis . . . in regno Armenie*.[33] Pagnac was an influential Hospitaller; he had been elected master of Rhodes in 1317 on the deposition of Fr Fulk of Villaret, but the pope quashed the election two years later. At this time the Hospital's lands were in fact in the hands of the Armenian king who had confiscated them.

[28] Hill, II, pp. 216–62; Riley-Smith, pp. 210–15; Luttrell, 'Hospitallers in Cyprus', pp. 165–7. These accounts are based mainly on the chronicles of Amadi and Bustron.

[29] Text in C. Perrat, 'Un Diplomate gascon au XIVe siècle: Raymond de Piis, nonce de Clément V en Orient', *Mélanges d'archéologie et d'histoire* XLIV (1927), pp. 70–1.

[30] Text in Finke, III, pp. 198–9.

[31] A. Luttrell, 'Feudal Tenure and Latin Colonization at Rhodes: 1306–1415', *English Historical Review* LXXXV (1970), pp. 755–7.

[32] Text of 1336 in C. Trasselli, 'Sugli Europei in Armenia', *Archivio storico italiano* CXXII (1964), p. 490, n. 25; cf. K. Forstreuter, *Der Deutsche Orden am Mittelmeer* (Bonn, 1967), pp. 59–67, 200, n. 21, 234–7.

[33] Text in J. Richard, *Chypre sous les Lusignans* (Paris, 1962), pp. 115–17. There seems to be no reference in the documents from which any of the Hospital's Cilician properties held during the period after 1291 can be identified.

The Hospitallers were still closely involved in Cypriot affairs, and they arranged the marriage of the king of Cyprus' daughter to James II of Aragon which took place in 1315.[34] The Hospitallers' support of the regime in Cyprus may have increased King Oshin's antagonism towards them. Pope John XXII in a bull of 5 May 1318 commended to the Hospitallers his legates to Armenia, who were to request the cessation of persecutions against the Hospital there.[35] On 13 August 1319 John XXII instructed Pagnac and the papal collector in the East to exhort King Henry of Cyprus and King Oshin of Armenia to observe the truce they had made,[36] and the two papal agents did succeed in securing a new truce.[37] Over a year later, on 22 September 1320, the pope wrote to Leon, the new king of Armenia, requesting the return of the Hospital's properties and promising that Pagnac would reside on these estates and defend them. This bull rehearsed the story of how, following the fall of Acre, the Hospitallers had failed to defend their Armenian lands so that the Crown had justifiably confiscated them, and of how for a space of time they had served once again so that Oshin, who became king in 1308, had returned their properties, only to take them away again when the Hospitallers once more failed to provide the service due.[38] A similar bull of the same date instructed that Pagnac or a substitute should take up residence in Armenia and assist in its defence.[39]

The situation in Armenia became desperate when the Mongols, Turks and Mamluks all attacked in 1321. Discussions about a projected Armenian expedition had been dragging on for years at the papal and French courts;[40] and in response to the new crisis Pope John XXII arranged for money to be sent to the Armenians. In fact a total of only 37,722 florins was paid to the bankers, who were to send it to the Armenians, during the whole of John XXII's long pontificate; some of this money was used to rebuild the fortifications at Ayas and elsewhere, while ships were constructed in Cyprus and supplies sent to Cilicia.[41] Fr Maurice of Pagnac, the preceptor of Armenia, apparently did serve

[34] A. Luttrell, 'The Aragonese Crown and the Knights Hospitallers of Rhodes: 1291–1350', *English Historical Review* LXXVI (1961), pp. 5–6.

[35] Archivio Vaticano, Reg. Vat. 109, ff. 207v–208; text in S. Pauli, *Codice diplomatico del Sacro Militare Ordine Gerosolimitano* II (Lucca, 1737), p. 67.

[36] Archivio Vaticano, Reg. Aven. 12, ff. 83v–84.

[37] Reg. Aven. 14, ff. 124–24v.

[38] Reg. Aven. 14, f. 426v (text *infra*, pp. 135 and 137).

[39] Reg. Aven. 14, f. 123–23v.

[40] G. Tabacco, *La casa di Francia nell'azione politica di Papa Giovanni XXII* (Rome, 1953), pp. 218–34.

[41] Texts and references in Richard, pp. 36–49.

with a force of horse and foot in defence of the kingdom; on 25 October 1324 the pope exempted him from the payment of papal tenths in Cyprus on the grounds that he had maintained *plures equites et armigeri* for the defence of Armenia at his own expense, and that the destruction inflicted on Armenia by the Muslims had reduced his Armenian incomes to little or nothing.[42] At this time there was possibly some sort of rapprochement between the Hospital and the powerful baron Oshin of Gorighos, the leading member of the regency council which sent John and Bohemond, sons of Aimery of Lusignan, lord of Tyre, into exile at Rhodes; they were courteously received by the Hospitallers and stayed in Rhodes for three years. Subsequently Bohemond became count of Gorighos while John, who was constable of Armenia, ruled the country for a brief spell in 1341.[43] Pagnac himself was one of three agents instructed by the pope on 9 April 1323 to work for a peace between King Leon of Armenia and King Henry of Cyprus.[44]

Meanwhile plans for more active assistance remained under discussion in Avignon until news arrived that the Armenians had made a truce with the Mamluks, that they had agreed to pay tribute, and that they were themselves opposed to the idea of an armed expedition.[45] None of the many crusading schemes presented to John XXII in 1323 envisaged any Hospitaller participation in such a crusade,[46] but the *Ramenbranze* which Marino Sanudo wrote when presenting his crusade treatise to the king of France in 1323 did call for a force which would defend Armenia and to which Cyprus and Rhodes were to provide galleys; Sanudo added: *Les Isles de Cypre et de Rodes pourront bien aider Armenie continuellement de cccl. hommes a cheual.* A Latin variation of this preface, written at about the same time, claimed that the Hospital, which was by then spending less on the defence of Rhodes, could afford 150 armed horsemen from its Cypriot and Armenian incomes: *Hospitale tum propter diminutionem custodiae Rodi Insulae, tum de redditibus quos in Cypro et Armenia percipit posset large dicto regno Armeniae de cl. armatis equitibus subuenire.*[47] On 1 September 1326 James II of Aragon had heard that the master of the Hospital and Louis of Clermont, who had been nominated as the commander of an eventual French

[42] Reg. Aven. 22, ff. 338–338v.

[43] According, at least, to Jean Dardel, *Chronique d'Arménie*, in *RHC.Arm.* II, p. 19; cf. ibid., II, p. 21 notes.

[44] Reg. Vat. 62, ff. 12v–13.

[45] Tabacco, pp. 234–7.

[46] Texts in *Lettres secrètes et curiales du pape Jean XXII (1316–1334) relatives à la France*, ed. A. Coulon (Paris, 1906), nos. 1682–1711.

[47] Texts in G. Bongars, *Gesta Dei per Francos* II (Hanover, 1611), pp. 5–7.

expedition, were proposing to lead a force of nobles to Armenia.[48] Meanwhile Pagnac died in Armenia and was buried in Cyprus.[49] Following his death, and acting upon the master's request, John XXII wrote once again on 25 September 1328 demanding that the Hospitallers' Cilician estates be returned to them.[50] In effect the preceptory of Armenia was gradually disappearing; from about 1330 it was not expected to pay *responsiones*, though it still existed on paper.[51] There was a preceptor of Armenia, Fr Nienaut of Pomiers, in 1340,[52] and there were *gubernatores* in the preceptory as late as 1347.[53]

By 1332 the Armenian king was in such trouble that he begged John XXII to persuade the Hospitallers to accept the offer, as a gift in perpetuity, of two castles which the Armenians could not defend and would otherwise have to sell to the Turks or raze to the ground; the Hospitallers were to undertake the defence of the castles, and the pope wrote on 2 August 1332 exhorting them to do so. The papal bull referred to *duo Castra situata in marchia paganorum Turchorum, quorum unum Siquinum prope mare ad miliare, et aliud Anthioceta in Rupe supra mare posita* . . .[54] Both these places were on the coast and accessible to the Hospital's vessels. The former was apparently Sechin, on the Cilician coast between Anamur and Silifke; the latter was Anthiochia Parva or *ad Cragum* just west of Anamur.[55] In April and May 1336 the new pope, Benedict XII, unable to arrange immediate military aid, responded to desperate pleas from Armenia by sending grain and according indulgences to any inhabitants of Sicily, Cyprus, Rhodes and other eastern islands who would serve against the infidels in Cilicia.[56] Ayas was lost to the Mamluks in the following year.[57] The

[48] Barcelona, Archivo de la Corona de Aragón, Reg. 249, ff. 218–218v. (Señorita Mercedes Costa kindly traced this document, misleadingly cited in Finke II, p. 742).

[49] According to one version of a brief chronicle of the Masters of the Hospital: Toulouse, Archives départementales de la Haute-Garonne, H Malte 12, f. 56.

[50] Reg. Vat. 115, f. 92 (*olim* 64).

[51] Text in C. Tipton, 'The 1330 Chapter General of the Knights Hospitallers at Montpellier', *Traditio* XXIV (1968), pp. 302–3, 308.

[52] Valetta, Royal Malta Library, Archives of the Order of St. John, cod. 280, f. 46.

[53] Reg. Vat. 140, f. 280 (text *infra*, p. 141).

[54] Reg. Vat. 102, ff. 104v–105: text in Pauli, II, pp. 81–2 (inaccurately), and Raynaldus, 1332, xxiv. *RHC.Arm.* I, p. xxxiv, wrongly gives 22 August. O. Raynaldus, *Annales ecclesiastici*, 15 vols. (Lucca, 1747–56), is the edition used here, with references *ad annum* and by paragraph.

[55] Cf. L. Alishan, *Sissouan ou l'Arméno-Cilicie* (Venice, 1899), pp. 352–4, 377, 383.

[56] C. Daumet, 'Benoît XII et la Croisade', in his *Benoît XII 1334–1342: lettres closes, patentes et curiales se rapportant à la France* (Paris, 1920), p. liv; texts ibid., nos. 109, 151–2, 155, 175–6.

[57] *Infra*, pp. 137ff.

Hospitallers had done nothing; in fact, they were at last solvent and preparing for some sort of expedition in 1336 when Benedict himself cancelled any further crusading activity, partly perhaps because the Hospital's considerable credits were deposited with the pope's own hard-pressed bankers. Thereafter the Latins were increasingly preoccupied in the Aegean rather than in Cilicia, and this concern resulted in the Latin crusade which captured Smyrna from the Turks in 1344.[58] In any case, while the Latin and ecclesiastically Roman elements in Armenia looked to the West for support, the 'national' party was suspicious of papal aid since it was accompanied by strong pressure on the Armenian Church. An Armenian appeal for aid, made in 1343, produced no effective response from the West,[59] though on 8 September 1344 Clement VI did instruct the papal legate at Smyrna to send vessels to assist the king of Armenia.[60]

During 1346, in the face of renewed Mamluk attacks, King Constantine of Armenia sent his *secretarius* Constantius to seek help in the West.[61] Clement VI in turn ordered the bishops of Gaeta and Coron to inspect the orthodoxy of the Armenian Church, and on 3 September 1346 he recommended them to the master of the Hospital, who was to secure their passage from Rhodes to Cyprus;[62] they reached Cilicia in March 1347.[63] Following their report, Clement took action. On 26 September 1347 the pope sent Constantius back to the Armenian king to urge him to settle the doctrinal differences between the Roman and Armenian Churches, hinting that this would be the prerequisite for Latin assistance.[64] Clement also instructed the archbishop of Crete, who was his legate in the East and captain of the Latin fleet in the Aegean, to send vessels to provide help if the Armenian king requested it, but only in so far as this would not prejudice the Latin position at Smyrna: . . . *auxilijs et fauoribus oportunis quantum poteritis sine preiudicio negociorum fidei, ad que estis specialiter*

[58] Luttrell, 'The Crusade', pp. 133–5, with references.

[59] J. Gay, *Le Pape Clément VI et les affaires d'Orient: 1342–1352* (Paris, 1904), pp. 133–46.

[60] Text in C. Kohler, 'Lettres pontificales concernant l'histoire de la Petite Arménie au XIVe siècle', *Florilegium . . . Melchior de Vogüé* (Paris, 1909), p. 320.

[61] Reg. Vat. 140, ff, 210v–11.

[62] Reg. Vat. 140, ff. 111–12.

[63] Reg. Vat. 141, ff. 88–88v: text in G. Golubovich, *Biblioteca biobibliografica della Terra Santa e dell'Oriente francescano* IV (Quaracchi, 1923), p. 374. *Clément VI (1342–1352): Lettres closes, patentes et curiales intéressant les pays autres que la France*, ed. E. Déprez–G. Mollat (Paris, 1960), no. 1488, wrongly gives May.

[64] Reg. Vat. 141, f. 90: text in Raynaldus, 1347, xxix, and Déprez–Mollat, no. 1493.

deputati, efficaciter assistere studeatis.[65] On the same day, 26 September, the pope wrote to the master of Rhodes, Fr Dieudonné of Gozon, and to Hugh of Lusignan, king of Cyprus, encouraging them to continue to provide assistance or *auxilia* for the defence of the Cilician coast; these bulls stated that the Hospitallers and Cypriots had already made some contribution to the defence of Cilicia: *oportunis favoribus potenter assistere studuisti.*[66] The Hospitallers were involved and may have recovered some of their Armenian possessions, for on 29 April 1347 Clement had recommended Fr Dalmacius de Baucio to the *Gubernatores Prioratus Armenie hospitalis Sancti Johannis Jerosolomitani, eodem Prioratu uacante*, whom the bull did not actually name.[67] In addition, on 25 September, Clement wrote requesting the doge of Venice to use his influence with the Mamluk sultan in Cairo to obtain the restitution of Ayas, Constantine having sent envoys who were to ask the Venetians for help in the recovery of the town.[68]

Following various negotiations conducted by the Armenian envoy Constantine of Portella, who had been three years in Avignon, Clement sent him on 24 September 1351 to the kings of Armenia and Cyprus and to the master of the Hospital; on the same day he ordered the master of the Hospital, the king of Cyprus and the captain of Smyrna to send aid to Cilicia. As in so many papal exhortations of the period, no specific action was suggested in these bulls, which simply referred to assistance in the most general terms.[69] Clement also sent Fr Raymond Berenguer, preceptor of Castelsarrasin, with a message to the master but his letter of credence, dated 12 September 1351, gives no hint as to the nature of the message.[70] These appeals produced no action. At this time the Hospitallers in particular and the Latins in general were concerned with the retention of Smyrna, and they were also planning to aid Byzantium against the

[65] Reg. Vat. 141, f. 89v.

[66] Reg. Vat. 141, f. 89v: both texts in Kohler, *Lettres*, p. 323. Gay, p. 148, wrote of 'quelques vaisseaux . . . peut-être aussi quelques troupes de terre'; presumably he followed Bosio, who wrote of 'ships' and 'soldiers', which are not explicitly mentioned in the bull (*infra*, p. 140).

[67] Reg. Vat. 140, f. 280: text *infra*, p. 141.

[68] Reg. Vat. 141, ff. 89–89v: text in Raynaldus, 1347, xxviii; partially, in Déprez–Mollat, no. 1489; and *infra*, pp. 146, 147. Reg. Vat. 62, ff. 86–7, also contains the bulls of September 1347.

[69] Reg. Vat. 145, ff. 83–4: texts in Déprez-Mollat, nos. 2502–4: cf. nos. 2306, 2306 bis, 2498, 2501, 2505.

[70] Reg. Vat. 145, ff. 63v–64: text in *Clément VI (1342–1352): Lettres se rapportant à la France*, ed. E. Déprez–G. Mollat III (Paris, 1959), no. 5057.

Ottomans, who established themselves across the Dardanelles in 1354. Only for a brief period did effective Latin assistance reach Armenian Cilicia; this came after the papal legate Peter Thomas had abandoned the Greeks in 1360 and 1361 and, in alliance with Peter of Lusignan king of Cyprus, had transferred the centre of crusading activity to the Southern Levant. The Hospitallers provided four galleys and a number of brethren for the campaign in which King Peter captured Adalia in Cilicia in August 1361, their experienced troops playing a distinguished part at a difficult moment in the battle. The Hospital participated fully in Peter's great crusade of 1365 which set out from Rhodes and might well have attacked the Muslims in Armenia, though in fact it sailed to capture Alexandria in Egypt. In 1367 the Hospitallers again sent four galleys and a good number of other vessels to assist Peter, whose action included the restoration of order among the Latins at Adalia, a period of refitting at Rhodes, and the temporary recapture of one of the castles at Ayas.[71]

After the assassination of Peter of Lusignan in January 1369 no further Latin help reached Armenia. However on 7 April 1369 Pope Urban V, realising that both Adalia and Smyrna were in danger as a result of King Peter's death, wrote to the master and convent of the Hospital to send help to both cities if need be; he also appealed to the other petty Latin powers in the Aegean to give assistance, presumably to Smyrna rather than to Adalia.[72] Early in 1372, on 22 January, having received news from Armenia that much of the country had fallen to the infidels, the next pope, Gregory XI, sent an appeal to Venice, Genoa and the Eastern Latin powers, including the Hospital, to give assistance in Armenia.[73] The Latins, however, were divided among themselves; in fact, the master of the Hospital, Fr Raymond Berenguer, died in Cyprus in February 1374 whilst attempting to settle the quarrels between the Genoese and King Peter II,[74] and nothing was done to prevent Leon VI, the last king of Armenia, being captured by the Mamluks at Sis in April 1375. In that year Pope Gregory XI was organising a *passagium* of Hospitallers, destined to intervene against the Turks in 1377. The bull of 8 December 1375 by which Gregory convened

[71] Delaville, *Rhodes*, pp. 140–2, 158–60. On 8 February 1366 the Hospitallers granted favourable terms for certain Armenians from Mytilene to settle on Kos, an island north of Rhodes. Delaville, p. 155 and n. 1, gives details of this and assumes that the Armenians came from Cilicia, but the document (Malta, cod. 319, f. 270v) shows that their envoy was a *Vanes de Cafa Armenus*, and presumably they were from the Black Sea, as were other Armenians who in 1363 received similar concessions to settle in Crete: cf. F. Thiriet, *Régestes des délibérations du sénat de Venise concernant la Romanie* I (Paris–The Hague, 1958), pp. 105, 107.

[72] Reg. Vat. 244M, ff. 44–5.

[73] Texts in Kohler, *Lettres*, pp. 324–7.

[74] Hill, II, pp. 402–3.

this expedition did refer to Armenia, along with Serbia, Bulgaria and Constantinople, among the places suffering from the Turks,[75] but other similar documents concerning the scheme made no mention of Armenia at all.[76] In the event everything to do with the organisation of the *passagium* made it clear that the plan was to intervene in the Aegean; in fact, the expedition eventually sailed to Epirus.[77]

King Leon was taken in chains to Cairo, and on 20 March 1382 King Peter of Aragon wrote to Fr Juan Fernández de Heredia, the master at Rhodes, asking him to assist an Aragonese messenger being sent in an attempt to secure the liberation of Leon and his family.[78] On 21 October of the same year Leon reached Rhodes, where he found his kinswoman Isabella of Lusignan. While he was at Rhodes news arrived of the death of Peter II of Cyprus, and the master agreed to lend Leon a ship to take letters of condolence to Cyprus. Leon thought of trying to assert his rights to the throne of Cyprus but the Hospitallers, afraid of the Genoese who had their own interests in the island, prevented him from going there himself; so Leon left Rhodes on 21 November to seek aid in the West, accompanied by the Hospitaller Fr Domenico de Alamania and by the Rhodian landholder Giovanni Corsini, who in 1383 became Leon's Chancellor.[79] In May 1385 the Avignonese pope, Clement VII, sent Giovanni Corsini back to Rhodes and Cyprus on certain affairs connected with Leon, with a recommendation addressed to the master of the Hospital, who was then at Avignon, or to the lieutenant master and convent at Rhodes; he was to return within a fixed period of time.[80] Giovanni Corsini was well established at Rhodes,[81] and King Leon must still have hoped to secure or

[75] Text in Pauli, II, pp. 97–8.

[76] Eg. text in F. Cerasoli, 'Gregorio XI e Giovanna I regina di Napoli: documenti inediti dell'Archivio Vaticano', *Archivio storico per le provincie napoletane* XXV (1900), pp. 6–8.

[77] Details and references in Delaville, *Rhodes*, pp. 184–91, 199–204; O. Halecki, *Un Empereur de Byzance à Rome: vingt ans de travail pour l'union des Églises et pour la défense de l'empire d'Orient: 1355–1375* (Warsaw, 1930), pp. 248–329. *RHC.Arm.* I, 721, is clearly wrong in stating that the expedition was intended for Armenia.

[78] Text in M. Sáez Pomés, 'La ayuda de Valencia a León V de Armenia, I de Madrid', *Estudios de Edad Media de la Corona de Aragón* III (1947–8), p. 413.

[79] Dardel, in *RHC.Arm.* II, pp. 103–5.

[80] Reg. Vat. 296, ff. 1v–2v, in which Corsini is *Senescallus Regni Armenie*; cf. N. Valois, *La France et le Grand Schisme d'Occident* II (Paris, 1896), p. 221 n. 3.

[81] Cf. A. Luttrell, 'Interessi fiorentini nell'economia e nella politica dei Cavalieri Ospedalieri di Rodi nel Trecento', *Annali della Scuola Normale Superiore di Pisa: lettere, storia e filosofia*, 2nd ser., XXVIII (1959), p. 325.

recover some sort of advantage in Cyprus or Armenia. Such initiatives were however in vain and the Hospitallers were unlikely to give aid. At some point after 1377 the master, Fr Juan Fernández de Heredia, had the crusading tract composed by Prince Hetoum of Gorighos, who had included in it a wealth of information about Armenia, translated into Aragonese along with many other chronicles and treatises,[82] but Cilician Armenia was in Muslim hands and the Hospital's interests there were extinct.

The Christian Kingdom of Armenia, which ceased to exist in 1375, had been in a state of siege, turmoil and internal strife for the best part of a century. Ayas in particular had an economic importance for the Latins, and the kings of Cyprus had dynastic and strategic interests in the country. The papacy recognised a general duty to assist the Armenians, but this did not go beyond diplomatic and financial support. When the popes were looking for a military force capable of serving in Cilician Armenia they often turned to the Hospital, but Cilicia can seldom have represented an attractive objective for the Hospitallers. The Hospital had been quite securely established in the Armenian kingdom during the thirteenth century; then in the difficult period after 1291, when the Hospitallers were seeking an alternative to their base in Cyprus, they sent forces there on several occasions and may even have considered some more permanent form of involvement. However, the conquest of Rhodes, completed by 1310, provided the Hospital with a permanent base, and thereafter their interests were in the Aegean, in Smyrna or the Morea, rather than further south. Crusading was the principal *raison d'être* of the Hospitallers and from time to time, when encouraged by the pope or dragged in the wake of the king of Cyprus, they did participate in expeditions to Armenia, yet on the whole, once they were established at Rhodes and had lost any effective control of their Armenian properties, their interest in Cilicia was very marginal. After about 1345 the Hospitallers were largely responsible for the defence of Smyrna. Furthermore the Hospital lacked a fleet, so that for military activity it was dependent on the maritime powers. The great plague came in 1347, and war between Venice and Genoa began in 1351; effective action was scarcely possible. Only after 1358, in the time of Peter I of Cyprus, were the Hospitallers again galvanised into active, but temporary, intervention in Armenia.

* * *

This preliminary sketch of the Hospitallers' involvement in Cilician Armenia

[82] W. Long, *Flor de las ystorias de Orient, by Hayton, Prince of Gorigos* (Chicago, 1934).

in the period after 1291, a topic never before treated, is not based on any exhaustive examination of original documents and chronicles or even of all the sources in print; the Armenian sources in particular may have more to reveal. Nor has any detailed description of the obscure and chaotic course of political and religious events in the decadent Armenian kingdom been attempted. One question of general importance which does, however, merit more detailed treatment concerns the myth of a Christian recapture of Ayas with Hospitaller assistance in 1347. This myth, together with certain other errors examined below, derives from the works of Giacomo Bosio and of other sixteenth-century historians of the Hospital, notably Fr Joan Antoni de Foxa, whose writings require examination. Bosio and his predecessors as official historiographers of the Hospital worked in the Vatican and other archives, but they made or repeated a number of careless errors. Subsequent historians, many of whom still use the first edition rather than the far superior second edition of Bosio's work, have treated him as a reliable authority. Certain mistakes he made are reproduced in such standard publications as the continuations of Cardinal Baronius' *Annales Ecclesiastici*; the relevant sections of the first edition of this were published in 1618 by Abraham Bzovius, who cited Bosio, though the key documents of 1347 appeared only in the later edition by Raynaldus of 1652. From the *Annales*, these errors passed into another standard work, the two *Documents arméniens* volumes of the *Recueil des historiens des Croisades*, which appeared in 1869 and 1906. What follows shows, once again, that it is essential to check the documents before following Bosio.[83]

According to Bosio, Hetoum of Armenia sought aid in Cyprus during 1295 against his brothers who had ousted him. The king and the Military Orders favoured Hetoum but lacked the strength to assist him; subsequently they did provide a small force (*poche genti*) in 1298 or 1299 when Hetoum recovered his throne. When Fr William of Villaret reached Cyprus – Bosio wrongly gives the date of his arrival as 1298 rather than 1300 – Hetoum's envoys arrived to congratulate him on his election as master; to give thanks to the Hospital and Temple, with whose assistance their king had reduced his kingdom to obedience and had forced his brother Constantine into exile; and to ask Villaret to exhort the king of Cyprus and the master of the Temple to participate with the Tartar and Armenian forces in an attack on the Mamluks in Syria. The gist of all this

[83] G. Bosio, *Dell'Istoria della Sacre Religione . . . di San Giovanni Gierosolimitano* II (1st ed. Rome, 1594; 2nd ed. Rome, 1630). On Bosio, Foxa and their predecessors, and their sources and inaccuracies, see A. Luttrell, 'The Hospitallers' Historical Activities: 1530–1630', *Annales de l'Ordre Souverain Militaire de Malte* XXVI (1968).

was to be found in Foxa's manuscript history of the Hospital, from which Bosio presumably took it.[84] The sources for it are unknown though the general inaccuracy over dates suggests that it was derived from chronicles rather than documents. The story that the Hospitallers and Templars assisted Hetoum in deposing his brothers Sempad and Constantine is given, again without any source, in the *Recueil*,[85] which presumably derived it from Bosio; there may be some truth in it. There seems to be no evidence of any significant Latin cooperation with the Mongols or Armenians, except in amphibious attacks on the coasts, yet in Bosio's long and confused account of the Mongol campaigns of 1299 and 1300 he states that the Hospitallers and Templars sent the largest possible force to Ruad, and that they were still there when the Mongols won their great victory near Homs in December 1299; in fact, it seems that the Orders sent forces to Ruad only in 1300. Bosio was again following Foxa in much of this, though he does differ from him and adds a considerable amount of detail not found in Foxa; Foxa's chronology was also confused. Bosio wrote that after Homs, the Hospitallers and Templars collaborated in attacks on the retreating Mamluk forces and were left to garrison Jerusalem until the Tartars withdrew; the Hospitallers and Templars then lacked the force to defend Jerusalem on their own and were compelled to withdraw to Cyprus. Bosio also describes an expedition of the two Orders to Ruad in 1300, which did in fact take place, and their supposed participation, together with the Armenian king, in another Tartar campaign in Syria which failed to take Damascus in 1303. The only source for all this which Foxa and Bosio actually mentioned was a crusading treatise, the *Flos Historiarum* of the Armenian Hetoum of Gorighos.[86]

Bosio, like Foxa before him, had some idea of the papal bulls of 5 May 1318 and 20 September 1320 which showed that King Oshin had confiscated the Hospital's Armenian lands.[87] The latter bull, addressed to Leon of Armenia, read:

> Carissimo in Christo filio Leoni Regi Armenie Illustri Salutem. Dudum pro parte clare memorie Ossinj Regis Armenie genitoris tui dum adhuc uiueret fuit expositum coram nobis quod olim quidam [de] pro genitoribus tuis Regibus Armenie opera pietatis que magister et fratres

[84] Bosio, II (1594), pp. 4, 6; (1630), pp. 11–12, 17; Foxa, in Madrid, Biblioteca Nacional, MS. 3027, ff. 159–163v.

[85] *RHC.Arm.* I, p. 545, presumably followed, e.g., by H. F. Tournebize, *Histoire politique et religieuse de l'Arménie* I (Paris, 1900), p. 224, who also gives no source.

[86] Foxa, ff. 159–163v; Bosio, II (1594), pp. 6–11; (1630), pp. 17–18, 20–3, 26–7; cf. Hetoum, II, pp. 197–9 and *supra*, pp. 121–3.

[87] Bosio, II (1630), pp. 50–1; Foxa, ff. 173v–174.

V

(N.B. p.136 omitted)

hospitalis sancti Johannis Jerosolimitani [tunc] in illis partibus exercebant diligentius attendentes et considerantes attentius, quod fratres ipsi hostibus catholice [fidei] continue se [uir]iliter exponentes, contra eos strenue dimitabant, quasdam terras infra Regnum suum Armenie sitas, eidem hospitali sub certis conditionibus concesserunt. Cunque postmodum eiusdem hospitalis [fratres], Terris Tiri, et Ciuitate Acconensis, ab eisdem hostibus occupatis, a dictis cessarent operibus, [et] circa defensionem dicti Regni Armenie quamuis super hoc fuissent cum instantia requisiti intendere non curarent, idem Rex, undique dictorum hostium circumseptus insultibus, et grauatus inportabilibus oneribus expensarum, ad se terras huiusmodi reuocauit, nonnullos stipendiarios ad Regni defensionem eiusdem necessitate cogente, de ipsarum terrarum redditibus conducendo. Et licet demum magister et fratres hospitalis prefati, eidem Regi circa Regni defensionem eiusdem, per aliquod temporis spatium fideliter astitissent, tamen quia postmodum, jidem magister et fratres ab huius assistencia destiterunt, Rex prefatus terras ipsas quas eisdem magistro et fratribus restituerat, ad se iterum reuocauit. Cum autem dilectus filius Morisius de Ponacho frater hospitalis eiusdem, terras ut accepimus repetat supradictas nos intendentes, ut idem Morisius pro terrarum ipsarum tuitione resideat in eisdem, damus, ei, per nostras litteras in mandatis ut in eisdem terris pro ipsarum tuitione resideat, uel alium loco suo faciat residere, tot de redditibus dictarum terrarum ad tuitionem ipsarum, fratres hospitalis eiusdem, uel alios ydoneos, usque ad apostolice sedis beneplacitum retinendo, quot redditus ipsi comode poterunt sustinere. Alioquin tibi memoratas terras, usque ad beneplacitum dicte sedis, ut de ipsarum redditibus circa custodiam et defensionem ipsarum ualeas prouidere in pace dimittat. Volumus autem quod idem Morisius si eum in dictis terris residere, uel alium ad residendum deputauerit, ut prefertur, nemini teneatur interim de prefatis redditibus respondere, quodque tibi, uel hospitali predicto seu nature uel conditioni concessionis eiusdem nullum propter hoc jmposterum preiudicium generetur. datum Auinione .x. kalendas Octobris Anno Quinto.[88]

It is certain that the Mamluks took Ayas in 1337 and they still held it in and after 1347, yet the secondary works repeat a strong, though evidently erroneous,

[88] Reg. Aven. 14, f. 426v, damaged but completed from the similar bull of the same date addressed to Pagnac in Reg. Aven. 14, ff. 123–123v=Reg. Vat. 71, ff. 133–133v.

tradition according to which the Mamluks took Ayas only in 1347, or alternatively that the Christians retook Ayas and lost it again in that year. As late as 1966 the *Cambridge Medieval History* spoke of the Armenians defeating the Mamluk invaders with the aid of the king of Cyprus and the Hospitallers in 1356, the date presumably being a printing error for 1346,[89] while the revised *Encyclopédie de l'Islam* stated in 1960 that Ayas finally fell into Muslim hands in 1347.[90] In a book which appeared in 1930 Niculai Iorga wrote that Ayas was retaken in 1347 with the aid of the Hospitallers, citing a work published in 1899 by L. Alishan.[91] The latter gave no source for the same affirmation but reproduced a picture painted by Henri Delaborde for Louis-Philippe in 1844, which showed the Mamluks surrendering Ayas after their supposed defeat by the Hospitallers.[92] Jules Gay wrote in 1904 of the Mamluks taking Ayas in 1347, a misinterpretation of the bull of 25 September 1347, which he cited.[93] Iorga had already, in a work published in 1896, stated that 'Lajazzo et Alexandrette furent prises par les Égyptiens', and that the Hospitallers and the Armenians recaptured 'Alexandrette'; his source was Giacomo Bosio.[94] Iorga even cited the description given by the pilgrim 'Jacob von Bern' or 'Jacques de Berne' of the refugees reaching Famagusta from Ayas after its fall in '1346';[95] Iorga was citing a German translation of this text, wrongly dated to 1346 because the editors found in the standard works that Ayas fell in 1346 or 1347,[96] whereas this account was actually written in Latin by Jacopo da Verona and described his experiences in 1335.[97] Iorga also used De Mas Latrie who wrote of Ayas being taken by 'les Arabes d'Égypte' in 1320, being reconquered by the Armenians in 1347, and being lost again soon after; De Mas Latrie took this information from A. Saint-Martin, who in turn cited the work of M. Tchamt-

[89] *Cambridge Medieval History* IV, part 1 (revised ed. Cambridge, 1966), p. 636.

[90] *Encyclopédie de l'Islam* I (revised ed. Leyden–Paris, 1960), p. 802.

[91] N. Iorga, *Brève Histoire de la Petite Arménie: l'Arménie cilicienne* (Paris, 1930), p. 144.

[92] Alishan, pp. 470–1. Tournebize, p. 677, also stated that Ayas was retaken with Hospitaller and Cypriot assistance.

[93] Gay, p. 148; cf. *infra*, pp. 142, 143.

[94] N. Iorga, *Philippe de Mézières (1327–1405) et la Croisade au XIVe siècle* (Paris, 1896), pp. 60, 369.

[95] Ibid., p. 3 n. 1.

[96] R. Röhricht–H. Meisner, *Deutsche Pilgerreisen nach dem Heiligen Lande* (Berlin 1880), pp. 46, 51.

[97] *Liber Peregrinationis di Jacopo da Verona*, ed. U. Monneret de Villard (Rome, 1950), pp. 17–18. Ayas finally fell in 1337 but the first attack did come in 1335, according to the chronicle of the Constable Sempad (*RHC.Arm.* I, pp. 671–672).

chian published in 1786.[98] Tchamtchian used Nerses Balientz' chronicle and made it clear that Ayas remained in Armenian hands in 1321 and 1322; but he also wrote of the king of Cyprus and the master of Rhodes assisting the Armenians in 1347, and he stated that 'the infidels took Ayas' at that time, giving his source as Raynaldus.[99]

Nerses Balientz, who inserted passages concerning Cilician events into his Armenian version of Martin of Poland's Chronicle of the Popes and Emperors which he translated between 1347 and 1362, stated that Ayas was attacked by the Mongols, who withdrew in the spring of 1321; that it was then temporarily captured by the Mamluks who destroyed the fortresses, an event which he wrongly dates to 1321 rather than 1322; and that subsequently the Armenians rebuilt the castles with the help of 30,000 gold florins sent by the pope. Some sixteen years later, that is in 1337, the Muslims forced the Armenians to give up Ayas, 'and they took it and the same Muslims hold it to this day'.[100] This last remark is quite explicit, and nothing is known which contradicts it. A note in an Armenian short chronicle confirms this: 'In the year 1337 the lawless nation of Ismail took Ayas.'[101] In a colophon added in 1337 to a manuscript dated 1297, the writer Vasil relates how the sultan took Ayas in that year,[102] as does a detailed letter written by the sultan himself.[103] The anonymous continuator of the chronicle of the Constable Sempad confirms that Ayas was destroyed by the Mamluks in 1322, and gives no hint that they retained the town,[104] while it is known that in 1323 the sultan undertook to rebuild the *castrum* he had destroyed there.[105] John XXII's letters also spoke of Ayas being

[98] L. de Mas Latrie, *L'île de Chypre* (Paris, 1879), p. 234; A. Saint-Martin, *Mémoires historiques et géographiques sur l'Arménie* I (Paris, 1818), p. 198.

[99] M. Tchamtchian, *History of Armenia* [in Armenian], III (Venice, 1786), pp. 320, 350.

[100] Text in V. Hakopian, *Short Chronicles: XIII–XIV Centuries* [in Armenian], 2 vols. (Erevan, 1951–6), II, pp. 188–9.

[101] Text ibid., I, p. 88.

[102] Text (in English) in A. K. Sanjian, *Colophons of Armenian Manuscripts: 1301–1480* (Cambridge, Mass., 1969), p. 79. The inhabitants of Ayas had killed certain Muslims in 1335 (ibid., p. 75). All the information in the first part of this paragraph was most kindly supplied by Miss Sirapie der Nersessian.

[103] Translation in M. Canard, 'Les Relations entre les Mérinides et les Mamelouks au XIVe siècle', *Annales de l'Institut d'Études orientales: Université d'Alger* V (1939–41), pp. 53–4 and notes; this article provides a number of details concerning Cilician history drawn from Mamluk sources.

[104] *RHC.Arm.* I, p. 667.

[105] Text in Langlois, pp. 232–3.

taken by the Mamluks in 1322, and they made it clear that the castles at Ayas were in Christian hands and awaiting repair.[106] A text of 1325 confirmed that 30,000 florins were put aside to repair the *castra de Alaiacio maris et terre et alia loca regni Armenie*, though the money was not all spent.[107]

Gay, Iorga and De Mas-Latrie were presumably influenced by the *Recueil des historiens des Croisades*, which stated that Hospitaller and Cypriot forces aided the Armenians and which cited the bulls of September 1347, apparently taking them from Raynaldus. The *Recueil* spoke of the Mamluks taking and sacking Ayas in 1347, of Pope Clement VI sending money and a body of Hospitallers in 1348, and of the Armenians and Hospitallers in the year following 22 December 1348 taking 'Alexandrette'; no source was given, but presumably this too was taken, somewhat inaccurately, from Raynaldus.[108] Raynaldus, in describing the bulls of September 1347, made the assumption, which Gay subsequently made, that Ayas was recaptured in that year. In commenting on the bull of 25 September 1347 addressed to the doge of Venice, Raynaldus wrote: *Expugnatum est ab infidelibus Ajacium.* He also wrote of *Isso, . . . olim dictam Alexandretam, . . . a Constantio Rege recuperatam*, giving his source as Giacomo Bosio.[109]

Many of these confusions, therefore, derived from Bosio. In 1347, according to Bosio, the master of Rhodes learnt that the Mamluks had attacked various parts of Armenian Cilicia and had newly taken *Isso*, also known as *Alessandria* or *Alesandretta*; forgetting the damages which earlier Armenian kings had inflicted on the Hospital, the master at once despatched galleys and other ships with Hospitallers and their soldiers to assist the Armenians; together with the king, the Hospitaller forces repulsed the Mamluks and recovered Ayas; and, on hearing this in a letter from the king's ambassador *Costanzo*, the pope wrote to congratulate the master. This story appears in both editions of Bosio. In the second edition Bosio added that at this time the Hospital's grand preceptory of Armenia, called a *prioratus* in the papal registers, became vacant and the master and convent at Rhodes sent several governors or lieutenants instead of

[106] Texts in Coulon, nos. 1571–2.

[107] Texts in Richard, pp. 37–49.

[108] *RHC.Arm.* I, pp. 708–9.

[109] Raynaldus, 1347, xxviii–xxix; these phrases appear in the 1652 edition. V. Langlois, 'Documents pour servir à l'histoire des Lusignans de la Petite Arménie: 1342–1375', *RA.* XVI (1859), pp. 146–7, spoke of the Muslims taking Ayas despite the Hospitallers' participation in its defence in 1346/7, and of Hospitaller troops intervening in Armenia in 1349 (!), and he too cited Raynaldus and Bosio.

appointing a new preceptor; Clement VI therefore wrote to them on 5 May 1347 recommending the provision of Fr *Damario* de Baucio to the preceptory; Bosio cited *epistola* no. 1248 in the Vatican register for 1347.[110] This *epistola mccxlviij*, actually dated 29 April 1347, recommended Fr Dalmacius de Baucio to the governors of the *prioratus* of Armenia, the *prioratus* being vacant:

> Dilectis filijs . . Gubernatoribus Prioratus Armenie hospitalis Sancti Johannis Jerosolimitani eodem Prioratu uacante.
> Cum dilectum filium Dalmacium de Baucio hospitalis Sancti Johannis Jerosolimitani audiuerimus fidedignorum testimonijs multis uirtutum meritis adiuuari, Nos ipsum quem obtentu meritorum suorum huiusmodi, ac consideratione quorundam amicorum suorum deuotorum nostrorum et ecclesie Romane fauore dilectionis specialis prosequimur, ut uos, qui meritorum huiusmodi habere potestis noticiam pleniorem, eum super promotionem sua prout ipse petierit, et per vos honeste fieri poterit fauorabiliter prosequamini, uestre beniuolentie propensius propensius [*sic*] commendamus. Datum Auinione iij kalendas maij Anno Quinto.[111]

Bosio had three main sources: copies of documents from the Hospital's archives which had been transferred to Malta after the loss of Rhodes; the papal registers at the Vatican, from which much of the additional material in the second edition was drawn; and the manuscript history of the Hospital written by his predecessor as official historiographer of the Hospital, the Catalan Hospitaller Fr Joan Antoni de Foxa. The Vatican documents, discussed below, provide no evidence that Ayas fell to the Christians in 1347. Nor is there any evidence for this in the records of the Hospital now at Malta, though a fragment of the master's *liber bullarum* for the year 1347 to 1348 does survive. Furthermore it is unlikely that any relevant documents for this period which were then at Malta have been lost since Bosio's time. Bosio, therefore, presumably based his statement about the recovery of Ayas on Foxa, though he added information not given by the latter. Foxa wrote that in 1348 the Hospitallers, in response to a papal appeal, assisted Constantine of Armenia to retake *Issa* and to expel the Mamluks who had taken Ayas: . . . *le havia tomado en Cilicia la uila de issa.* The version of Foxa preserved at Malta, which Bosio may have used, gives a confusing variant: *la villa de Layassa.* Foxa wrote that, with the assistance of the master, *se covro la çiudad de la issa, no e podido hallar como ni otra cosa sobre esto mas de lo que tengo dicho y sea sacado de unas notas de fray antonio*

[110] Bosio, II (1594), p. 48; (1630), pp. 75–6.

[111] Reg. Vat. 140, f. 280.

Jofre, en que dize aver leydo esto en unos cuadernos viejos de nuestra canzilleria. Fr Antoine Geoffroi was Foxa's predecessor as historiographer, and in addition to various papers and old *cuadernos* Geoffroi may have seen at Malta, he had himself used copies of documents from the Vatican registers. It seems likely, therefore, that Geoffroi or Foxa either copied or made an error, which may possibly have arisen through confusing the events of 1347 with those of 1367 when the Hospitallers did participate in the temporary recapture of Ayas. It seems most probable that this error arose from the misinterpretation of documents in the Vatican registers which were available to Geoffroi, Foxa and Bosio, and which have subsequently been interpreted wrongly by other historians. The events of 1347 should therefore be reconstructed from the Vatican bulls.[112]

In his bull of 25 September 1347 Clement wrote of the sultan taking Ayas:

> Dilectis filijs Nobili Viro Andree Dandulo Duci et Communi Venetiarum. Occurrunt frequenter considerationis nostre conspectu deuotionis et fidei studia quibus insignis Terra uestra, erga deum et Romanam ecclesiam euidentibus signis et operibus claruit occurrit qualiter uos pro defensione fidei christiane ac ipsius cultu diffusius dilatando, tan quam Viri catholici et uere fidei prefate cultores aduersus ipsius persecutores et hostes labores et solicitudines subijstis hactenus et subitis propter quod in hijs que christi et ipsius ecclesie beneplacitis conueniunt et eiusdem fidei fauorem concernere dinoscuntur tanto [fiducialius?] eadem requirit ecc[lesi]a, quanto sperat in hijs per uos satisfieri promptius uotis suis. Sane ad notitiam uestram iam dudum credimus peruenisse qualiter Soldanus Babilonie immanis persecutor nominis christiani ad eiusdem fidei hanhelans exitium post impugnationes hostiles post uexationes innumeras post clades depopulationes et spolia aduersus Christianos orientalium partium per eum ut nostis a longis retro temporibus crudeliter peccatis exigentibus perpetrata Ciuitatem Aiacen. insignem utique locum Armenie prodolor occupauit et eam detinet occupatam Christianos illius ciues et incolas affligens iugo miserabilis seruitutis de cuius Ciuitatis recuperatione Carissimus in Christo filius noster Constantius Rex Armenie Illustris anxia cura

[112] Foxa, f. 185 (variant in Royal Malta Library, Biblioteca, MS. 314, II, p. 79); cf. Luttrell, 'Hospitallers' Historical Activities'. In addition to Raynaldus and Gay, others, such as Golubovich, IV, pp. 371–8, cited and discussed the bulls of 1346–1351, but further reference below is mostly to originals and published texts.

solicitus, ad uos quorum interuentionibus apud eundem confidit diuina fauente gratia, super hoc exaudiri ut intelleximus Nuncios suos mittit, petiturus a uobis ut pro recuperatione huiusmodi, uel aliqua cum eodem Soldano super hoc habenda conuentione siue concordia ad prefatum Soldanum speciales Nuntios destinetis. Quocirca Vniuersitatem uestram attente rogamus, quatenus, diuine remunerationis intuitu ac pro nostra et apostolice sedis reuerentia eisdem Regi et Regno, consueti fauoris auxilia impendentes, petitionibus Regis ipsius super hijs et alijs que deo gratia et ipsi fidei pro futura noueritis liberaliter condescendere prudentia uestra uelit ut redemptor noster cui prestabitis in hac parte gratum obsequium mercedis uobis premium tribuat, Nosque deuotionem uestram dignis gratiarum actionibus prosequamur in domino. Datum Auinione vij kalendas Octobris Anno Sexto.[113]

It seems clear that Clement was referring to the capture of Ayas, not 'a few months earlier', as Gay interprets the bull,[114] but several years earlier, that is in 1337, and that Clement considered that the Mamluks still held the city. Raynaldus printed the text of the bull of 1347, but glossed it *Expugnatum est ab infidelibus Ajacium* probably because Bosio, whom he cited on the next page, had written of the Christian recovery of Ayas in 1347. Presumably Bosio found *Ciuitatem Aiacen.* in the bull, but in a misguided display of classical erudition, and with Foxa's mistake to mislead him, he rendered it in his history as *Isso, Alessandria* or *Alesandretta*, not realising that Alexandretta, a name not mentioned in any of the documents cited here, is not the same as Ayas, but lies in the place now known as Iskenderum. Raynaldus glossed his printed text correctly, but then followed Bosio in writing of *Isso, . . . olim dictam Alexandretam, . . . a Constantio Rege recuperatam.*[115] Medieval Alexandretta was of very minor importance,[116] yet Iorga, citing Bosio, later wrote of the Mamluks capturing *Lajazzo et Alexandrette*, and of *Alexandrette* alone being recaptured. In fact, all this derived from the bull which mentioned only Ayas, and referred to its loss in 1337. Presumably the errors in Bosio and Foxa originated in a misinterpretation of the same bull. In any case, the myth that the Mamluks captured Ayas in 1347 was established.

A similar pattern of errors was repeated with regard to the events of 1351. Iorga wrote that a Latin league was formed in 1350 and that *Alexandrette*,

[113] Reg. Vat. 141, ff. 89–89v (=Reg. Vat. 62, ff. 86–86v).

[114] Gay, p. 148.

[115] Raynaldus, 1347, xxviii–xxix.

[116] Alishan, pp. 499–501.

which he thought of as a different place from Ayas but which was not mentioned as such in any of the sources discussed here, was retaken with the aid of the Hospitallers. Iorga cited the *Recueil*, which in fact simply stated that the Armenians were working to secure the formation of a league in which the kings of France and England as well as the Hospitallers were to join, and that the pope called upon the Hospitallers and others to assist the Armenians; in fact, neither the *Recueil* nor the relevant section in Raynaldus made any mention of Alexandretta.[117] Bosio provided correct information clearly derived directly from the papal registers: in response to an appeal from the king, Pope Clement VI instructed the master of the Hospital to send aid to Cilicia; in a separate letter of the same date he also recommended to him the Armenian envoy, Constantine of Portella, who was returning to Armenia after three years at Avignon; Clement also sent the preceptor of Castelsarrasin, Fr Raymond Berenguer, with a letter to the master and convent of the Hospital.[118] Foxa provided similar information apparently derived from the same source.[119] Once again, the correct version of events can be deduced from the Vatican bulls discussed above, but in this case the errors embedded in modern scholarship were not the fault of Foxa or Bosio.

[117] Iorga, *Brève Histoire*, p. 144; *RHC.Arm.* I, pp. 710–11; Raynaldus, 1350, pp. xxxviii–xxxix.

[118] Bosio, II (1630), p. 81; cf. *supra*, p. 130.

[119] Foxa, f. 187.

VI

Slavery at Rhodes: 1306-1440 (1)

Some forms of slavery already existed on Rhodes and the surrounding islands when, in the summer of 1306, the Hospitallers of the Order of St. John began the four-year campaign which culminated in the complete conquest of Rhodes from the Greeks. Conditions there were certainly unstable, and the islands of the archipelago had probably been the object of Turkish razzias (2). As a result the Greeks of Rhodes, and especially the women, were liable in one way or another to become slaves, and some of them passed into Latin hands. Thus on 10 March 1306 Gufredus Lupinus of Candia sold to a Jew at Candia a female slave he had acquired at Rhodes; the girl had a Christian name, *Ebdochia de Romania*, but was declared to be Jewish, presumably in order to justify the sale of a Christian to a Jew (3); she could have been a Rhodian or a Greek from some other

(1) Information comes mainly from the manumissions and other documents in the Masters' *libri bullarum* from Rhodes, now in Valletta, National Library of Malta, Archives of the Order of St. John; such documents are calendared, and specimen texts published, below. It must be emphasized that the fragmentary nature of the records, which mostly mention slaves only when they belonged to the Hospital or to individual Hospitallers, permits no proper statistical conclusions, though they do provide an unusual type of documentation. I am most grateful to Professor Lionel Butler, who first drew my attention to these texts, and to Professor Charles Verlinden, who most kindly provided much information and advice.

(2) For the general situation in 1306 and thereafter, see A. LUTTRELL, "The Hospitallers at Rhodes: 1306-1421," in *A History of the Crusades*, ed. K. SETTON, iii (Madison, Wisconsin, 1975), 282-283 *et passim*, and the bibliography given there. The Turks sacked Rhodes in 1303: GEORGIUS PACHYMERES, *De Michaele et Andronico Paleologis*, ed. E. BEKKER, ii (Bonn, 1835), 344. Before 1306 the Greeks on Rhodes were paying tribute to the Turks, according to LUDOLPHUS DE SUCHEM, *De itinere Terrae Sanctae*, ed. F. DEYCKS (Stuttgart, 1851), 28. A later version which says of Rhodes *Que olim fuit Turchorum* is clearly corrupt: LUDOLPHUS DE SUDHEIM, *De itinere Terre Sancte*, ed. G. NEUMANN, in *Archives de l'Orient latin*, ii (1884), documents, 333.

(3) Venice, Archivio di Stato, Notariato di Candia: Notary Nicolò Pizzolo de Candia (unfoliated) [ex inf: C. Verlinden].

part of *Romania*. On 16 August 1309 a notary at Palermo recorded the sale of Arena, a *sclava greca de Rhodo* aged ten (4). Another female slave from Rhodes who was freed at Candia on 25 May 1313 may have been the victim of a Turkish raid upon the island, as she had been purchased at Satalia on the Anatolian coast by an inhabitant of Rhodes (5).

The port of Rhodes grew into a major Latin trading post under the control of the Order of St. John. It was also a centre of the slave traffic, particularly for slaves being moved by Genoese and other Latin slavers from the Aegean and Black Sea area towards the Mamluk domains in Egypt and Syria (6). One motive for the conquest of Rhodes had been that it would provide a base from which the Hospitallers could enforce the papal prohibitions against trade with the infidels. By May 1310 the Venetians were particularly alarmed at this prospect and when in 1311 the Hospitallers interfered with Genoese shipping, a sharp conflict ensued (7). This initial threat to the trading activities of the great maritime powers was brief in duration, and Greek slaves were soon arriving in Rhodes where the Hospital was anxious to attract a variety of settlers and workers for the defence and agriculture of the island. As early as 1311 the Chapter-General of the Hospital held at Rhodes was legislating about the slaves on the Hospitallers' estates (8). In 1319 there were official Byzantine complaints that in March 1313 a Venetian from Crete named Nascimbene had sold at Rhodes thirty-six Greeks from a place called *Ceconi*. The Byzantines also alleged that in July 1316 the Venetians had seized many men at Monemvasia who were subsequently transferred to galleys of the Hospital off Cape Malea and that the Hospitaller galleys then sold them, it was not said where but quite possibly at Rhodes, for 500 hyperpers ; and furthermore that

(4) C. Verlinden, «L'esclavage en Sicile au bas moyen âge,» *Bulletin de l'Institut Historique Belge de Rome*, xxxv (1963), 45.

(5) Venice, Archivio di Stato, Cancelleria Inferiore D.4 : Notary Marino Dato (unfoliated) [ex inf : C. Verlinden]. There are several places called Episkopia but it is conceivable, although he had been purchased from a Catalan, that the Johannes *qui fuit de Piscopia de natione Grecorum* and who was manumitted before the same notary at Candia on 6 September 1312, came from the island of Piskopi in the Rhodian archipelago.

(6) C. Verlinden, «Mamelouks et Traitants», *Economies et sociétés au Moyen Age : Mélanges offerts à Edouard Perroy* (Paris, 1973), citing many of his earlier works touching on the topic. A ship left Rhodes for Cyprus on 21 March 1345 *cum marinariis Janue ac quibusdam mercatoribus habentibus viros et mulieres captivatos, quos sclavos vocant, vendendos*, ... : text in G. Golubovich, *Biblioteca biobibliografica della Terra Santa e dell'Oriente francescano*, iv (Quaracchi, 1923), 445.

(7) Luttrell, in *History of Crusades*, iii. 281-287, and text of 13 May 1310 in Venice, Archivio di Stato, Lettere di collegio rectus Minor Consiglio, f. 83-83v.

(8) *Infra*, 85.

Venetian subjects from Corone and Methone had carried off four hundred people from the region of Maina and that these Venetians had sold them in Cyprus, Crete and Rhodes (9). Following the Latin conquest, Rhodes evidently provided a market for Greek slaves from the Morea and probably from elsewhere in *Romania*, and some of them presumably remained on the island.

Slaves from Rhodes continued to be sold in the West. At Genoa on 10 June 1374 Theramus de Savignono, an inhabitant of Rhodes, sold a Tartar named Margherita to Antonius de Savignono of Genoa (10), while in 1445 the ship of Pietro Lomellino reached Siracusa in Sicily from Rhodes and disembarked seventy-four slaves belonging to various Catalan merchants (11). In 1391 the Venetian senate instructed that Venetian galleys returning from Syria should not carry off slaves from Rhodes (12). The Catalans were equally involved at Rhodes (13). At least from 1349 onwards contracts made in Barcelona sometimes envisaged the purchase of slaves, particularly females, at Rhodes (14), while in 1382 a Catalan established at Candia had purchased at Rhodes a Greek named Anthony who was twenty years old and had originally come from Thebes (15). Traders from Narbonne and Montpellier, who lacked Levantine colonies of their own, found advantageous conditions at Rhodes which was dominated by the French, and

(9) Text in G. Thomas, *Diplomatarium Veneto-Levantinum*, i (Venice, 1880), 124-127. In 1316 Marco Contarini of Venice was protesting that he had been fined at Nigroponte for carrying to Rhodes, contrary to the interdict, sixty slaves he had purchased: F. Thiriet, *Délibérations des Assemblés Vénitiennes concernant la Romanie*, i(Paris-The Hague, 1966), 167. The text of this interdict, imposed by Venice in 1313, is in C. Verlinden, «La Crète, Débouche et plaque tournante de la traite des ésclaves aux xive et xve siècles», in *Studi in onore di Amintore Fanfani*, iii (Milan, 1962), 607-608.

(10) Genoa, Archivio di Stato, Notary Bartholomeus Gattus, Reg. 1, f. 18v [ex inf: C. Verlinden].

(11) D. Gioffrè, *Il mercato degli schiavi a Genova nel secolo XV* (Genoa, 1971), 171, n. 14.

(12) Venice, Archivio di Stato, Misti del Senato, xlii, f. 23v.

(13) A. Luttrell, «Aragoneses y catalanes en Rodas: 1350-1430», *VII Congreso de Historia de la Corona de Aragón* (Barcelona, 1962). On 19 November 1430 the *curya comerchi* at Rhodes registered the sale of a Caucasian slave aged twelve and named Maria by Niccolò Doria of Genoa to Piero Barbarigo of Venice: text in G. Dennis, «Un fondo sconosciuto di atti notarili veneti in San Francisco», *Studi Veneziani*, vii (1965), 429-430.

(14) J. Ma. Madurell Marimón and A. García Sanz, *Comandas comerciales barcelonesas de la baja edad media* (Barcelona, 1973), 229-234 (1349), 324-325 (1417), 335 (1425); such contracts did not, of course, necessarily result in purchases at Rhodes, but they indicated current practice.

(15) Venice, Archivio di Stato, Notariato di Candia: Notary Manoli Bresciano (unfoliated) [ex inf: C. Verlinden].

especially by Southern French, Hospitallers. In 1356 the Master of Rhodes, Fr. Roger de Pins, made special commercial agreements with the merchants of Narbonne and Montpellier. However, the exemptions granted to them were not to apply to dues levied on soap or slaves, unless they were the merchants' own personal domestic slaves :

> excepto sapone, et exceptis sclavis sexus promiscui utriusque, de quibus nobis et nostre domui solvi volumus jura illa que per alios talia portantes et extrahentes ad Rodum et de Rodo sunt dari et solvi consueta, preterquam de sclavis sexus utriusque qui et que pro eorum domestico servitio per dictos mercatores emerentur seu alias haberentur, a quibus jus aliquod exigi nolumus nec haberi ([16]).

On 8 November 1381 a Narbonnese shipper sold at Marseille a Tartar boy aged fifteen whom he had in that year purchased at Rhodes from Paganeo de Marquesato of Rhodes ([17]), while on 13 September 1418 at Montpellier Corrado Gentile, *mercator et burgensis Rodi*, sold a Russian slave to a merchant of Barcelona, the vendor guaranteeing the purchaser against legal action to recover this slave by pledging his goods in court, the *curia commercii*, at Rhodes ([18]). This traffic was certainly recognized by the government and courts of that island.

In addition to those who were merely being imported and exported, there were slaves at Rhodes who belonged to the Hospital or to individual Hospitallers, despite the ambiguities involved in a Christian order or its members holding slaves. In Syria, where it was technically illegal to enslave Christians of any sect, the Hospitallers certainly had non-Christian slaves as well as dependent peasants, *rustici* or *villani*, whose status varied considerably ([19]). A papal bull of 28 July 1237 commanded the Hospitallers to permit the baptism of those of their slaves in Syria whose desire for baptism was a genuine one and who were prepared to remain in slavery ; this was because slaves were feigning conversion in order to secure the liberty which,

(16) Text partially cited in C. VERLINDEN, *L'esclavage dans l'Europe médiévale*, i : *Péninsule ibérique-France* (Bruges, 1955), 780 n. 164 ; vol. 2 is in press.

(17) *Ibid.*, i. 769 and n. 98.

(18) Text *ibid.*, i. 890-893.

(19) J. RILEY-SMITH, *The Knights of St. John in Jerusalem and Cyprus : c. 1050-1310* (London, 1967), 426-429, 433-439 ; see also IDEM, *The Feudal Nobility and the Kingdom of Jerusalem : 1174-1277* (London, 1973), 40-49, 53-56, 62-63.

according to Syrian custom, accompanied baptism, and the Hospitallers were in consequence refusing to allow them to be baptized (20). Another problem was the tendency of individual brethren to free their own personal slaves. Statutes of 1262 forbade Hospitallers either to baptize or to manumit slaves without a special licence from the Master ; nor could they be given away or sold unless they were old or sick, but slaves could secure enfranchisement in return for a payment equivalent to the price of two or three slaves :

> Statutum est quod baylivus, nec alius quisquam frater, non vendat nec det extra domum ullum sclavum, nisi sclavus sit senex aut machatus, seu aliquis velit redimere se, de cujus precio duo aut tres possint haberi sclavi.
> Statutum est quod baylivus nec quisquam frater alius nullum sclavum baptizari faciat sine magistri licencia speciali (21).

There was no new legislation concerning the manumission of slaves during the period after 1310, but the Chapter-General of 1311 laid down that in the case of the death of brethren who held lands on Rhodes, the slaves were to stay on their estates rather than be seized by the Treasury of the Order :

> ... que toutes les bestes e bestial de noireture e les esclaf qui seroyent troues au dit luoq doient demorent en la reparation dou dit luoq e le sur plus veigne au trezor sauue la rayson dou mareschal (22).

This statute was replaced in 1332 by a slightly different one which stated again that the slaves on the *casale* of a deceased Hospitaller were to remain on the *casale* :

> Item establi est des freres qui tenoient casal en lisle de Rodes que se dieus fasoit son Comandament de eaus que le bestial demoure touz alestat du casal et les esclaus ausi, et que soit mis en escrit au Trezor, Jardins vingnes bestial tant de ceaus qui non tienent cazal come de ceaus qui les tienent uiegne tout au Trezor (23).

(20) *Cartulaire général de l'Ordre des Hospitaliers de S. Jean de Jérusalem*, ed. J. Delaville le Roulx, 4 vols. (Paris, 1894-1906), ii. 513-514 (no. 2168).

(21) *Ibid.*, iii. 53-54 (no. 3039), paras. 48-49 ; cf. Riley-Smith, *Feudal Nobility*, 62-63, 258, n. 10.

(22) Biblioteca Vaticana, Ms. Vat. Lat. 3136, f. 68.

(23) Original in Malta, cod. 280, f. 24v ; Latin translation of ca. 1357 in cod. 69, f. 15v. An Italian version of this statute, datable to 1461/67, gives a quite different interpretation of the final section, ... *Ma li possessioni, li schiaui, el bestiame, lentrate con altra comoditate che se ne potra cauare, sera del thesoro* : Malta, cod. 1700, f. 59v-60.

This legislation concerned slaves who were attached to an agricultural estate rather than to an individual Hospitaller. Brethren of the Convent at Rhodes did have personal slaves who, unless they had been freed with a proper licence, passed to the Treasury when their owner died. Another statute of 1332 established that the Marshal had a right to take up to four such slaves for the service of his *hospicium*, all other slaves of deceased Conventual brethren reverting to the Treasury :

> Item establi est que le Mareschal puisse auoir iusque a iiij. esclaus des freres du Conuent quant morront pour lus de son ostel, et li remanans des esclauans uiengue au Tresor et du bestial qui seront troues aus dits freres ce est a sauoir champestre viegne tout au Tresor (24).

This clause was clarified in 1354 when it was enacted that each Marshal could only take his four slaves once, even if he lost any by death or in some other way :

> Item pro declaratione statuti Magistri Elioni quo cauetur quod marescallus habere possit usque ad quatuor sclauos fratrum decedentium in Conuentu ordinatum est quod quilibet marescallus non possit habere nisi dictos quatuor sclauos semel q[uod] ipsi moriantur uel al[iter] deficiant non obstante (25).

The Turkish slaves were infidels and naturally they presented problems. A statute of 1357 decreed that thenceforth, for reasons of security, no Turkish slave should remain in the service of any Conventual Hospitaller, that is that no such slave should be kept within the fortified town of Rhodes ; nor should the brethren send Turkish slaves out with their horses to seek hay or grass. Each hostel was, however, allowed to keep one Turkish slave as a servant :

> Item pro euitandis scandalis et periculis, que in nostro castro possent evenire et per consequens toti terre, Statutum est, ne fratrum Conuentus ullus teneat nec tenere debeat in seruicio suo inantea sclauum turcum illi uero qui eos presentialiter tenent infra sex menses ipsos aliqualiter a se abicere teneantur,

(24) Original in Malta, cod. 280, f. 24 ; Latin translation of ca. 1357 in cod. 69, f. 15v.

(25) Malta, cod. 69, f. 20v. This is the Latin translation of ca. 1357. The original of this statute does not survive, but a Provençal version of 1366, probably close to the original, gives the final section as *la sia ayso que li morissan sen autra maniera li defalhissan* : National Library of Malta, Biblioteca Ms. 460, f. 92v-93. The Italian version of 1461/67 changes the sense ... *Excepto se li manchassero per morte, o, per qualche altra via* : Malta, cod. 1700, f. 74.

Nec interea illos cum eorum equis quesitum paleam seu herbam extra debeant destinare saluo tamen et retento quod in unaquaque albergia pro eius seruicio possit haberi unus (26).

Some of the Turkish slaves involved may have been taken in battle, though the brethren often massacred their Turkish prisoners. One such massacre was reported as occurring in about 1319 (27), and when 250 Turks were taken by the Hospitallers at sea in 1458 and were fortunate enough not to be taken to Rhodes, a traveller wrote that normally they would have been slaughtered in the customary way : *doueuano essere tagliati a peze o ficati in palli, come usanza farli, quando sono presi da li caualieri di Rodi* (28). Hospitallers sometimes kept slaves on their preceptories in Western Europe (29), especially in Spain (30). In about 1446 a French Hospitaller had a Greek slave with him in France (31). In addition to the Hospitallers' slaves, there were also the slaves of Latins who settled at Rhodes. The fourteenth-century *Capitula Rodi* said of these :

Item, quod qui habebit sclavum suum seu sclavos, qui non sint de Insula Rodi possit ipsos extrahere de dicta insula.

This passage implied that some slaves at Rhodes were themselves of Rhodian origin. In the margin was added *Additio : de licentia domini*, an addition which possibly reflected a tightening of controls (32). Unusually perhaps, a licence of 1438 permitted a Jewish couple at Rhodes to keep a Saracen female as a domestic slave (33).

The majority of manumissions registered in the mid-fourteenth century at Rhodes concerned slaves with Greek names. A number of these came from

(26) Malta, cod. 69, f. 21.

(27) Ludolphus de Suchem, 29.

(28) *Viaggio in Terra Santa fatto e descritto per Roberto da Sanseverino*, ed. G. Maruffi (Bologna, 1888), 58.

(29) Eg. Verlinden, *Esclavage*, i. 754.

(30) On 9 November 1332 the King of Aragon granted ten *sarraceni* to the Hospitaller Preceptor of Onda in Valencia : text *ibid.*, i. 864-865. The Templars of Aragón-Catalunya had an average of twenty Moorish slaves on their commanderies in 1289 and some had many more, many of whom had been purchased, but these were not personal domestic slaves : A. Forey, *The Templars in the 'Corona de Aragón'* (London, 1973), 285-286, 303, 398-399.

(31) Verlinden, *Esclavage*, i. 818.

(32) Text in P. Ewald, «Reise nach Spanien im Winter von 1878 auf 1879», *Neues Archiv*, vi (1881), 268.

(33) Register no. 49.

the shores or islands of the Aegean or were descendants of such Greeks, some of whom may have been among those imported with Venetian complicity in the years immediately following the completion of the conquest of Rhodes in 1310. Places suggested by the names of slaves included Thebes, Athens, Nigroponte, Salonika, Sikaminon, Monemvasia, Phocaea and Mytilene (34). It may have been that Greek names figured prominently in the registers, especially before about 1360, because Greeks were favoured as personal or domestic slaves and these could expect manumission, while there may have been slaves of other origins who were seldom freed and therefore not recorded. After about 1380 the non-Rhodian Greek names disappeared, and there were at least some Russian, Armenian and Bulgar slaves at Rhodes, while in 1414 a female Hungarian slave was working as a nurse in the hospital (35). These trends were probably the result of changing political conditions in the Levant and of variations in the general currents of the slave-traffic, rather than of new attitudes towards Greeks as such. For long the enslaving of schismatic Greek Christians, who constituted something of a special case, was not explicitly forbidden by the Latin Church, though during the fourteenth century opinion was moving towards its prohibition, especially in Sicily and Catalunya-Aragón. Baptized Christian slaves increasingly received more humane treatment in the West and Urban V, pope from 1362 to 1370, proclaimed that Greek slaves should be freed after seven years of servitude (36). Such pronouncements seem to have had no particular effect at Rhodes, where they may even have remained unknown. The papal bull of 1237 concerning baptisms had possibly been forgotten completely and may have been lost, along with many other documents, at the fall of Acre in 1291 (37).

Slaves, male and female, might belong to the Master in person (*sclauus noster*) or to the Hospital as an order (*sclauus noster et dicte domus nostre*), though the exact nature of this distinction was not always made clear in the magistral bulls ; other slaves belonged to particular Hospitallers. Individual brethren usually manumitted only one or two slaves at a time, and the case

(34) Register nos. 2-4, 8, 10, 17, 19, 21-22. A person such as *Micalj de Athena* did not, of course, necessarily himself come from Athens.

(35) Register nos. 29, 34 (*bulgaro*), 39 (*burgaria*), 40, 44 (*armenus*), 42 (*hungaria*), 48 (*Russo*).

(36) C. Verlinden, «Orthodoxie et esclavage au bas moyen âge», in *Mélanges Eugène Tisserant*, v = *Studi e Testi*, ccxxxv (Vatican, 1964).

(37) The bull survives in the papal registers but not in the archives now in Malta : *Cartulaire*, ii. 513.

of Margarita de Nigroponte, a *soror* of the Hospital who in 1347 freed no less than fourteen slaves and their children, must have been quite exceptional (38). Margarita, possibly a Latin from Nigroponte — the classical Euboea, was a widow who had considerable property on Rhodes (39) and apparently devoted herself to good works such as the freeing of slaves. To judge by their names, many of those she manumitted came from Greece. The Hospitallers had slaves in Kos as well as on Rhodes (40). Some slaves worked on the *casali* of the Hospital in the Rhodian countryside (41). Serfs were also used and in 1359, for example, one *casale* contained two *hospicia seruorum* (42), while in 1390 there were *serui* and others who were *experti in agrisculturis* (43). One of Margarita de Nigroponte's slaves was a *custos molendinj* and another was described as *tauernaria*, while a slave on one *casale* was a baker or *paneterius* (44). There was little sign of plantation-type slavery involving really large numbers of slaves such as the Templars were said to have employed on the vineyard of Engadi on Cyprus, a property which passed to the Hospital after 1312 (45). On Rhodes itself considerable efforts were made to settle both Latins and Greeks in the countryside, and to farm the island through non-feudal grants of land leased in perpetual emphyteusis, rather than to create large-scale agricultural units cultivated with slave labour (46).

Manumission could take a number of forms. Often the Master's bull contained a standard formula, or variations on it, giving generic pious reasons for granting the slave his freedom and making him technically a *civis*

(38) Register no. 4.

(39) On 3 and 7 November 1347 she was disposing of a house, an oven, a windmill and a bath, all inside Rhodes town, to her daughter Simone, and previously she had a garden, a mill, vines and lands outside the town: Malta, cod. 317, f. 242, 242v, 242v-243, 243v.

(40) Register nos. 9, 38, 43-45.

(41) *Supra*, 85; Register nos. 12, 31, 46.

(42) ... *casale ... dictum Veruorj in quo sunt hospicia seruorum duo et molendinum aque unum*: Malta, cod. 316, f. 307-307v.

(43) On 13 August 1390, the Master instructed his proctor, Dragonetto Clavelli, to import oxen (*boues*) into Rhodes and to distribute them to *serui* and others: *Prout accepimus sunt in insula nostra Rodj serui plures et alij experti in agrisculturis quj boues arabiles non habent deffectum quorum sustenemus incomoda plurima*: Malta, cod. 324, f. 149. The condition of the Rhodian serf awaits detailed investigation.

(44) Register nos. 4, 22.

(45) ... *semper centum sclavi, id est Sarraceni capti*: LUDOLPHUS DE SUCHEM, 32. There is little evidence on Hospitaller slaves in Cyprus, but see Register nos. 34 (1381), 50 (1439), and possibly no. 41 (1413).

(46) A. LUTTRELL, «Feudal Tenure and Latin Colonization at Rhodes: 1306-1415», *English Historical Review*, lxxxv (1970).

Romanus (47). Sometimes there was reference to service, to long service, or to the service of the slave's father. The Master had to licence or confirm manumissions by individual brethren, and this was often necessary when a Hospitaller had freed a slave but had then died without securing a licence or a written document from the Master (48). In some cases the slave being manumitted had to make a payment or to provide a slave or slaves in exchange for his freedom (49). Often the freed slave was bound to continue to give service during the life of the Master who manumitted him, as happened to a group of slaves in 1358, or for some other period (50). In one such case he was to receive a stipend (51), and in another the service of a slave of a deceased Hospitaller was granted for five years to a leading official, the Prior of the Convent, who was to pay the Treasury twenty-five ducats ; then the slave was to be free (53). Occasionally, the documents mentioned the price of a slave ; twenty-five florins for a female in 1374/7, and forty ducats for a female in 1435 (54).

Manumission normally made the slave or *sclauus* a free man. In many cases manumitted serfs, that is *serui* or in the fifteenth-century documents *parichi*, became *marinarii* or marine serfs ; *marinarii*, or their children if they were women, owed hereditary service on the Hospital's galleys to which they were liable by reason of the status to which they had been born or manumitted. This did not, strangely perhaps, happen to freed slaves, who were not made *serui* or *marinarii* on their manumission. Nor were slaves employed as oarsmen. The Hospital could not afford to maintain a permanent force of slaves to row its galley or galleys ; in any case, galley-slaves were seldom employed in the Mediterranean during the fourteenth century (55). Confusing situations could arise, as in 1347 when a free man,

(47) Eg. Register no. 8.
(48) Register nos. 7, 29, 33, 35, 44.
(49) Register nos. 2, 3, 5, 12.
(50) Register nos. 18-21, 24, 26, 32, 43, 43-45, 51.
(51) Register no. 26.
(52) Register no. 32.
(53) Register no. 51.
(54) Register nos. 28, 46.
(55) Cf. A. Luttrell, «The *Servitudo Marina* at Rhodes : 1306-1462», in *Serta Neograeca*, ed. K. Dimaras and P. Wirth (Amsterdam, 1975), where p. 65 n. 60, should be amended to read as follows : «The whole process of the introduction of slaves to row galleys awaits study ; possibly the Hospital began at about this time to use serfs or *parichi* recruited by press-gang, as was the case in Cyprus in the later fifteenth century : G. Hill, *A*

a *liber homo*, married a *serua*, the husband giving the Hospital a female slave; his wife was manumitted from serfdom, but their children were all to be *marinarii* (56). A text of 1445 recorded the case of a *marinarius* who was manumitted from that condition and who gave in exchange a male slave and a female one (57). All these matters could be regulated by the Master, or the Master and Council, who issued sealed bulls attesting the status of those involved. Some of these were copied with only minor abbreviations into the current *liber bullarum*; sometimes merely a brief note or calendar was entered, occasionally with a formula such as *ut in forma* (58).

History of Cyprus, iii (Cambridge, 1948), 653, n. 1. See also J. GUILMARTIN, *Gunpowder and Galleys: Changing Technology and Mediterranean Warfare at Sea in the Sixteenth Century* (Cambridge, 1974). The condition of the *paroikoi* around Smyrna and on the islands, including Leros and Kos, during the thirteenth century is discussed in M. ANGOLD, *A Byzantine Government in Exile: Government and Society under the Lascarids of Nicaea, 1204-1281* (Oxford, 1975), 132-140.

(56) Register no. 6.

(57) Malta, cod. 357, f. 222.

(58) The distinction between documents given by the Master acting alone and those issued by the Master with the counsel of the brethren, by the Master and Council or by the Master and Convent, has not been indicated in the registers below; in fact, the abbreviations in the registered form of the original text often make it impossible to say what the form of the original would have been.

REGISTER

The manumissions in the surviving *libri bullarum* of the Masters of the Hospital preserved in the National Library of Malta at Valletta are mostly in the sections usually headed *partes cismarine* and *libertates*. Cod. 316 contains bulls for 1346, none of which mention slaves, and for 1358/9 ; cods. 317-319 cover 1347/8, 1351/2 and 1365/6, while cod. 321 covers 1380/1. Cod. 320 contains only bulls issued in France and Italy. Cods. 322-329 contain bulls issued while the Master, Fr. Juan Fernández de Heredia, resided at Avignon between 1382 and 1396 ; texts nos. 36 and 37 may have concerned slaves who were not at Rhodes, Kos or Cyprus. For this period, therefore, there are few manumissions in the *libri bullarum* ; there are none in cod. 281, the register for 1384-1386 of the Urbanist, Roman «anti-Master» Fr. Riccardo Caracciolo. As a result, the documentation is extremely fragmentary, and nothing about the numbers of slaves at Rhodes can safely be deduced from the comparative scarcity of manumissions for the period after 1381. The registers for 1397/8 and 1398/9 are lost. With a number of exceptions, for example in certain registers kept while the Master Fr. Philibert de Naillac was in the West from 1409 to 1420, cods. 330-354 contain documents issued at Rhodes from 1399 to 1440. Chancery scribes may sometimes have been Greeks ; no attempt has been made to improve their texts, doubtful readings being given in square brackets, but in the summaries names are normally given in the nominative form. Brethren of the Hospital are given as «Fr.» ; the phrase «in common form» denotes the formula, or variations of it, found in text no. 8. A few texts concerning *serui* are registered since they involved the provision of slaves in exchange for the freedom of the serf. All documents, except nos. 36-38 given at Avignon and no. 40 given in Paris, were issued at Rhodes. Where entries are marked with an asterisk (*) the passage given represents the complete text in the more or less abbreviated form actually given in the register now at Malta.

*1. 20 June 1347 [cod. 317, f. 236]
die .xx[a]. mensis Junij. data est licentia fratri francisco dacre manumitendi et francos faciendi Dimitrium et Stamati eius sclauos etc in forma.

2. 8 July 1347 [cod. 317, f. 234v]
Manumission in common form of *Aporictus sclauus noster*, since *Georgius de Nigroponte pater tuus sclauus noster* had paid 7 gold florins to Fr. Guillelmus de Sparano, Seneschal of the Master's household.
3. 20 September 1347 [cod. 317, f. 239v]
Manumission in common form of *Gorgius de Nigroponte noster et domus nostre sclauus*; he had paid Fr. Guillelmus de Sparano 22 gold florins, and the lead bull of the Master was attached to the document.
*4. 26 September 1347 [cod. 317, f. 241v]
Frater Deodatus de Gosono et cetera, dilecte nobis, in christo Sororj, margarite, de nigroponte domus eiusdem, salutem et c. Illa uobis libenter annuimus que satisfactionem, uestrj desiderij ac anime uestre consolationem, et salutem pariter, concernere, dignoscuntur, Igitur manumitendj, liberandj, francosque, et liberos faciendj, Calj de Squiro, Micalj de athena, cum eius tribus liberis Erinj de Saloniquj, et Vallaco eius viro, Georgium mandachi, et mariam eius consortem cum duobus suis liberis, Costam Sactj, Johani maronitj Costam ces[cr]unt, micalj custodem molendinj, et eius filium, Nicolaum cauulla, de Stiues, Erinj saronissa, Calj tauernaria, et mariam spanuda, sclauos uestros, in anime uestre salutare remedium, vobis tenore presentium, concedimus, et donamus, licenciam et plenariam potestatem, Ea consideratione motj potissime, quia sicut uestra, nobis exhibita supplicatio continuit, Vobis tanto seruiuerant, tempore, quod dictam manumissionem, merito meruerunt, data Rodj die vicesima sexta mensis, sete[m]bris Anno Incarnationis dominj, m°.ccc°, quadrigesimo septimo
5. 15 October 1347 [cod. 317, f. 242]
Manumission of Nicola Corupi *sclauus noster et domus nostre*, who had given the Hospital a slave in return for his own freedom: *Gorgium de [li]mjne sclauum nobis et domus (sic) nostre dedisti.*
6. 23 October 1347 [cod. 317, f. 241v-242]
Licence to Costecome *homo liber et francus* to marry Anna, daughter of Leo Cauasilla *seruus noster et domus nostre*. Costecome and Leo have given the Hospital a female slave; Costecome's children were to be *marinarij*, and he was to owe the Hospital *pronagium* (?) on all goods received as Anna's dowry.
7. 8 February 1348 [cod. 317, f. 245]
Manumission of Estomaquo Thomasij *Sclauus domus nostre*, who had

petitioned for his freedom, since his owner, the late Fr. Petrus Oliti, had secured a licence to free him but had died before he actually did so.

*8. 24 March 1348 [cod. 317, f. 226v]
Frater Deodatus et c. Dilecto nobis in christo Cristodolo de lo Sicamino sclauo nostro. Salutem in domino. Cum redemptor noster tocius humane conditor creature, ad hoc propiciatus humanam uoluit carnem assumere, ut diuinitatis sue gratia, dirupto quo tenebantur captiuj uinculo seruitutis, pristine, nos restitueret libertati, salubriter agitur, si homines quos ab inicio natura liberos protulit, et ius gencium iugo substituit seruitutis, ut ej in qua natj fuerant manumitentis beneficio libertatj reddantur, atque ideo pietatis intuitu, et huius rej consideracione comotj, de et cum consilio fratrum et procerum conuentus nostrj Rodj nobis assistencium in hac parte, te dictum Cristodulum sclauum nostrum, libertum ex hac die inantea ciuemque romanum efficimus, omneque tuum tibi seruitutis peculium tenore presencium de certa nostra Scientia et specialj gratia relaxamus. In cuius rej et c, data Rodj die .xxiiij. Mensis Marcij. Anno Septimo

9. 10 June 1351 [cod. 318, f. 210v]
A *sclauus* belonging to Fr. Johannes de Valensa was said to have been killed on the island of Kos by Fr. Petrus Ortis; if this were found to be correct, Fr. Petrus was to compensate Fr. Johannes.

10. 12 October 1351 [cod. 318, f. 213]
Manumission in common form, in consideration of his long service, of *Nichola Grossero de Saloniq. sclauus noster.*

11. 25 December 1351 [cod. 318, f. 216v]
Manumission in common form, in consideration of his service, of *Theodorus Vasillico noster et domus nostre sclauus.*

12. 29 December 1351 [cod. 318, f. 216v]
Manumission of *Johannes Apocogano domus nostre sclauus conmorans in Cazali nostro de Apidi*, on condition he pay 4 gold florins; Fr. Rostagnus de Serueria, formerly *baliuus* of the island of Rhodes, had promised him his freedom in return for 28 gold florins, 24 of which had been paid before Fr. Rostagnus died.

*13. 1351/2 [cod. 318, f. 219v]
Fr. Deodatus etc. Dilecto nobis in christo Jorgio otutis nostro et domus nostre sclauo. Salutem in domino. Cum redemptor noster totius humane conditor creature, ad hoc propiciatus humanam uoluit carnem assumere ut diuinitatis [*no more copied; the whole entry, evidently a manumission, was crossed out.*]

*14. 2 February 1352 [cod. 318, f. 218]
die ijda. februarij data fuit licentia fratri Bertrando amici faciendj francum et liberum Jannj sclauum suum ut in forma.

15. 24 March 1352 [cod. 318, f. 219]
Manumission in common form of *Giorgius de dispotato sclauus noster et domus nostre*, who gave the Hospital a *Sclauus unus bonus et sufficiens* in return for his freedom.

16. 24 March 1352 [cod. 318, f. 219]
Manumission in common form, with reference to long service, of *Nichola Agripiotj Sclauus noster et domus nostre.*

*17. 20 July 1358 [cod. 316, f. 298v: in same form as no. 22]
die xx. mensis Julij mecalj de Methelino sclauus fuit manumissus in forma Nicole de Methelino superius immediate registrata.

*18. 1 August 1358 [cod. 316, f. 298: in same form as no. 24]
die prima mensis augusti, Nicola de Tyna filius magistri yannj Changari generi paramati sclauus dominj magistri fuit manumissus in forma qua manumissus fuit Jannj Esmerilonj in folio retro contenta.

19. 20 August 1358 [cod. 316, f. 298]
Manumission, in same form as no. 18, of *Costa morayti de focia sclauus.*

20. 20 August 1358 [cod. 316, f. 301, 301-301v]
Manumissions in common form of *Maria filia Teodori Sequiadia sclaua nostra* and of *Erinj de Maquidioci sclaua nostra,* with reference to long service and the condition *Sic tamen dictam tibi facimus gratiam ut nobis quam diu in humanis agemus prout seruiuisti hactenus fideliter et legaliter obsequi tenearis.*

21. 20 August 1358 [cod. 316, f. 303v-304, 304, 309v]
Manumissions in common form of *Michaeli de Saloniqui*, of *Nicola de Monouassia filius petri de Monouassia*, and of *Philippus de hioty filius de Strouliaty*; each of these was described both as *sclauus noster* and as *sclauus noster et dicte domus nostre*, and in each case there was a reference to long service and the condition *Sic tamen ... tenearis* [as in no. 20].

22. 15 December 1358 [cod. 316, f. 298v]
Manumission in common form of *Nichola de Metellino sclauus noster ac paneterius in casali nostro de Mora*, with reference to long service but without the condition *Sic tamen ... tenearis*; the text added *duplicata fuit.*

*23. 15 December 1358 [cod. 316, f. 305]
Fr. Rogerius etc. fratrj ferdinando petrj de deza domus eiusdem Salutem etc. Vota uestra illa precipue que pietatem sapi[unt] et anime uestre salutem concernere dignoscuntur exaudientes benigne, quod duos sclauos uestros manumitere francos et libero (*sic*) facere et ab omnj nexu seruili liberare ualeatis, Vobis hac serie licenciam elargimur, data Rodj die xv[a] mensis decembris anno Lviij°.

24. 1358 [cod. 316, f. 297v]
Manumission in common form of *Johannes esmerlionj filius Costantini sclauus noster*, with reference to his services and the condition *Sic tamen ... tenearis* ; ... *data Rodi Anno Lviij.*

25. 1 May 1366 [cod. 319, f. 295]
Manumission in common form of *Georgius marmara sclauus noster et dicte nostre domus*, with reference to his services.

26. 15 May 1366 [cod. 319, f. 294v]
Manumission in common form of *Antonius ysmaillj sclauus noster et dicte nostre domus,* with reference to his service and the condition *Sic tamen ... tenearis* ; *tenearis* was followed by the marginal insertion *conpetens stipendium tibi dando.*

*27. 15 May 1366 [cod. 319, f. 295, immediately following no. 26]
Item sub tenore inmediate prescripto et sub eadem data et anno, Georgius guillelmj, Petrus Sullemne, Martinus cousan, Johannes Auguat, Johannes Brachierij, et Bertrandus saguat, Johannes ysob, Georgius assan, Johannes et Holamis cum uxore et filijs suis, Caloguero, Guillelmo Jacob, ferrandi yacxi, Martinus ysmaillj, Bernardus Orouggaichi, et Astasius maraclerius sclaui fuerunt manumissi et facti liberi atque franci.

28. 1374/7 [cod. 347, f. 214]
Manumission of Papa Costa Chrimeli, *seruus noster et dicte domus nostre*, on account of his services and in return for *unus sclauus et vigintiquinque floreni pro una sclaua.* On 20 July 1427 this manumission of *Papa Costa chrimeli Casalis nostri de Arcangelo*, originally made by Master Fr. Robert de Juilly [1374-1377], was confirmed, the relevant documents having been produced, since Papa Costa's children were being impressed for marine service.

29. 6 July 1381 [cod. 321, f. 243]
Manumission, in abbreviated common form, of Georgio Bulgaro who had been freed, with the Master's licence, by Fr. Mauhettus de Caneo, Preceptor of *Cournal et bangi*, whom he had faithfully served ; the

earlier manumission had not been written down, so that it was repeated (*te de nouo manumictere*) in writing.

*30. 6 July 1381 [cod. 321, f. 243; cf. no. 29]
Similis manumissio facta fuit Jacomino de licustony sclauo Jam dicti fratris Mauhetti dictis die et anno et mandatum fratribus ne contraueniant ut prefertur

31. 27 August 1381 [cod. 321, f. 225]
Lease to Fr. Domenico de Alamania, Preceptor of Naples and Cicciano, and lieutenant in Italy of the Master and Convent, of various *hospicia* and *jardina* in the *contrata* of Passimade on Rhodes *cum molendino duobus sclauis mulo et equo.*

*32. 14 October 1381 [cod. 321, f. 243]
die quartadecima mensis octubris Annj octuagesimj primj per dominum magistrum de consilio procerum Georgius de Salochio sclauus ipsius et Religionis manumissus fuit et ciuis Romanus liber effectum et omnem suum peculium remissum Retento quod seruire teneatur dicto domino magistro et Religionj Anno uno ut in forma, mandando fratribus uniuersis ne contraueniant.

33. 14 October 1381 [cod. 321, f. 243 (partly damaged)]
Confirmation, at his request, of the manumission of Johannes de Licosteme, *sclauus* of Fr. Jacobus de Vincestre [Winchester], Preceptor of Yeavely and Barrow; Fr. Foucaud de Cognac, Treasurer of the Hospital, had confirmed that Fr. Jacobus had freed him but that the previous Master had died before the licence was granted.

34. 30 November 1381 [cod. 321, f. 243v]
Confirmation of the manumission of *Theodorus bulgaro sclauus domus nostre*, at the request of Fr. Antonius de Sellani, Prior of the Hospital's church of *Santa Maria quondam templj* at Nicosia in Cyprus.

35. 23 March 1382 [cod. 321, f. 227]
Fr. Arnaldus de Castillione, Preceptor of *Raçach*, was confirmed in his rights to the *bona quondam michallj de lestella sclauj quondam fratris manuelis de carretto* conceded to him by the Master Fr. Robert de Juilly [1374-1377] but without a written document.

*36. 13 October 1384 [cod. 322, f. 257v]
[Avinione] die decima tercia mensis octobris Anno .lxxxiiij. dominus magister concessit licenciam priorj pisarum fratri Johanni siffe manumictendj Jacobum ... sclauum suum.

37. 10 May 1386 [cod. 323, f. 212-212v]
Confirmation, given by the Master at Avignon, of the manumission of *Katherine negre sclaua nostra et dicte domus* and of her son, freed by the late Fr. Rigotus de Nicossa, Preceptor of Barcelona, in consideration of her services but without the licence of the Master, which was now given with a version of the common form.

38. 29 August 1391 [cod. 325, f. 155-155v]
Manumission, granted by the Master at Avignon, of *Georgius calamia noster et dicte domus seruus*, who was a serf because while his father Micali Protutameno was *francus*, his mother, Cali tu Mangipa, was a serf from Kos, *serua nostra et dicte domus insule Langonis*; in return he promised to give *sclaui greci quatuor* to the *baiulia* of Kos.

39. 19 January 1404 [cod. 332, f. 171]
Manumission in common form of *Maria de burgaria sclaua nostra et dicte domus*; a full version of the text, it concluded *In Cuius Rei testimonium bulla nostra plumbea presentibus est appensa.*

40. 12 April 1413 [cod. 338, f. 230]
Manumission in common form, given in Paris by the Master, of *petrus dictus georgius armenus sclauus noster acquisitus*, in recognition of his services *ultra mare* [presumably at Rhodes].

41. 8 October 1413 [cod. 339, f. 289v-290]
Manumission of *Stratj de Casalj Corsorto* [possibly on Cyprus] who was *seruus noster*, granted at the petition of Fr. Johannes Claretj, lieutenant in the Preceptory of Cyprus; *Addita tamen talj condicionj quod tu stratj tenearis et debeas emere quendam sclauum christianum qui in dicto casalj seu villagia seruorum more morarj uxorare debeat et in loco tuo esse subrogatus.*

42. 22 December 1414 [cod. 339, f. 295]
Manumission in common form of *helena nationis hungarie sclaua nostra*, in recognition of her services to the sick in the *infirmaria* of the Hospital.

43. 22 April 1415 [cod. 339, f. 295v]
Manumission in common form of *Jany pully Sclauus noster et dicte domus nostre* for his services to Fr. Hesso Schlegelholtz, late Preceptor of Kos; but first he was to give three more years of service.

44. 8 January 1421 [cod. 345, f. 197v-198]
Declaration by the Master and Convent, *Sub impressione sigillj nostrj quo utimur in cera nigra*, that the late Fr. Petrus de Balma, lieutenant

on the island of Kos, had at the moment of death manumitted *Jacobinus armenus sclauus*, in return for his services on condition that he serve in the infirmary of the Convent at Rhodes for three years, which service he had commenced on 1 March 1420.

*45. 5 October 1421 [cod. 346, f. 164]
de precepto dominj magistrj, et dominorum de conuentu fratre Jeno de Boys requirente fuerunt manumissi Janj sergentin, et Anthoni soupy, sclauj Insule, siue preceptorie langonensis, cum hac condictione quod toto eorum tempore seruire debeant, et neccessaria ut similibus aliis manumissis, eisdem per preceptorem, siue nostrum locumtenentem prestentur. data Rhodj die .V. mensis Octubris .m.ccccxxj. sub Impressione etc.

46. 24 February 1435 [cod. 351, f. 151v]
Manumission from serfdom of *Xeni Angelina filia costa plandia, et Ereni tis mangaffadenas serua seu aschiticia nostra et dicte domus nostre casalis de cosquino, conmorans presentialiter in parambolino*, who was also described as *serua seu parichissa*; she had paid the Master 40 *ducati ... causa emendi loco tui vnam sclauam, ut in similibus est consuetudo.*

47. 20 April 1436 [cod. 352, f.67]
Fr. Joan de Vilagut, Castellan of Amposta [ie. Prior of Aragon], was licensed to free various slaves he had purchased on account of their domestic service to him (*non nullos sclauos vsque a pueritia eorum emptos propter eorum domesticam seruitutem et fidem erga vos ...*), and lest they kept in slavery after his death; he had had them baptized.

48. 22 May 1438 [cod. 353, f. 184]
Manumission in common form, by the *Magnus Preceptor* and Convent at Rhodes, of *Andrea Russo sclauus quondam Reuerendissimj dominj magistri nunc vltimate defuncti*, who was freed according to the late Master's will.

*49. 14 September 1438 [cod. 353, f. 192v (almost illegible)]
die xiiij Septembris 1438. Data fuit licentia Abro de cipro et Elie sue vxorj Ebreis Emendi unam sclauam saracinam antiquam Et qua filij procrearj minime possit, et Eam pro usu Seruicij domus sue Retinendj ut Alij faciunt.

50. 26 July 1439 [cod. 354, f. 250]
Manumission at the petition of Katherine de Lusignan, *admiratissa* of the Kingdom of Cyprus, of *Caly georgii tu latrioti sclaua empti[o]ne* of the Hospital's *casale* of Finika on Cyprus.

*51. 31 August 1439 [cod. 354, f. 250]
die ultima mensis Augusti, fuit transactum per Consilium quod Cosmas sclauus quondam fratris G[e]raudj de ceruilion, debeat seruire pro Annos quinque venerando domino priori conuentus Rhodj. Et ipse dominus prior pro ipso debet soluere comuni tesauro, Infra dictum tempus quinque Annorum ducatos Rhodj viginti quinque. Et dicto termino transacto dictus Cosmas remanere debeat franchus et liber.

VII

VONITZA IN EPIRUS AND ITS LORDS: 1306-1377 (*)

Vonitza, a port in Acarnania situated within the Gulf of Arta close to its entrance on the southern side, occupied a strategic position in an area which was for long a centre of Greco-Latin struggles for control in Epirus. Though the Latins' seapower enabled them to hold Corfu and the other Ionian islands, particularly mountainous Cephalonia, they could never permanently subdue the mainland territories. The possession of Vonitza, however, allowed access to the country southwards towards Lepanto, and facilitated attacks against Arta on the far side of the gulf to the north. Vonitza was an obvious base for an invasion of Greece and was easily reached from Leucadia, an island just outside the Gulf of Arta. Leucadia, like Cephalonia, Ithaka and Zante which lay further to the south, was itself attractive as a naval base, a commercial entrepôt or a pirate hideout. To the east of Vonitza stretched the Greek hinterland, to the west the sea and the islands of the Mediterranean. In this environment there flourished an unstable, multilingual society of adventurers and corsairs. The Greeks and Albanians of the mainland mingled and intermarried with the feudal Frankish lords from Southern Italy who came in search of lands, rents and castles, and with the Venetians who were interested in strategic harbours on their vital shipping lanes and, secondarily, in trade (1).

(*) This note, intended merely to establish certain fundamental points, is largely based on a re-examination of documents in the Archivio di Stato at Venice [= Venice]; note that the pencil foliations have generally been cited. These documents were used in K. Hopf, *Geschichte Griechenlands vom Beginn des Mittelalters bis auf unsere Zeit*, 2 vols. (= J. Ersch-J. Gruber, Allgemeine Encyklopädie der Wissenschaften und Künste, 85-86: Leipzig, 1867-1868); Hopf cited the modern copies. Partly because the Angevin archives at Naples have been destroyed, a large number of Hopf's statements can never be controlled; yet many of them, repeated in numerous subsequent works, require modification. The older unreliable narratives and genealogies so often used have here been ignored. These points once made, no systematic indication of past errors has been included in the notes below.

(1) Cf. F. Braudel, *La Méditerranée et le monde méditerranéen à l'époque de Philippe II* (Paris, 1949), 116-131, *et pass.*

The Latins were attacking the Ionian islands and the coast of Epirus long before the crusade of 1204 and the consequent destruction of the Byzantine empire. Cephalonia, Ithaka and Zante were conquered by the Normans in 1185 and later passed by marriage to the Orsini family. After 1204 the Venetians held claims throughout this area and briefly occupied Corfu, but the whole region of Epirus, including Leucadia and Vonitza, escaped permanent Latin settlement and came under the rule of Michael I Angelos, the independent Greek Despot of Epirus. The Orsini retained their islands, surviving as best they could. They married into the Angelos family and did homage both to Venice and to the Villehardouin rulers of the Latin Principality of Achaea, of which they became barons. In 1259, following his defeat by Michael VIII Palaeologus, the Despot Michael II Angelos withdrew to Vonitza and then to Leucadia before taking refuge with his Orsini kinsmen at Cephalonia. Shortly after, Vonitza served as the base for Michael II's reconquest of Epirus (1).

After the Palaeologi had reestablished their imperial rule at Constantinople in 1261 the Despots of Epirus were forced to rely increasingly on Italian support against the Byzantines. Michael II's son Nicephorus I allied with the Angevin rulers of Naples, who through conquest and marriage were acquiring extensive interests and a complex series of dynastic claims in Epirus and throughout Greece. In 1294 Charles II of Anjou transferred these lands and claims to his fourth son Philip of Taranto, and in the same year Philip married Nicephorus' daughter Thamar, whose dowry was supposed to include the towns of Lepanto, Vrachova, Angelokastron and Vonitza. In 1303, following the refusal of Nicephorus' widow the *Despoina* Anna, acting as regent for their young son Thomas, to do them homage, the Angevins invaded Epirus, passing through Vonitza but failing to take Arta. Philip of Taranto led another expedition to Epirus in 1306, partly at the instigation of Giovanni I Orsini, Count of Cephalonia and lord of Leucadia, whose wife Maria was also a daughter of Nicephorus. Giovanni had hoped for

---

(1) F. THIRIET, *La Romanie vénitienne au moyen âge; le développement et l'exploitation du domaine colonial vénitien* (*XIIe-XVe siècles*) (Paris, 1959), 36-86; E. LUNZI, *Della condizione politica delle isole Jonie sotto il dominio veneto* (Venice, 1858), 22-49; D. NICOL, *The Despotate of Epirus* (Oxford, 1957), 10, 16-20, 90-91, 187, 222.

conquests in Epirus, but the Despot Thomas defended himself well and secured Philip's withdrawal at the cost of conceding him Lepanto, Vonitza and Butrinto, a coastal fortress opposite Corfu (1). For a while Vonitza was in Angevin hands, then in 1314 the news that Corfu was in revolt and that Vonitza was besieged compelled the Angevins to prepare a relief force in Italy (2). Corfu was retained but during the years following the Angevins lost control of Vonitza, possibly to the Despot Thomas, or perhaps to the treacherous Giovanni Orsini, who changed sides twice in the civil war which began in the Morea in 1315 and who was suspected of poisoning Louis of Burgundy, Prince of Achaea, in 1316.

In 1318 Niccolò Orsini, Giovanni I's son and his successor as Count of Cephalonia, murdered his own step-uncle, the Despot Thomas. Then, after marrying Thomas' widow Anna Palaeologina and entering the Greek orthodox church, he ruled the Despotate of Epirus as Niccolò Orsini Angelos; presumably he controlled Leucadia and Vonitza as well. In 1320 Niccolò had to seek Venetian assistance against the Palaeologi, but when he offered to place the County of Cephalonia under Venetian protection as his ancestors had, the Venetians replied that they considered that Cephalonia, Ithaka and Zante rightfully belonged to them in any case (3). In 1323 Niccolò was assassinated by his brother Giovanni, who became Despot of Epirus in his turn and entrusted the government of Cephalonia to his uncle Guglielmo Orsini. In 1325, after several years of preparation, Philip of Taranto's younger brother Jean of Gravina landed on Cephalonia, imprisoned Guglielmo Orsini and established Angevin authority there (4). He probably secured Ithaka and Zante as well, but Leucadia and Vonitza remained in the hands of Giovanni II Orsini until 1331.

---

(1) J. LONGNON, *L'empire latin de Constantinople et la principauté de Morée* (Paris, 1949), 272-273, 285-287, 292; *Libro de los fechos et conquistas del principado de la Morea*, ed. A. Morel-Fatio (Geneva, 1885), 100-103, 115. The Orsini apparently secured control of Leucadia shortly before 1300: W. MILLER, *The Latins in the Levant* (London, 1908), 181.

(2) R. CAGGESE, *Roberto d'Angiò e i suoi tempi*, 2 vols. (Florence, 1922-1930), i.212.

(3) G. THOMAS, *Diplomatarium Veneto-Levantinum*, i (Venice, 1876), 146, 161-162, 168-170; R. CESSI-P. SAMBIN, *Le deliberazioni del Consiglio dei Rogati (Senato); serie 'mixtorum'*, i (Venice, 1960), 223.

(4) *Libro de los fechos*, 138, 144; CAGGESE, ii. 313-318.

In 1331 Gautier de Brienne, Count of Lecce and titular Duke of Athens, whose wife Beatrice was the daughter of Philip of Taranto and of Thamar of Epirus, invaded Greece through Epirus. He failed to recover Athens and Thebes from the Catalans who had usurped them, but he captured Leucadia, Vonitza and Arta, to which the Angevins had old claims, from Giovanni II Orsini. Gautier could not hold Epirus and his efforts to mount a new expedition in the years following were unsuccessful, but he did retain Leucadia and Vonitza, presumably as fiefs held from the Angevins (1). He placed them under the command first of Jean de la Mandelé and then of Jean Cligny; Cligny's administration gave rise to complaints and came to an end in 1343 (2). Meanwhile, in the years following Philip of Taranto's death in 1331, the Angevin rights in Greece and the control of the Morea, Lepanto, Corfu and Cephalonia passed to his second wife Catherine de Valois, who ruled them as regent for their son Robert of Taranto. And when Robert married Marie de Bourbon in 1347 the income he settled on her was partly secured on his possessions in Corfu and Cephalonia (3). In Epirus the Despot Giovanni II was assassinated in 1335 by his wife Anna, who then ruled as regent for their son Nicephorus II Orsini. When Anna proved unable to resist pressure from the Byzantine emperor Andronicus III Palaeologus, Catherine de Valois sent assistance to her, hoping to reestablish Angevin influence in Epirus in this way. But, as Andronicus' minister John Cantacuzenus pointed out, even with the consent of the rulers of Epirus the Angevins could secure no more than a few coastal positions at Lepanto, Vonitza and Butrinto (4). The Byzantines drifted into civil war and their predominance in Epirus lasted only a decade. It was replaced in 1349 by that of the great Serbian ruler Stefan Dushan, who established his half-brother Simeon Urosh as ruler at Arta.

---

(1) K. SETTON, *Catalan Domination of Athens: 1311-1388* (Cambridge, Mass., 1948), 38-43; CAGGESE, ii.338-340.

(2) HOPF, i.430, 441, citing Archivio di Stato, Naples; Reg. Ang. 1336 B (no. 303), f. 484v; 1343 D, f. 158 (documents now destroyed).

(3) J. BUCHON, *Nouvelles recherches historiques sur la principauté française de Morée*, 2 vols. (Paris, 1843), i.54, 304; ii.72, 103-104; E. LÉONARD, *Histoire de Jeanne I, reine de Naples*, i-iii (Monaco-Paris, 1932-1937), i.183-185; ii.678, n. 7.

(4) Iohannes CANTACUZENUS, *Historiarum libri IV*, ed. L. Schopen, i (Bonn, 1828), 529.

The Venetians retained their interest in the Ionian isles. In November 1348 they decided to approach the Angevin rulers of Naples with a view to securing Corfu. By September 1350 they were negotiating to acquire Corfu, Cephalonia, Zante, Butrinto and places nearby from Robert of Taranto, who was then in captivity and anxious to raise his ransom. On 30 January 1351, despite doubts in the senate as to whether the islands might not prove more of a liability than an asset, the Venetians formally agreed to expend 60,000 ducats for the islands. They then made detailed arrangements for the administration of these places, but by 11 February the whole agreement had been cancelled, apparently because negotiations for Robert's release were under way (1).

A few years later Venice did indirectly secure a foothold in the Ionian islands at Leucadia which, together with Vonitza, remained in the hands of Gautier de Brienne; in 1347 he had provided in his will for the constables of his castles there (2). The Venetians had long maintained relations with Gautier, though they were consistently reluctant to assist him in attacks on the Catalans at Athens. In 1344 Gautier became a Venetian citizen, and when they captured one of his pirate vessels in 1349 the Venetians subsequently, at Gautier's request, ordered its release. In 1352 they refused Gautier facilities for arming ships at Venice but were willing to supply him with provisions (3). The Brienne had long-standing connections with the Venetian family of Giorgio. On 5 November 1335 Gautier, while in Venice, confirmed Graziano Giorgio's claims to an abbey in the Duchy of Athens which Gautier's father had granted in 1310 to Graziano's grandfather Giovanni Querini. Twenty years later, on 18 October 1355 at Paris, Gautier granted Leucadia and its castle of Santa Maura to Graziano Giorgio to be held in fief with obligations of military and marine service (4).

---

(1) Venice, Deliberazioni del Senato (secreta): liber rogatorum B, f. 33v, 70v, 97v, 100v, 101v-102v, 105; R. Predelli, *I libri Commemoriali della Republica di Venezia: regesti*, ii (Venice, 1878), 188-189; Léonard, ii.159, 300-301, 305.

(2) K. Hopf, *Chroniques gréco-romanes* (Berlin, 1873), xxix-xxx.

(3) Setton, 38-43; C. Cipolla, 'Venezia e Gualtieri VI di Brienne', in *Archivio veneto*, xvii (1879), 141-144; Venice, Misti del Senato [= Misti], xxvi, f. 77v (2 January 1352).

(4) Texts in Lunzi, 121, n. 2, 124, n. 1.

Soon after, Robert of Taranto granted Cephalonia to a Neapolitan knight, Leonardo Tocco. Leonardo's father Guglielmo Tocco, who died in 1335, had been Philip of Taranto's chamberlain and his governor at Corfu. Guglielmo's wife may have been Margherita, sister of Giovanni I Orsini; his children perhaps grew up in the Ionian islands. Guglielmo's sons Lodovico and Pietro served the Angevins; both were seneschals of Robert of Taranto and were rewarded with lands and titles (1). Leonardo also served Robert for a number of years, and by 1353 had become his chamberlain (2). Shortly before May 1357 Robert made him Count of Cephalonia and Zante (3); when Leonardo witnessed an act of Robert at Taranto on 20 June 1357 he was described as Count of Cephalonia and lord of the Barony of Tocco (4). He married, perhaps at this time, Maddalena Buondelmonti whose Florentine parents, Manuele Buondelmonti and Lapa Acciaiuoli, had Neapolitan connections through Lapa's brother Niccolò Acciaiuoli, the powerful minister of the Angevins. By 1362 Leonardo and Maddalena had a daughter; and other children, including two sons Carlo and Leonardo, followed (5). Just as Robert granted Corinth to Niccolò Acciaiuoli in 1358 when unable to defend it himself, so the establishment of Leonardo Tocco at Cephalonia was probably intended to secure its defence. For, following the death of Stefan Dushan late in 1355, Nicephorus II Orsini reasserted his claims in Epirus and ousted Simeon Urosh from control at Arta (6).

---

(1) BUCHON, i.307, 410, mentioning but not citing a document referring to Guglielmo in 1330; LÉONARD, i.381, n. 3, 447; ii.300; C. D'ENGENIO, *Napoli Sacra* (Naples, 1624), 23. Clear evidence as to the identity of Guglielmo's wife seems to be lacking; Leonardo is sometimes said to have married an illegitimate daughter of Lodovico or Philip of Taranto.

(2) LÉONARD, ii.97; iii.342; HOPF, i.452.

(3) BUCHON, i.99, 305, n. 1, mentions a document — possibly that of 11 February 1356 which he saw at Corfu (i.411) — showing Robert still exercising direct jurisdiction over Cephalonia in 1356; Leonardo was count by May 1357 (below, p. 137, n. 2).

(4) Biblioteca Marciana, Venice, cod. lat., cl.x, no. 279 (= 2801), f. 84.

(5) On 18 May 1362 the Countess of Malta wrote to Lapa from Naples: " de la contessa de Cephalonia avemmo spisso novelle ch'essa e lo conte e la figlia stanno bene " (BUCHON, ii.207). HOPF, ii.36, gives three daughters: Petronilla, Giovanna, Susanna.

(6) S. CIRAC ESTOPAÑAN, *Bizancio y España: el legado de la basilissa María y de los despotas Thomas y Esaú de Joannina*, i (Barcelona, 1943), 118-121.

Nicephorus was interested in Leucadia and apparently he incited the population to revolt against Graziano Giorgio, who naturally turned to Venice for support. On 28 January 1357 the authorities agreed that, at the discretion of their captains, Venetian ships would call at Leucadia for victuals and repairs and would protect Graziano against " pirates "; they also undertook to purchase quantities of biscuit from him (1). On 15 May the Venetian commander Pietro Soranzo arrived at the castle of Santa Maura to collect the provisions due, only to find that Graziano's Greek subjects had rebelled and seized the provisions. Soranzo learned that a force of horse and foot from the Despotate of Epirus had landed on Leucadia and had captured two Venetian merchants, and that the Count of Cephalonia had recently been there for a while with two ships. Soranzo agreed to supply Graziano with 100 men off his galleys, and with these Graziano set out, without proper arms or supplies but confident of recovering the provisions. The Greeks declared that death was preferable to Graziano's rule. With a force reported by Soranzo as numbering 500 foot and 40 horse, they attacked and captured Graziano and his brother Niccolò; the Venetians were permitted to return to their galleys. Since Graziano's son had only fifteen men to hold the castle of Santa Maura, Soranzo left thirteen men there before sailing away. He later explained that he considered Leucadia to be worth over 2000 florins annually to Venice, and that he was anxious to prevent the Despot capturing the castle (2). Santa Maura apparently held out, and on 17 June 1357 the Venetians granted Graziano permission to send a Venetian notary to the Despot to negotiate his release (3).

Graziano Giorgio later attacked Vonitza. After Gautier de Brienne's death at Poitiers in 1356 the overlordship of Leucadia and the lordship of Vonitza passed to his nephew Jean d'Enghien, Count of Lecce. Jean d'Enghien, writing from Lecce on 24 August

---

(1) Misti, xxvii, f. 110.

(2) Soranzo's report of 23 May, in Venice, Libri Commemoriali, v, f. 101v. The *dispotus* and the *comes Zephalonie et Zante* were clearly different persons; Tocco was, therefore, already count by May 1357.

(3) Misti, xxviii, f. 6v. Nicephorus may have hoped to reestablish Orsini rule in the Ionian islands. On 5 September 1357 the Venetians told the envoys of the *dominus despotus* that they would supply him with a ship if one were available but that *ulterius in peticione sua non possumus nos intromittere* (Misti, xxviii, f. 13).

1359, complained to the Venetians that Graziano, though his vassal, was continually attacking his castle at Vonitza, damaging his lands, incomes and fisheries there, and imprisoning his subjects; he requested the cessation of the attacks, the payment of reparations, and the release of the prisoners. On 14 October the Venetians replied, evasively, that they had no competence to interfere in such a quarrel between a lord and his vassal. But, after some disagreement in the senate, they did write to admonish Graziano (1).

Meanwhile, in the spring of 1359, Nicephorus was defeated and killed by the Albanian chiefs whom Stefan Dushan had established in Epirus; one of them, Petros Losha, became lord of Arta. Orsini power around Arta was at an end. It was an empty gesture when in January 1361 the Serbian ruler Simeon Urosh confirmed the pretensions of John Tsaphas Orsini to the lordship of Arta and of other places in Epirus, including Leucadia; John Tsaphas was a kinsman of Simeon's wife Thomais, who was Nicephorus' sister (2).

At Cephalonia Leonardo Tocco behaved as a kind of maritime marcher lord. He failed to provide the feudal service due to the Prince of Achaea. Using a galley hired from Otranto and two other vessels, he made the waters between Clarenza and Corfu unsafe. And in 1360 he was waging war both against the Albanians in Epirus and the Catalans of the Duchy of Athens, forcing the Catalans to arm ships against his pirates from Cephalonia (3). It was apparently in this period that Leonardo seized Leucadia, perhaps to forestall an Albanian invasion, perhaps because the population appealed to him to liberate them from the Giorgio, or perhaps because the Enghien were anxious to be rid of their troublesome Giorgio vassals. And at this time or later Leonardo also occupied Vonitza, with or

---

(1) Venice, Libri Commemoriali, vi, f. 70: text in A. RUBIO I LLUCH, *Diplomatari de l'Orient català* (Barcelona, 1947), no. 238. Misti, xxix, f. 29v (14 October 1359).

(2) CIRAC, i.119-127.

(3) Bibliothèque Nationale, Paris; Ms. fran. 6537, f. 61, 75 (*circa* December 1360). Nicola de Boyano reports " che lu conte de Cefalonia fa gran guerra co lu dispotatu de li albanesi et co lu duzame de athena ". C. DU CANGE, *Histoire de l'empire de Constantinople sous les empereurs français*, ed. J. Buchon, ii (Paris, 1826), 265, caused confusion by reading this as saying that Tocco made war " au despote, aux Albanais, et aux Catalans ".

without the consent of the Enghien [1]. It may have been this last action which inspired Federigo III of Sicily to reassert his claims in Epirus; at Siracusa on 16 August 1363 he authorized Matteo de Moncada, his vicar-general in the Duchy of Athens, to conquer Vonitza and the lands between Vonitza and Arta [2]. Nothing came of this scheme and Leonardo retained his acquisitions. When on 19 February 1362, following the homage done by his proctor Giovanni Valaresso, Leonardo Tocco and his descendants were granted Venetian citizenship, the formal document described him simply as "Cephalonie comes palatinus" [3], but a papal bull dated 6 November 1367 entitled him " dux Lucate et comes Ihecefalionie " [4], and by September 1373, if not earlier, he was also styling himself " signor de la citade de Bondanza " [5].

Leonardo Tocco's piratical activities periodically brought him into conflict with Venice. On 15 March 1363 the Venetians agreed to sell him 200 oars for his galley. In December 1366, still searching for an Adriatic base, they reached a preliminary agreement, never actually put into effect, by which Robert of Taranto's successor, Philip of Taranto, would transfer control of Corfu and Butrinto to Venice as security for a loan. Venice's weakness in this area was emphasized when, on 28 March 1368, the Captain of the Adriatic fleet had to be instructed to secure the release of a ship allegedly seized by Leonardo Tocco from the Venetian Franceschino Venier; he was also to demand free access to Tocco's ports for Venetian ships and merchants. The Venetians subsequently wrote demanding that Leonardo cease harrassing and oppressing their merchants,

---

(1) There is no reliable evidence as to how or when Leonardo acquired Leucadia and Vonitza. B. REMONDINI, *De Zacynthi Antiquitatibus et Fortuna Commentarius* (Venice, 1756), 243, states, but with no source, that he acquired Leucadia in 1362, and most authors have accepted that date. Some (eg. MILLER, 292) repeat a story that Graziano died in 1362 and that the islanders revolted against his son and called in Leonardo; Graziano's son Bernardo did have some cause for complaint later. There is apparently no evidence as to the attitude of the Enghien, who seem to have abandoned their claims to Leucadia and Vonitza.

(2) Text in RUBIO, no. 254; read *Bondancie* as Vonitza.

(3) Venice, Libri Commemoriali, vi, f. 125v: text in LUNZI, 120, n. 1.

(4) O. HALECKI, *Un empereur de Byzance à Rome* (Warsaw, 1930), 170; there is no evidence as to the origin of the ducal title.

(5) HOPF, *Chroniques*, 182; *Bondanza* was Vonitza.

and since this had no effect they gave orders on 3 September 1371 for their Adriatic Captain to take action. Leonardo regained some favour when his eldest daughter married the Venetian Niccolò dalle Carceri, Duke of Archipelago. On 24 August 1372 Leonardo wrote from his castle of San Giorgio at Cephalonia asking for the use of Venetian galleys for the wedding, and on 28 October the Venetians graciously granted his request on condition that the galleys were not required in the Aegean (1). But on 20 March 1375, after Graziano Giorgio's son Bernardo had come forward with a copy of Gautier de Brienne's grant of 1355 and had requested assistance in recovering what he considered his legitimate position at Leucadia, the Venetians ordered their Captain in the Adriatic to visit Leonardo and claim either the restoration of Leucadia or suitable compensation to Bernardo for its loss; if need be he was to threaten Venetian action in support of Bernardo (2). These decisions seem to have had no effect.

Leonardo Tocco took his place among the Latin lords in Greece. In the ecclesiastical sphere, the Greek archbishop was expelled from Leucadia in about 1367; and Vonitza was the seat of a Latin bishopric. In 1372 the pope summoned Leonardo to a congress at Thebes, which never actually met but was intended to discuss an alliance against the Turks (3). After Philip of Taranto's death in November 1373 Leonardo was called to Clarenza in the Morea to decide the future of the Principality of Achaea with the other barons, and from there he sailed to Naples in his own galley as one of four barons sent early in 1374 to hand over the principality to Joanna of Anjou, Queen of Naples (4). Between September 1373 and August 1374 Petros Losha died and Arta came into the hands of Ghin Boua Spata, the Albanian lord of Angelokastron. In 1375 he formed an alliance with the Serbian Despot of Jannina, Thomas Preljubovich. Thomas' wife Maria was the daughter of Simeon Urosh and of Nicephorus II Orsini's sister Thomais, and Ghin Boua married Thomas' daughter

---

(1) Misti, xxx, f. 137 (1363); Venice, Sindicati, i, f. 106 (1366); Misti, xxxii, f. 119 (1368); xxxiii, f. 129v (1371); xxiv, f. 32 (1372).

(2) Misti, xxxv, f. 7v: text in LUNZI, 126, n. 1.

(3) CIRAC, i. 129; RUBIO, nos. 330, 336.

(4) *Libro de los fechos*, 156-157, confirmed in Misti, xxxiv, f. 102v (26 April 1374).

Helena, thus linking himself with the Orsini line of descent. Thereafter he turned to attack Vonitza (1).

At about this time Leonardo Tocco died, leaving his widow Maddalena Buondelmonti in a difficult position as regent for their young son Carlo. In the summer of 1377 she temporarily made Vonitza over to the Knights Hospitallers of Rhodes, who were to use Vonitza as a base for yet another dismally unsuccessful invasion of Epirus during 1378 (2). From the beginning of the century Vonitza was almost continuously in Latin hands and was normally controlled by whoever held Leucadia. The Italians ruled the seas, but only a considerable army, well led and well supplied, could make permanent conquests on the mainland in Epirus. Vonitza therefore remained a Latin bridgehead on Greek soil.

---

(1) CIRAC, i.125-127, 135-143; Laonicus CHALCOCANDYLES, *Historiarum Demonstrationes*, ed. F. Darkó, i (Budapest, 1922), 196-198. These events cannot be dated precisely from the chronicles.

(2) Leonardo was alive shortly before March 1375 (Misti, xxxv, f. 7v) but dead before August 1377; on the events of 1377, see A. LUTTRELL, ' Interessi fiorentini nell'economia e nella politica dei Cavalieri Ospedalieri di Rodi nel Trecento ', in *Annali della Scuola Normale Superiore di Pisa: lettere, storia e filosofia*, serie 2, xxviii (1959), 322-324. The document seen by Mazzella, which BUCHON, i.309, n. 3, cited as evidence that Leonardo was dead by 1377, was actually a document of 1477. The Albanians defeated the Hospitallers in 1378 but the Tocco retained Vonitza, and its subsequent history is recorded in their family chronicle; see G. SCHIRÒ, ' Struttura e contenuto della cronaca dei Tocco ', in *Byzantion*, xxxii (1962). This present note may serve as a partial substitute for the lost opening passages of this chronicle.

VIII

THE LATINS OF ARGOS AND NAUPLIA: 1311-1394

DURING the fourteenth century the Latins' hold on those fragments of the great empire of *Romania* which they had acquired after the overthrow of the Byzantine emperor in 1204 became increasingly precarious. In the Morea, as the Peloponnese was then known, the foremost Frankish houses, the Villehardouin, the Courtenay, the de la Roche and others, were extinguished. The French magnates faced hostility not only from the Greeks and Turks, but also from the Catalans and the Italianate elements to whom their lands passed through conquest, marriage or princely favour. A turning point in this process was the slaughter of many male members of the old Frankish aristocracy by the Catalan companies and their Turkish allies in a great battle near Thebes in 1311, at which Gautier de Brienne, who had succeeded his kinsman Guy de la Roche as Duke of Athens and Neopatras in 1309, was killed. Gautier's duchies were occupied by the Catalans, who were acting independently of the Aragonese King of Sicily, though they subsequently rendered a vague formal allegiance to a line of Siculo-Aragonese dukes. The Catalans did not take Corinth, which lay on the isthmus separating the Duchy of Athens from the Morea, and the Brienne family retained effective possession of its lands beyond Corinth, around Argos and Nauplia, which continued to form part of the Principality of Achaea. Gautier de Brienne's young son, also named Gautier, and his descendants failed however in their repeated attempts to recover Athens and Thebes, and in the years after the younger Gautier's death in 1356, when his Enghien nephews inherited his Greek claims and possessions, the great baronies of the Principality of Achaea were held by Italians: the Zaccaria of Genoa, Lords of Chalandritza; the Tocco of Naples who in 1357 became Counts of Cephalonia; and the Florentine Acciaiuoli who were granted Corinth in 1358.[1]

The struggle for possession of Athens and Thebes took place within the context of the great Mediterranean conflict between the royal houses of Aragon and Anjou. For a brief period in 1311 Gautier de Brienne's widow, Jeanne de Châtillon, defended Athens against the Catalans. When no help came, many of her subjects fled to seek protection from the Venetians on the island of Negroponte, while she travelled westwards with the young Gautier to secure the assistance of her father Gautier de Châtillon, Constable of France; at Naples on 22 November 1312 she formally

[1] For general background and extensive bibliographies, K. Setton, *Catalan Domination of Athens*: 1311–1388 (Cambridge, Mass., 1948); J. Longnon, *L'empire latin de Constantinople et la principauté de Morée* (Paris, 1949); *Cambridge Medieval History*, iv, part 1 (revised: Cambridge, 1966). Too much of what has been accepted in many standard works derives from K. Hopf, *Geschichte Griechenlands vom Beginn des Mittelalters bis auf die neuere Zeit*, 2 vols. (Leipzig, 1867–1868) [=Hopf, i-ii], which is unreliable and hard to control, especially since it is partly based on the Angevin documents in the Archivio di Stato, Naples [=Naples], which were destroyed in 1943. The undocumented and inaccurate genealogies in K. Hopf, *Chroniques gréco-romanes inédites ou peu connues* (Berlin, 1873) [=Hopf, *CGR*], are largely derived from his earlier work. The present study is based as far as possible on the original texts; it ignores many secondary works and attempts no systematic indication of the numerous past errors, but since so little material relating to fourteenth-century Greece survives considerable detail has been included. Inevitably, more material on the present topic remains to be exploited, especially among the sources of French and Italian history, and above all among material which does survive at Naples. The archives of the Counts of Conversano apparently contain nothing relevant to the present study: G. Monti, *Nuovi studi angioini* (Trani, 1937), 375.

constituted him bailli of the Brienne possessions.[2] Gautier de Brienne had come of age by January 1321, when he was compelled to accept liability for part of the debts incurred by his parents in the defence of the family lands in Greece.[3] His marriage to Beatrice, daughter of his overlord Philippe of Anjou, who was Prince of Taranto, Prince of Achaea and titular Emperor of Constantinople, increased Gautier's prestige,[4] though as titular Duke of Athens and Neopatras, Count of Brienne in Champagne and Count of Lecce in the Kingdom of Naples, he was a grand and influential magnate in his own right, with extensive possessions and interests. Gautier was always eager for power and ready to oppress his own vassals. The Florentine chronicler Giovanni Villani, naturally critical of Gautier after his tyrannical rule in Florence, described him as cruel, cunning, avaricious, proud and dictatorial, and noted that he was 'nourished in Greece and Apulia rather than France.'[5]

By March 1312 Jeanne de Châtillon was sending men and horses from Italy to Greece under Guillaume de Usez.[6] Support came from Robert of Anjou, King of Naples, and from the pro-Angevin French popes at Avignon, who excommunicated the Catalan usurpers and promoted attacks on them. In 1312 Pope Clement V ordered the Master of the Hospitallers at Rhodes to assist Philippe of Anjou, Prince of Achaea, in driving out the Catalans. In 1313 he permitted Gautier de Brienne's kinsman Gautier, Bishop of Negroponte, to reside away from Negroponte, for the Catalans were harassing the island. In 1314 Clement V instructed that the Templars' properties in the Duchy of Athens should be handed over to Gautier de Châtillon; he also invoked the intervention of Jaime II of Catalunya-Aragon against his fellow Catalans, and he commanded the Master of Rhodes to provide three or four galleys and a military force to defend those places, presumably in the Argolid, which were still holding out. Jeanne and Gautier de Châtillon sent provisions to their followers at Argos and Nauplia. They also tried to secure from the Venetians the shipping and the large sums of money necessary for an attack on Athens, but in 1318 the Venetians evaded these requests, reporting that the scheme could not succeed since the Brienne vassals at Argos and Nauplia had come to terms with the Catalans. In fact Gautier and François de Foucherolles were defending Argos for the Brienne, and in August 1319 Pope John XXII wrote to encourage their resistance. It was the Venetians who in 1319 made a pact with the Catalans, and in the coming decades a major reason for Gautier de Brienne's failure to reconquer Athens was the persistent refusal of Venice to provide military and naval assistance against its Catalan allies.

After 1321 Gautier continued to supply his Argolid castles from Italy, but his Apulian lands were continually being invaded, pawned and subjected to litigation, and he had long had great difficulty in paying his endless debts and providing the

[2] *Libro de los fechos et conquistas del principado de la Morea*, ed. A. Morel-Fatio (Geneva, 1885), 121; 1312 text in N. Vigner, *Histoire de la maison de Luxembourg* (revised: Paris, 1619), 245.

[3] Texts of 1321 (not 1320) in A. du Chesne, *Histoire de la maison de Chastillon sur Marne* (Paris, 1621), preuves, 212–214. Jeanne de Châtillon died only in January 1355 (not 1354: epitaph in Vigner, 261).

[4] Hopf, i, 424, and many others date the marriage to 1325, but R. Caggese, *Roberto I d'Angiò e i suoi tempi*, 2 vols. (Florence, 1922–1930), ii, 304, 335, n. 2, citing Naples, Reg. Ang. 221, f. 133–133 v; 239, f. 60–61 v, shows Gautier married by May 1321.

[5] Giovanni Villani, *Cronica*, ed. F. Dragomanni, iv (Florence, 1845), 6, 9 *et passim*.

[6] Hopf, i, 411, citing Naples, Reg.Ang. 195 (1310 C), f. 89.

70 knights whose service he owed to the crown. He repeatedly announced his coming invasion of Greece; this secured him exemptions and financial favours from the crown, but for years there was no effective action. In 1326 he was serving as a captain in Tuscany, and by 1328 he had even concluded a truce with the Catalans of Athens. Finally, strong Angevin backing enabled him to launch an expedition. In March 1331 he sent Corrado Guindazzo to Argos and Nauplia to inspect the terrain,[7] but when he left Brindisi in August he sailed not to the Argolid but to Epirus, which he invaded with a force which included 800 French cavalry and 500 Tuscan foot. Villani remarked that Gautier had too few troops for a quick victory but too many for the long, expensive siege campaign in which the Catalans tied him down. A year later Gautier was back in Italy. Possibly he had not even visited Argos and Nauplia, and his only permanent conquests were the Adriatic island of Leucadia and the nearby port of Vonitza in Epirus, to which he had claims through his wife Beatrice, whose mother Thamar was the daughter of Nicephorus I, Despot of Epirus.

Despite this failure, Gautier intermittently renewed his attempts to organise an attack on Athens. He negotiated with Venice, but he also fought against the English in France; and in 1342 he became *signore* of Florence, though the Acciaiuoli and other leading families soon expelled him. King Robert of Naples died in 1343 and the subsequent ascendancy at the Neapolitan court of Niccolò Acciaiuoli, who had his own Greek interests, further diminished Gautier's influence. In the same year Pope Clement VI, faced with mounting Turkish aggression in the Aegean, moderated the papal campaign against the Catalans.[8] None the less, in December 1351 Gautier was preparing to set out for Greece from Brienne in Champagne.[9] The Venetians had continued to refuse effective military aid, and on 2 January 1352 they once again declined to allow Gautier to arm ships at Venice although they were prepared to supply him with provisions.[10] By 17 February 1352 Gautier was in Lecce,[11] but in the following years he was distracted by campaigns at Taranto, Brindisi and elsewhere in Apulia, at a time when the whole Neapolitan kingdom was in confusion.[12] On 8 September 1354 he was at Naples,[13] but later he returned to France. At Paris on 18 October 1355 Gautier granted the island of Leucadia and its castles as a fief to Graziano Giorgio of Venice.[14] In the following year, on

[7] Hopf, i, 426, citing Naples, Reg.Ang. 282 (1330 C), f. 173.

[8] Details of Gautier's schemes, largely derived from Naples documents, in Hopf, i, 411–416, 424–430, 439–440 *et passim*; Caggese, i, 240; ii, 329–342; Setton, 22–49; P. Lemerle, *L'émirat d'Aydin, Byzance et l'Occident* (Paris, 1957), 118–122, 182; with numerous texts in A. Rubió i Lluch, *Diplomatari de l'Orient català*: 1310–1409 (Barcelona, 1947) [=*Diplomatari*].

[9] A document of Gautier (21 December 1351) referred to his kinsman Guillaume de Mello *qui nous doit suivre es parties de Romenie*: quoted in M. Huillard-Bréholles, *Titres de la maison ducale de Bourbon*, i (Paris, 1867), 451.

[10] Archivio di Stato, Venice; Misti del Senato [=Misti], xxvi, f. 77 v. Note that the pencil foliations of Venice documents are generally those cited; Hopf worked from and cited the unreliable modern copies.

[11] Text cited in H. d'Arbois de Jubainville, 'Catalogue d'actes des comtes de Brienne: 950–1356,' *Bibliothèque de l'École des Chartes*, xxxiii (1872), 185–186.

[12] Matteo Villani, *Cronica*, ed. F. Dragomanni, i (Florence, 1846), 223–224, 246–247; Naples documents cited in G. Guerrieri, *Gualtieri VI di Brienne, duca di Atene e conte di Lecce* (Naples, 1896), 40, 68–70.

[13] Text quoted in J. Buchon, *Nouvelles recherches historiques sur la principauté française de Morée*, i (Paris, 1843), 83, n. 1.

[14] A. Luttrell, 'Vonitza in Epirus and its Lords: 1306–1377,' *Rivista di studi bizantini e neoellenici*, xi (=ns. i) (1964), 135.

19 September 1356, Gautier de Brienne, Constable of France, was killed in battle at Poitiers.

Gautier de Brienne had drawn up his will at Hesdin in Flanders on 18 July 1347, and it reflected his Greek interests.[15] Having no surviving children, either by Beatrice of Anjou or by his second wife Jeanne de Brienne, he left his possessions in France, around Lecce and Conversano in Apulia, and in Greece and Cyprus to his sister Isabelle. In Greece he held Leucadia and Vonitza, in addition to Argos, Nauplia and two other castles in the Argolid, one at Thermision, the other at Kiveri on the coast near Nauplia; he bequeathed a month's wages to his constables and sergeants at these six castles. He endowed a chantry at Kiveri, and made bequests to the church at Argos, to the chapels of his castles at Argos and Nauplia, to the Franciscans at Clarenza and Patras, and to the Dominicans at Clarenza. Those he named as executors, a number of them Frenchmen with Greek connections, included his *tres chers et amez compaignons*: Renaud de Lor, Archbishop of Taranto, later Archbishop of Patras; his brother Gautier de Lor, who had been with Gautier de Brienne in Florence as his marshal in 1343[16] and who later became Angevin bailli or vicegerent in the Principality of Achaea;[17] Robert de Châteauneuf, Archbishop of Salerno, also to become Bailli of Achaea;[18] Nicolas de Foucherolles and Boniface de Prothimo, both Gautier's vassals in the Argolid;[19] Anthonace de Plancy;[20] and the Bishop of Argos.[21] In Cyprus, Gautier's proctor did homage to the king for his estates there.[22] These consisted of the *casali* of Dischoria, Conodra and Omorphita near Nicosia, which were producing some 16,700 besants annually in 1356; the lands were worked by slaves and the profits were sent westwards through Italian bankers. Gautier's bailli in Cyprus, Cosimo de' Medici of Athens, was replaced in about February 1354 by Raouche de Monteron. In 1356 Raouche journeyed to Lecce where he saw Gautier's nephew Jean d'Enghien, at whose command he then travelled to Nauplia and thence back to Cyprus.[23]

Gautier's lands in the Argolid, which he held as a vassal of the Angevin Princes of Achaea,[24] were of some value for their products and incomes. The Argolid had been ravaged by the Catalans during the decade following 1311[25] and apparently by Umur, the Turkish Emir of Aydin in Anatolia, in 1332;[26] in 1333 and 1334 large quantities of grain had to be sent to Gautier's castles in *Romania* following several years of famine.[27] Yet despite the plague, Turkish razzias and the consequent

[15] Text in C. Paoli, 'Nuovi documenti intorno a Gualtieri VI di Brienne, duca d'Atene e signore di Firenze,' *Archivio storico italiano*, III ser., xvi (1872), 39–52, with corrections in Hopf, *CGR*, xxix-xxx, 537–538.

[16] Text in C. Paoli, 'Della signoria di Gualtieri duca d'Atene in Firenze,' *Giornale storico degli archivi toscani*, vi (1862), 253–263.

[17] On the Lors, R.-J. Loenertz, 'Athènes et Néopatras: régestes et notices pour servir à l'histoire des duchés catalans: 1311–1394,' *Archivum Fratrum Praedicatorum*, xxv (1955), 430–431.

[18] *Libro de los fechos*, 150.

[19] *Infra*, 49, 52–53. In 1339 Petrus de Prothimo was granted a papal dispensation to marry Bonami, daughter of Symon Forese of Negroponte: text in F. Gregorovius—S. Lampros, *Historia tes poleos Athenon kata tous mesous aionas*, 3 vols. (Athens, 1904–1906), iii, 66–67.

[20] *Gille ae la Plainche*, Bailli of Achaea, sealed the will of Gautier's father at Zeitoun on 10 March 1311: text quoted in Hopf, *CGR*, 537.

[21] Unknown to C. Eubel, *Hierarchia catholica medii aevi*, i (Münster, 1913), 105–106.

[22] Text in *Recueil des historiens des croisades*: *lois*, ii (Paris, 1843), 386.

[23] E. Poncelet, 'Compte du domaine de Gautier de Brienne au royaume de Chypre,' *Bulletin de la commission royale d'histoire*, 98 (1934), 23–27 *et passim*.

[24] *Diplomatari*, doc. 171 (*ca.* 1338).

[25] *Diplomatari*, doc. 110.

[26] Lemerle, 122.

[27] Caggese, ii, 339, nn. 6–7, citing Naples, Reg. Ang. 289, f. 62; 293, f. 182 v, 188 v, 205.

depopulation, the Morea continued to enjoy a certain agrarian prosperity[28] and to support a not inconsiderable population; in fact, the inhabitants of Argos claimed in 1451 that the Turks had enslaved as many as 14,000 persons there in 1397.[29] There were vineyards around Argos[30] with grazing in the hills and plains, and fishing at Nauplia; other products included cereals, cotton and linen.[31] Carobs, raisins, resin and acorn dye for tanning were being exported in 1378;[32] there was a trade in cloth;[33] and there were valuable saltings at Thermision near the tip of the Argolid peninsula.[34] This economy supported the town of Argos, protected by its great fortress dominating the Argolid plain, while the port of Nauplia was well placed at the head of the Bay of Nauplia on a rocky promontory with an excellent fortified harbour and only a short landward wall to defend.[35]

On Gautier de Brienne's death in 1356 his lands and claims did not pass to his sister Isabelle, though she was apparently still alive in 1361.[36] They went to Gautier's nephews, the sons of Isabelle de Brienne and Gautier d'Enghien. The eldest son, Gautier, had died in 1340,[37] and it was Solier d'Enghien who became titular Duke of Athens and Count of Brienne, while Jean became Count of Lecce and Lord of Vonitza and Leucadia, and Louis received the County of Conversano. The Brienne lands in Cyprus passed to Engelbert,[38] who probably sold or abandoned them. Apparently Engelbert d'Enghien also received Argos and Nauplia but, being unwilling to defend them, he exchanged them for his brother Guy's part of the inheritance, Ramerupt in Champagne, where Engelbert took up residence. It was Guy d'Enghien who became Lord of Argos and Nauplia. Apparently he married into the local aristocracy and defended his lands stoutly against the Turks: *Guido fuit vir bellicosus et acer in hostes, qui fortissime quidem, quamdiu vixit, sed laboriosissime, propter Turquos qui sibi maximam inquietudinem ingerebant, terram suam rexit.*[39]

Guy's chief Frankish vassals were descended from a Jean de Foucherolles who married a daughter of Renaud de Veligourt, Lord of Damala. In 1309 Gautier de Brienne confirmed Jean's son François and François' son Nicolas in their succession to certain lands inherited from Renaud. In 1319 François and his brother

[28] D. Zakythinos, *Le despotat grec de Morée*, 2 vols. (Paris, 1932: Athens, 1953); P. Topping, 'Le régime agraire dans le Péloponnèse latin au XIVe siècle,' *L'Hellénisme contemporain*, II ser., x (1956); J. Longnon, 'La vie rurale dans la Grèce franque,' *Journal des Savants* (for 1965).

[29] F. Thiriet, *Régestes des délibérations du Sénat de Venise concernant la Romanie*, 3 vols. (Paris, 1958–1961) [=*Régestes*], iii, no. 2865; the chroniclers reported over 30,000 enslaved (Zakythinos, i, 157).

[30] Texts in *Diplomatari*, 407 note; C. Sathas, *Documents inédits relatifs à l'histoire de la Grèce au moyen âge*, 9 vols. (Paris, 1880–1890), ii, 18–20, 123–124.

[31] *Régestes*, iii, nos. 2598, 2694, 2866, 2888, 3093 (mid fifteenth-century documents).

[32] Misti, xxxvi, f. 56.

[33] The *comercle des fustaines* at Argos in 1347 (Hopf, *CGR*, xxix, 537).

[34] A document of 1451 reported: *in el castello de Termissi, se trova le piu notabile saline che sia in tuto Levante, de lequal se poria cavar un pozo d'oro . . .* (*Régestes*, iii, no. 2866); on salt exports in 1384, *infra*, 45.

[35] G. Gerola, 'Le fortificazioni di Napoli di Romania,' *Annuario della Regia Scuola archeologica di Atene e delle missioni italiane in Oriente*, xiii-xiv (1930–1931); K. Andrews, *Castles of the Morea* (Princeton, 1953), 90–115, with photographs and plans.

[36] Du Chesne, 354.

[37] Epitaph in E. Matthieu, *Histoire de la ville d'Enghien* (Mons, 1876/8), 68; Hopf, *CGR*, 474, wrongly gives 1358.

[38] According to a document cited in O. Vredius, *Genealogia comitum Flandriae*, ii (Bruges, 1643), 258.

[39] All this appears in *Chronographia regum francorum*, ed. H. Moranvillé, ii (Paris, 1893), 321–322 (inaccurately annotated); apparently composed in France soon after 1415, this contains some accurate or partly accurate information about the Enghien in Greece and gives Guy's wife as a daughter of the 'Lord of Arkadia' (possibly Érard le Maure). Vredius, ii, 263, gives her as a Greek named Bonne or Maria (*cf. infra*, 55, n. 159).

Gautier, who was then Captain of Argos, were defending the Brienne possessions in the Argolid. On François' death his lands passed to his son Nicolas, and thence to Nicolas' daughter who married Jacomo, Lord of Tzoya in the Western Morea. The Assizes of Romania, the old feudal customs of Achaea, stated that the husband of a wife who held a fief should do homage for it to the lord, and in December 1364 Guy issued letters from his castle at Nauplia reducing to four armed men the service due from Jacomo de Tzoya, his 'dear and well-loved knight and companion,' and from Jacomo's heirs in perpetuity, for the fief which Jacomo held 'by reason of his wife.' Following his wife's death, there was trouble over her fief, for according to the Assizes of Romania fiefs passed by primogeniture to the children, and on the death of his mother her son Niccolò had to ask to be invested with the fief. Jacomo de Tzoya, having held the fief while his wife was alive, contested his son's rights. On 15 February 1376 a court consisting mostly of Italians found in Jacomo's favour, and Guy d'Enghien subsequently decided that he should hold the fief and owe the service of three armed men for it.[40]

Though the Enghien were among the last of the great French families established in the Morea, their position in Greece, like that of the Angevin themselves, partly depended on their strength as Italian magnates. Jean and Louis inherited lands in Apulia and married into the Neapolitan nobility, but they did not acquire sufficient power to exert any great influence in the Morea, which was suffering from Turkish invasions and the unruliness of the great barons and the local populace. In 1360 the Greek and other inhabitants of Argos and Nauplia shut up Guy d'Enghien's men in their strongholds in protest against restrictions on the sale of figs and raisins imposed by Guy's bailli, Averardo de' Medici.[41] The Enghien position at Vonitza and Leucadia was even more precarious. On 24 August 1359 Jean d'Enghien wrote from Lecce complaining to the Venetian government that Graziano Giorgio, who held Leucadia as his vassal, was attacking Vonitza, damaging lands and fisheries there and imprisoning the inhabitants. The Venetians refused to enforce the cessation of the attacks or to secure the payment of reparations, but they did write admonishing Graziano. At some point in the next few years Leucadia was, apparently, seized by Leonardo Tocco, who by 1373 at the latest had also secured Vonitza, with or without the consent of the Enghien who seem to have abandoned their claims both to Leucadia and Vonitza.[42]

During this period the brothers were distracted by events outside Greece. In 1356 Jean d'Enghien was serving in Apulia as a captain under Robert of Anjou, Prince of Taranto and Achaea, titular Emperor of Constantinople,[43] and in August 1359 he was at Lecce.[44] On 27 March 1363 Pope Urban V called upon Jean and Louis, among many other Neapolitan nobles, to give assistance to Jaime of Mallorca, husband of Jeanne of Anjou, Queen of Naples. Guy was in Greece, and on 19 September 1363 the pope exhorted him, with the other magnates in the Morea, to

[40] Texts and discussion *infra*, 52–55; *cf.* texts in P. Topping, *Feudal Institutions as revealed in the Assizes of Romania* (Philadelphia, 1949), 34, 41, 48, 52, 65, 145.

[41] Text *infra*, 51.

[42] Luttrell, 138–139; exactly how and when Tocco acquired Leucadia and Vonitza is still unclear.

[43] Text in E.-G. Léonard, *Histoire de Jeanne Ire, reine de Naples, comtesse de Provence*: 1343–1382, iii (Monaco-Paris, 1936), 607–608.

[44] *Diplomatari*, doc. 238.

support the newly-elected Archbishop of Patras.[45] Then in March 1364 Solier d'Enghien, who had remained in Flanders, was beheaded by Albert of Bavaria. His title as Duke of Athens and Count of Brienne passed to his young son Gautier, and by 12 July 1364 Pierre d'Ameil, Archbishop of Naples, had written to Jean d'Enghien at Lecce urging him to go to look after the young Gautier's affairs in Flanders. The archbishop was scheming to marry Gautier to a Sicilian noblewoman, Costanza, the daughter of Giovanni di Randazzo, the Siculo-Aragonese Duke of Athens and Neopatras, from whom she took her courtesy title of Duchess of Athens; but nothing came of these plans for an alliance which could have united the two rival claims to the duchies.[46] On Solier's death, Engelbert d'Enghien summoned his brothers Jean and Louis from Italy. Jean had reached Flanders by about June 1364, and he launched a war of revenge which was only concluded by a peace on 11 April 1367; Louis was also in Flanders in December 1366.[47] Jean was still at Enghien on 6 June 1367 when he wrote to the Venetian consul at Bruges about a galley left at Venice by Gautier de Brienne, which Jean had subsequently sold.[48]

On 22 July 1362 Guy d'Enghien, 'Lord of Argos and Nauplia in *Romania*' became a citizen of Venice, where a proctor swore fealty on his behalf.[49] In December 1364 he was in his castle at Nauplia,[50] and soon after he became involved in the civil war which followed the death of Robert of Anjou, Prince of Achaea, in September 1364. Robert left no direct heir and the rival claimants were his younger brother Philippe of Taranto and his widow Marie de Bourbon, who claimed the Principality of Achaea as part of her dowry on behalf of her son by an earlier marriage, Hugues de Lusignan, titular Prince of Galilee. Philippe of Taranto appointed Simone del Poggio of Perugia to rule in the Morea as his bailli, but Guillaume de Talay, who was defending the castle of Navarino for Marie de Bourbon, captured the new bailli and held him prisoner. During the ensuing siege of Navarino Guillaume de Talay sought help from Guy d'Enghien and from Manuel Cantacuzenus, the Greek Despot of the Morea, who raised their followers and overran the plain behind Clarenza, doing damage estimated at over 20,000 florins. There was a temporary peace in 1366 but Hugues de Lusignan was able to continue the struggle, still with the assistance of Guy and Manuel, until by an agreement concluded at Naples on 4 March 1370 Hugues was bribed to abandon his claims to the Principality of Achaea.[51]

Since their inheritance of the Brienne lands in 1356, the position of the Enghien in Greece had been weak. Leucadia and Vonitza were lost; the Bourbon attachment involved them on the weaker side in prolonged civil strife; they lacked powerful

[45] *Lettres secrètes et curiales du pape Urbain V*: 1362–1370, ed. P. Lecacheux, fasc. 1 (Paris, 1902), nos. 245, 247, 620.

[46] Matthieu, 77; K. Setton, in *Speculum*, xxviii (1953), 682–683, n. 116; Loenertz (1955), 118–120, 156. *Diplomatari*, docs. 312, 314–315, belong to 1364; Setton shows that Hopf, i, 453, and others, including recently L. Nicolau d'Olwer, *La duquèssa d'Atenes i els 'documents misteriosos'* (Barcelona, 1958), 59–62 *et passim*, contain serious chronological and other confusions on these points.

[47] *Chronographia regum francorum*, ii, 320–324; Matthieu, 78–92; F. Quicke, *Les Pays-Bas à la veille de la periode bourguignonne*: 1356–1384 (Paris-Brussels, 1947), 86–101, with references to sources.

[48] Archivio di Stato, Venice; Libri Commemoriali [=Commemoriali], vii, f. 92; reply in Gregorovius-Lampros, iii, 366–367.

[49] Commemoriali, vi, f. 143.

[50] *Infra*, 53.

[51] *Libro de los fechos*, 152–155, but many details await elaboration; the date of 4 March 1370 is given in Hopf, ii, 9, citing Naples, Arche Angiov. K.m. 31, n. 18; D.m. 31, n. 83; Fasc. Ang. BBB, f. 71; DDD f. 76, 78.

allies. Then in 1370 Philippe of Taranto sent Louis d'Enghien, Count of Conversano, to govern the Morea as Bailli of Achaea, and during the brief period in which Louis held that office[52] the Enghien made a serious attempt to recover the Duchies of Athens and Neopatras from the enfeebled Catalans. This new project, which meant that the Enghien exchanged their opposition to the Angevin in the Morea for an attack on the Catalans made with Angevin encouragement, apparently formed part of the general settlement of March 1370. At Naples on 28 March Queen Jeanne of Naples granted a request from Jean d'Enghien, Count of Lecce, to be allowed to use vessels from her ports to transport 1000 men and 500 horses, and Jean subsequently tried to collect shipping in Apulia, at Bari and along the coast as far as Brindisi.[53] At the same time Jean, Louis and Guy sent envoys to Venice claiming the duchies as heirs of Gautier de Brienne, no mention being made of their nephew Gautier d'Enghien. They stated that they were about to attack the Catalans with a large army and, as citizens of Venice, they requested: firstly, that their shipping should be free from attacks by the Venetians; secondly, that they should be allowed to set up stores of provisions on the island of Negroponte; thirdly, that the Venetian bailli at Negroponte should be ordered always to give prompt justice to their men; and finally, that these favours should be guaranteed for the future by letters from the Doge. The Venetian senate replied on 22 April, accepting the first demand, rejecting the second on account of their truce with the Catalans, declaring that the third required no special order, and evading the fourth. Early in 1371 Jean d'Enghien sent envoys who again pointed out his family claims to the duchies, reminding the Venetians that the Catalans were usurpers and excommunicates. He demanded that the Catalans should not be allowed to send their cattle to safety on Negroponte, that the subjects of the Prince of Achaea who inhabited the island should be able freely to join the Enghien, that the Enghien soldiers should be permitted to forage and secure provisions and supplies there, and that Venice should provide them with a large galley. On 2 February 1371 these requests were politely rejected, the Venetians again emphasizing their truce with the Catalans.[54]

In the following months Louis d'Enghien, having made a pact with Manuel Cantacuzenus, ruler of the Greek despotate in the south-east of the Morea, set about raising troops. Assembling the men of the Morea, he invaded the Catalan duchies and ravaged the land. He occupied Athens but the castle on the Acropolis was too strong for him; after a while he fell ill and returned with his men to the Morea.[55] By August 1371 his brother Guy had concluded a truce with the Catalans; announcing this to the Venetian government on 9 August, Giovanni Delfin the Venetian bailli on Negroponte sought permission, granted him by the senate on 23 September, to occupy the Catalan castle at Megara, perhaps in the capacity of arbitrator between the Enghien and the Catalans. Soon after, the treaty was modified, and it was agreed that the projected marriage between Joan de Lluria,

[52] According to *Libro de los fechos*, 155, Louis became bailli some time after the conclusion of peace (*i.e.* after 4 March 1370 ?), and was replaced after his campaign against Athens, apparently late in 1371.

[53] Text in S. Santeramo, *Codice Diplomatico Barlettano*, iii (Barletta, 1957), 21–22.

[54] *Diplomatari*, docs. 317 (correct date 1371), 320.

[55] *Libro de los fechos*, 155, without precise date, but the invasion presumably took place after the appeal answered from Venice in February 1371.

Lord of Stiris near Thebes and probably the son of the late Catalan marshal Roger de Lluria, and Guy's daughter Marie, heiress apparent to Argos and Nauplia, should after all take place, despite the clause in the treaty revoking it.[56]

In the end there was no Catalan marriage. The Enghien position in Greece worsened and they lost the initiative in pressing their claims, while as the Catalans grew weaker and the Ottomans more aggressive, the papacy could no longer sanction attacks on Athens and Thebes. In 1372 Pope Gregory XI summoned a congress of almost all the Latin rulers of Greece and the Aegean who were to meet at Thebes to discuss measures against the Turks; the congress never took place, but the Enghien were conspicuous absentees from the list of those invited.[57] Even after the truce of 1371 Guy d'Enghien would scarcely have visited the capital of his greatest enemies. The Enghien lacked strength and allies, and they were again distracted by events outside Greece. Jean and Louis were both in Apulia for at least part of 1372;[58] then in 1373 Jean, who had married Sancia de Baux, died and was succeeded as Count of Lecce by their son Pierre; he also left two daughters, Marie and Francesca.[59] In May 1374 Louis, Count of Conversano, was fighting in Apulia against Sancia's brother François de Baux, who had risen in revolt against Jeanne of Anjou, Queen of Naples.[60] After the death of Philippe of Taranto in November 1373, the barons of the Morea had recognised Jeanne as Princess of Achaea, but François claimed the principality through his wife Margherita of Taranto, who was Philippe's sister. This quarrel was settled later in 1374, and towards the end of the year Pierre d'Enghien was planning a pilgrimage; on 1 October 1374 he received a papal licence to send a ship to Egypt or Syria, and to visit Jerusalem.[61] Not until 6 May 1376 did Pierre make his formal entry into Lecce, accompanied by his uncles Louis d'Enghien and François de Baux.[62]

The Enghien claims suffered a further blow when Megara, which lay between Corinth and Athens, was seized from the Catalans, in 1374 or very early in 1375, by Nerio Acciaiuoli. Nerio's father Niccolò Acciaiuoli had been granted Corinth by Robert of Anjou in 1358 and had been expected to help the Enghien during the revolt at Argos and Nauplia in 1360, but Nerio, unlike his father, did not depend on the favour of the Angevin, and at Megara he was occupying territory claimed by the Enghien.[63] Guy d'Enghien was alive at Nauplia in October 1376,[64] but he died soon after and for a short time his brother Louis, Count of Conversano, administered Argos and Nauplia on behalf of Guy's young daughter Marie. While acting as Marie's guardian Louis settled a debt of a 1000 ducats, which Guy had owed to his vassal Jacomo de Tzoya, by granting Jacomo another fief. More important, he arranged Marie's marriage, which was apparently concluded by Louis' proctor at Venice on 17 May 1377, to Pietro Cornaro of Venice;[65] possibly Louis was still

[56] *Diplomatari*, docs. 331–332; *cf.* Loenertz (1955), 132, 183–184.

[57] *Diplomatari*, docs. 336–337; there is no evidence that the congress took place.

[58] D. Morea—F. Muciaccia, *Le pergamene di Conversano* (Trani, 1942), doc. 140.

[59] A. Cutolo, *Maria d'Enghien* (Naples, 1922), 19.

[60] *Lettres secrètes et curiales du pape Grégoire XI (1370–1378) relatives à la France*, ed. L. Mirot *et al.* (Paris, 1937–1957), no. 3372.

[61] Archivio Vaticano, Reg. Aven. 229, f. 290–290 v.

[62] Cutolo, 20.

[63] Setton, 65–68, 78; text of 1360, *infra*, 51.

[64] Text *infra*, 53.

[65] A. Luttrell, 'The Principality of Achaea in 1377,' *Byzantinische Zeitschrift*, lvii (1964), 340–341 (correcting Hopf). The confused and unreliable passages from Theodore Zygomalas and Dorotheos of Monemvasia who wrote long after the events

hoping to involve Venice against the Catalans. On 16 July at Venice the senate gave Pietro's father Federigo Cornaro permission to arm a galley to bring his daughter-in-law Marie to Venice, and on 8 March 1378 it conceded him a ship to carry supplies for the defence of 'his places' of Argos and Nauplia.[66]

Louis d'Enghien's control in the Argolid presumably came to an end at about this time. Enghien influence in Greece had almost evaporated, but Louis may have undertaken a final sortie against the Catalans. During 1378 Latin Greece was in turmoil. Federigo III of Aragon, King of Sicily and Duke of Athens and Neopatras, died in July 1377. For a while his daughter Maria acted as Duchess of Athens, but in 1379 the inhabitants of the duchies recognised King Pedro IV of Catalunya-Aragon as Duke of Athens and Neopatras. Venice and Genoa were at war, and Queen Jeanne of Naples, having leased the Principality of Achaea to the Hospitallers of Rhodes in mid-1377, became involved in the conflicts provoked by the schism in the papacy in 1378. An invasion of Epirus by an expedition of Hospitallers, launched by Pope Gregory XI and led by Juan Fernández de Heredia, Master of Rhodes, sailed to Vonitza in Epirus early in 1378, and was defeated by the Albanian Lord of Arta during the summer. Probably in 1379, possibly in the spring, the Navarrese mercenaries, who were at one point employed by the Hospitallers, attacked the Catalans and captured Thebes with the assistance of Nerio Acciaiuoli, Lord of Corinth and Megara, and of certain Hospitallers.[67] In 1378 Marie d'Enghien's Catalan ex-fiancé Joan de Lluria, Lord of Stiris, had become the prisoner of Louis d'Enghien, who still held him captive in 1381.[68] Possibly therefore Louis, while acting as Marie's guardian in the Argolid, had launched a raid against the Catalans during the year before the Navarrese campaign.

The Venetian family which gained control of Argos and Nauplia was extremely powerful. The Cornaro had long held lands and offices in Crete, which Andrea Cornaro governed as Duca di Candia from 1341 to 1343; they were lords of Skarpathos and other islands between Crete and Rhodes;[69] and when Andrea Cornaro married the widow of the last Pallavicini Marquis of Boudonitza in 1312, they gained a temporary foothold on Negroponte and at Boudonitza in mainland Greece.[70]

(texts in Hopf, *CGR*, 236–239) are here ignored. According to Dorotheos, Marie was Guy's wife (!) and the Venetians bribed two citizens of Nauplia, Kamateros and Kaloethes, to arrange her marriage to a Barbaro!

[66] Misti, xxxvi, f. 23 v, 56.

[67] R.-J. Loenertz, 'Hospitaliers et Navarrais en Grèce, 1376–1383 : regestes et documents,' *Orientalia Christiana Periodica*, xxii (1956), 330–336; A. Luttrell, 'Interessi fiorentini nell'economia e nella politica dei Cavalieri Ospedalieri di Rodi nel trecento,' *Annali della Scuola Normale Superiore di Pisa : lettere, storia e filosofia*, II ser., xxviii (1959), 322–324. When Thebes fell is uncertain; the evidence is discussed by K. Setton, in *Cambridge Medieval History*, iv, part 1, 420, n. 1, rejecting a date in 1378.

[68] On 8 May 1381 Pedro IV of Aragon, from distant Zaragoza, wrote : *quod dictus Johannes, tres anni afluxerunt, fuit et adhuc detinetur captus in posse comitis de Conversa* . . . (*Diplomatari*, doc. 714). This gives 1378; Loenertz (1955), 136, dates Joan's capture to 1377, and mistakenly describes Louis as Angevin bailli. No more is known of Joan de Lluria. Louis' movements are obscure. On 20 November 1378 the pope, at Fondi, granted him a supplication : K. Hanquet, *Documents relatifs au Grand Schisme*, i = *Analecta Vaticano-Belgica*, viii (Rome, 1924), 188. An inscription formerly at Conversano read, *Hoc opus fieri fecit Lodovicus de Enchineo Comes Cupersani. Anno Domini* 1380 : G. Bolognini, *Storia di Conversano* (Bari, 1935), 91, n. 5.

[69] Hopf, i–ii, *passim*; S. Borsari, *Il dominio veneziano a Creta nel XIII secolo* (Naples, 1963), 21, n. 37, 23, n. 52, 77, n. 56, 81–82, 90, 102–103, 153–154; F. Thiriet, *La Romanie vénitienne au moyen âge* (Paris, 1959), 162–163, 274–276, 296, 330–333; *Régestes*, i, nos. 32, 34, 64, 118, 147, 172, 197, 286, 322, 446, 555.

[70] References in Setton, 30–34.

They were one of the few Venetian families which successfully maintained a certain independence of their government. The greatest and wealthiest member of the house, Federigo Cornaro di Santa Lucia, developed something approaching a foreign policy of his own. By about 1360 he was advantageously established in Cyprus in partnership with his brothers Marco and Fantin. A financier and business magnate, Federigo raised money in Italy and invested it in his extremely lucrative sugar plantations in Cyprus; in 1379 he was the richest man in Venice. King Pierre I of Cyprus, to whom Federigo loaned 60,000 ducats, three times stayed at Palazzo Cornaro in Venice. Federigo stood proxy for King Pierre II of Cyprus at the king's marriage to Valentina Visconti at Milan in April 1376, and he was employed on diplomatic missions by the King of France as well as by the Venetian republic.[71]

It was Federigo's son Pietro Cornaro who married Marie d'Enghien in 1377; she was less than fourteen years old,[72] and he was probably young as well. It is unlikely that Marie brought the Cornaro any considerable dowry in cash, and presumably their interest was in Argos and Nauplia. Federigo Cornaro may have felt that difficulties lay ahead in Cyprus and that he should diversify his operations by establishing a branch of his family in the Argolid, with its commercial opportunities and its salt. Support was forthcoming from the Venetian government, which must have sensed the long-term possibility of securing a naval base at Nauplia. On 16 July 1377 the senate, acting *pro honori nostri dominii*, lent Federigo a galley which he was to arm at his own expense to transport Marie to Venice; on 8 March 1378 he was conceded a ship to take supplies to defend 'his places' of Argos and Nauplia, and to bring raisins, resin, carobs and acorn dye back to Venice.[73] Meanwhile the Venetians had launched upon a great war with Genoa, and Federigo Cornaro was hard hit by heavy war taxation and by his failure to recover monies lent to the King of Cyprus. Yet when peace came in 1381 Federigo secured favourable privileges for his family in Cyprus, and though his executors faced bankruptcy proceedings after his death in 1382, the Cornaro were able to sustain their interest in the Argolid.[74]

Pietro Cornaro ruled with Marie d'Enghien at Argos and Nauplia. For example, they confirmed Jacomo de Tzoya in possession of the fief he had received from Louis d'Enghien, while Pietro granted a vineyard at Argos to a certain Leo Pigassi.[75] On 14 November 1381 the Venetians conceded Federigo Cornaro, acting for Marie d'Enghien, permission to buy a galley to defend Argos and Nauplia against the Turks 'and other pirates,' and when on 16 March 1383 Pietro Cornaro was permitted to travel with his company on a Venetian galley to defend Argos and Nauplia, the senate considered those places more or less as Venetian possessions:

> *Cum loca nobilis viri ser Petri Cornario, quondam ser Phederici, scilicet Argos et Neapolis, fuerint et sint ad honorem nostri dominij, et pro omni bono respectu, pro statu nostro, faciat quod dicta loca conserventur in manibus dicti ser Petri, ad honorem nostri dominij . . .*[76]

[71] L. de Mas-Latrie, *Histoire de l'île de Chypre sous le règne des princes de la maison de Lusignan*, ii–iii (Paris, 1852–1855), ii, 363, 372–373; iii, 817; G. Hill, *A History of Cyprus*, ii (Cambridge, 1948), 328, n. 1, 423, n. 3, 427, n. 2; G. Luzzatto, *Studi di storia economica veneziana* (Padua, 1954), 118–123, 135–136, 281 (but Luzzatto, 119, 121, confuses Marie d'Enghien with Marie de Bourbon); F. Lane, in *Nuova rivista storica*, xlix (1965), 71–75. The Cornaro deserve further study.

[72] *Infra*, 47.

[73] Misti, xxxvi, f. 23 v, 56.

[74] Mas-Latrie, ii, 378–381; Hill, ii, 428–429; Luzzatto, 122, 281.

[75] *Infra*, 49.

[76] Misti, xxxvii, f. 25 v; xxxviii, f. 14 v.

On 25 April 1384 Pietro was licensed to import into Venice 150 *modia* of salt from Argos and Nauplia.[77] Early in 1385 Pietro was in Venice and due to return to Argos in March. The Dominican Jacopo, Bishop of Argos since 1367 and an agent of the Acciaiuoli, who was to return with Pietro Cornaro, referred to him as *dominus patrie Argolicensis*; he had, in effect, become Lord of Argos and Nauplia, and was addressed as such by the King of Aragon on 17 August 1386.[78] The towns may have suffered from the Turkish raids on the Morea during 1387, and the Venetian envoy commissioned on 3 October to treat with the Ottoman ruler Murad about these attacks was Daniele Cornaro.[79] But by 1388 Pietro Cornaro was dead, and in that year Marie sold Argos and Nauplia to Venice.

After 1388 the Enghien were completely without influence in Greece, but they did retain certain claims the precise nature of which was of considerable importance, since they could be used as a legal basis for new interventions there. Louis and Pierre d'Enghien became involved in the struggles of the Neapolitan kingdom. In January 1380 when Louis, Duke of Anjou and younger brother of Charles V of France, was negotiating to be adopted as the heir of Jeanne of Naples, the French envoys were empowered to secure the allegiance of the Counts of Lecce and Conversano, who as Frenchmen were expected to support Louis of Anjou.[80] Jeanne was captured by her rival Charles of Anjou in July 1381 and assassinated in July 1382; Charles became King of Naples and was supported by Jacques de Baux, whose claims to the Principality of Achaea were recognised by the barons in the Morea late in 1381.[81] In 1382 Louis d'Enghien and his nephew Pierre d'Enghien, Count of Lecce, rallied to Louis of Anjou,[82] while Charles of Anjou confiscated and attacked their Apulian lands and on 11 February 1383 formally declared them rebels.[83] Pierre d'Enghien was at Venice in 1382, where on 27 November, after a delay there of many days, he secured permission from the senate to hire or purchase a ship to take him *ad domum suam*.[84] Louis was in Flanders, for on 7 July 1381 Gautier d'Enghien was killed at Ghent, and Louis, who inherited from him the County of Brienne, had travelled northwards from Italy to secure his new lands against the pretensions of his brother Engelbert; by 2 July 1382 he was at Hesdin, and he stayed in Flanders until 1384.[85] Louis d'Enghien was at Troyes on 3 May 1384, on his way to support Louis of Anjou in Apulia,[86] and he was present when Louis of Anjou made his will at Bari on 15 September 1384, shortly before his death; Louis d'Enghien was named an executor and swore to defend the rights of the young Louis II of Anjou.[87]

A final abortive scheme for the revival of the Enghien claim to Athens seems to have been considered early in 1386 when Juan Fernández de Heredia, Master of

[77] Archivio di Stato, Venice; Notatorio del Colegio, ii, f. 24.

[78] *Diplomatari*, docs. 574, 592.

[79] *Régestes*, i, nos. 736, 742.

[80] Text in E. Jarry, 'Instructions secrètes pour l'adoption de Louis Ier d'Anjou par Jeanne de Naples: Janvier 1380,' *Bibliothèque de l'École des Chartes*, lxvii (1906), 248.

[81] Loenertz (1956), 335, 339–341.

[82] Text in N. Valois, *La France et le grand schisme d'Occident*, ii (Paris, 1896), 64, n. 6 (Pierre wrongly given as Nicolas).

[83] Naples, Reg. Ang. 358, f. 40 v; 359, f. 262 v, 281 v, cited in Cutolo, 22, 27–29.

[84] Misti, xxxvii, f. 122.

[85] Matthieu, 95–101.

[86] Text cited in Vredius, ii, 261; *cf. Chronographia regum francorum*, iii (1897), 69.

[87] Text in Valois, ii, 79, n. 4.

the Hospitallers of Rhodes, who was already negotiating to secure from Louis II of Anjou his claims to the Principality of Achaea,[88] instituted an inquiry in Flanders as to who was the true heir to the Enghien claim.[89] The position was somewhat doubtful, for at that point Louis d'Enghien was still alive but he had no surviving son. His nephew Pierre d'Enghien, Count of Lecce, who had married a sister of Waleran de Luxembourg, Count of Saint Pol,[90] had died without issue in 1384; the County of Lecce then passed to Pierre's sister, another Marie d'Enghien, who married first Raimondo de Baux-Orsini, and later, in 1407, Ladislas of Anjou, King of Naples.[91] Louis d'Enghien, who remained in opposition to Charles of Anjou, apparently died between April 1387 and, at the latest, September 1390.[92] Louis had married Giovanna di San Severino, and the County of Conversano passed to their daughter Margherita, whose husband Jean de Luxembourg became Count of Enghien, Brienne and Conversano. Jean was dead by 5 May 1395 and was succeeded by his son Pierre de Luxembourg, who was ultimately chased out of his Italian county by King Ladislas of Naples in 1407. In their documents neither Louis, Margherita, Jean nor Pierre took the title of Duke of Athens which technically passed to them.[93] The Enghien claims to Athens and Neopatras had in effect lapsed, and their two Luxembourg marriages reflected a shift of interest away from the Mediterranean lands of which they gradually lost control. The Aragonese claim to the duchies also became merely theoretical when, in 1388, Athens itself was captured from the Catalans by Nerio Acciaiuoli; and on 11 January 1394 Nerio was created Duke of Athens by King Ladislas of Naples.[94] When Nerio made his will at Corinth on 17 September 1394, just before his death, he directed that the property he had by then acquired in Argos should be used to endow both a weekly mass for his soul at Argos and a hospital for the poor to be established at Nauplia. His agent Jacopo Bishop of Argos was made an executor with powers to administer the nunnery Nerio had already founded at Nauplia.[95]

The Enghien connection with Greece was all but ended, though after Marie d'Enghien's death, in or before 1393, her uncle Engelbert d'Enghien sent letters to Venice, dated at Bruges on 24 June 1393, claiming Nauplia, Argos and Kiveri as Marie's heir. The Venetians pointed out on 25 August 1393 that they had purchased full rights to these places in 1388, though Argos was not yet in their possession. However they agreed, cynically enough, that Engelbert should have both Argos

[88] Hopf, ii, 47–49; J. Delaville le Roulx, *Les Hospitaliers à Rhodes jusqu'à la mort de Philibert de Naillac*: 1310–1421 (Paris, 1913), 220–224 (both with errors).

[89] In May 1386 the Hospitallers' treasurer at Avignon paid eight francs 'pour envoier en brabant par devers frere henry de saincteron et autres commandeurs du paiz pour faire faire informacion si comme par monsser le maistre me fut expressement mande de ceulx qui sont vraix heretiers du duchesme dathenes' (Royal Malta Library, Valletta; Archives of the Order of St. John, codex 48, f. 124 v). Henri de Saint Trudon was Preceptor of Avalterre in Brabant (Delaville le Roulx, 193, 206, n. 7).

[90] *Chronographia regum francorum*, iii, 38; her name was Marguerite (Vredius, ii, 260).

[91] Cutolo, 32 *et passim.*

[92] Naples, Reg. Ang. 361, f. 1; 365, f. 35, cited by N. Barone, in *Archivio storico per le province napoletane*, xii (1887), 499, 501; Matthieu, 101, without evidence, gives 1390; Hopf, i, 453, gives 17 March 1394.

[93] Morea—Muciaccia, xviii–xxiii; docs. 151–152, 156. In these documents Margherita, Jean and Pierre are not styled as Dukes of Athens; nor were Pierre's descendants (Vigner, 621–622 *et passim*; Matthieu, 102–125 *et passim*). Vigner and subsequent authors contain numerous errors and confusions regarding the Enghien genealogy, but an undocumented seventeenth-century heraldic work (Biblioteca Nazionale, Naples; Ms. Brancacciana II A 7, f. 176) concords exactly with the details established in this paper.

[94] *Diplomatari*, docs. 622, 643.

[95] Text in Gregorovius—Lampros, iii, 146–152.

and Nauplia if he would pay all the expenses incurred by Venice in acquiring and defending them. Engelbert was not satisfied and on 5 November 1394 the Venetians agreed to show his envoy the act by which Marie had sold the towns, and to tell him they were ready to give him both places, provided he paid the cost of the occupation of Nauplia and of the siege and conquest of Argos, which by then they held.[96] The matter apparently ended there, and when Engelbert died on 12 February 1403[97] the Enghien interest in the Argolid was extinct. Few male members of the family had survived, and they lacked the allies or resources necessary to combat the new powers which controlled the Morea.

From about 1377 onwards the Morea was increasingly unsettled, while the Ottomans were making rapid advances in Northern Greece and the Balkans. In 1387 the situation worsened following the fall of Thessalonika and the subsequent Turkish razzia in the Morea. Theodore Palaeologus, the Despot of the Morea, paid tribute to the Ottomans and in August 1388 the Venetians, fearful of the consequences, sent a mission to try to wean him from the Turks. In that year Pietro Cornaro died; thereafter both Argos and Nauplia were left with no adequate defender, and Pietro's widow Marie d'Enghien, to whom the towns belonged, became an important prize. Late in 1388, with the backing of his Turkish allies and his father-in-law Nerio Acciaiuoli, and with the support of the Greek and probably also some of the Latin inhabitants, Theodore attacked Argos and Nauplia.[98] The Venetians were forced to act to secure a strategic base, in which a number of Venetians were already settled. By December Marie d'Enghien was at Venice and had agreed to sell Argos and Nauplia. On 12 December the government at Venice declared that this acquisition was not only useful but that it was necessary in order to prevent the towns falling to Nerio Acciaiuoli, *tirannus crudelissimus* and an enemy of Venice, in whose hands they would be dangerous:

> *nam sunt situata et potentia ad adquirendum totum residuum Amoree; et in dictis partibus, et in toto duchamine [Athenarum], non est aliqua terra nec aliquod castrum quod habeat portum pro defensione navigiorum nisi terra Neapolis, que est etiam potens ad armandum duas galeas, . . .*

Giovanni Gradonico of Venice had been sent from the Argolid with letters in which certain citizens and nobles begged the Venetians to take over Argos and Nauplia and thus exclude Nerio Acciaiuoli, and it was decided, by 51 votes against 7 with 4 abstentions, to purchase the places on certain conditions.[99] On the same day, 12 December, Marie d'Enghien, then in Venice and said to be between 14 and 25 years of age, agreed to sell Argos and Nauplia to Venice; she and her heirs were to have an annual income in perpetuity of 500 gold ducats; she herself was to have an additional 200 ducats annually during her lifetime; and if she died without heirs, she might leave 2000 gold ducats to whom she pleased. On 17 December, in the house

[96] Misti, xlii, f. 129 v; xliii, f. 34. According to *Chronographia regum francorum*, ii, 322, Engelbert went to Venice and sold Argos, Nauplia and 'Thebes' *pro magna pecuniarum summa*!

[97] Epitaph in Matthieu, 69 (Hopf, i, 453, wrongly gives 1392); Vredius, ii, 265, names Engelbert's descendants.

[98] R.-J. Loenertz, 'Pour l'histoire du Péloponèse au XIVe siècle,' *Études byzantines*, i (1943), 167–170.

[99] Archivio di Stato, Venice; Secreta Consilii Rogatorum [=Rogatorum], E. f. 46 v.

of the heirs of Federigo Cornaro, she also promised, on pain of losing her incomes from Venice, that she would not remarry except to a Venetian noble.[100] The Venetians thus acquired another naval base, but their enemies accused them of exerting pressure on Marie d'Enghien. Nerio's brother Donato Acciaiuoli wrote that her relations treated her badly and that the Venetians 'have kept the woman in Venice against her will and married her as they wish, so that they retain that barony.'[101]

It required several years of energetic diplomatic campaigning before the Venetians were able to secure actual possession of both Argos and Nauplia. On 22 December 1388 the government at Venice decided to write to Albano Contarini of Venice, who was thought to be still holding the castle at Argos in the name of Marie d'Enghien against Theodore's attacks, urging him to resist until 15 April when help would arrive; it was also decided to write to Marco Morosini at Nauplia, to the Bishop of Argos and to Jacomo de Tzoya. On 26 January 1389 Perazzo Malipiero was appointed *provisor* of Argos and Nauplia, but it was doubted whether he could secure either place; indeed by February it was believed in Venice that the walls of Argos had been knocked down. The Venetians had succeeded in occupying Nauplia by May, and in June they still hoped that at least the castle at Argos was resisting. Perazzo Malipiero had been ordered on 18 February to raise the local nobility in the Venetian cause, and on 22 June he was instructed to make payments to the faithful subjects of Venice who were in the castles at Argos, Nauplia and Kiveri.[102] The Venetians were determined to win control of Argos from Theodore but they were divided as to how to do so, being reluctant to embark on large-scale military operations against Theodore and the Turks on a mainland reduced almost to anarchy. They attempted to impose an economic blockade; they tried to bribe Theodore; and they engaged in the most treacherous and complex negotiations with Pedro de San Superan, the Navarrese Prince of Achaea, who in 1389 captured Nerio Acciaiuoli and held him prisoner. In the end, however, Theodore had trouble with his own Greek nobles, and early in 1394 he broke with the Turks, who had demanded that he should cede Argos to them. A rapprochement with Venice naturally followed, and the Venetians occupied Argos on 11 June 1394. The treaty with Theodore previously concluded at Modon on 27 May provided that Argos, Kiveri and Thermision should be handed over to Venice with all rights enjoyed there by Pietro Cornaro and Marie d'Enghien. There was to be an amnesty for all those at Argos who were politically culpable towards Venice, and up to twenty families were to be allowed to leave Argos, provided they were free from debt.[103]

There was already a considerable Venetian presence in the Argolid by 1388, and the new rulers sought to win the favour of the local notables. One of these, Jacopo Bishop of Argos, was in Venice in December 1389 and again early in 1391, acting

[100] Texts in *Diplomatarium Veneto-Levantinum*: 1300–1450, ed. G. Thomas—R. Predelli, ii (Venice, 1899), 211–215.

[101] Text in J. Buchon, *Recherches historiques sur la principauté française de Morée*, ii (Paris, 1845), 433. Apparently Marie married Pasquale Zane of Venice and died before 28 January 1393 (Hopf, ii, 50).

[102] Rogatorum E, f. 46 (22 December 1388); Misti, xl, f. 151 (26 January), 162–163 (18 February) [the text printed by E. Gerland from Hopf's notes is seriously unreliable]; xli, f. 9 v (31 May), 19 v–20, 20 v (22 June 1389). *Cf. Régestes*, nos. 745, 748, 753, 757.

[103] R. Cessi, 'Venezia e l'acquisto di Nauplia ed Argo, '*Nuovo archivio veneto*, n.s. xxx (1915); Zakythinos, i, 130–143; Loenertz (1943), 168–185; Setton, 190–193; *Régestes*, i, nos. 753–865. This affair requires further study.

once more as an envoy for the Acciaiuoli.[104] Another was the *nobilis miles* Gerardo de Laburda, a Venetian subject, who was confirmed on 23 April 1390 in the possession of the fief which had previously been conceded to Jacobus de Castronovo by the 'former lords' of Argos and Nauplia.[105] On a later occasion in 1400, however, the Venetians refused to accept a privilege granting to a Leo Pigassi a vineyard at Argos which had once belonged to a priest called Nicholas Cocho, on the grounds that Pietro Cornaro had been wrongly informed when granting the privilege.[106] Probably the most important of Venice's new vassals was Jacomo de Tzoya. In 1389 he was in Venice, and on 22 June he was ordered to remain there until news arrived from the Argolid; he was granted a small pension to cover his expenses in Venice since all his goods were in the city and territory of Argos. On 17 August he was at last permitted to leave for home, since his stay in Venice was affecting his health and his affairs.[107] On 31 August 1389 the senate gave him permission to leave to one of his younger sons the fief in the Argolid which had once belonged to Boniface de Prothimo, and which Louis d'Enghien had granted to Jacomo after Guy d'Enghien's death in lieu of 1000 ducats owed him by Guy. He produced privileges to show that Pietro Cornaro and Marie d'Enghien had confirmed his possession of the fief. By the customs of the country it was due to pass on his death with all his other possessions to his eldest son, but since he had two other small sons who could expect no inheritance at all, and on account of the services he might be able to render the Venetians, they agreed to allow this fief to be left to whichever of the other sons he might choose, on condition that the eldest son was agreeable and that thereafter it should always pass to the eldest son, according to custom.[108]

Argos and Nauplia were governed in much the same way as the other Venetian colonies in *Romania*, though with certain concessions to local conditions. Venetian officials were instructed to observe the customs of Argos and Nauplia, and to send a text of them to Venice for correction. Old privileges, such as exemptions from payments of wax granted in the times of Guy d'Enghien and his predecessors the Dukes of Athens, were recognised. The castles were repaired and kept in Venetian hands; the Venetians maintained garrisons in the towns and a galley at Nauplia; the population had to work on the fortifications, to guard the walls, to serve on the galley, and to assist in the manufacture of wax. Nauplia came under attack by the Turks in 1391, and even after 1394 Venetian lordship did not bring peace. Apart from the wars against the Greeks of the Morea, the plain of Argos suffered devastation by the Count of Cephalonia in 1395, and in 1397 Argos was overrun by the Turks, who enslaved large numbers of persons there. The Venetians imposed an effective taxation system and attempted to repopulate the Argolid by settling Albanians. For several decades there was a measure of prosperity, and it was only later in the fifteenth century, with the general crisis of the Latin Levant, that this turned into decline at Argos and Nauplia.[109] The old de la Roche lands there,

[104] Misti, xli, f. 52 v; *Régestes*, i, nos. 792, 800.

[105] Misti, xli, f. 76.

[106] Texts in Sathas, ii, 2–3, 18–20.

[107] Misti, xli, f. 20 v, 32 v. A letter of 15 December 1379 had listed Jacomo among those in Greece to whom Lorenzo Acciaiuoli was advised to write (text in Gregorovius—Lampros, iii, 129–132).

[108] Misti, xli, f. 35.

[109] *Régestes*, i, nos. 748, 761, 784, 792, 831, 861, 865, 886, 904–905, 936, 950, 967; ii–iii, *passim*. The numerous documents at Venice (*cf.* texts in Sathas, *passim*) would permit a much more detailed study of conditions in the Argolid during the period after 1394.

having passed to the Brienne and the Enghien, Italianate Frankish families with Apulian possessions, and from them to the great Venetian house of Cornaro with its wide Levantine interests, had become a link in the long chain of Venetian naval bases.

APPENDIX I

The Medici in Greece

The Medici were not among those Florentine houses which extended their business activities to Greek lands in the late thirteenth and early fourteenth centuries.[110] In fact, by the 1340's a number of the Medici were far from prosperous; some gave up banking and business and devoted themselves primarily to their estates, while others turned to crime.[111] When Gautier de Brienne became *signore* of Florence in 1342 he had Giovanni di Bernardino de' Medici decapitated, and other members of the family played a leading part in securing Gautier's expulsion from Florence in 1343.[112] Yet several Medici served Gautier in Greece. By the 1350's certain Medici were well enough established there to have hellenized their name to *Iatros*; they described themselves as 'of Athens' although the Brienne whom they served had not held Athens itself since 1311. A certain *Cosma d'Athaines dit Yatro* was Gautier de Brienne's bailli in Cyprus. He was replaced in about February 1354 by Raouche de Monteron, whose accounts show that in 1356, on Gautier's instructions, he paid 1000 besants owed by Gautier to *Piere Yatro d'Ataines*.[113] Cosimo apparently went to the Argolid, for a *Cosmas ntatennes* was a witness to the act, given in Greek at Nauplia in April 1357, by which *Piere tantenes* called *Iatros*, who was acting as bailli and captain-general at Argos and Nauplia, confirmed the purchase of a house at Nauplia by Gregorio di Michele Catello of Messina.[114]

[110] S. Borsari, 'L'espansione economica fiorentina nell'Oriente cristiano sino alla metà del Trecento,' *Rivista storica italiana*, lxx (1958).

[111] G. Brucker, 'The Medici in the Fourteenth Century,' *Speculum*, xxxii (1957), 13–14 *et passim*.

[112] Giovanni Villani, iv, 7, 28, 31, 45. Presumably it was only a coincidence that between 1314 and 1316 Gautier and his mother borrowed considerable sums from, and pawned lands in Apulia to Pierre Miège (also known as *Petro Medico* or *Petrus Mezi seu Medici*) of Toulon, galley-owner and money-lender at Marseille and Naples: details in Caggese, i, 217, n. 7, 240, n. 3; ii, 178, n. 5, 328, n. 1, 331; *Histoire du Commerce de Marseille*, ed. G. Rambert, ii (Paris, 1951), 29–31, 36, n. 1, 151, n. 2.

[113] Poncelet, 14, 26 *et passim*. Niccolò Acciaiuoli may have been referring to Piero de' Medici in writing, on 14 March 1356: . . . *e Piero riavera la sua terra plu tosto che non pensa* (text in Léonard, iii, 589–590).

[114] This document survives in a sixteenth-century copy (executed by Janus Lascaris and attested by Alexius Celadonius, Bishop of Molfetta (not Amalfi) 1508–1517) from the Medici archives. It is now in Archivio di Stato, Florence; Carte orientali e greche, busta 2: text in Gregorovius—Lampros, ii, 738–740. Two drawings on the parchment, clumsily reproduced in W. Miller, *Historia tes Phrangokratias en Helladi*: 1204–1566, trans. S. Lampros, ii (Athens, 1909/10), 10, purport to show the bailli's 'seal and counter-seal (*antiboulla*)' mentioned in the text. One drawing depicts the Brienne seal with the inscription: GAVLTIER DVC DE ATHENES CONTE DE BRENE ET DE LICCE SEIGNOR DE FIORA(N)CE 1342. The second drawing shows a seal with the Medici arms inscribed: PIERRE DE MEDICIS DE ATHENIS BAIVLVS ET GNAL. CAP. DE ARGOS ET DE NEAPOLI DE ROMA; the date 1342 also appears, though not as part of the inscription on the seal but beneath the drawing. The document does not mention Gautier, who was dead by 1357; the drawings look suspect; and the date 1342 suggests that the inscriptions are at least partly unreliable. It seems unwise to conclude (as in Gregorovius—Lampros, ii, 232, n. 2, 670–671, and elsewhere) that Piero was already bailli in 1342. Professor Peter Topping of Cincinnati University most generously supplied information and advice on this question, as on many others.

Piero was presumably acting for Guy d'Enghien, and he was apparently succeeded by another Medici. On 3 July 1360 a *Bartolo Talenti* wrote from Venice to Giovanni Acciaiuoli of Florence, Archbishop-elect of Patras:

> Sapiate monsingniore chome avemo per novele che lo cholettore del santo padre che mando in Patraso vende tutta biava e fa danari quanto elo pode, e per zo monsingniore farete bene a dare i spaco o di venire o di mandare per vedere i fatti vostri. Anchora ordinate di dire o di far dire a monsingniore lo grade sinischalcho la dove fose chome avemo per novele che i greci e altra gente citadini d'Argo e di Napoli di Romania si anno asediati queli d'Anghi dentro nel donzo dele dette Argo e Napoli per che messer Arardo avea fatto dare bando per le dette tere che niuno dovese vendere ne fiche ne uva pasa senon ala chorte, e per zo ordinate che monsingniore lo sapia tosto per che sapra quello chara a fare.
>
> Bartolo Talenti vi si rachomanda,
>
> fatta in Vinega a di 3 di luio 1360.
>
> (*reverse*)
>
> Reverendissimo in Christo patri, et domino suo, domino Johanni, ecclesiae Patracensis Archiepiscopo dignissimo.[115]

The writer, probably Bartolomeo di Talento de' Medici, was invoking the assistance of Niccolò Acciaiuoli, Grand Seneschal of the Kingdom of Naples, who had become Lord of Corinth in 1358. The Enghien bailli of 1360 was apparently an Averardo de' Medici.

These Medici may well have been descendants of the Averardo de' Medici who died in 1318/9, and whose sons included Talento, Salvestro, Jacopo and Giovenco *detto* Venturo. Talento's son Bartolomeo was presumably the *Bartolo Talenti* who wrote from Venice in 1360. Salvestro's son Averardo *detto* Bicci, the grandfather of the famous Cosimo, was in Florence in 1360, and the *Arardo* then at Argos was possibly Jacopo de Averardo's son Averardo, who was certainly still alive in 1353.[116] Averardo di Jacopo's wife Giovanna di Bencivenni Baroncelli[117] was perhaps related to Aldobrando Baroncelli of Florence, who acted in Greece as an agent for the Acciaiuoli.[118] Giovenco *detto* Venturo's grandson Piero di Francesco[119] may have been Piero de' Medici of Athens. This Piero de' Medici was still alive at Nauplia in October 1376.[120] He held lands around Corinth from the Acciaiuoli Lords of Corinth, and his son Niccolò de' Medici married the daughter of the Greek notary Damianos Phiomachos, who became Nerio Acciaiuoli's secretary. After Piero's death, Nerio confirmed Niccolò de' Medici in the possession of his father's

[115] Biblioteca Laurenziana, Florence; Carteggio Acciaiuoli, Cassetta II A, lettera 101, partly quoted in E.-G. Léonard, 'La nomination de Giovanni Acciaiuoli à l'archeveché de Patras: 1360,' in *Mélanges offerts à M. Nicholas Iorga* (Paris, 1933), 523, n. 4.

[116] Brucker, 9, 25 *et passim*; R. de Roover, *The Rise and Decline of the Medici Bank*: 1397–1494 (Cambridge, Mass., 1963), 385. Professor Brucker most kindly searched his notes for more information on these Medici, as did Professor F. Gaupp of Southwestern University (Texas).

[117] P. Litta, *Famiglie celebri italiane*, fasc. xvii (Milan, 1827–1830), tavola III.

[118] *Cf.* Topping, 'Régime agraire,' 290–291; Luttrell, 'Interessi fiorentini,' 324; *Dipolomatari*, doc. 622.

[119] Litta, fasc. xvii, tavole XVII, XIX.

[120] Text *infra*, 54. Hopf, ii, 20, gives Piero as a son of Lapo *delle brache*, which seems quite unfounded (*cf.* Brucker, 24).

lands and granted him other properties which lay within the Duchy of Athens by an act of January 1387 recorded in Greek at Athens.[121] The Medici of Athens subsequently remained in Greece for many decades.[122]

APPENDIX II

The Foucherolles and their Argolid Fiefs[123]

The Foucherolles acquired at least some of their Argolid lands by marrying into a cadet branch of the de la Roche family. Guy de la Roche, Lord of Athens, was granted Argos and Nauplia by the Prince of Achaea, and his younger brother Guillaume de la Roche married a daughter of Mathieu de Walincourt de Mons, Lord of Veligourt (or Veligosti) in the Morea. In 1276 their son *Jaque de Veligourt* did homage for the fief of *la Valte, ou tout le casal de la Regranice et cellui de Coscolomby*, possibly places in the Argolid, while in about 1304 Jacques' son *Regnaux de Veligourt* held Damala as liege vassal of Nicolas de Saint-Omer, Co-seigneur of Thebes.[124] Renaud, whose father *Jacomo de Viligort* or *de la Rocia* married Marie, daughter of Guillaume Aleman Lord of Patras,[125] was still alive in April 1309;[126] Renaud probably died fighting the Catalans in March 1311.[127] By 1325 Damala had passed to Martino Zaccaria,[128] apparently through his marriage to Renaud's daughter Jacqueline. Another daughter of *Rinaldo di Valgonato* or *delle Porte* married Jean de Foucherolles, through whom some of Renaud's lands passed to Jean's son François. In 1309, in an act witnessed by François, the elder Gautier de Brienne confirmed François' son Nicolas in the inheritance of these lands.[129] By this time the Foucherolles were firmly established in the Argolid, where their holdings included three knight's fees : *en la partida de Corento et de Argo tres cavallerias de tierras et de villanos*.[130] So their lands seem to have lain north of Argos towards Corinth and perhaps towards Damala. A Nicolas de Foucherolles was a canon at Argos 1311;[131] François and Gautier de Foucherolles were defending Argos, Gautier as Captain of Argos, in 1319;[132] and François' son Nicolas was named in Gautier de

[121] *Diplomatari*, doc. 600.

[122] References in W. Miller, *The Latins in the Levant* (London, 1908), 338, 510, 553–554.

[123] The Foucherolles' history derives, only with considerable uncertainty, from the two documents printed here. These survive only in modern copies which, whether the originals were in Latin, French or Italian, are clearly corrupted, confused and unreliable; so are Hopf's interpretations of them (i, 390, 424; ii, 19–20; *CGR*, 472–473).

[124] *Livre de la conqueste de la princée de l'Amorée*, ed. J. Longnon (Paris, 1911), 44, 71, 208, 379.

[125] *Libro de los fechos*, 30, 87, anachronistically stating that Jacques was granted Veligourt in 1209.

[126] J. de Saint Génois, *Droits primitifs des anciennes terres et seigneuries du pays et comté de Haynaut*, i (Paris, 1782), 215 (as cited in Hopf, i, 369).

[127] Hopf, i, 391, without evidence, regards this as certain.

[128] Text in C. Minieri Riccio, *Saggio di codice diplomatico*, supplemento, part ii (Naples, 1883), 75–77 (date corrected in Hopf, i, 408, n. 13). Hopf, *CGR*, 502, gives Martino as Lord of Veligosti and Damala in 1324, but as marrying Jacqueline in 1327! Hopf, i, 413, supposes that Martino helped defend the Argolid after 1311, but the 1318 text (*Diplomatari*, doc. 102) only shows, without specifying where, that the Catalans had captured his brother Niccolò.

[129] This genealogy derives from the 1376 text; Hopf's version (*CGR*, 472) is hopelessly confused.

[130] *Libro de los fechos*, 31, anachronistically stating that the Foucherolles acquired them in 1209; the other versions of the Chronicle of the Morea make no mention of this (*Livre de la conqueste*, 44, n. 2, 45, n. 5).

[131] Text in *Regestum Clementis Papae V*, vi (Rome, 1887), no. 6776.

[132] *Diplomatari*, doc. 110. Bulls of 14 January 1314 mention an unnamed captain of Argos (*ibid.*, docs. 63–66); Hopf, *CGR*, 472, without evidence, gives Gautier as captain from 1311 until 1324.

Brienne's will in 1347.[133] Nicolas was dead by 1364, the fief passing, apparently under some kind of entail,[134] to his daughter. Her husband Jacomo, who was Lord of *Joya* in the *Grisera*,[135] that is of Tzoya just south of Clarenza in the west of the Morea,[136] was holding the fief from Guy d'Enghien by 1364; after his wife's death his right to it was confirmed by Guy d'Enghien in 1376, though only after a dispute with Jacomo's son Niccolò. Jacomo continued to participate in Argolid affairs and was still alive in 1391.[137]

Guy d'Enghien: Nauplia, December 1364[138]

Noi Gui d'Anguiano Signor di Argues, et di Napoli facciamo a saper a tutti per la tenor di queste presente lettere, che in compenso di boni agradi, et accettabili servitii, che nostro caro, et bene amato Kavalier, et Compagno il Signor miser di Zoia noi ha fatto, et speriamo chel farà per l'avenire a Noi et nostri heredi di nostra buona volontà, et proprio moto per noi e nostri heredi al ditto signor Jacomo, et alli suoi heredi habbiamo fatto, che per la servitu di tutti possessi, che egli tiene di Noi in nostro detto paise d'Argues, et di Napoli per causa di sua mogliere, che'l detto Signor Jacomo, ne li suoi heredi non siano obligati d'altro nome di fornire quatro huomini d'arme a Cavallo, et arme alla guardia, et diffesa del nostro detto paese d'Argues et Napoli non ostante, che li detti possessi, et terre secondo il tenore di privilegij soleva dever, et esser obligati di più gran servitio, il qual di gratia speciale l'habbiamo assoluto, et assolvemo, senza che l'ha obligato di sopradetti quatro huomini d'arme, et non più esser di quelli tenuto, et stretto. Promettendo in buona fede, et lealmente per noi et nostri Heredi al detto Signor Jacomo et alli suoi heredi di non andar mai, ne far andar in alcun modo al contrario di questa gratia, anzi la tenimo et faremo tenire rata, ferma, et stabile imperpetuo, et per più sigurezza di verità habbiamo fatto fare queste presente lettere bollate del nostro bollo grande, pendente, et scritte nel nostro Castello di Napoli il mese di Decembrio l'anno di gratia 1364.

Guy d'Enghien: Nauplia, October 1376[139]

Noi Gui d'Anguiano Signor d'Argues, et de Napoli faciamo saper alli nostri Nobili il Signor Miser Nicolo de Zoia figliuolo del Signor Jacomo de Zoia, et Zise, et Laurento,[140] che è verità, che noi habbiamo fatto fare una rivestitione per il Signor Jacomo di Zoia di Argues, per che la rivestitione non poteva fare rinvestire il Signor Jacomo di fossieres[141] che sariano datte a sua mogliere, et figlio di sua

[133] *Supra*, 37. A Ferry de Foucherolles was Marshal of the Hospital at Rhodes from 1330 to 1335, and later Prior of Champagne; Gérard de Foucherolles held preceptories at Châlon, Metz and Beaune, became Hospitaller of the Hospital, and in 1400 was empowered to treat with the Despot Theodore in the Morea (Delaville le Roulx, 278).

[134] *Infra*, 55, n. 159.

[135] Luttrell, 'Principality of Achaea,' 344.

[136] 1516 portolan in Sathas, i, endpiece. Hopf (i, 424; *CGR*, 472) places Tzoya in the Argolid and gives Nicolas de Foucherolles as Baron of Tzoya in 1324!

[137] *Supra*, 48–49. Hopf, ii, 20, wrongly states that Jacomo died in 1376, and that Niccolò died in 1382 leaving a son Jacomo, Lord of Tzoya!

[138] Modern copy from a codex entitled *Famiglia Cornera* in Archivio di Stato, Venice; Miscellania codici I, Storia veneta no. 149 (*olim* Brera, Milan, Ms. I, 58), f. 66 (punctuation as in Ms.); printed, inaccurately, in Hopf, *CGR*, 240.

[139] *Ibid.*, f. 66–66 v (punctuation as in Ms.); printed, inaccurately, in Hopf, *CGR*, 240–242 (only significant errors noted here).

[140] Reading *et Lise de Laurento*, Hopf, ii, 19–20, deduces a first husband for *Lise* named *Laurento* or *Lorient*! *Laurento* remains a puzzle.

[141] Or *fontieres*(?); Hopf *forestieretis*.

mogliere, et che saria stato solo miser Nicolo[142] setetn'ia,[143] et riposto il XVe di fevraro ultimo passato in presentia di noi tutti homini delegati Signor Miser Piero d'Athene ditto medico,[144] et Signor Miser Giorgio della Borda,[145] et miser mistro Nicolo Alemano,[146] et Signor Miser Arduno Pisan et Miser Joanne di Brisano, et Joanne Battista et Zanetto Buccone, et Galleace Meno[147] Marco et Nicolo Canaz[148] nostro Thesauriero d'argues a Porta Castelli[149] nostro Thesauriero di Napoli tal revistitione non potter esser fatta, ma si bene di rivestire il Signor Jacomo, come herede di sua mogliere, perche egli e figliolo del Signor Nicolo di fosserole,[150] et non altrimente[151] ha rimandata tal rivestitione, la quale non si poteva fare,[152] et ha richiesto Niccolo di Zoia in Nostra presenza, che la era figlia[153] de chi era sua Madre, et noi ha mostrato, che quel possesso solo del signor Rinaldo delle porte, et con quello l'heredità, perche da egli è venuto uno suo figliolo il Signor Francesco faulseron, come noi è stato mostrato per una investitione fatta del tempo di Gualtiero duca d'Athene, e di Brin, et, e stata fatta l'anno 1304,[154] la qual è stata fatta inanzi Miser Francesco figliolo del Signor Zuane, e di quelle, e rivestito il signor Miser Nicolo de Faulseroni figliolo del Signor Francesco suo Padre di tutti li possessi del Signor Joanne di faulseroni figliolo del signor Rinaldo delle Porte,[155] et del signor Nicolo di Caves secundo il modo, che teneva Nurdo di Carghi[156] quando haveva il Castello di raggione[157] con tutte sue adherentie, et le Cassalle di Chitadenes con tutte sue adherentie, et le Cassale delle forne, che sono appartinente al signor Rinaldo di Valgonato con tutte le sue adherentie dalla serada che va di santa Marina alle Castri del ponente la marina, La Borria le adherentie di Santa Marina d'Austro le adherentie del Castri,[158] et li Casali chiamati messacorio con tutte adherentie, et il Cassallo della macrona con tutte sue adherentie, gli monti confini, et da levante il monte per onde si va in Argues, sino a Macronam da Ponente li monti della Pastura, che va di boiere alla fumara per tutto, che e possesso serve, et appartiene tutto al signor Nicolo di fouguerolles, et a miser Nicolò di Zoija, che e figliolo del signor Jacomo con privileggio, che'l nostro possesso, che hebbe una nostra Sorella al Signor Gulielmo Conte con Signor d'Argues, et Napoli, chi naque del Signor Nicolo, et tutti li suoi heredi leggitimi che sarano di lui discendenti, et con quello è stata

[142] This obscure passage might mean that Guy had re-invested Jacomo with certain lands but that others (*fossieres* = Foucherolles?) could only pass through his wife to their son Niccolò.

[143] =*sentenza*?

[144] Piero de' Medici (*supra*, 50–51).

[145] Possibly Gerardo de Laburda (*supra*, 49); Hopf, ii, 20 gives Peter!

[146] Possibly *messer Janni Misido* and *Nicola alamangno* who held castles in the Morea in 1377 (Luttrell, 'Principality of Achaea,' 344).

[147] Possibly Galeazzo Nani, Venetian consul at Clarenza in 1356 (*Régestes*, i, no. 282).

[148] Or *Cavaz*(?); Hopf *Catello*, but Hopf, ii, 20, gives Marco and Niccolò Cavaza. Johannes Cavaza was castellan of Nauplia castle in 1400 (Sathas, ii, 13–14).

[149] *Sic.* Hopf *Petro Castelli*, but Hopf, ii, 20, gives Aporito Catello. Niccolò and Aporico Catello were inhabitants of Nauplia in 1400 (Sathas, ii, 14).

[150] *I.e.* Jacomo de Tzoya is son-in-law (*figliolo*) of Nicolas de Foucherolles.

[151] *Sic.* Hopf *altrui, unde.*

[152] *I.e.* on 15 February 1376 Guy's court judged, against Niccolò, that Jacomo should be invested as his wife's heir.

[153] *Sic.*

[154] Read 1309: Gautier only reached Greece and became duke in 1309 (Setton, 6–7).

[155] *I.e.* the lands passed from Renaud de Veligourt *alias* de la Roche (*Rinaldo di Valgonato* or *delle Porte*) to his son-in-law (*figliolo*) Jean de Foucherolles, to Jean's son François (given as Renaud's *figliolo*!), to François' son Nicolas, and to Nicolas' daughter; in 1309 Gautier de Brienne confirmed them, in François' presence, to Nicolas. Niccolò de Tzoya obviously argued that the rule of primogeniture should continue so that he inherit from his mother, who was the daughter of Nicolas.

[156] *Nicolo di Caves* and *Nurdo di Carghi* remain unidentified.

[157] Possibly the *casal de la Regranice* held by Jacques de Veligourt in 1276 (*supra*, 52).

[158] Possibly Kastri (Hermione) on the Argolid coast near Thermision (Sathas, i, endpiece; Andrews, 249 and pl. xxvii).

rivestita sua detta Madre, faciamo saper, che è fatto, et scritto privileggio l'anno 1328 del mese d'Aprile datto al Castello d'Argues[159] et facciamo saper, et recchime diamo a tutti nostri suggetti, che sia investito il Signor Jacomo come herede di sua mogliere nominato nella sopra detta nominatione, come si la detta investitione di sua detta mogliere fosse stata fatta in nome del detto Miser Jacomo, deve ancora simile investitione tenere, galder et posseder il detto signor Jacomo nella forma, et modo che la teneva sua detta mogliere inanzi ch'ella moresse, con gli fonti, mollini, Ville con tutte le sue ordinanze, et tutto il detto possesso, et uno corpo, come e apparito per il paese, et non soleva per il possesso esser obligato nome di tre huomini a Cavallo bene Armati, et Cavali sufficienti, et buoni, et ha promesso il Signor Jacomo, et iurato nella mano dell'homo delegato esser contra tutti li nostri nemisi, et noi promettiamo, et faremo restare questo previleggio stabile, durabile et valabile, sino che il sole lusara a gli huomini, et per certezza, et corroboratione di Verita del detto Privileggio habbiamo fatto bollare quel detto Privileggio del nostro bollo grande pendente. scritto, et datto il detto Privileggio l'anno 1376 al mese d'Ottobre nel nostro Palazzo di Napoli.

[159] This most obscure passage conceivably means that—in accordance with a privilege granted at Argos in April 1328 (though this date is suspect) to a Guillaume (*Gulielmo*) de Foucherolles, son of Nicolas and Captain (*Conte*) and Seigneur (*Signor*) of Argos and Nauplia, and to his descendants—Nicolas de Foucherolles' lands were to pass to Niccolò de Tzoya as they had passed to Niccolò's mother (who was Nicolas's daughter), her brother Guillaume presumably having died before his sister without an heir; alternatively, though the text says *qui naque del Signor Nicolo*, the *Gulielmo* was possibly Nicolas' brother Gautier who was Captain of Argos in 1319. Hopf reads *una nostra Sorella Antonia*(!) *signor Gulielmo Conte consolo*(!) *d'Argues*, . . . Hopf then invents (ii, 19–20; *CGR*, 472) two other daughters for Nicolas, an Antonia (*al!*) de Foucherolles, wife of a Guillaume, Count of Plancy, and a Bona de Foucherolles-Zoia, the wife of Guy d'Enghien, making Antonia Guy's sister-in-law (*nostra Sorella*) and Jacomo de Tzoya his brother-in-law! But the Anthonace de Plancy of 1347 (*supra*, 37) was presumably a man; the *Sorella* and much else await explanation.

IX

JOHN CANTACUZENUS AND THE CATALANS AT CONSTANTINOPLE: 1352-1354 *

The majority of those subjects of the King of Aragon who fought or traded in *Romania* and who were generally known to the Greeks as *Katelánoi* did come from Catalunya, although some were from Aragon, Valencia, Majorca and the other dominions of the Aragonese Crown. The colony they founded at Constantinople during the second half of the thirteenth century was never large. Facing powerful and privileged Italian competition, the Catalano-Aragonese kingdoms lacked the incentives and the resources either to develop their own limited commercial interests in the Aegean or to pursue an active imperial policy in *Romania*. Catalans and Greeks however shared a common hostility towards the House of Anjou which ruled in Naples and in the Morea, as the Peloponnese was then known, and after 1282 both benefitted from the Sicilian Vespers which, not without a measure of Aragonese-Byzantine collusion, had replaced Angevin rule in Sicily with that of the Aragonese Crown. In 1293 an Aragonese fleet sacked a number of Byzantine ports, and reprisals against Catalan merchants at Constantinople followed. Yet in 1296, at the request of their consul there, the emperor granted to the small number of Catalans at Constantinople certain commercial privileges, though these were not as advantageous as those already enjoyed by most of the other Latin powers established there. In 1303 a body of unemployed Catalan mercenaries from Sicily reached Constantinople to serve the Emperor Andronicus II. At first they fought successfully against the Turks, but soon there were dissensions and the Catalans began to pillage the country. In 1305 the Greeks murdered many of the mercenaries at Constantinople and elsewhere, and the

* For Jesús Ernesto Martínez Ferrando who was Director of the Archivo de la Corona de Aragón when I first worked there. I am deeply grateful to my former colleague at Edinburgh University, Dr. Donald Nicol, who kindly indicated and translated certain Greek passages and provided other invaluable help.

rest finally moved out of the empire; in 1311 they set up an independent state based on Thebes and Athens. Tenuous diplomatic relations between Byzantium and the Aragonese Crown survived these hostilities and, following an embassy despatched by Jaime II of Aragon, the imperial privilege of 1296 was extended and confirmed in October 1315. Catalan merchants continued to trade at Constantinople, and by 1325 their community in the city was large enough to be involved in a major riot with the Venetians [1].

After the death of the Emperor Andronicus III in 1341 the Byzantine state entered a period of increasing disruption. Andronicus' son John V Palaeologus was only nine years old and John Cantacuzenus, who had long been the chief minister, had himself declared emperor. The ensuing civil wars were complicated by profound social and religious disturbances, by plague and economic depression, and by further inroads from Serbs, Turks and Latins. John Cantacuzenus was an able statesman and one of his ambitions was to restore Byzantine control over the Latins in Greece, the Catalans of Athens included. He expressed his hopes in a speech which he reported in his own somewhat tendentious memoirs: «Should we succeed with God's help in bringing the Latins in the Peloponnese under the control of the empire, then the Catalans in Attica and Boeotia will acknowledge us either voluntarily or by compulsion» [2]. But far from restoring the empire, Cantacuzenus gradually lost control of it. The powerful Serbian ruler Stephan Dushan advanced overland, and the Genoese seized the island of Chios, assaulted Constantinople and destroyed the Byzantine fleet. From 1350 onwards John V Palaeologus was actively seeking to undermine Cantacuzenus' position and to assert his own. In the spring of 1351 Genoa's enemies, the Venetians, sacked Galata or Pera, as the Genoese suburb across the Golden Horn from

[1] C. Marinesco, *Notes sur les Catalans dans l'empire byzantin pendant le règne de Jacques II: 1291-1327*, in *'Mélanges d'histoire du moyen âge offerts à M. Ferdinand Lot'* (Paris, 1925); D. Geanakoplos, *Emperor Michael Palaeologus and the West: 1258-1282* (Cambridge, Mass., 1959), 304, 344-358, 375-377 *et passim;* F. Giunta, *Aragonesi e Catalani nel Mediterraneo*, II (Palermo, 1959), 38-39, 57-64, 82-85, 140-145, 163-192 *et passim*. The standard work, L. Nicolau d'Olwer, *L'expansió de Catalunya en la Mediterrània oriental* (Barcelona, 1926), is now seriously outdated but Giunta revises it only down to 1327. Documents in *Diplomatari de l'Orient català: 1301-1409*, ed. A. Rubió i Lluch (Barcelona, 1947); recent bibliography in A. Luttrell, *La Corona de Aragón y la Grecia catalana: 1377-1394*, «Anuario de Estudios medievales» (forthcoming).

[2] Ioannes Cantacuzenus, *Historiarum libri IV*, ed. L. Schopen, 3 vols. (Bonn, 1828-1832), III, cap. 12 (II. 80).

Constantinople was then called, and compelled Cantacuzenus, who lacked military force and a strong fleet, to accept an alliance designed to expel the Genoese from *Romania* [3].

John Cantacuzenus thus became an ally of the Catalans since Venice, seriously short of men and ships, had already made a treaty with the Aragonese Crown, the rival of Genoa throughout the Western Mediterranean and especially in Sardinia. King Pedro of Aragon realized that this meant war in the Eastern Mediterranean, and on 1 June 1351 he sent an appeal to the Aragonese and Catalans at Athens and elsewhere in *Romania,* calling on them to support their distant fatherland [4]. Pedro drove a hard bargain with the Venetians, who had to finance twelve out of eighteen galleys to be contributed by the Aragonese to a fleet dedicated to the destruction of Genoese strength in the East. Pope Clement VI intervened in vain as the opposing powers gathered their forces. Open warfare between Venice and Genoa had already begun, and in August 1351 sixty-two Genoese vessels under Paganino Doria attacked the Venetians in port on their Aegean island of Negroponte. The Catalans of the Duchy of Athens sent three hundred horse and many foot to relieve the town, while the Venetian fleet, strengthened by the Aragonese galleys under Pons de Santa Pau and by reinforcements from Venice, eventually forced the Genoese to abandon the siege, which lasted from 15 August to 20 September. Both Cantacuzenus and Santa Pau then urged the Venetian commander Niccolò Pisani to take the offensive. He was reluctant to do so, but eventually the allies sailed to join the Greek fleet at Constantinople [5].

In one of the greatest battles ever fought in the Bosphorus, which

[3] References in P. SCHREINER, *La chronique brève de 1352: texte, traduction et commentaire,* «Orientalia christiana periodica», 31 (1965); 34 (1968).

[4] *Diplomatari,* doc. 199.

[5] In addition to CANTACUZENUS, see especially Nicephorus GREGORAS, *Byzantina Historia,* III, ed. I. BEKKER (Bonn, 1855), XXV-XXVI *et passim; Chronique catalane de Pierre IV d'Aragon, III de Catalogne,* ed. A. PAGÈS (Toulouse-Paris, 1942), 290-297; *Documentos concernientes a la armada que en 1351 mandó aprestar el rey don Pedro IV de Aragón en contra de genoveses,* ed. J. SANZ Y BARUTELL, in *Memorial Histórico Español,* II (Madrid, 1851). To the detailed analysis in A. SORBELLI, *La lotta tra Genova e Venezia per il predominio del Mediterraneo: 1350-1355,* «Memorie della R. Accademia delle Scienze dell'Istituto di Bologna», classe di scienze morali, I ser., 5 (1910-1911), and the recent amendments in SCHREINER, add M. BRUNETTI, *Contributo alla storia delle relazioni veneto-genovesi dal 1348 al 1350,* «Miscellanea di storia veneta», III ser., 9 (Venice, 1916); S. DUVERGÉ, *Le rôle de la papauté dans la guerre de l'Aragon contre Gênes: 1351-1356,* «Mélanges d'Archéologie et d'Histoire», 50 (1933); C. KYRRIS, *John Cantacuzenus and the Genoese: 1321-1348,* «Miscellanea storica ligure», 3 (Milan, 1963).

took place in a colossal gale on 13 February 1352, there were apparently some forty Venetian, twenty-five Aragonese and ten Greek vessels facing about sixty-five Genoese galleys [6]. The Genoese, who had failed to prevent the junction of the allied and Greek fleets, were sighted off the Asiatic coast opposite Constantinople. They were fresh from port, while the allied fleet had been battered by severe storms. Yet it was Santa Pau and the Catalans who took the initiative, compelling the Venetians to follow them. As a great wind blew up the Genoese retreated past Pera into rocky waters near Diplokionion, a short way up the Bosphorus on the European side. The allies were blown right past the Genoese, but rowed their ships against the wind to attack the enemy. An extraordinarily confused action or series of small battles began shortly before sunset and lasted much of the freezing night. Neither side could manoeuvre with ease to order its line of battle, or even distinguish friend from foe, so that Genoese fought ferociously against Genoese, and Venetian against Catalan. The Greeks seem to have withdrawn at nightfall, while some of the Aragonese galleys, not knowing the waters, were blown into the sunken rocks; many of their sailors were drowned and others were captured when they attempted to land on Genoese territory at Pera under the impression that it was Constantinople. Dawn broke on a scene of carnage. The icy sea was full of wrecks and corpses, while the crews of ships driven ashore fought each other on land. The Genoese retired to Pera but, to the disgust of Cantacuzenus and Santa Pau, the timid Pisani refused to follow up his limited advantage by besieging them there. Instead the allied fleet withdrew up the Bosphorus to Therapia, allowing the initiative to pass to the Genoese, who even attacked the allies there. Santa Pau reluctantly refused to join Cantacuzenus in an attack on the Genoese, since his orders were to follow and obey the Venetians and he was unable to persuade Pisani to take action. When, after some weeks, the Catalan admiral died, his lieutenant and successor Bononat Dezcoll also rejected Cantacuzenus' suggestion that he should lead the Greek fleet against the Genoese. Even when three large Catalan warships joined him, Pisani still refused to attack. Instead he insisted, against all advice, on anchoring his fleet off Constantin-

[6] References in Sorbelli, 145, n. 7; in addition, King Pedro (*Chronique*, 297) gave 34 Venetian, 25 Catalan and 9 Greek ships, while the 1352 Chronicle gave 60 allied and 10 Greek (Schreiner [1968], para. 56).

ople by the Gate of Santa Barbara, where a sudden squall sank four Venetian and three Catalan ships, though their crews were saved [7].

Both sides suffered heavily and both claimed the victory, so that there was little agreement as to the number of ships sunk [8]. Success was not to be measured numerically, and the real victors were the Genoese who retained their position at Pera and imposed a treaty on Cantacuzenus, while their enemies ultimately sailed away. Venice lacked a proper base in or near the Bosphorus and its fleet was seriously demoralized, for after the great plague of 1348 the republic was short of men, conditions aboard ship were poor, and discipline was lamentable. The Venetians put no trust in their own allies, and the government's general reluctance to fight was reflected in the excessive prudence of their admiral [9]. The Aragonese commander Santa Pau was some way up the Bosphorus at Hieron on 2 March, and the Aragonese fleet was at Constantinople selling its booty by 13 March [10]. The Catalans were far from home, short of supplies and paralyzed by the Venetians' timidity. As Bononat Dezcoll explained in a letter written to the Doge on 7 August 1352, the Catalans had stayed on only in order to honour their treaty with Venice, remaining in the Bosphorus about fifty-four days until around 7 April, and by that time they were so seriously short of victuals that hunger had finally compelled them to sail to Negroponte, Modon and Coron, where they found money and supplies [11]. Soon after the battle the Venetians had sent urgently to Venice and Crete for more money in order to prevent the Catalan fleet from leaving [12], while on 21 May 1352 the Senate voted to allow a Catalan *coca* which had recently arrived in Venice to export a certain quantity of grain [13]. By 15 April, however, Dezcoll had already reached Negroponte [14].

7 SORBELLI, 145-155, utilizing the conflicting chroniclers; add King Pedro's account (*Chronique*, 297-298). On the topography, R. JANIN, *Constantinople byzantine* (Paris, 1950); on the double columns at *Diplochioni*, G. GEROLA, *Le vedute di Costantinopoli di Cristoforo Buondelmonti*, «Studi bizantini e neoellenici», 3 (1931) 267 *et passim*.

8 References in SORBELLI, 149-152.

9 BRUNETTI, 7-28, 107-115 *et passim*.

10 *Diplomatari*, docs. 202, 209 (p. 275).

11 Venice, Archivio di Stato; Libri Commemoriali, IV, f. 212 v.

12 LORENZO DE MONACIS, *Chronicon de rebus venetis ab U. C. ad annum MCCCLIV*, ed. F. CORNELIUS (Venice, 1758), 214.

13 Venice, Archivio di Stato; Misti del Senato, XXVI, f. 93 v.

14 *Diplomatari*, p. 265, n. 4.

The Aragonese fleet had been more pugnacious than that of Venice, and the *Katelánoi* obviously enjoyed good relations with the Greeks and with Cantacuzenus, who gave high praise to Santa Pau and his men while criticizing the Venetians bitterly. The Catalans were operating in largely unknown waters. It was true that Bononat Dezcoll, for example, had been captain of a ship sailing for Constantinople in 1342 [15], while Santa Pau's two councillors Guillem Morey and Francesc de Finestres, both citizens of Barcelona, were described by King Pedro as the most able and accomplished seamen in all his domains [16], but on the whole the Catalans seldom ventured past Constantinople into the Black Sea and they were unlikely to be familiar with the Bosphorus. On 2 March Santa Pau reported that the Aragonese had lost twelve galleys [17], and by 18 May Pedro had received news from the Doge at Venice that Santa Pau himself had died after the battle *per mort natural* [18]. Cantacuzenus wrote, contradictorily, that *Poúnson* son of *Ntesánta* — as he called him — became so angry with Niccolò Pisani that, partly for that reason, he died of a fever he had caught and was succeeded by *Monenán te Skoltois* — Bononat Dezcoll, whom Cantacuzenus vainly persuaded to act independently of the Venetians [19]. King Pedro's chronicle described how Santa Pau died of his wounds a few days after the battle and was initially buried at Constantinople; it also mentioned that his body was on a Catalan galley captured by the Genoese off Navarino [20].

In addition to the Catalan dead, there were a number of prisoners who were transferred from Pera to Genoa where they remained in captivity for several years. One of these was Pere Escrivà, a merchant of Majorca who had been one of several Aragonese subjects aboard a Greek boat which was seized at the island of Tenedos in the mouth of the Dardanelles by the Venetians under Niccolò Pisani on Easter Friday 1351. Escrivà had subsequently followed the Venetians to Constantinople where Pisani had promised to refund him the value of the goods he had lost at Tenedos, but there, while aboard a Catalan galley, he was captured in the great battle of 13 February.

15 *Diplomatari*, doc. 178.
16 *Chronique*, 295.
17 *Diplomatari*, doc. 202; King Pedro (*Chronique*, 298) later reported 14 galleys lost.
18 *Documentos*, docs. 34-37.
19 Cantacuzenus, IV, cap. 31 (III. 230).
20 *Chronique*, 298; Santa Pau died on 9 March (Postscript *infra*).

On 2 September 1352 Pere Escrivà wrote a pathetic and rather ungrammatical letter, addressed from his prison in Genoa to the Doge at Venice: *Et fui captus, et sum ductus in carceribus*... He wanted the money Pisani had owed him; and later, after five years spent in prison, he began a long lawsuit, hoping to recover his losses [21].

Pedro of Aragon did not abandon the struggle against Genoa. On 18 May 1352 he gave instructions for the continuation of operations, and on 2 August he replied to letters from Cantacuzenus that he was resolved to sustain the war; he inquired if it were true that Cantacuzenus wanted peace with Genoa. On 20 August Pedro ordered that ten galleys under Mateu Mercer should join Bononat Dezcoll in Crete [22], but in fact the Catalan fleet had already left Greek waters. After sailing from Constantinople to seek supplies at Negroponte, Coron and Modon, Dezcoll had moved to the island of Cerigo, where provisions reached him. On 7 August he wrote from Crete to inform the Doge that he had decided, after taking council with his captains and also with Niccolò Pisani, to sail away; he was to be given an escort of four Venetian galleys. The Genoese had appeared off Crete and then moved westwards without making an attack, and Dezcoll considered it his duty to follow them. He formally acknowledged that he had received some 56,811 ducats from the Venetians together with biscuit, oars and other supplies, but he avoided payment on the grounds that he did not know the price of biscuit [23]. By September the Aragonese galleys under Bononat Dezcoll, Guillem Morey and Francesc de Finestres, were reaching their home ports with considerable spoil, including the profits from booty sold at Constantinople and in Crete [24].

At Constantinople the departure of the allies encouraged the Genoese and their Turkish allies to besiege the city, and Cantacuzenus had to accept a separate peace, dated 6 May 1352, which contained clauses excluding Venetian and Catalan galleys from Byzantine ports [25]. The Venetians subsequently made an abortive appearance off Pera, sinking some Genoese shipping and then withdrawing; the

[21] Venice, Commemoriali, IV, f. 213 (text in Appendix); VI, f. 73 v-76, 86 v, 90 v, 113, 139-140; *Diplomatari*, doc. 243.

[22] *Documentos*, docs. 34-37, and apéndice, docs. 25-29; *Diplomatari*, docs. 204-205.

[23] Venice, Commemoriali, IV, f. 212 v, 213.

[24] Details in *Diplomatari*, docs. 207-209.

[25] H. Riccotius, *Liber Jurium reipublicae Genuensis*, II (Turin, 1857), doc. 203.

Catalans were not involved [26]. Then on 10 October 1352 the Venetians also reached an agreement with one of their opponents, John V Palaeologus; by it they were to hold the island of Tenedos, which controlled the Dardanelles, for the duration of the war with Genoa [27]. Aragonese involvement in *Romania* had in effect come to an end, but the war continued and in August 1353 the Genoese were seriously defeated off Alghero in Sardinia by a combined Aragonese and Venetian fleet. Negotiations for the return of prisoners were already under way in March 1353 [28], and on 23 April 1354 Pedro of Aragon agreed to exchange his Genoese captives for Aragonese subjects in prison at Genoa, most of whom had been captured in *Romania* [29]. Meanwhile the Aragonese alliance with Venice was breaking down in mutual recriminations; Pedro of Aragon claimed that Venice owed him money, while the Venetians accused him of refusing to send his fleet further east than Sicily [30]. In fact, the Aragonese never again intervened in force in *Romania* and Genoa's position there was strengthened; in November 1354 the Genoese defeated a Venetian fleet off Modon in Southern Greece.

There were however a number of Catalans who remained in Constantinople. The contemporary historian Nicephorus Gregoras reported that the Catalans had fought harder than anyone, falling on the enemy in hand-to-hand conflict as if in a land battle, so that some ships sank from the sheer weight of men leaping on them in the darkness. He described how men who had been pitched ashore from galleys which had hit rocks wandered helplessly around unable to speak the language, some dying of wounds or collapsing on the sands, while others staggered along the road to Constantinople where they found help [31]. The surviving Aragonese galleys also landed their wounded in the capital to be cared for by the citizens and hospitals, and Cantacuzenus wrote a graphic account of these unclothed starving Catalans, who were scarcely able to move on account of the

[26] Lorenzo de Monacis, 214-215, and Gregoras, XXVII, cap. 55 (III. 171-172), but neither mentioned any Catalan participation.

[27] G. Thomas, *Diplomatarium Veneto-Levantinum,* II (Venice, 1899), doc. 8.

[28] Venice, Misti, XXVI, f. 111 v.

[29] Venice, Commemoriali, V, f. 15: *quod cum plures* [Catalani] *sunt capti in Janue et maior pars in bello Romanie.* Cf. *Diplomatari,* p. 303, n. 2.

[30] Venice, Commemoriali, V, f. 29-33; details of these and other documents here cited are registered, but unreliably, in R. Predelli, *I libri commemoriali della Republica di Venezia: regesti,* II (Venice, 1878), 223-225 *et passim.*

[31] Gregoras, XXVI, caps. 22-23 (III. 88-89).

cold and hunger to which, according to Cantacuzenus, they had been condemned by Niccolò Pisani, whom he accused of being interested only in the welfare of his own Venetians. Many of the Catalans, full of gratitude to the Greeks, subsequently left on their own ships, and two thousand of them whose vessels had been destroyed were sent home by Cantacuzenus; over three hundred of the Catalans voluntarily remained in Constantinople to serve the emperor, who later praised their warlike qualities [32]. These mercenaries attracted little attention in distant Catalunya. Pons de Santa Pau informed King Pedro in his letter of 2 March that the crews of ten out of the twelve lost galleys had reached Constantinople under cover of darkness, and Pedro's own chronicle briefly stated that the Greeks had saved a number of the galleys which had been thrown onto the shore [33]. Some of the survivors made their way to the Catalan Duchy of Athens, and during the summer Bononat Dezcoll tried to get them to rejoin the fleet in Crete [34]. Those who took service with Cantacuzenus must simply have been abandoned.

There was a long-established mercenary tradition among the Catalans, many of whom had served the Muslim rulers of North Africa or fought in Sicily and Italy [35]. Despite the unhappy history of the Catalans engaged by Andronicus II in 1303, Cantacuzenus put his trust in some of the survivors of the battle in the Bosphorus. According to Nicephorus Gregoras, some five hundred of them, who had reached Constantinople «naked and begging for help», were armed and organized as a bodyguard by Cantacuzenus, who mistrusted his own people [36]. The leader of this force, a certain *Ioannes* Peralta, had a strange career. He had served Cantacuzenus during his stay in Serbia and in the civil war from 1342 onwards [37], and he was a com-

[32] CANTACUZENUS, IV, cap. 30 (III. 225-228).

[33] *Diplomatari*, doc. 202; *Chronique*, 298. LORENZO DE MONACIS, 214, reported that the crews of only 7 out of 12 galleys were saved. Apart from A. RUBIÓ I LLUCH, *La expedición y dominación de los catalanes en Oriente juzgados por los griegos*, «Memorias de la Real Academia de Buenas Letras de Barcelona», 4 (1887) 67-68, and a few passing references (eg. NICOLAU, 129), modern historians have ignored these Catalans, whose history is known only through Cantacuzenus' account and some references in Gregoras. Cantacuzenus wrote a biased personal apologia, but much of his information is correct.

[34] *Diplomatari*, doc. 205.

[35] C. DUFOURCQ, *L'Espagne catalane et le Maghrib au XIIIe et XIVe siècles* (Paris, 1966); Ma. T. FERRER I MALLOL, *Mercenaris catalans a Ferrara: 1307-1317*, «Anuario de Estudios medievales», 2 (1965).

[36] GREGORAS, XXVII, cap. 30 (III. 151).

[37] CANTACUZENUS, IV, cap. 41 (III. 301-302).

petent architect who assisted in the reconstruction of the dome of the great church of Santa Sophia in Constantinople following the earthquake of 1346 [38]. Though presumably of Catalan origin, Peralta probably came from Sicily rather than Catalan Athens, and he may have been a kinsman of Guglielmo de Peralta Count of Caltabellotta, who married Leonora the daughter of Giovanni di Randazzo, titular Duke of Neopatras and Athens. Other members of this family who moved to Greece were Matteo de Peralta, who became Vicar-General of the Duchy of Athens in 1370, and Galcerán de Peralta, who in 1371 was confirmed in his office of Castellan of the castle on the Acropolis at Athens [39].

The Catalans must have seen much service in the disturbed period from 1352 to 1354. For example, when John V Palaeologus seized Adrianople in the autumn of 1352 and besieged the citadel, Cantacuzenus rushed with his Turkish and Catalan troops to relieve the town, which they then plundered [40]. This reliance on barbarian Turks and schismatical Latins increased Cantacuzenus' unpopularity, and Nicephorus Gregoras described how deeply the Greeks hated the foreign mercenaries [41]. At the end of 1354 the number of Catalan guards available in the palace amounted to about a hundred [42], and this reliable band must have been of great value to Cantacuzenus, who was otherwise heavily dependent on his Turkish allies. When Palaelogus fought his way into Constantinope on the night of 22 November 1354, Cantacuzenus' military advisers encouraged him to resist and, as he himself reported, the most insistent were his Catalan mercenaries who urged him to lead them out against Palaeologus, for they were sure that they could easily drive him out of the city. The mob rose in support of Palaeologus and attacked the fortified area of the imperial palace, but the Catalans broke out and drove the rioters back, burning down some of the houses in front of the palace. On 24 November however Cantacuzenus came to terms with Palaeologus and agreed to hand over the almost impregnable for-

[38] C. Mango, *Materials for the Study of the Mosaics of St. Sophia at Istanbul* (Washington, 1952), 67-68; thirteen ribs repaired by Peralta and the Greek architect Astros have been identified. Mango, like most writers on these repairs, somewhat misleadingly describes Peralta as an Italian called Giovanni.

[39] References in K. Setton, *Catalan Domination of Athens: 1311-1388* (Cambridge, Mass., 1948), 150-151; Peralta's career remains largely obscure.

[40] Cantacuzenus, IV. cap. 33 (III. 243-245).

[41] Gregoras, XXVIII, cap. 2 (III. 177).

[42] According at least to Gregoras, XXIX, cap. 28 (III. 242).

tress at the Golden Gate which was manned with his Catalan guards.

Three days later Cantacuzenus went to persuade the sturdy garrison of the Golden Gate to surrender. The Catalans welcomed the emperor and offered to protect him, for they thought that the fighting was still going on and that Cantacuzenus was expecting reinforcements, and they were confident that they had enough supplies to hold the fortress for three years. They begged Cantacuzenus not to give in, their leader Peralta recalling his own long and faithful service to the emperor in the face of many dangers. When Cantacuzenus insisted, the Catalans asked for time to consider, and while he remained in the courtyard they went inside the citadel to deliberate. Peralta wanted Cantacuzenus to renounce his agreement with Palaeologus and to stay and hold out with them, or to go back to his palace and let them resist on their own; alternatively, if Cantacuzenus was determined to hand over the fortress, he should first secure them a safe and honourable discharge. The Catalans accepted the advice of Peralta, knowing him to be a loyal supporter of Cantacuzenus, but when they bolted the gates of the fortress and announced their decision from the battlements Cantacuzenus was furious. He addressed the Catalans, so he claimed, in «the Latin language», presumably in Italian, asking them if they acknowledged him as their master, and they replied that he was their lord. He then threatened to write to their king denouncing each by name as a traitor and mutineer who had disobeyed his commands, so that they would be dishonoured and outlawed for ever. At this the Catalans surrendered, and on the next day John V Palaelogus drove them out of their fortress [43].

John Cantacuzenus abdicated on 10 December, and the subsequent fate of his Catalan followers was not the concern of any contemporary; they remained anonymous and Cantacuzenus himself gave no more information about them in his memoirs. The company must have disbanded. Some perhaps returned to Sicily or Spain; others may have joined their fellow Catalans at Athens; a few possibly remained to serve John V Palaeologus. One or two Catalans may even have joined the Turks: a Latin architect who was also familiar with Byzantine building methods certainly played some part in designing the Westernized semi-Gothic façade of the mosque at

[43] Cantacuzenus, IV, caps. 39-41 (III. 286-287, 290-293, 300-304); D. Nicol, *The Abdication of John VI Cantacuzene*, «Byzantinische Forschungen», 2 (1967).

Bursa built for Murad I in the years after 1361 [44], while the author of the Catalan version of an Oriental historical romance, the *Història de Jacob Xalabín* which was apparently written soon after 1389, was possibly a Catalan in Turkish service [45]. At Constantinople itself the Genoese were in the ascendant, and though peace of a sort came in 1355 it is doubtful if there were many Catalans settled there in the following decade.

Appendix

Exemplum litterarum missarum per Petrum [46] scribanum de maiolica pro damnis de quibus conqueritur.

Illustri magnificentie vestre domine Dux veneticorum, ac vestri prudenti Consilio, supplicatur pro parte vestri servitoris, Petrus scribanus de civitate maioliche. Cum eram super quodam navem Grecorum, et dicta navis erat quodam homo nomine Vopulo, et dominus Nicolaus pisanus Capitaneus galee quatuordecim communis Venetie, capit dictam navem ad locum ubi dicitur tenedum, et me derobavit in rauba et denarios tot et tantum que valebat florinos quatuor centum auri, et me conquerivi coram dicto domino Nicolao, dicendo quod eram de civitate mayoliche, et quod ego et omnes subditi domini Regis Aragonensius eramus amici et servitores communis venetie. Et dictus dominus Nicolaus vidit et hoc cognovit per veritatem, et fecit scribere in suo libro nomen meum et illud quod me derobavit, et inter aliis rebus que ipse fecit scribere, fecit scribere florenos auri centum quadraginta octo quod habebam. Et dictus dominus Nicholaus promisit me de restituere omnia que me derobavit quando fuisset in Constantinopoli, et ego eundo super galeis domini nostri domini Regis Aragonensis una cum dicto domino Nicolao et cum galeis armate communis Venetie in Constantinopoli, Invenimus ad dies .xiij. februarij Galee armate communis Janue. Et fui captus, et sum ductus in carceribus communis Janue. Cum ego non possum esse coram vestri magnificentie, Ideo quod sum in dictis carceribus, Rogo magnificentie vestre quod placeat facere quod dicta mea bona me derobata per dictum dominum Nicolaum fiat depositata penes dominis procuratoribus communis vestri Venetie, Ad hoc quod fiat salve, quod quando placuerit domino deo ego refiebo de carceribus ubi sum, et coram vestri magnificentie accedam.

Data Janue in carceribus malpage. M.ccc.lij. die secundo septembris.

Venice, Archivio di Stato; Libri Commemoriali, vi, f. 213.

[44] U. Vogt-Göknil, *Living Architecture: Ottoman* (New York, 1966), 48-49.

[45] *Història de Jacob Xalabín*, ed. A. Pacheco (Barcelona, 1964).

[46] Ms: *Nicolaum.*

Postscript

Señorita Mercedes Costa most generously supplied references to certain documents, some of them to be published, which primarily concern Venetian-Aragonese relations and the preparations for war, but which provide a few details bearing more directly on the present topic [47].

On 20 March 1351 King Pedro rather naively wrote urging both Cantacuzenus and Palaeologus to join the coalition against Genoa [48], and on 30 July the Doge informed the Pope that Venice had made alliances with Aragon and with the *Imperator Constantinoplis.* On 3 March 1352 the Doge retailed to Pedro news of the allied fleet as reported from Crete on 31 December 1351, and only on 21 April did he write to the king about the battle of 13 February, giving the date of Santa Pau's death *morte naturali* as 9 March. The letter of 21 April also referred to an anti-Genoese pact between Cantacuzenus and Palaeologus:

> Habemus etiam quod Imperator Constantinopolis, ad honorem nostrum et vestrum exposuit et exponit cotidie liberaliter personam suam et gentes suas, et quod est optime dispositus ad perseverandum constanter ad omnia que cedant in nostrum honorem et confusionem hostium iamdictorum. Et quod Imperator Iuvenis est concors cum Imperatore Catacuseno, et fuit in Constantinopoli, ac juramento firmavit et approbavit unionem nobiscum, et est similiter bene dispositus ad felicem exitum agendorum [49].

[47] «A propósito de la batalla del Bósforo: 1352», presented to the Convegno on *Venezia e il Levante fino al secolo* XV (Fondazione Georgio Cini, Venice; June 1968).

[48] Barcelona, Archivo de la Corona de Aragón, Reg. 1065, f. 50-50 v.

[49] Barcelona, Archivo de la Corona de Aragón, Pergaminos extra inventario de Pedro III, 1031 (30 July 1351), 1053, 1054 (3 March 1352), 1075 (21 April 1351).

X

VENEZIA E IL PRINCIPATO DI ACAIA: SECOLO XIV

La grande ricchezza di fonti negli archivi e nelle biblioteche di Venezia ci ha fornito una serie di idee generali sulla *Romania* veneziana.[1] È certo che, anzichè occupare i vasti territori sui quali essi poterono accampare diritti dopo la crociata del 1204, i Veneziani evitarono una gran parte dei problemi e delle spese dell'amministrazione coloniale, stabilendosi solo in alcune basi lungo la rotta per i ricchi mercati orientali. Creta fu la principale colonia del loro grande impero marittimo, mentre essi fondarono scali a Modone e Corone nel Peloponneso sud-occidentale, inviandovi coloni latini e instaurandovi una efficiente amministrazione locale, sul modello e sotto lo stretto controllo del governo metropolitano. L'importanza di Modone e Corone, che non facevano parte del Principato di Acaia, e delle altre basi veneziane che circondavano la Morea, derivava non solo dal commercio con l'Oriente, ma dal fatto che esse erano centri di un colonialismo di tipo indiretto che sfruttava economicamente il Principato di Acaia. Per certi aspetti, quindi, la posizione veneziana in Acaia era diversa da quella nella *Romania* in generale. A parte questo, la politica veneziana del duecento dovette essere modificata nel trecento alla luce del crollo del dominio greco come di quello latino in *Romania*, e dell'avanzata dei Turchi ottomani nei Balcani. In generale le attività veneziane in Acaia, che non era sottoposta al dominio di Venezia, hanno suscitato meno interesse che non il colonialismo veneziano a Creta ed altrove, e molti problemi rimarranno

1. Vedi le numerose pubblicazioni di F. Thiriet, in particolare *La Romanie vénitienne au moyen âge: le développement et l'exploitation du domaine colonial vénitien* (*XIIe-XVe siècles*), Parigi 1959; è comunque bene notare che il suo sistema di *régestes* è stato ripetutamente criticato, per esempio da D. Jacoby, in « Byzantion », 36 (1966), pp. 627-634, e da U. Tucci, in « Rivista Storica Italiana », 70 (1968), pp. 131-137. Vedi inoltre S. Borsari, *Studi sulle colonie veneziane in Romania nel XIII secolo*, Napoli 1966. Ma nessuna di queste opere tratta in modo particolare l'argomento in questione. (Vorrei ringraziare vivamente la signorina Luciana Valentini, che ha curato la traduzione).

in ogni caso insoluti, fino a quando la stessa storia generale del principato sarà così oscura.

Un ostacolo generale sta nella difficoltà di scoprire come la politica coloniale si formò a Venezia, e come e quando venivano prese le decisioni governative. I documenti del Senato forniscono una quantità di dettagli; essi contengono in molti casi affermazioni esplicite circa i motivi all'origine degli accordi stessi, e riportano le cifre delle votazioni che indicano frequenti diversità di opinione. Eppure, mentre tanto è stato fatto per illustrare la storia economica di Venezia,[2] non esiste un'analisi veramente soddisfacente della situazione socio-politica.[3] Uno dei risultati di questa deficienza è la tendenza ingannevole a generalizzare le abitudini veneziane, a parlare sempre in termini di « stato » o di « governo », a pensare ad una inesorabile, monolitica oligarchia anzichè ai singoli individui, fazioni ed interessi. E questa tendenza è accentuata dal fatto che il problema può essere studiato soprattutto sulla base dei documenti emanati dal governo centrale stesso.

I Principi di Acaia erano normalmente cadetti della casa di Angiò, che dominava il Regno di Napoli; essi erano anche Principi di Taranto, e per tanto risiedevano in Italia meridionale. La propria potenza marinara fu il fattore decisivo che permise a Venezia di dominare le acque del Golfo Adriatico che separava questi due principati, di escludere i Genovesi sia dell'Adriatico che dalla Morea, di proteggere le sue rotte mercantili, e di imporre quasi un monopolio in Puglia, dove essa aveva considerevoli privilegi ed interessi commerciali. La posizione di Venezia in Acaia deve essere esaminata sullo sfondo di questa sua egemonia adriatica, e delle sue relazioni con gli Angioini in tutta l'Italia. Il governo veneziano poteva imporre blocchi e minacciare di

2. Cfr. F. C. Lane, *Recent Studies on the Economic History of Venice*, in « Journal of Economic History », 23 (1963), che esamina le opere di G. Luzzatto, R. Cessi ed altri.

3. Ma vedi l'interessante opera di G. Cracco, *Società e stato nel medioevo veneziano*, Firenze 1967, che ha iniziata una tale analisi, anche se essa non si riferisce particolarmente alla Morea.

richiamare i suoi mercanti dalla Puglia e dall'Acaia. C'era una vera e propria pirateria, da ambo le parti, ed i mercanti veneziani e le autorità angioine si odiavano tanto che tutta una serie di trattati ufficiali non riuscirono mai ad evitare che essi si attaccassero e provocassero a vicenda.[4] I Veneziani si imposero sempre più; e nel 1376, quando il console veneziano a Clarenza, la sede del governo del principato, riferì che il *bailli* o governatore angioino opprimeva i mercanti di Venezia, Giovanna d'Angiò fu subito costretta a sostituire il *bailli* ed a confermare i vantaggiosi privilegi dei Veneziani.[5]

La politica veneziana procedeva abilmente fra collaborazione, minaccia e velata ostilità. Ogni tanto Venezia si univa in coalizioni contro i Turchi, ma si rifiutò costantemente di aiutare gli Angioini nei loro tentativi di recuperare il Ducato di Atene usurpato dai Catalani. Quando nel 1321 i baroni di Acaia dovettero fronteggiare la disintegrazione del governo angioino, un partito pro-veneziano, guidato dal Cancelliere Beniamino di Calamata, chiese a Venezia di assumersi il governo del principato, ma la repubblica non accettò.[6] Solo dopo il crollo definitivo del potere angioino in Grecia, Venezia fu costretta, dal 1380 in poi, a cambiare attitudine ed a trattare con le nuove forze nella Morea: con i mercenari navarrini, i quali avevano assunto il controllo di una buona parte del principato; con Nerio Acciaiuoli, il signore fiorentino di Corinto; e con i principi bizantini del Despotato di Mistra.[7] I Veneziani dovettero occupare nuove posizioni strategiche a causa della minaccia ottomana come della caduta del governo latino, mentre la presa di Corfù nel 1386 ebbe in parte lo scopo di escludere i Genovesi dall'isola. I Veneziani

4. R. Caggese, *Roberto d'Angiò e i suoi tempi*, 2 voll., Firenze 1921-1922, I, pp. 542-546 *et passim*; vedi inoltre É. - G. Léonard, *Histoire de Jeanne Ière, reine de Naples, comtesse de Provence: 1342-1382*, 3 voll., Parigi-Monaco 1932-1937.

5. R. Predelli, *I libri Commemoriali della Republica di Venezia: regesti*, III, Venezia 1883, pp. 129-131.

6. J. Longnon, *L'empire latin de Constantinople et la principauté de Morée*, Parigi 1949, pp. 311-312; ma la breve sezione sul trecento ha bisogno di una revisione.

7. G. Dennis, *The Reign of Manuel II Palaeologus in Thessalonika: 1382-1387*, Roma 1960.

appoggiarono crociate sia contro i Greci che contro i Turchi, quando fece loro comodo, ma più spesso preferirono trattare anzichè combattere; di fatto essi inviarono flotte molto più forti contro Genova che non contro i Turchi. Quando le infiltrazioni ottomane minacciarono perfino l'Adriatico, e la crociata contro i Turchi si identificò con la difesa della Morea, allora Venezia, con riluttanza e cautela, rafforzò le sue posizioni in Acaia. Argo e Nauplia furono acquistate dopo il 1388; Tino e Micono nel 1390; Atene nel 1395. Il rifiuto dei Veneziani di difendere Corinto ebbe come conseguenza che Argo fu saccheggiata dai Turchi nel 1397; e nei decenni che seguirono i Veneziani si sentirono obbligati ad assumere il controllo di Navarino, Patrasso e Lepanto.

Il Principato di Acaia comprendeva un certo numero di signorie feudali che erano in possesso di cittadini veneziani, quali il Ducato di Nasso, appartenuto per lungo tempo ai Sanudo; Tino e Micono, tenute dai Ghisi; l'isola di Negroponte che poco alla volta finì sotto il completo dominio di Venezia; e Boudonitza, appartenuta ad Andrea Cornaro e più tardi a Francesco Giorgio. Alcuni di questi magnati si dedicarono al commercio; altri si impegnarono nella politica. Quasi tutti mostravano una tendenza al separatismo. Essi tenevano a sottolineare la loro posizione di vassalli del principato per sfuggire all'ingerenza di Venezia, ma la repubblica riusciva di solito ad imporre ai suoi cittadini di compiere il loro dovere. Per esempio, il governo veneziano vinse la resistenza angioina assicurandosi che Fiorenza Sanudo di Nasso non sposasse un non-Veneziano come ella intendeva fare nel 1363.[8] Salvo poche eccezioni,[9] tali uomini non acquistarono mai nè terre nè castelli sulla terraferma della Morea. Laddove i Veneziani esercitarono un diretto dominio, come nel caso di Argo e Nauplia, essi dovettero governare la popolazione locale, organiz-

8. Vedi i molti articoli di R. -J. Loenertz che controbattono gli innumerevoli errori di K. Hopf; il libro del Loenertz sui Ghisi è in corso di stampa.

9. 17 marzo 1372: *Capta. Quod in favorem nobilis viri Johannis Michaelis pro quodam pheudo, quod nomine Elene uxoris sue, asseruit se tenere a principatu Achaye possint scribi litere domino imperatori Constantinopolis, Achaye et Tarenti principi, in forma que videbitur dominio.* (A. S. V., *Misti del Senato*, xxxiii, f. 150v).

zare la difesa delle città, e regolare le attività agricole dei contadini greci. Malgrado che le decisioni venissero prese soprattutto nella metropoli, i dirigenti delle colonie erano disposti, fino ad un punto sorprendente, a mantenere e adottare sistemi bizantini, piuttosto che creare guai, imponendo le loro proprie istituzioni.[10]

L'acquisto di Argo e di Nauplia da parte del governo veneziano è un esempio della difficoltà di stabilire come e perchè le decisioni venissero prese a Venezia. Quando la giovane Maria d'Enghien ereditò le due città verso il 1377, le fu subito fatto sposare Pietro, figlio di Federigo Cornaro di Venezia; nel 1388, in seguito alla morte di Pietro, Maria fu persuasa a vendere la sua eredità alla repubblica, che in seguito dedicò notevoli mezzi nell'intento di assicurarsi il possesso di questi territori che il Despota greco della Morea aveva occupato. La zona forniva vino, sale ed altri prodotti, ed un certo numero di Veneziani vi si erano stabiliti. Nauplia non era proprio essenziale per Venezia come porto, ma nel 1388 i Veneziani giustificarono il suo acquisto sostenendo che essa non doveva essere fatta cadere nelle mani del nemico; i documenti ufficiali sostenevano inoltre che queste città erano *situata et potentia ad adquirendum totum residuum Amoree*.[11] Ma se c'erano uomini che desideravano una espansione nella Morea, l'amministrazione in generale non aveva intenzione di acquistare il resto della penisola. Di fatto, anche dopo il grande disastro del 1396 a Nicopoli, quando gli Ottomani sembrarono avere la possibilità di travolgere l'intera penisola, il governo veneziano rifiutò di intervenire; esso rimase ad osservare gli eventi con sospetto, mentre gli Ospedalieri di Rodi occupavano parte della Morea e difendevano l'istmo di Corinto.[12]

Non è chiaro per quale motivo Federigo Cornaro, l'uomo più

10. D. JACOBY, *Un aspect de la fiscalité vénitienne dans le Péloponnèse aux XIVe et XVe siècles: le Zovaticum*, in «Centre de recherche d'histoire et civilisation byzantines: travaux et mémoires», 1 (1965).

11. A. LUTTRELL, *The Latins of Argos and Nauplia: 1311-1394*, in «Papers of the British School at Rome», 34 (1966).

12. A. LUTTRELL, *Venice and the Knights Hospitallers of Rhodes in the Fourteenth Century*, *ibid.*, 26 (1958), p. 210.

ricco di Venezia, il quale sfruttava le ricche piantagioni di canna da zucchero di Cipro, abbia deciso di investire le sue risorse in un luogo dove le prospettive economiche erano ovviamente limitate, e la situazione politica dei latini probabilmente suscettibile di deterioramento. Se egli voleva semplicemente creare una signoria semi-indipendente per il figlio, il governo veneziano, che normalmente non l'avrebbe aiutato, in questo caso, per motivi ancora sconosciuti, lo appoggiò. Solo una ricerca particolare sugli interessi e le attività economiche e sull'ambiente sociale e culturale di tali famiglie potrà fornire le risposte a problemi di questo genere.[13]

Ai Veneziani non interessavano solo le basi e gli empori nelle isole e nei porti. Venezia ed il suo retroterra necessitavano di viveri e di materie prime. La Morea, malgrado le guerre e le epidemie aveva una sana economia agricola, industrialmente sottosviluppata e di tipo coloniale, ma tuttavia ricca di vino, olio, miele, seta, sale, uva passa ed altri prodotti.[14] D'altro canto essa costituiva un buon mercato per i tessuti di qualità scadente prodotti in Occidente.[15] Questi fatti non sono sempre messi in rilievo. I Veneziani erano nella posizione di sfruttare il paese economicamente, evitando le complicazioni di un diretto controllo politico; il Principato di Acaia era quasi una colonia veneziana. Avremmo però bisogno di un maggior numero di dettagli circa i privilegi di Venezia, i suoi mercanti, i suoi cittadini residenti in Acaia, i prodotti scambiati, e così via.[16] Per ora disponiamo solo di notizie frammentarie: i sei Veneziani che perdettero tanto denaro quando portarono stoffe alla fiera di San Demetrio a Clarenza nel 1338,[17]

13. G. LUZZATTO, *Les activités économiques du patriciat vénitien*, nel suo *Studi di storia economica veneziana*, Padova 1954, iniziava tale studio.

14. P. TOPPING, *Le régime agraire dans le Péloponnèse latin au XIVe siècle*, in « L'Hellénisme contemporain », II ser., 10 (1956).

15. Che i Veneziani stessi abbiano esportato schiavi dal principato non è ancora chiaramente provato.

16. Cfr. V. HROCHOVÁ, *Le commerce vénitien et les changements dans l'importance des centres de commerce en Grèce*, in « Studi veneziani », 9 (1967), la quale delinea alcuni dei problemi, ma fornisce solo una documentazione frammentaria.

17. F. THIRIET, *Régestes des délibérations du Sénat de Venise concernant la Romanie*, I, Parigi-L'Aia 1958, p. 39.

o gli 80.000 ducati di mercanzie inviati a Patrasso nel 1400.[18] Sappiamo comunque che non esisteva un mercato di merci di lusso, e che in Acaia molti mercanti operarono probabilmente con un piccolo capitale, trasportando i prodotti di porto in porto. Anch'essi erano soggetti al regime metropolitano; erano, per esempio, normalmente obbligati a servirsi, per le loro merci, di navi veneziane.

I mercenari e gli ecclesiastici veneziani beneficiavano anch'essi delle opportunità offerte dalla Morea. Malgrado i Veneziani al servizio del governo angioino, quali Nicoletto Foscarini, che fu capitano ed ammiraglio a Clarenza nel 1348,[19] fossero abbastanza rari; Paolo Foscari di Venezia, arcivescovo di Patrasso, comunque, divenne perfino il *bailli* di Acaia. La carriera del Foscari, il quale era stato precedentemente vescovo di Corone, ci dimostra quanto vantaggioso potesse essere avere un Veneziano come arcivescovo.[20] Se si estraessero, dagli archivi Vaticani e da altri fonti, liste più complete dei vescovi e canonici della Grecia latina, apparirebbe chiaramente quanti uomini di chiesa, alcuni di essi non-residenti, sfruttarono i benefici greci. Un esempio eccezionale fu l'ammiraglio veneziano Carlo Zeno, il quale, in veste di canonico di Patrasso, ebbe in gioventù un ruolo importante nella guerra civile fra il 1364 e il 1370. Un caso più tipico fu invece quello di Rodolfo de Sanctis, altro canonico di Patrasso e dottore in diritto canonico, la corrispondenza del quale rivela sia i vari doveri ufficiali della curia vescovile di Patrasso, nei quali era coinvolto, sia le sue attività personali: l'acquisto di uno schiavo a Patrasso; l'amministrazione delle sue proprietà in Grecia; le sue amanti ed i suoi debiti.[21]

18. THIRIET, *La Romanie...*, p. 349.
19. 22 gennaio 1348: *Capta. Quod fiat gratia viro nobili, Nicoleto fuscareno, facto capitaneo et armiralo in Clarentia per dominum Imperatorem et principem Tarentini, quod cum quatuor famulis, et suis levibus arnesiis levetur, super galeis nostris unionis, et portetur ad partes clarentie* (*Misti del Senato*, XXIV, f. 58).
20. DENNIS, *The Reign of Manuel II...*, pp. 142-144.
21. G. DENNIS, *The Correspondence of Rodolfo de Sanctis, Canon of Patras: 1386*, in « Traditio », 17 (1961).

Che cosa la maggioranza dei Veneziani pensasse della Grecia è difficile da stabilire. Alcuni, certo, sapevano parlare greco. Lo studioso burocrate Paolo di Bernardo, il quale si trovava a Negroponte nel 1380 ed aveva portato con se alcuni dei suoi autori classici, scriveva lamentandosi del suo esilio fra barbari che mancavano di una cultura letteraria e non conoscevano nemmeno il latino. Eppure egli stesso annotò nella sua copia di Livio il passaggio: *Graecis, gente lingua magis strenua quam factis.*[22]

È ovvio che la presenza veneziana in Acaia deve essere interpretata nel più vasto contesto della sua politica sulla *terraferma*, in Puglia, ed altrove nell'Oriente latino. Di fatto, esiste il pericolo che la grande ricchezza di documentazione sopravissuta per quanto concerne la *Romania* veneziana possa produrre certe distorsioni, e che tutta la storia del Principato di Acaia possa essere vista troppo ed esclusivamente attraverso i documenti veneziani. L'attiva pubblicazione delle fonti veneziane, e la distruzione degli archivi angioini ha reso questo processo inevitabile; ma esistono altre fonti per la storia della Morea, e la riunione di questo materiale, per quanto possa essere una impresa lenta e faticosa, deve essere intrapresa. Da tale studio risulterà più chiaramente come Catalani e Navarrini, Napoletani e Fiorentini, Greci e Turchi, avessero anch'essi interessi nella Morea del trecento. Solo quando tutto il quadro sarà più completo, sarà possibile valutare pienamente la posizione di Venezia in Acaia.

22. L. Lazzarini, *Paolo di Bernardo e i primordi dell'umanesimo in Venezia*, Ginevra 1930, pp. 86-89, 136, 222-223.

XI

LA CORONA DE ARAGÓN Y LA GRECIA CATALANA: 1379-1394

El destino de la Grecia latina en el siglo XIV fue determinado en gran parte por el cambiante equilibrio del poder en el mundo mediterráneo. La desintegración del imperio bizantino ocasionó el enfrentamiento de los turcos otomanos, cada vez más poderosos, con los latinos de Grecia. El propio mundo latino atravesaba un período de crisis que comprendía la decadencia económica, la guerra universal y el cisma eclesiástico. Los franceses habían perdido su antiguo predominio en Grecia a principios del siglo XIV. La casa de Aragón, que reinaba en Cataluña, Aragón, Valencia y Mallorca, había ya reemplazado a los angevinos en Sicilia en 1282. En 1311 los almogávares catalanes —junto con aventureros aragoneses, valencianos, sicilianos y otros— conquistaron los ducados de Atenas y Neopatria; a fines de siglo unos cuantos mercenarios navarros controlaban gran parte de la Morea, como se denominaba entonces al Peloponeso. Pero fueron sobre todo los italianos quienes sustituyeron a los franceses. En particular, Niccolò Acciaiuoli se aseguró el señorío de Corinto, que se encontraba en la frontera meridional del ducado de Atenas, y su hijo Nerio se convirtió en el mayor enemigo de los catalanes en Grecia. Cuando en 1379 Atenas y Neopatria pasaron a depender directamente del rey Pedro IV de Aragón, la amenaza otomana era demasiado grave, el poderío latino en Oriente demasiado fragmentado y dividido, y la Corona de Aragón demasiado débil para que los ducados pudieran tener muchas esperanzas de supervivencia.

Durante el heroico período de las hazañas de los almogávares en Anatolia y los Balcanes, que llevaron al establecimiento del dominio catalán en Atenas después de 1311, los catalanes de Grecia no estaban ligados formalmente a la Corona de Aragón. Aceptaban, sin embargo, el flojo dominio de los gobernantes de Sicilia, que pertenecían a una rama de la casa real de Aragón, mientras que la Grecia catalana se beneficiaba de la protección de los reyes de Aragón. Los gobernantes aragoneses de Sicilia tomaron el título de duques de Atenas y Neopatria, pero raramente pudieron ocuparse de manera efectiva del gobierno y defensa de los ducados. A la muerte de Federico III de Sicilia el 27 de julio de 1377, Pedro IV de Aragón, que era a la vez suegro y cuñado del rey difunto, heredó la pretensión directa a los ducados griegos, porque el padre de Federico había excluido explícitamente a las mujeres de la sucesión en su testamento, y a Federico le sobrevivió únicamente una hija de quince años, María, a quien, sin embargo, dejó en testamento la corona de Sicilia y los ducados griegos [1].

La aceptación por Pedro IV de estos títulos y responsabilidades en Grecia señaló un viraje de la política de la Corona de Aragón. A principios del siglo XIV Jaime II de Aragón había mantenido en Oriente ambiciones que se debían a una mezcla de intereses comerciales catalanes, extemporáneos sentimientos de cruzada y peregrinación, y perspectiva imperialista en general. Jaime se había casado con una princesa chipriota y apoyó la invasión de la Morea por su pariente Ferran de Mallorca en 1315. Pero Jaime II había perdido con anterioridad el control directo del reino de Sicilia, y fueron los reyes sicilianos quienes trataron infructuosamente de utilizar a los ducados catalanes como un medio de extender a tierras griegas su pugna con los gobernantes de la casa de Anjou, que reinaban en la Morea, así como en Nápoles y en Provenza. Después de 1336 Pedro IV de Aragón concentró su atención en Cerdeña y Mallorca, aunque tenía pretensiones sobre Sicilia a través de su tercera esposa, Leonor de Sicilia, que murió en 1375. Este matrimonio podía haber proporcionado Atenas y Neopatria a Pedro IV, porque en 1357 Federico III de Sicilia legó tanto Sicilia como los ducados griegos a su hermana Leonor y a su esposo, Pedro IV, en caso de morir sin sucesión masculina ni femenina. En 1370 Leonor llegó a proponer el cambio de Atenas a Federico por unos 100.000 florines que éste debía pagar a los aragoneses por la dote de Blanca de Sicilia. Señalaba a Federico que él no obtenía ningún provecho de los ducados griegos

[1] La obra clásica K. SETTON, *Catalan Domination of Athens: 1311-1388*, Cambridge, Mass., 1948 [= SETTON], es muy detallada y contiene una bibliografía muy completa, pero trata de los acontecimientos de Grecia más que de la política aragonesa hacia Grecia, en tanto que el presente trabajo intenta aproximarse e interpretar estos acontecimientos desde el punto de vista de los que se encontraban en España. Debe tenerse en cuenta, sin embargo, que la obra de Setton fue escrita antes de la aparición de la magnífica colección de documentos de A. RUBIÓ I LLUCH, *Diplomatari de l'Orient català: 1301-1409*, Barcelona, 1947 [= *DOC*], aunque Setton utilizó plenamente los diversos artículos de Rubió en el «Anuari de l'Institut d'estudis catalans» y en otros sitios. Véanse también las importantes adiciones y rectificaciones en los artículos de R.-J. LOENERTZ, citados más adelante, y D. JACOBY, *La «Compagnie catalane» et l'état catalan de Grèce: quelques aspects de leur histoire*, «Journal des Savants» (1966); para otra bibliografía reciente: S. TRAMONTANA, *Per la storia della «Compagnia Catalana» in Oriente*, «Nuova rivista storica», XLVI (1962).

y era incapaz de defenderlos, en tanto que ella se proponía conservarlos para la Corona de Aragón; alegaba también que estaban perdiendo sus habitantes y que se enfrentaban con tal peligro, por parte de los turcos, que los catalanes de Grecia le habían solicitado repetidamente que se convirtiese en su señor feudal [2].

Tal vez fuese cierto que, en tanto que el control del Mediterráneo occidental aseguraba un equilibrio del intercambio económico entre los países de la Corona de Aragón, era del comercio con Oriente de donde podían obtenerse algunos de los más importantes beneficios. Pero en realidad el Mediterráneo oriental no podía convertirse nunca en un lago catalán. El poderío naval catalán era limitado en comparación con el de Génova y Venecia [3], y tanto política como económicamente los intereses fundamentales de la corona consistían en ocupar y retener las islas del Mediterráneo occidental —Mallorca, Menorca, Cerdeña, Sicilia, Malta— que eran esenciales para el importantísimo comercio con el norte de África y la ruta del oro y que estaban situadas en aguas limitadas por tierras cuyo control ejercían la Corona de Aragón o su rama menor de Sicilia. Los países de la Corona, en conflicto con Castilla en la península y con Génova en el mar, no tenían los recursos básicos ni la potencia naval para proseguir una política imperial en el Mediterráneo oriental, en tanto que los venecianos tenían buen cuidado de impedir el desarrollo de una base naval potente en los ducados catalanes. Desde mediados de siglo la población y la economía catalano-aragonesas estaban descendiendo, alcanzando su más bajo nivel hacia 1381, cuando los financieros italianos comenzaron a jugar un papel predominante en Cataluña. Los verdaderos intereses de la Corona en Oriente eran los de las ciudades marítimas: en la ruta de las especias a Egipto y Siria y, en menor grado, en la piratería. Los navíos y mercaderes catalanes viajaban a través de todo el Mediterráneo oriental, por el Adriático y el Egeo y en aguas de Cilicia y Siria, pero estos intereses catalanes no requerían la ocupación militar de posiciones estratégicas, porque podían conservarse utilizando medios que no fuesen militares: la alianza con Venecia, las embajadas a los sultanes mamelucos y las intervenciones diplomáticas en Aviñón, Nápoles o cualquier otro lugar. Después de la muerte de Federico III en 1377, Sicilia volvió a

[2] *DOC*, docs. 234, 323-324.

[3] J. Robson, *The Catalan Fleet and Moorish Sea-Power: 1337-1344*, «English Historical Review», LXXIV (1959).

la órbita aragonesa, y los ducados catalanes volvieron con Sicilia, pero en el momento en que Pedro IV se convirtió en duque de Atenas en 1379 la economía catalana no estaba en condiciones de sostener una política imperial efectiva en Grecia [4].

Desde el punto de vista comercial, los ducados catalanes fueron perdiendo importancia sin cesar durante el siglo XIV, a medida que la peste, el retroceso económico y la guerra disminuían la prosperidad de Grecia. Tebas y Atenas tenían escasa o nula importancia por lo que se refiere al comercio de lujo a larga distancia y, exceptuando tal vez algunas manufacturas de la seda, no poseían industria alguna. Los ducados no estaban situados en rutas marítimas importantes y el interior de Grecia sólo tenía un valor secundario para los catalanes como mercado de intercambio o de consumo. Sin embargo, Atenas podía haberse utilizado como base de los piratas catalanes, y se exportaban esclavos, especialmente por los mallorquines que traficaban en el puerto de Livadostro, en el golfo de Corinto [5]. Pero, el tráfico de esclavos no era un elemento importante en 1379 y, en efecto, en 1382 la Corona de Aragón inauguró una serie de actas prohibiendo que se hiciera esclavos a varios griegos de religión ortodoxa, hacia los que se mostraba una nueva y más humanitaria actitud [6]. Los mer-

[4] La obra de L. NICOLAU D'OLWER, *L'expansió de Catalunya en la Mediterrània oriental*, Barcelona, 1926, requiere ahora una profunda revisión. J. VICENS VIVES, *et. al.*, *La economía de los países de la Corona de Aragón en la Baja Edad Media*, «VI Congreso de Historia de la Corona de Aragón» (Madrid, 1959), págs. 103-113, afirman que «la Corona de Aragón se estableció *sobre la ruta de las especias* y que gran parte de su política estribó en la conservación y defensa de la misma». Esta tesis ha sido en general rechazada: F. GIUNTA, *Aragonesi e Catalani nel Mediterraneo*, II, Palermo, 1959, págs. 7-18, 163-192 *et passim*; F. SOLDEVILA, *Història de Catalunya*, 3 vols., Barcelona, 2.ª edición, 1962, I, págs. 403-486; II, págs. 487-510; P. VILAR, *La Catalogne dans l'Espagne moderne*, I, Paris, 1962, págs. 410-420, 461-490 *et passim*; A. BOSCOLO, *Geronimo Zurita e i problemi mediterranei della Corona d'Aragona: II, dal trattato di Anagni ai Martini*, «VII Congreso de Historia de la Corona de Aragón: Crónica, ponencias y comunicaciones», I (Barcelona, 1962), págs. 219-228; M. DEL TREPPO, *L'espansione catalano-aragonese nel Mediterraneo*, «Nuove questioni di storia medioevale», ed. «Marzorati» (Milán, 1964); S. TRAMONTANA, *La Spagna catalana nel Mediterraneo e in Sicilia*, «Nuova rivista storica», L (1966); C. DUFOURCQ, *L'Espagne catalane et le Maghrib aux XIIIe et XIVe siècles*, Paris, 1966, págs. 571-588 *et passim*; V. SALAVERT ROCA, *La Corona de Aragón en el mundo mediterráneo del siglo XIV*, «VIII Congreso de Historia de la Corona de Aragón» (Valencia, 1967); C. CARRÈRE, *Barcelone, centre économique, à l'époque des difficultés: 1380-1462*, Paris-La Haye, 1967, 2 vols. Ha sido tendencia de muchos historiadores el exagerar la importancia tanto política como económica de los ducados para la corona aragonesa y el interés regio hacia ellos. Han tendido también a concentrar sus estudios en el período anterior al reinado de Pedro IV.

[5] Además de los documentos de *DOC* y la escasa evidencia restante examinada en SETTON, págs. 35, 71-72, 85-87, 90-91, véase A. CAPMANY, *Memorias históricas sobre la marina, comercio y artes de la antigua ciudad de Barcelona*, I, Barcelona, 2.ª edición, 1961, págs. 264-265 *et passim*, donde permanece sin modificar la idea de que la posesión de los ducados facilitaba el comercio en *Romania* y Constantinopla. Cf. V. HROCHOVÁ, *Le commerce vénitien e les changements dans l'importance des centres de commerce en Grèce du 13e au 15e siècles*, «Studi Veneziani», IX (1967), pág. 19, propone que la ocupación catalana provocaba la oposición veneciana e impedía el desarrollo del comercio.

[6] C. VERLINDEN, *Orthodoxie et esclavage au bas moyen âge*, «Mélanges Eugène Tisserant», V [= «Studi e testi, CCXXXV] (Vaticano, 1964), págs. 427-440.

caderes independientes catalanes traficaban en el Egeo, pero cuando una flota aragonesa intervino contra los genoveses en Constantinopla en 1352, los catalanes se dieron cuenta de que los venecianos no eran dignos de confianza como aliados, y sufrieron severas pérdidas que les desanimaron de emprender nuevas expediciones de este tipo. La presencia de seis galeras catalanas cruzando el Egeo en septiembre de 1363 debió ser excepcional [7]. Entre tanto, la penetración progresiva de los turcos otomanos en el norte de Grecia y en Servia hizo que los mercados de especias de Beirut y Alejandría resultasen más provechosos y seguros que el de Constantinopla. El resultado fue que el comercio catalán a larga distancia, lo mismo que el de Venecia, se alejase cada vez más de la *Romania* y se volviese hacia *Ultramar*, a los puertos de Egipto y Siria y a las bases de Rodas y Chipre [8].

Los ducados no constituían la única preocupación de Pedro IV, porque los catalanes ejercían sus actividades a través de toda la *Romania*. Probablemente porque sus posesiones españolas estaban amenazadas, el rey emitió el 21 de febrero de 1378 una orden que prohibía a cualquier *fusta de rems* navegar más allá de Sicilia y Túnez o atravesar el estrecho de Gibraltar. Sin embargo, en enero y marzo de 1379 el rey dio licencia a dos *naus* de Mallorca para navegar hasta *Romania* [9]. Los catalanes se movían activamente en el Adriático, donde la propia Corona se procuraba algunas provisiones de madera. El 10 de enero de 1378, el senado veneciano permitió a un catalán, que actuaba como representante de Pedro IV, que alquilase en Venecia un bote para ir a Senj, en Dalmacia, a cargar madera con destino a Cataluña [10]. El 26 de febrero de 1379 Pedro IV protestó del secuestro en Dubrovnik de mercancías pertenecientes a varios catalanes y que un mercader catalán transportaba de Turquía a Barcelona [11]. En 1381

[7] F. Thiriet, *Délibérations des assemblées vénitiennes concernant la Romanie*, I, Paris, 1966, núm. 707 (septiembre, de 1363).

[8] A. López de Meneses, *Los consulados catalanes de Alejandría y Damasco en el reinado de Pedro el Ceremonioso*, «Estudios de Edad Media de la Corona de Aragón», VI (1956); *Correspondencia de Pedro el Ceremonioso con la Soldanía de Babilonia*, «Cuadernos de Historia de España», XXIX-XXX (1959); A. Luttrell, *Aragoneses y catalanes en Rodas: 1350-1430*, «VII Congreso de Historia de la Corona de Aragón: Crónica, ponencias y comunicaciones», II (Barcelona, 1962). Cf. F. Thiriet, *Observations sur le trafic des galées vénitiennes d'après les chiffres des incanti: XIV-XV siècles*, «Studi in onore di Amintore Fanfani», III (Milán, 1962). En efecto, faltan las estadísticas necesarias para medir la importancia del comercio catalán en *Romania* y a través de todo el Oriente. Las teorías actuales, que se basan únicamente en las referencias a la presencia de barcos y mercaderes, no resultan muy concluyentes, aunque Carrère, *ob. cit.*, proporcione datos en abundancia.

[9] *DOC*, doc. 370 y nota.

[10] Archivio di Stato, Venezia; Misti del Senato, XXXVI, fol. 49.

[11] Archivo de la Corona de Aragón, Barcelona [=ACA], Reg. 1486, fol. 41v-43; 78v-79; cf. Capmany, *ob. cit.* II, pág. 99. Algunos de estos documentos de interés primordialmente comercial no fueron incluidos en Rubió, *DOC*.

intervenía en favor de Simón Tanyana de Barcelona y de otros catalanes que habían sido atacados por los venecianos y habían visto sus mercancías capturadas o destruidas mientras se encontraban en territorio húngaro de Dalmacia, donde Tanyana actuaba en representación del rey comprando madera para remos, mástiles y lanzas con destino a las galeras reales[12].

Estas molestias se hicieron mas serias durante la guerra naval en gran escala entre Génova y Venecia, que duró de 1377 a 1381 y que produjo una serie de incidentes en los que se vieron envueltos mercaderes catalanes. En abril de 1379, en el Adriático, cerca de Ancona, los genoveses capturaron una coca barcelonesa que transportaba mercancías venecianas de Creta a Venecia; se llevaron también de la coca algunas mercancías catalanas[13]. En el Egeo tenían lugar parecidos incidentes. A fines de 1378 galeras venecianas obligaron a una *nau* de Barcelona a entrar en el puerto de Modon y robaron de ella ciertas mercancías que declararon ser genovesas. El 8 de mayo de 1379 unos mercaderes valencianos que iban en una *navis* de Barcelona se vieron forzados a atracar en Tenedos, donde fueron maltratados y sus mercancías tomadas por los venecianos[14]. El 13 de septiembre de 1379 los venecianos robaron los bienes de Pere Andrea, un comerciante de Mallorca, de ciertas galeras napolitanas que volvían de Beirut y fueron atacadas cerca de Castellorizzo, una isla situada al este de Rodas[15]. Algún tiempo antes de abril de 1381 los venecianos habían atacado a ciertos comerciantes mallorquines cerca de Corfú, cuando volvían de *partes Romanie*[16]; el 7 de mayo de 1381, en Quíos, una *galiota* genovesa armada en Pera se apoderó de las mercancías de un comerciante de Perpignan, transportadas en una coca de Mallorca[17]; y en octubre de 1382 los genoveses robaron cierta cantidad de azúcar propiedad de otro mercader de Perpignan[18]. Los catalanes y sicilianos actuaban también como agresores. En 1380 Luis Fadrique de Aragón, vicario general de los ducados catalanes, se apoderó de las mercan-

[12] Documentos de 1 de marzo, 28 de agosto y 13 de septiembre de 1381 (ACA, Reg. 1276, fol. 47 v-48 v; Reg. 1488, fol. 18-20). Los catalanes fueron atacados en «castrum Besche insule v[er]glen comitis segnien». VILAR, *ob. cit.*, I, pág. 418, escribe como si los catalanes no frecuentasen los puertos dálmatas antes del siglo XV.

[13] Protesta de 11 de febrero de 1380 (ACA, Reg. 1486, fol. 113 v-114 v).

[14] *DOC*, docs. 387-388.

[15] Protesta de 2 de septiembre de 1382 (ACA, Reg. 1488, fol. 68-72).

[16] Protesta de 3 de octubre de 1381 (ACA, Reg. 1488, fol. 27-28).

[17] Protestas de 14 de marzo y 3 de septiembre de 1382 (ACA, Reg. 1488, fols. 45 v-48 v, 66 v-68).

[18] Protesta de 24 de enero de 1383 (ACA, Reg. 1488, fols. 102 v-103). La captura tuvo lugar «in quadam insula vocata al mil».

cías de un barco de Ancona[19]. En marzo de 1382 Pedro IV ordenó que se indemnizara al griego Juan Lascaris Kaloferos por cierta cantidad de seda tomada en Sicilia por galeras catalanas en abril de 1381. Posteriormente, en 10 de febrero de 1383, el *consell* de Barcelona solicitó que Pedro pagase la indemnización, puesto que Kaloferos era conde de Zante y Cefalonia y los *consellers* temían represalias en estas islas, donde —decían— se dedicaban al comercio muchos súbditos de la Corona[20].

Las disputas comerciales pusieron también en contacto a la Corona de Aragón con Bizancio. Durante largo tiempo había existido en Constantinopla una comunidad mercantil catalana, y mercenarios catalanes, supervivientes en su mayor parte de la batalla de 1352, habían servido allí a Juan VI Cantacuzeno[21]. El 29 de septiembre de 1380, el hijo de Pedro IV, Juan, duque de Gerona, escribió al emperador bizantino pidiéndole la libertad de Joan Ferrer, mercader de Perpignan, que había permanecido ocho meses en prisión, aparentemente por no haber efectuado ciertos pagos. El 25 de febrero de 1383, los *consellers* de Barcelona nombraron un cónsul en Pera, el suburbio genovés de Constantinopla, pero el emperador Juan V protestó ante el nombramiento de un genovés, de modo que el 23 de diciembre de 1383, Pedro IV revocó el nombramiento y escribió prometiendo designar a un catalán o a un griego, como requería el emperador. Al mismo tiempo intercedía ante Juan V por dos mercaderes catalanes, Guillem Pons y un tal Canyelles, cuyos bienes habían sido requisados en Constantinopla durante la guerra de 1377 a 1381, bajo pretexto de que eran genoveses y por tanto enemigos. Guillem Pons había perdido gran cantidad de tejidos, y después de realizar una investigación, Juan V había escrito a Pedro el 26 de agosto de 1383 prometiendo su restitución si conseguía averiguar quien se había apoderado de las telas[22]. Estos dos comerciantes parece que hicieron en Pera ciertas promesas a Manuel II Paleólogo, el emperador en Tesalónica, que posteriormente utilizó el pretendido incumplimiento de estas promesas para apoderarse de mercancías catalanas. El 15 de mayo de 1386 Pedro escribió a Manuel acerca de las mercan-

[19] F. Thiriet, *Régestes des délibérations du sénat de Venise concernant la Romanie*, I, Paris, 1958, núms. 743 758, 788.

[20] *DOC*, docs. 508, 541.

[21] A. Luttrell, *John Cantacuzene and the Catalans at Constantinople: 1352-1354*, «Martínez Ferrando, Archivero: Miscelánea de estudios dedicados a su memoria» (Barcelona, 1968).

[22] *DOC*, docs. 426, 542, 556-557.

cías arrebatadas en Tesalónica a los catalanes Francesc Cerdà, Francesc Solanes, Joan Valls y otros, que estaban en una coca perteneciente a Jacob Furno, Pere Quintana, Guilabert Gurri y Guillem Tria, la cual fue también confiscada [23]. Una carta semejante, fechada en 18 de octubre de 1386, se quejaba a Manuel en nombre de Joan Guillaniu, que tenía mercancías en el mismo barco, negando las acusaciones originales hechas por Manuel acerca de promesas incumplidas como pretexto para el embargo. Pedro manifestaba su sorpresa ante tal acción de Manuel en una época de amistad entre la Corona de Aragón y el emperador de Bizancio [24]. En realidad a esto se reducía casi por completo en aquel momento el alcance de las relaciones entre las dos potencias.

La desesperada situación de los ducados catalanes en el momento en que Pedro se convirtió en duque de Atenas en 1379 se debía en parte a los propios latinos. El siciliano Roger de Lauria se había sublevado en Tebas en 1362, gobernando la ciudad como tirano durante cuatro años; después de 1370 la desunión política se vió acompañada por la desintegración territorial. La familia Enghien, que dominaba Argos y Nauplia y había heredado las antiguas pretensiones francesas a los ducados, sitió Atenas en 1371. En noviembre de 1372 el papa Gregorio XI convocó una asamblea de gobernantes cristianos, a celebrar en Tebas, para discutir las medidas a tomar contra los turcos, pero esta asamblea no llegó a reunirse nunca. En cambio las facciones de nobles catalanes luchaban entre sí en Tebas en 1373, y en abril de 1375 Nerio Acciaiuoli, señor de Corinto, había tomado a los catalanes el castillo de Megara, que defendía la frontera de los ducados contra los ataques procedentes del istmo de Corinto. En 1377 tuvo lugar la muerte de Federico III de Sicilia, a la que siguió la incertidumbre sobre quien habría de sucederle como duque de Atenas y Neopatria. Al mismo tiempo la situación general de los latinos en Grecia continuaba empeorando. En el verano de 1378 un *passagium* de la Orden de los Hospitalarios de Rodas, que había sido organizado por Gregorio XI, fue derrotado por los albaneses en Epiro. Los Hospitalarios retrocedieron para defender Lepanto y las tierras

[23] ACA, Reg. 1487, fols. 149 v-150 v.

[24] *DOC*, doc. 598, tratado en G. Dennis, *The Reign of Manuel II Palaeologus in Thessalonica: 1382-1387*, Roma, 1960, págs. 130-131. En 1389 Joan Guillaniu, mercader de Barcelona, tenía su domicilio en Rodas: Biblioteca Real de Malta, Valletta, Archivo de la Orden de San Juan, cod. 324, fol. 10. Carrère, I, pág. 263, n. 4, pág. 315, n. 3; II, pág. 640 *et passim*, proporciona ulteriores datos sobre el comercio catalán en *Romania*.

de la Morea que les habían sido arrendadas en 1377 por Juana de Anjou, reina de Nápoles y princesa de Acaya. El cisma en la iglesia de Roma a fines de 1378 significó que poca o ninguna ayuda efectiva podía esperarse del Occidente latino en general. Y sin embargo la amenaza inmediata para los catalanes procedía aún principalmente de sus vecinos más cercanos. Parece que Louis d'Enghien capturó a Joan de Lauria, señor de Stiris, en 1378. Probablemente fue en la primavera de 1379 cuando Tebas, careciendo de fortificaciones adecuadas y traicionada desde el interior, cayó en poder de Juan de Urtubia, capitán de un grupo de aquellos mercenarios navarros que quedaron perdidos en Albania, faltos de recursos y de jefes, en 1376. Estos navarros parecieron encontrar un aliado en Nerio Acciaiuoli, que pudo haber instigado el ataque contra los catalanes, así como en varios súbditos descontentos de los ducados y en ciertos Hospitalarios. En septiembre de 1379 Pedro IV había recibido en Barcelona algunas noticias de esto, y ese mismo mes comenzó a actuar formalmente como duque de Atenas y Neopatria [25].

Si bien Pedro tenía al menos algunas nociones de la difícil situación de los ducados y de su limitado valor económico, existían otras razones para hacerle cambiar su política anterior a la aceptación de responsabilidades en Grecia en septiembre de 1379. Los ducados catalanes podían resultar un útil peón en la embrollada diplomacia del Mediterráneo occidental, complicada como estaba por el cisma eclesiástico, en tanto que las pretensiones en Grecia iban unidas a sus pretensiones sobre Sicilia, y a la necesidad de conservar el control aragonés sobre esta isla [26]. En 1379 Pedro era un anciano dominado

[25] Los detalles en Setton, con enmiendas y adiciones en R.-J. Loenertz, *Athènes et Néopatras: régestes et notices pour servir à l'histoire des duchés catalans: 1311-1394*, «Archivum Fratrum Praedicatorum», XXV (1955), págs. 116-141, 193-194, 428-430; *Hospitaliers et Navarrais en Grèce, 1376-1383: régestes et documents*, «Orientalia Christiana Periodica» [= «OCP» (1956)], XXII (1956), págs. 329-334; *Athènes et Néopatras: régestes et documents pour servir à l'histoire ecclésiastique des duchés catalans: 1311-1395*, «Archivum Fratrum Praedicatorum», XXVIII (1958), págs. 66-70; A. Luttrell, *The Latins of Argos and Nauplia: 1311-1394*, «Papers of the British School at Rome», XXXIV (1966), págs. 41-43. Cuando Bernat Ballester dejó Grecia en la primavera de 1379, no había caído aún Tebas, como se ve claramente en los documentos de Pedro de septiembre; el 13 de septiembre el rey se dirigía a la *universitat* de Tebas como una de las ciudades de los ducados. Las noticias de la caída de Tebas llegaron probablemente con Francesc Ferrer de Salona hacia el 30 de septiembre, cuando Luis Fadrique era confirmado como vicario general; Pedro mencionó por vez primera la reciente (*nuper*) caída de Tebas el 19 de octubre de 1379 (*DOC*, docs. 372-384). La evidencia en G. Dennis, *The Capture of Thebes by the Navarrese* (*6 March 1378*), «OCP», XXVI (1960), deriva de una breve crónica que no parece muy digna de confianza; cf. como la rechaza K. Setton en *Cambridge Medieval History*, IV, parte 1, Cambridge, reedición, 1966, págs., 420, nota. No existe evidencia de que Louis d'Enghien fuese derrotado en Atenas en 1379, como se afirma en Soldevila, *ob. cit.*, I, pág. 485.

[26] A. Boscolo, *La affermazione aragonese in Sicilia dopo la morte di Federico il Semplice: 1377-1396*, «Homenaje a Jaime Vicens Vives», I (Barcelona, 1965).

cada vez más por sus sentimientos. La adquisición de los ducados significaba que al fin podría proclamar su dominio directo sobre todas aquellas tierras gobernadas por catalanes y aragoneses. El rey era también víctima en parte de su propia propaganda efectiva sobre la unidad de las tierras y súbditos de la Corona de Aragón, con sus lenguajes y sus lealtades comunes. Los catalanes de Grecia, que recordaban su país de origen, respetaban a la Corona de Aragón, que les había proporcionado ayuda mientras buscaba su fidelidad: por ejemplo, en 1351, durante la guerra con Génova, Pedro IV había apelado elocuentemente a los aragoneses y catalanes de *Romania* como a sus «naturales», cuya fidelidad a la Corona no había de ser disminuída por la distancia. Aún cuando los ducados estaban técnicamente sujetos al rey de Sicilia, Pedro había intervenido en sus asuntos en algunas ocasiones[27]. En 1360, después de haber protestado los venecianos de que los catalanes no tenían derecho a descargar madera en Livadostro, puesto que no formaba parte de los dominios de la Corona de Aragón, Mateu de Moncada, el vicario general siciliano de los ducados, declaró: «com entre les jurisdiccions del dit seyor rey d'Aragón e del molt alt príncep e senyor, senyor nostre don Frederich per la gràcia de Déu rey de Cicília e duch dels dits ducats, no.s dega fer neguna differència, com lo dit seyor rey nostre sia al dit senyor rey d'Aragón cosí e frare e fill e gendre ...»[28]

Era también significativo el aumento del elemento humanista en la cancillería real, acompañado de un interés literario de tipo clásico por Grecia, su idioma y su historia. El propio Pedro IV se interesaba por los autores antiguos, y sus secretarios insertaban en los documentos reales pasajes referentes a las gestas de los griegos, tomados de Salustio y de otros autores clásicos. Una sorprendente carta real, fechada en 11 de septiembre de 1380, llama a la Acrópolis, que había sido convertida en fortaleza, «la pus richa joya qui al mont sia». Además, en la introducción de textos griegos en Cataluña-Aragón, representó un papel preponderante el Hospitalario aragonés Juan Fernández de Heredia; éste, íntimo amigo del rey, se vio profundamente envuelto en los asuntos de la Grecia latina[29].

A la muerte de Federico de Sicilia en 1377, algunos al menos de

[27] Rubió, *DOC*, págs. XLIII-XLIV; Setton, pág. 37; Soldevila, *ob. cit.*, I, págs. 484-485.

[28] *DOC*, doc. 245.

[29] K. Setton, *The Byzantine Background to the Italian Renaissance*, «Proceedings of the American Philosophical Society», 100 (1956), págs. 64-69; M. de Riquer, *Medievalismo y humanismo en la Corona de Aragón a fines del siglo XIV*, «VIII Congreso de Historia de la Corona de Aragón» (Valencia, 1967).

los súbditos de los ducados griegos reconocieron a su hija María como duquesa [30]. Probablemente encontró apoyo en Tebas. Pudo existir un elemento que prefería la independencia al dominio siciliano o catalán, y continuaron las disputas locales y la rivalidad de las facciones [31]. Incluso antes de 1370 había existido un grupo pro-catalán que había intentado traspasar el ducado de Atenas a la esposa de Pedro IV, Leonor. Asimismo, la toma de Tebas, su capital, a principios de 1379, que marcó un momento decisivo en la decadencia de los ducados, subrayó la necesidad de un gobernante capaz de defender la Grecia catalana. Las *universitats* y gran parte de los barones y del clero de la Grecia catalana se volvieron a Aragón en busca de ayuda. Pedro no tomó ninguna medida para ratificar sus pretensiones en Grecia antes de la llegada de mensajeros que traían peticiones de ayuda en septiembre de 1379. Hasta cierto punto debió sufrir por la dificultad de conseguir noticias ciertas acerca de una situación distante y confusa en un país que nunca había visitado. Sólo como respuesta a estas llamadas, y después de haber fracasado en el intento de casar a su primogénito Juan con María de Sicilia, comenzó a actuar como duque de Atenas y Neopatria en septiembre de 1379 y a emitir un raudal de documentos referentes a sus nuevos súbditos de Grecia.

Entre los que reconocieron a Pedro en 1379 se encontraba Luis Fadrique de Aragón, conde de Salona —la antigua Anfisa— y señor de Zitounion, que era el primer magnate de los ducados y había sido nombrado vicario general de Atenas y Neopatria por Federico de Sicilia en 1375. El 30 de septiembre de 1379 el rey le dio instrucciones para que continuase gobernando los ducados hasta la llegada de un nuevo vicario general. En septiembre de 1380 Pedro aceptó los *capítols* y peticiones enviados por el capitán y *universitat* de Atenas, y por las *universitats* de Tebas y Livadia que se habían reunido en Salona a fines de mayo. Estos *capítols* insistían en la pobreza y apuros de sus habitantes, y Pedro aceptó sus demandas de incorporación perpetua de los ducados a la Corona de Aragón. En estos años el rey respondió a los requerimientos de nobles, castellanos, clérigos y otros habitan-

[30] LOENERTZ (1955), págs. 137, 202. Lo mismo ocurrió en Sicilia donde, por ejemplo, el testamento del magnate Manfredi Chiaromonte, fechado en 1380, titulaba a María como *Athenarum et Neopatrie ducissa*: texto en G. PIPITONE-FEDERICO, *Il testamento di Manfredi Chiaramonte*, «Miscellanea di Archeologia, Storia e Filologia dedicata al Prof. Antonino Salinas» (Palermo, 1907), págs. 332-339.

[31] Varios historiadores han interpretado las querellas internas de los ducados como una extensión de las luchas sicilianas entre una *parzialità catalana* y una *parzialità latina* siciliana, pero la evidencia no apoya tal interpretación. En efecto, los historiadores de Sicilia están abandonando esta interpretación; cf. V. D'ALESSANDRO, *Politica e società nella Sicilia aragonese*, Palermo, 1963.

tes, tanto latinos como griegos, con gran número de concesiones, donaciones, confirmaciones, licencias, pensiones y privilegios referentes a toda clase de asuntos, de mayor o menor importancia. Recompensó a los que habían sido fieles, y se ocupó de ciertos rebeldes y traidores, muchos de los cuales eran de origen siciliano. En particular concedió a Luis Fadrique, que poseía ya la fortaleza de Salona, tanto Siderocastron como la isla y castillo de Egina, que el rey confiscó a Pedro Fadrique de Aragón, el cual se había rebelado contra su primo Luis Fadrique. Pedro procuró terminar con las viejas luchas de facciones entre los nobles, la mayoría de los cuales le aceptaron como señor. Trató de contrarrestar la tendencia de las ciudades hacia la independencia comunal fortaleciendo los poderes del vicario general. Se interesó por las tierras de la iglesia y por los nombramientos eclesiásticos; intentó obtener de Livadia la cabeza de San Jorge. A pesar de su política neutralista de indiferencia ante el cisma, el rey solicitó del papa de Roma que levantase el entredicho que pesaba sobre los ducados y que colocase a Joan Boyl, el obispo de Megara, que había venido de Grecia para ver a Pedro, en el puesto de Simón Atoumanos, arzobispo de Tebas, a quien Pedro acusaba de ser uno de los que habían entregado traidoramente la ciudad de Tebas a los navarros.

El rey se lanzó también a una ofensiva diplomática menor. Buscó la ayuda de los venecianos, que protegieron a los refugiados catalanes en la isla de Negroponte; la de los albaneses sometidos al conde de Mitra —la antigua Demetrias; la del arzobispo de Patras; y la de Mateo Cantacuzeno, cuya hija Helena se había casado con Luis Fadrique, y que había enviado ya ayuda desde el despotado griego de la Morea, del que era entonces regente. El 10 de septiembre de 1380 Pedro solicitó de los Hospitalarios que lograran la libertad de uno de sus principales partidarios, Galceran de Peralta, el siciliano castellano de Atenas, el cual era prisionero de los navarros. A fines de 1380 o principios de 1381 los navarros tomaron Livadia, pero durante 1381 se trasladaron hacia el sur y se establecieron en la Morea, probablemente porque al fin habían llegado refuerzos a los ducados catalanes. Los doce arqueros que el rey, al recibir noticias de que Atenas había resistido un sitio, mandó enviar en septiembre de 1380 con el obispo de Megara para la defensa de la Acrópolis, representaban poco más que un gesto, pero en mayo de 1381 Pedro reclutaba trescientos soldados de a pie. Las noticias de la caída de Livadia habían llegado a Zaragoza en abril de 1381, y el 28 del mismo mes el rey designó formalmente a un gran magnate catalán, el poderoso vizconde de Rocabertí, Felip Dalmau, como su *vicarius, viceregius et locumtenens* en los ducados. Rocabertí había sido nombrado en principio en 13 de septiembre de 1379, pero en aquel momento acababa de ser enviado con una expedición a Cerdeña. Pedro le había dado instrucciones de navegar desde Cerdeña a Grecia, pero se retrasó, y su nombramiento, aunque permaneciendo técnicamente válido, quedó en suspenso. En efecto, el 30 de septiembre de 1379, tras recibir noticias de la situación en Grecia, que empeoraba rápidamente, Pedro dio instrucciones a Luis Fadrique de Aragón, que representaba ya la ley y el orden en los ducados, para que continuara actuando como vicario general.

En 1381 Pedro estaba preparado para afrontar considerables gastos a fin de enviar a Rocabertí con dos galeras a Grecia. Además de las numerosas cantidades de menor importancia para donaciones, pensiones y mensajeros, Pedro entregó a Rocabertí bastante más de 9.000 florines de oro para la expedición a Grecia. El 10 de mayo de 1381 dio instrucciones para que Rocabertí recibiese 1.500 florines para *certes lances*, suma que había de tomarse de las rentas eclesiásticas que técnicamente debían pagarse a uno u otro de los papas rivales. Los reacios representantes de Barcelona y de otros puertos fueron obligados a abastecer y proporcionar tripulación a las galeras, que habían de ser equipadas con la renta de un año del obispado de Lérida y con otros fondos. Otros pagos ulteriores incluían los 4.000 florines prometidos a Bernat Ballester de Tèbas; 4.000 florines para pagar a la tripulación de las galeras; y otros 6.000 florines concedidos a Rocabertí a fines de 1382. Aún cuando Pedro era lento para pagar sus deudas, todos estos gastos representaban un auténtico esfuerzo por parte de la Corona, hecho en un momento de grandes dificultades en Cerdeña y en otros lugares, y sin el respaldo de las ciudades catalanas ni de los nobles, que tradicionalmente habían apoyado la política de expansión mediterránea, pero que ahora demostraban escaso entusiasmo hacia una aventura en Grecia. En agosto de 1381 Pedro llegó a un acuerdo en Cerdeña, lo cual supuso la pacificación provisoria de la isla, de modo que pudo ocuparse de Grecia. El 6 de agosto el rey, irritado por el largo retraso, dio instrucciones a Rocabertí para que embarcase inmediatamente hacia Grecia, cosa que hizo éste. En julio de 1382 Rocabertí estaba ya de regreso en Barcelona. Había obtenido por la fuerza 1.000 ducados de varios florentinos de Cefalonia, había hecho naufragar una de sus galeras en Naxos y había rescatado a María, princesa de Sicilia, de Augusta, en la misma Sicilia. En la propia Grecia había acordado una tregua con Nerio Acciaiuoli y con los navarros y se había asegurado los castillos de Atenas y Neopatria, aunque había fracasado en el más importante de sus objetivos: la reconquista de Tebas. Los catalanes ya no se encontraban en tan inmediato peligro, pero habían quedado seriamente debilitados y, en un intento de remediar la despoblación ocasionada en los años anteriores, Pedro ofreció la exención de impuestos a todos los griegos y albaneses que se establecieran en los ducados. Los habitantes supervivientes de éstos habían sido incorporados a los países de la Corona de Aragón, y tenían que continuar viviendo conforme a los Usatges de Barcelona[32].

Después del regreso de Rocabertí en 1382, Pedro envió ya poca ayuda a los ducados, donde la situación empeoraba constantemente. A continuación del matrimonio del anciano rey con Sibila de Fortià en octubre de 1379, tanto las cortes, que se mostraban reacias a entregar dinero para las expediciones a Cerdeña hasta que sus agravios fueran resueltos, como los magnates, que veían con resentimiento la ascensión del clan Fortià, disputaron cada vez más agriamente con Pedro. Se oponía al rey su propio hijo Juan, que trastornó la política mediterránea de Pedro al negarse a contraer matrimonio con María de Sicilia. Enfrentado en su propia patria con la depresión económica, la quiebra financiera, la peste, la guerra y el descontento social, pocos recursos podía allegar Pedro para sus lejanos súbditos de Grecia. Ellos continuaban apelando a la Corona de Aragón, y recibían a cambio poco más que promesas. El 12 de septiembre de 1382 Pedro anunciaba ya que Rocabertí volvería a Grecia al año siguiente, promesa repetida con frecuencia. El 20 de junio de 1383 afirmaba que, aunque Rocabertí se había visto retrasado por las cortes y por los problemas de Cerdeña, estaba a punto de partir para Grecia con refuerzos. El 16 de septiembre, Pedro escribió a Rocabertí diciéndole que los ducados estaban en gran peligro y llamándole a su presencia, y el 23 de octubre, habiendo oído que Rocabertí estaba enfermo, envió a Bernat Ballester para que tratase con él acerca de los asuntos de los ducados. Al año siguiente sucedió lo mismo. El 20 de abril de 1384, Pedro escribió a su hijo Juan que aunque las cortes no habían proporcionado

[32] Los detalles en A. Rubió i Lluch, *La Grècia catalana des de la mort de Frederic III fins a la invasió navarresa: 1377-1379*, «Anuari de l'Institut d'estudis catalans», VI (1915-1920); Setton; y *DOC*, docs. 372-536, 711-717 *passim*. Adiciones y enmiendas en Loenertz (1955), págs. 138-152; «OCP» (1956), págs. 334-346; (1958), págs. 69-75. Loenertz (1958), pág. 69, describe equivocadamente a Pedro IV como un urbanista. Véase también R.-J. Loenertz, «Revue des Études Byzantines», XXIV (1966), págs. 230-232.

ayuda para Grecia, «el fet languiariassa tant que.ls dits ducats se porien perdre». Pedro afirmaba que Rocabertí estaba dispuesto a llevar tropas a Grecia y a adelantar 25.000 florines, siempre que se le dieran las garantías que pedía. El 30 de mayo de 1384 Pedro informaba a los catalanes de Atenas y a Helena Cantacuzena, la viuda de Luis Fadrique de Aragón, de que tan pronto como terminasen las cortes, se les enviaría un «gran esforç de gents d'armes e de ballesters» [33].

Una parte de las dificultades radicaba en los escasos deseos de Rocabertí de volver a Grecia. Rocabertí era un gran magnate catalán, un guerrero y diplomático experimentado, que había servido a la Corona durante largo tiempo, aunque se había enemistado con Pedro en varias ocasiones y había servido incluso a Enrique de Trastámara durante algún tiempo. Además, Rocabertí estaba estrechamente relacionado con el infante Juan, cuyo chambelán había sido desde 1371. Juan y Rocabertí estaban entre los dirigentes de la oposición de los magnates, y a medida que la disputa se iba agriando cada vez más, resultaba menos probable que Rocabertí dejase Cataluña para ir a Grecia como vicario general del rey, sobre todo si Pedro no podía proporcionar el dinero necesario [34]. Aparentemente Rocabertí había tenido intenciones de establecer intereses serios en Grecia, porque antes de dejar los ducados en 1382 había acordado con Luis Fadrique de Aragón, que poseía el condado semiindependiente de Salona y que era el jefe de los barones sículo-catalanes en Grecia, que su hijo Bernat Hug, conocido por Bernaduc, se casaría con María Fadrique, hija de Luis. Esta alianza, planeada probablemente para cimentar la unidad de los dirigentes catalanes de los ducados, así como para llevar Salona y Zitounion a la familia Rocabertí, fue apoyada por Pedro. El 18 de noviembre de 1382, a continuación de la muerte de Luis Fadrique, el rey escribió a Helena Cantacuzena, su viuda, ofreciéndole entregar de por vida el castillo de Siderocastron a María Fadrique si ésta se casaba con Bernaduc. Sin embargo, el matrimonio no llegó a efectuarse, tal vez porque la condesa viuda se daba cuenta de que el regreso de Rocabertí a Grecia era poco probable, o quizá porque deseaba retener el control del condado de Salona [35].

[33] *DOC*, docs., 520-521, 533-534, 546, 548-550, 552-553, 559, 562-563.

[34] S. Sobrequés Vidal, *Els barons de Catalunya*, Barcelona, 1957, págs. 222-225.

[35] *DOC*, docs. 525-528; *infra*, págs. 236, 250-251.

Pedro tuvo que enfrentarse a la negativa de su propio virrey de volver a Grecia, y el 30 de mayo de 1384 tuvo que escribir a Ramón de Vilanova, a quien Rocabertí había dejado en Grecia como lugarteniente, para persuadirle de que no abandonase Atenas. Pedro temía que la Acrópolis se perdiese si el hijo de Galceran, Albertí de Vilanova, sustituía a su padre al mando del castillo, pero a pesar de todo, en septiembre, Albertí dejaba España con rumbo a Grecia. El 30 de mayo, Pedro escribió también a Nerio Acciaiuoli, dándole las gracias por haber mantenido la tregua concertada con Rocabertí dos años antes y por la ayuda prestada en la defensa de Atenas [36]. En realidad Pedro apenas tenía idea de lo que estaba sucediendo en la lejana Grecia. Luis Fadrique de Aragón murió en 1382, dejando el condado de Salona a su esposa Helena, cuyo padre, el pro-catalán Mateo Cantacuzeno, murió también en 1383 en Mistra [37]. No había señales de ayuda procedente de España y en 1385 los ducados sufrían los ataques no sólo de griegos y turcos, sino también de Nerio Acciaiuoli. Desde su base de Corinto, Nerio disponía de unas setenta lanzas, ochocientos jinetes albaneses y numerosos soldados de a pie. Su poderoso aliado y yerno, Teodoro Paleólogo, que había sucedido a Manuel Cantacuzeno como gobernante del despotado griego de la Morea, no tomaba parte aparentemente en los ataques contra los catalanes. Los aliados venecianos de Nerio le alquilaron una galera que utilizó contra los turcos. En el mismo año Nerio atacaba también el condado de Salona, que invadió con grandes fuerzas de caballería, después de que Helena Cantacuzena rehusase casar a su hija María con el cuñado de Nerio, Pietro Saraceno de Negroponte. En julio de 1385 Nerio se llamaba a sí mismo señor del ducado de Atenas: *dominus Choranti et Ducaminis*. Allá en Cataluña, Pedro tardaba en comprender que Acciaiuoli era su enemigo. El 17 de julio de 1385, al escribir agradeciendo su ayuda a los navarros, que disponían de unos 1.300 jinetes con los que se oponían a Nerio y a Teodoro, Pedro mencionaba solamente a los «griegos y turcos» que, decía, atacaban diariamente Atenas [38].

En diciembre de 1383, Pedro enviaba a Bernat Ballester a tratar

[36] *DOC*, docs. 561-564, 568.

[37] R.-J. Loenertz, *La Chronique brève moréote de 1423*, «Mélanges Eugène Tisserant», II [= «Studi e testi», CCXXXII] (Vaticano, 1964), 419, n. 30.

[38] *DOC*, docs. 574-575; Setton, págs. 174-175; Thiriet, *Régestes*, I, núms. 639, 700, 707; R.-J. Loenertz, *Une page de Jérôme Zurita relative aux duchés catalans de Grèce: 1386*, «Revue des Études Byzantines» = «REB» (1956), XIV (1956), págs. 159, 161-163. Los venecianos alquilaron a Nerio una galera con la que según parece atacó a los turcos, pero las fuentes citadas por Setton, pág. 174, no parecen demostrar que Nerio ocupase el puerto de Atenas en el Pireo y las alturas de Munychia.

con el barón siciliano Guglielmo Raimondo de Moncada, cuyo padre Mateo de Moncada había sido una vez vicario general de los ducados, «sobre.l fet dels ducats de Athenes e dels capítols que vos nos donàs» y a convocar a Moncada a presencia del rey. En agosto de 1384, se dieron instrucciones a Guillem Torrelles y Albertí de Vilanova, que partían para *Romania*, de ejecutar ciertos *afers* reales [39]. Pedro estaba tratando acerca de los asuntos griegos con Juan Fernández de Heredia, maestre de los Hospitalarios de Rodas, los cuales tenían intereses en Grecia [40]. El rey planeaba también una expedición al mando de Galceran de Vilanova, quizá un pariente de Ramon de Vilanova, que había servido con Rocabertí en los ducados en 1381 y 1382. En 1385 Galceran de Vilanova presentó a través de Bernat Ballester proposiciones para emprender un *passatge*, y el 18 de julio Pedro aceptó el plan de Galceran y le llamó urgentemente a la real presencia. El 29 de noviembre Pedro escribió a Galceran diciéndole que «lo fet dels ducams de Athenes», que habían tratado juntos recientemente, había sido retrasado, pero que el negocio debía seguir adelante y que Galceran había de presentarse nuevamente ante el rey. El 4 de enero de 1386 el rey enviaba a Bernat Ballester a Galceran; Pedro había firmado los *capítols* presentados por Galceran a través de Ballester «sobre lo fet dels bacinets i ballesters que vos havets menar per haver e pendre la possessió del castell nostre de Cetines e de la Pàtria». Una vez más, parece ser que este proyecto no condujo a nada. El 29 de marzo de 1386, tras la vuelta de Ballester a Pedro con otros *capítols* de Galceran, Pedro aceptaba los nuevos *capítols* y de nuevo llamaba a Galceran urgentemente a su presencia [41]. El agente principal en casi todas estas negociaciones fue Bernat Ballester de Valencia, que había estado en Tebas en 1362, que era capitán de Livadia en 1367 y que poseía tierras en los ducados. En 1379, había actuado como procurador de Luis Fadrique de Aragón y de los catalanes de los ducados, y él había organizado probablemente el llamamiento al rey de Aragón, en un intento de salvar los ducados. Posteriormente había sido un intermediario activo en los tratos de Pedro referentes a los asuntos griegos [42].

Finalmente, el rey se vio obligado a destituir a Rocabertí. El 12

[39] *DOC*, docs. 554, 566 (suponiendo que *Ombertic* fuese Albertí).
[40] *Infra*, págs. 237-248.
[41] *DOC*, docs. 560, 576, 583, 585, 588.
[42] *DOC* (índice: vid *Ballester*); LOENERTZ (1955), págs. 189-192.

de septiembre de 1385 Pedro le escribió que Ramon de Vilanova estaba en peligro de perder la Acrópolis por falta de hombres y de provisiones. A petición de Ramon, el rey daba instrucciones a Rocabertí para que desligase a Ramon de su juramento de homenaje como lugarteniente del vicario general; afirmaba también que enviaría a alguien de su propia elección para sustituir a Ramon. Pedro repitió varias veces estas instrucciones y encontró inaceptables las primeras excusas de Rocabertí. El 6 de enero de 1386 Rocabertí escribió desde Zaragoza, protestando de su lealtad, pero señalando que Pedro le debía aún 5.000 florines y la paga de veinticinco lanzas utilizadas en su anterior expedición a Grecia. El rey le contestó desde Barcelona el 17 de enero, repitiendo sus instrucciones referentes a Ramon de Vilanova y ofreciéndose a discutir los agravios financieros de Rocabertí. Esto no solucionó nada y el 26 de junio Pedro informó a Ramon de Vilanova de que el vicariato de Rocabertí había sido revocado y que Pedro de Pau, que actuaba como lugarteniente de Ramon en Grecia, debía entregar los ducados al vicario general recién nombrado cuando éste llegase. El nuevo virrey era Bernat de Cornellà, un noble miembro de la casa real, pero no un gran magnate con recursos propios como Rocabertí. Pedro escribió a diversas autoridades en Grecia, incluyendo al arzobispo de Patras y a los navarros, excusándose por el retraso en el envío de refuerzos, prometiendo que Bernat de Cornellà llevaría fuerzas de a caballo y de a pie en la primavera y anunciando la llegada de Guillem de Cornellà para gobernar los ducados hasta entonces, pero en diciembre de 1386 Bernat de Cornellà seguía aún en España [43].

Sin embargo, Pedro podía ver que el retraso era peligroso. Helena Cantacuzena, atacada por Nerio Acciaiuoli y por los griegos, había roto el compromiso de su hija María con Bernaduc de Rocabertí, cuya llegada era claramente improbable, y había prometido a María con Esteban de Pharsalos, hijo del emperador serbio Simeón Uroš. Pedro, al escribir a Helena en 17 de agosto de 1386, le manifestaba su descontento por no haber casado a María con Bernaduc o con otro súbdito de la Corona de Aragón, pero reconocía que no podía culparse a Helena por haber buscado protección en otra parte [44]. Al mismo tiempo Pedro envió a los navarros una nueva petición de ayuda, agradeciéndoles la que le habían prestado en el pasado y tomándoles *per naturals nostres*. Sin embargo, el rey no parecía darse cuenta aún de que

[43] *DOC*, docs. 577-578, 584, 586-587, 590-597, 599.
[44] *DOC*, docs. 591; Loenertz, «REB» (1956), págs. 159, 163-164.

Nerio Acciaiuoli atacaba a sus súbditos. En enero de 1387 Acciaiuoli había penetrado en la parte baja de Atenas y, tras un sitio que duró más de un año, tomó al fin la Acrópolis el 2 de mayo de 1388 [45]. Entre tanto Pedro había muerto el 5 de enero de 1387.

Después de 1382 ninguno de los esfuerzos hechos por Pedro IV a fin de obtener aliados y asistencia para sus ducados consiguió gran éxito, pero tenía una posible fuente de ayuda en los Hospitalarios de Rodas y en su Maestre Juan Fernández de Heredia, que durante su larga y variada carrera había estado relacionado estrechamente con el rey Pedro. Este Hospitalario aragonés debía su pronta promoción y su afortunada carrera en Aragón a la influencia de Pedro IV [46], y había actuado durante muchos años como principal agente aragonés en la curia pontificia, encargándose de toda clase de negocios, diplomáticos o no, en Aviñón [47]. En 1375, la Corona de Aragón consiguió un cardenal en la persona de Pedro de Luna, y Fernández de Heredia perdió parte de su importancia como agente de Pedro en Aviñón. Al mismo tiempo se veía cada vez más envuelto en los designios papales, especialmente al ser nombrado jefe del *passagium* de Hospitalarios que Gregorio XI planeaba enviar para oponerlo a los turcos. Se produjo cierta frialdad, y Pedro y su hijo Juan opinaban que su protegido no hacía avanzar sus asuntos, pero no llegó a efectuarse una verdadera ruptura entre Fernández de Heredia y el rey [48]. El 24 de septiembre de 1377 el papa proveyó en Fernández de Heredia el maestrazgo del Hospital y poco después partía éste hacia el Epiro, en Grecia, con una pequeña expedición de Hospitalarios [49]. En los meses siguientes tanto Pedro como Juan escribieron a Fernández de Heredia manifestando su complacencia ante esta elección, su interés por el *passagium* de los Hospitalarios y su pesar por su fracaso y por la captura del maestre cerca de Arta, en Epiro, en 1378 [50]. Juan contribuyó, además, al res-

[45] *DOC*, docs. 593, 600, 620-622; cf. SETTON, págs. 175-182.

[46] A. LUTTRELL, *The Aragonese Crown and the Knights Hospitallers of Rhodes: 1291-1350*, «English Historical Review», LXXVI (1961), págs. 13-19.

[47] A. LUTTRELL, *Juan Fernández de Heredia at Avignon: 1352-1367* (de próxima aparición).

[48] J. DELAVILLE LE ROULX, *Les Hospitaliers à Rhodes jusqu'à la mort de Philibert de Naillac, 1310-1421*, Paris, 1913; J. VIVES, *Juan Fernández de Heredia, Gran Maestre de Rodas: vida, obras, formas dialectales*, «Analecta Sacra Tarraconensia», III (1927). Otros numerosos detalles en A. LUTTRELL, *Juan Fernández de Heredia Castellan of Amposta (1346-1377), Master of the Knights of St. John at Rhodes (1377-1396)*, tesis doctoral sin publicar, Oxford, 1959.

[49] A. LUTTRELL, *Interessi fiorentini nell'economia e nella politica dei Cavalieri Ospedalieri di Rodi nel Trecento*, «Annali della Scuola Normale Superiore di Pisa: lettere, storia e filosofia», IIª ser., XXVIII (1959), págs. 322-324.

[50] *DOC*, doc. 369; VIVES, *ob. cit.*, docs. 15, 19; ACA, Reg. 1256, fol. 123; Reg. 1261, fol. 65 v, 91 v-92; Reg. 1745, fol. 33-33 v.

cate de su portaestandarte, Luis Cornell, que tomó parte en la campaña y resultó apresado [51].

En mayo de 1378, Pedro prohibió a cierto número de Hospitalarios abandonar sus dominios para participar en el *passagium* a Grecia [52]. Tales prohibiciones eran cosa corriente, especialmente en momentos de peligro para Aragón, y no indicaban oposición por parte del rey a la política del Hospital en Grecia; Pedro había impedido a los Hospitalarios aragoneses emprender viaje para reunirse con Fernández de Heredia en Provenza en septiembre de 1376, y las prohibiciones de 1378 fueron impuestas claramente como medida de seguridad contra un ataque al reino [53]. El maestre había sido liberado de la cautividad y estaba en Clarenza, en la Morea, en 1 de marzo de 1379 [54]; el 20 de mayo seguía aún allí [55], pero en 9 de agosto había llegado ya a Rodas [56]. En algún momento Pedro envió una petición a Fernández de Heredia. Hizo referencia a esta petición en una carta posterior, de 2 de agosto, en la que mencionaba su complacencia ante la recién llegada noticia de la liberación del maestre; enviaba además un mensajero para llamarle a su presencia a fin de tratar importantes asuntos [57]. El negocio en cuestión pudo haber sido el cisma eclesiástico o algún problema doméstico; el interés activo de Pedro por los ducados griegos no empezó hasta septiembre de 1379.

Hasta septiembre de 1380, Pedro no expresó sospechas sobre las actividades de los Hospitalarios. Las misivas reales dirigidas en 10 de septiembre a los Hospitalarios de Grecia y a Fernández de Heredia, que estaba entonces en Rodas, manifestaban que algunos *—aliqui—* Hospitalarios habían amenazado con invadir los ducados catalanes. El rey exhortaba a Fernández de Heredia y a los capitanes Hospitalarios a que desistieran de injuriar y oprimir a sus súbditos y a que les hicieran la debida restitución; pedía que cesaran de ayudar a los navarros y que asegurasen la liberación de Galceran de Peralta, a quien los navarros tenían cautivo. Otra carta de 23 de septiembre, dirigida solamente a los capitanes de los Hospitalarios en la Morea, manifestaba que Pedro había sabido por Luis Fadrique y sus enviados que los

[51] ACA, Reg. 1657, fol. 112 v.

[52] *DOC*, docs. 367-368.

[53] Vives, *ob. cit.*, doc. 10; ACA, Reg. 1261, fol. 65 v, 91 v-92; Reg. 1743, fol. 115-116; Reg. 1745, fol. 75 v-77. No puede demostrarse que Pedro se opusiera al *passagium* de los Hospitalarios, como afirma Setton, pág. 129.

[54] Archivo Histórico Nacional, Madrid, Órdenes Militares, Sección de Códices, 604-B, fol. 6 v-7.

[55] Delaville, *ob. cit.*, pág. 206.

[56] Archivio Vaticano, Reg. Aven. 216, fols. 171-172.

[57] *DOC*, doc. 371.

Hospitalarios amenazaban con atacar a Luis Fadrique si no hacía las paces con los navarros. Pedro declaraba que, a menos que los Hospitalarios abandonasen tal línea de conducta, procedería contra sus considerables propiedades y rentas dentro de los dominios aragoneses [58]. La información de Pedro acerca de estos distantes y confusos acontecimientos procedía con frecuencia de hombres tales como Bernat Ballester y Joan Boyl, obispo de Megara, que obtenían del rey considerables posesiones y favores en los ducados. Las noticias que proporcionaban no eran totalmente dignas de crédito, como se desprende de las diversas y absurdas acusaciones que el rey hizo en septiembre de 1380 contra Simón Atoumanos, arzobispo de Tebas. Es cierto que los Hospitalarios habían empleado durante cierto tiempo a algunos de los mercenarios navarros, y que estaban en contacto con Nerio Acciaiuoli, que había participado en los ataques contra los catalanes. «Ciertos» Hospitalarios, tales como el gascón Gautier de la Bastide, prior de Tolosa, habían ayudado aparentemente a los navarros contra los catalanes. Probablemente Fernández de Heredia no estaba envuelto de cerca en el asunto. Había permanecido prisionero durante muchos meses y estuvo sólo unas semanas en la Morea antes de embarcar para Rodas; en efecto, Pedro IV no presentó contra él ninguna acusación personal [59]. El 25 de abril de 1381 el infante Juan escribió a Fernández de Heredia una carta amistosa pidiéndole que eximiera a cierto Nicola Estratigon del servicio como marino en Rodas [60], cosa que hizo el maestre en 8 de julio de 1381 [61]. Galceran de Peralta fue liberado en seguida, y en mayo de 1381 Pedro enviaba a los Hospitalarios de Grecia la noticia de la próxima llegada de la expedición de Rocabertí, pidiéndoles que le ayudaran a expulsar a los navarros. Escribió también a Fernández de Heredia pidiéndole que prestara ayuda a Rocabertí si éste la requería, y anunciaba que Rocabertí tenía instrucciones de ayudar a los Hospitalarios en caso de necesidad [62].

Los Hospitalarios devolvieron el principado de Acaya a Juana de

[58] *DOC*, docs. 398, 400, 425.

[59] LOENERTZ, «OCP» (1956), págs. 331-333; LUTTRELL, *Interessi fiorentini*, pág. 324, n.6.Cf. *DOC*, doc. 406, y K. SETTON, *The Archbishop Simon Atumano and the Fall of Thebes to the Navarrese in 1379*, «Byzantinisch-neugriechische Jahrbücher», XVIII (1945-1949 [1960]); G. FEDALTO, *Simone Atumano: monaco di studio arcivescovo latino di Tebe (secolo XIV)*, Padova, 1968, págs. 100-107. No puede demostrarse que el propio Fernández de Heredia ayudase a los navarros *vergonyosament* como se alega frecuentemente (por ejemplo, SOLDEVILA, *ob. cit.*, pág. 485).

[60] *DOC*, doc. 454.

[61] Malta, cod. 321, fol. 243.

[62] *DOC*, docs. 467, 487, 715.

Anjou en la primavera de 1381, y evacuaron la Morea, según parece, durante aquel verano [63]. Mientras tanto, Rocabertí dejaba Cataluña en agosto y debió llegar a los ducados griegos durante el otoño; es posible que recibiera algún apoyo de los Hospitalarios a su llegada [64]. El propio Fernández de Heredia partió de Rodas en abril de 1382 y en julio estaba en Aviñón, donde permaneció el resto de su vida, ya que él y la mayoría de los Hospitalarios apoyaban al papa de Aviñón [65]. El maestre efectuó una breve visita a Barcelona en junio de 1382 [66], pero se apresuró a partir hacia aquella ciudad sin ver a Pedro IV, que el 8 de noviembre de 1382 invitó calurosamente al maestre a volver a España y visitarle [67]. Esta visita no llegó a efectuarse, y en cambio surgieron ciertas diferencias entre Fernández de Heredia y el rey. El maestre, como el infante Juan, era un partidario convencido del papa de Aviñón, y se produjeron disputas, motivadas por el cisma, sobre las rentas y el control del Hospital en Aragón. Pedro se encolerizó cuando el maestre consiguió para su propio sobrino, García Fernández de Heredia, el importante arzobispado de Zaragoza. Sin embargo, el rey, viejo y aislado, necesitaba amigos, y siguió confiando en Fernández de Heredia, pidiéndole favores en Aviñón, recibiendo sus consejos y confiándole asuntos secretos [68].

El interés de Juan Fernández de Heredia por Grecia parecía haber surgido de sus experiencias allí en 1378 y 1379 y durante su posterior estancia en Rodas; sólo entonces comenzó a patrocinar traducciones y compilaciones de historias griegas, incluídas la traducción al aragonés de las *Vidas* de Plutarco y la versión aragonesa de la Crónica de Morea. Políticamente, la expedición de los Hospitalarios a Grecia

[63] LOENERTZ, «OCP» (1956), pág. 337.

[64] Según G. ZURITA, *Anales de la Corona de Aragón*, II, Zaragoza, 1668, fol. 337 v, generalmente digno de confianza, Fernández de Heredia y sus Hospitalarios constituian «el mayor socorro, y amparo que aquellos Estados [los ducados] tuvieron, despues de la ida del Vizconde...» Zurita pudo haber tenido evidencia de esto o pudo basarse en las anteriores *peticiones* de ayuda. Hacia principios de 1381, Fernández de Heredia y Pedro mantenían, una correspondencia amistosa sobre la encomienda del Hospital en los ducados (*infra*, pág. 241.). Existe la posibilidad de que al mismo tiempo que los Hospitalarios dejaban la Morea, Fernández de Heredia pagase a los navarros para que partiesen de los ducados catalanes hacia la Morea; esto podría explicar por qué el Hospital estaba aún en deuda con los navarros *pro quodam passagio* en 1385 (*infra*, pág. 244, n. 87).

[65] A. LUTTRELL, *Intrigue, Schism, and Violence among the Hospitallers of Rhodes: 1377-1384*, «Speculum», XLI (1966), págs. 40 *et passim*.

[66] Archivo Histórico Nacional, Madrid, Órdenes Militares, Sección de Códices, 604-B, fol. 147 v-148 v.

[67] A. LÓPEZ DE MENESES, *Documentos culturales de Pedro el Ceremonioso*, «Estudios de Edad Media de la Corona de Aragón», V (1952), pág. 746.

[68] VIVES, *ob. cit.*, pág. 126, n.15, 130, n. 30, y docs. 21-24; J. VINCKE, *Die Krone von Aragon und das Grosse abendländische Schisma*, «Staatliche Akademie von Braunsberg Personat und Vorkungs-Verzeichnis» (Gumbinnen, 1944), págs. 36, 43, 46, 60-62, 79-89 *et passim*; ACA, Reg. 1817, fol. 88-88 v; Reg. 1267, fol. 26-26 v; Reg. 1274, fol. 78 v-79 v; Reg. 1287, fols. 60 v-61; Reg. 1278, fols. 73-74; Reg. 1289, fol. 104 v.

en 1377 había sido inspirada por el papa Gregorio XI y sólo a partir de entonces demostró Fernández de Heredia un especial interés en que los Hospitalarios se establecieran en la Morea o en algún otro lugar del interior de Grecia [69].

El Hospital retuvo algunas tierras en la Morea, aunque no fuesen de gran importancia. La encomienda de la Morea incluía tierras, situadas alrededor de Modon, en el sur [70], y los castillos de Paleópolis y Phostena [71]. Existía también una encomienda del ducado de Atenas, con tierras en Negroponte y en Sykaminon, al norte de Atenas, que fue confiada frecuentemente a algún súbdito de la Corona de Aragón. Al aragonés Lop de Pomar se le concedió la encomienda de Atenas en 1340; el lugarteniente del maestre en esta encomienda era en 1347 el castellano Adán Arias de Lemos, y algún tiempo antes de 1362 era comendador el catalán Pere de Castellsent [72]. En 1362 Berenguer Soler actuaba como procurador para recibir las rentas de la encomienda de Corinto, situada entre los ducados de Atenas y Neopatria [73]. En abril de 1381, la reina Sibila de Aragón escribió a Fernández de Heredia pidiéndole que diera la encomienda vacante de Sykaminon, en el ducado de Atenas, a un tal Berenguer Batlle [74]. El 5 de junio el maestre le nombraba su lugarteniente en el ducado de Atenas, con plenos poderes para gobernar la encomienda, la cual se decía que tenía grandes deudas por falta de gobierno adecuado; el 31 de junio se dio licencia a Berenguer Batlle para abandonar Rodas con rumbo a Grecia. El 20 de marzo de 1382 se nombró a Ramón de Mallorca comendador del ducado, así como del *domus* de la isla de Negroponte, eximiéndole durante los dos primeros años de las rentas que se debían pagar a Rodas para que pudiese reparar los daños causados por las incursiones de los navarros, que probablemente se habían ya retirado [75]. Estas tierras en realidad habían sido empeñadas a Nerio Accia-

[69] A. LUTTRELL, *Greek Histories translated and compiled for Juan Fernández de Heredia, Master of Rhodes, 1377-1396*, «Speculum», XXXV (1960), pág. 402, n. 5 *et passim*. El maestre estuvo relacionado con la expedición de 1378 y con los primitivos planes de 1356, pero la evidencia no demuestra que los inspirase.

[70] THIRIET, *Régestes*, I, núms. 583. 715.

[71] A. LUTTRELL, *The Principality of Achaea in 1377*, «Byzantinische Zeitschrift», LVII (1964), pág. 344; *Libro de los fechos et conquistas del principado de la Morea*, ed. A. MOREL-FATIO, Ginebra, 1885, pág. 129.

[72] Malta, cod. 280, fol. 46; cod. 317, fol. 127 v., 232-232 v; cod. 319, fol. 143. En 24 de noviembre de 1347, Arias de Lema recibió instrucciones para que pagase su *vestiarium* anual a Guillermo Alfonso, que se había quejado a Rodas de que no se le había pagado (cod. 317, fols. 243 v-244). K. HOPF, *Geschichte Griechenlands von Beginn des Mittelalters bis auf die neuere Zeit*, 2 vols., Leipzig, 1867-1868, I, pág. 439, considera erróneamente a Alfonso como comendador de Atenas.

[73] *DOC*, doc. 301: fecha corregida en LOENERTZ (1955), pág. 114.

[74] *DOC*, doc. 449.

[75] Malta, cod. 321, fol. 212 v-213, 217 v-218.

iuoli y algún tiempo antes del 25 de febrero de 1382 el Hospital pagó 3.000 florines para redimirlas [76]. Pero estos intereses de menor importancia no explican los persistentes intentos por parte de los Hospitalarios de establecerse en Grecia, donde en 1377 habían arrendado todo el principado de Acaya. Estos intentos se remontaban a la primera parte del siglo XIV, antes de la época de influencia de Fernández de Heredia, y continuaron después de su muerte [77].

Tras su regreso a Aviñón en 1382, Fernández de Heredia trataba aparentemente de ajustar sus ambiciones en Grecia a la nueva situación de la Morea. Los Hospitalarios habían abandonado la Morea durante la primavera de 1381, y en julio de 1381 Juana de Anjou, reina de Nápoles y princesa de Acaya, fue apresada por Carlos de Anjou, que se convirtió en rey de Nápoles; Juana fue asesinada en julio de 1382, dejando a Luis, duque de Anjou, como heredero de sus derechos al reino de Nápoles. Jacques de Baux, que reclamaba el principado de Acaya desde la muerte de su tío Felipe de Anjou, príncipe de Taranto y de Acaya, en 1373, consiguió el apoyo de unos latinos de la Morea. Jacques de Baux llegó también a un acuerdo con los mercenarios navarros en la Morea, los cuales a su vez concertaron alianzas durante 1382 tanto con los venecianos como con Rocabertí y los catalanes; después murió en julio de 1383 [78]. El 15 de julio Jacques de Baux hizo testamento, dejando todas sus posesiones, incluídas sus tierras y sus pretensiones en Grecia, a Luis, duque de Anjou, hermano de Carlos V de Francia y heredero de la reina Juana de Nápoles; Luis, el 19 de septiembre de 1376 había comprado ya a Isabel de Mallorca, nieta de Isabel de Villehardouin, princesa de Acaya, todos sus derechos en Italia y *Romania* por 20.000 francos de oro [79]. Después de julio de 1383 los dominios principescos de la Morea permanecieron en su mayor parte en manos de los navarros, con los que Fernández de Heredia se veía obligado a negociar si quería instalar a los Hospitalarios en la Morea. El maestre podía también negociar

[76] LUTTRELL, *Interessi fiorentini*, pág. 324, n. 6.

[77] A. LUTTRELL, *Venice and the Hospitallers of Rhodes in the Fourteenth Century*, «Papers of the British School at Rome», XXVI (1958), págs. 207-210. [H.] ZEININGER DE BORJA, *Les Hospitaliers de Saint-Juan de Jérusalem en Grèce continentale*, «Rivista araldica», LVI-LIX (1958-1961), contiene gran cantidad de información, pero mucha está tomada de las obras de K. Hopf y no es digna de confianza.

[78] LOENERTZ, «OCP» (1956), págs. 335-349. No hay evidencia de que Jacques de Baux lanzase a los navarros contra los catalanes, como se afirma con frecuencia (por ejemplo, en SOLDEVILA, *ob. cit.*, I, pág. 485).

[79] Archives Nationales, Paris: Fonds chambres des comptes d'Anjou, côte P. 1354 (2), n.os 865-870 (19 de septiembre de 1376), n.os 871-872 (15 de julio de 1383).

sobre las pretensiones de Luis de Anjou. Pero, como decidido partidario del papa de Aviñón, Clemente VII, difícilmente podía Fernández de Heredia tratar con Carlos de Anjou, rey de Nápoles y pretendiente también al principado de Acaya, que estaba estrechamente relacionado con el papa de Roma, Urbano VII.

Era natural que Fernández de Heredia se volviese también hacia el rey a quien había servido durante tanto tiempo, y que buscaba a su vez aliados en Grecia. Tras el retorno de Rocabertí de Atenas en 1382, Pedro no consiguió enviarle nuevamente a Grecia y al parecer buscaba otras soluciones; en diciembre de 1383 envió a Bernat Ballester a tratar con Guglielmo Raimondo de Moncada y en agosto de 1384 Guillem Torrelles y Albertí de Vilanova partían hacia Grecia. El 9 de agosto de 1384 el rey llamó a Ballester urgentemente a su presencia para tratar de los asuntos de Grecia y el 11 de septiembre envió a Ballester a que discutiese con Juan Fernández de Heredia «alguns fets nostres tocants los ducats de Athenes et de Neopatria». [80]. Dos importantes Hospitalarios, el catalán Pere de Vilafranca, *Drapier* del Hospital y después prior de Cataluña, y Hugues de Giraud, Comendador de Niza y luego Gran Preceptor del Hospital [81], llevaron al rey desde Aviñón la respuesta del maestre, y el rey volvió a enviarles con un mensaje para Juan Fernández de Heredia el 15 de noviembre [82]. Sin embargo, este intercambio no produjo resultados. Algún tiempo antes de mayo de 1386 Fernández de Heredia mandó a Flandes un enviado para que averiguase «ceulx qui sont vraix heretiers du duchesme d'athenes». Gautier d'Enghien, duque titular de Atenas, que murió en 1381, había heredado el título de su bisabuelo Gautier de Brienne, el duque de Atenas muerto por los catalanes en 1311. Después de 1381, las pretensiones de los Enghien sobre Atenas y Neopatria parecieron cesar, a pesar de que sobrevivía cierto número de posibles pretendientes, entre los que se contaba Marie d'Enghien, que gobernaba sobre Argos y Nauplia, en la Morea. Es posible que Fernández de Heredia estuviera considerando la adquisición de esta pretensión de los Enghien, incluso aunque chocase directamente con los títulos del rey Pedro sobre los ducados [83].

[80] *DOC*, docs. 554, 565, 566, 570; cf. *supra*, págs. 232-235. El 10 de septiembre se envió también a Ballester a tratar con el siciliano Berenguer de Cruilles, que quizá estuviera también por entonces en Aviñón (*DOC*, doc. 569).

[81] Delaville, *ob. cit.*, pág. 219, n. 8, pág. 220, n. 1.

[82] ACA, Reg. 1290, fol. 26; este documento no contiene detalles del asunto en discusión.

[83] Luttrell, *Intrigue, Schism and Violence*, págs. 45-47. El pago del viaje a Flandes se registró en mayo de 1386.

En aquel tiempo la propia Atenas estaba siendo atacada. Pedro IV mantenía su alianza con los navarros, planeaba enviar a Galceran de Vilanova a Grecia y empezaba a pensar en sustituir a Rocabertí [84]. En octubre y noviembre de 1385 envió cuatro llamadas urgentes a Bernat Ballester, que en enero de 1386 actuaba como mensajero entre Pedro y Galceran de Vilanova; el 29 de marzo Ballester se había reunido con el rey llevándole noticias de Galceran [85]. En este momento Pedro no depositaba muchas esperanzas en la ayuda de Fernández de Heredia o de los Hospitalarios.

Entretanto los Hospitalarios consideraban otras posibilidades. Luis, duque de Anjou, murió el 21 de septiembre de 1384, y sus pretensiones pasaron a su hijo, el joven Luis, a quien Fernández de Heredia planeaba comprárselas. Los Hospitalarios negociaban también con los navarros, que ejercían control efectivo sobre gran parte de la Morea. El Hospitalario Adam Boulart, que se convirtió en prior de Francia en 1387 [86], fue elegido en Aviñón el 15 de mayo de 1385, como hombre con experiencia en estos problemas, para ir a la Morea a fin de reclutar nuevos hermanos y de restaurar las posesiones del Hospital tras los destrozos de la guerra y el peso de las deudas; debía tratar con Mahiot de Coquerel, Pedro de San Superan y los navarros, que, efectivamente, retenían en prenda diversas tierras de la encomienda del Hospital [87]. Los navarros, que disponían de unos 1.300 hombres de a caballo, se encontraban en una fuerte situación, y en su oposición a Nerio Acciaiuoli y a su yerno Teodoro Paleólogo, déspota de la Morea, contaban con el apoyo de los catalanes y de los magnates rebeldes del propio Teodoro [88]. Cuando, alrededor de 1385, los Hospitalarios propusieron a los navarros la cesión del principado de Acaya, los navarros pudieron exigir unas condiciones realmente imposibles. Pedían 70.000 ducados para su paga y los gastos de su compañía; que se diera a su jefe un castillo durante el resto de su vida; confirmación del derecho de la compañía a sus posesiones fuera de los dominios reales y garantía de que el acuerdo se mantendría

[84] *Supra*, págs. 233-235.

[85] *DOC*, docs. 579-582, 585, 588.

[86] Delaville, *ob. cit.*, pág. 221, n. 3.

[87] Malta, cod. 323, fols. 31,237 (citado parcialmente y erróneamente, con fecha equivocada por Delaville, pág. 221). El dinero que se debía a los navarros era *pro quodam passagio ipsis dari promisso per dictus domus* [*Hospitalis*] *fratres... sub obligacione bonorum domus nostre.* Este *passagium* estaba posiblemente relacionado con los acontecimientos de 1378-1381; cf. Loenertz, «OCP» (1956), págs. 331-337. No hay razón para suponer —como hacen Hopf, *ob. cit.*, II, pág. 47 y Delaville, *ob. cit.*, pág. 221—, que se había prometido el dinero para un viaje a Aviñón.

[88] *Supra*, pág. 234; cf. Dennis, *Thessalonica*, págs. 114-128.

secreto hasta que los Hospitalarios hubieran tomado posesión del principado y de que el Hospital enviaría fuerzas suficientes para defenderlo. También pedían los navarros pruebas de que Jacques de Baux había legado el principado a Luis de Anjou, de que el papa y los cardenales reconocían al joven Luis como rey de Sicilia, y de que el papa, el rey de Francia y el joven Luis aprobaban el acuerdo [89].

Aunque había fracasado con los navarros, Fernández de Heredia siguió orientando sus negociaciones hacia la compra de los derechos de Luis de Anjou. La regente y madre de Luis, María de Bretaña, estaba siempre necesitada de dinero y en octubre de 1386 aceptó la enajenación del principado de Tarento o su equivalente a Otto de Brunswick [90]. Por entonces debía también estar negociando con los Hospitalarios para venderles el principado de Acaya y el 5 de enero de 1387 el papa Clemente VII, actuando —como declara la bula— a petición de Luis, que necesitaba el dinero, ordenó una investigación de la venta [91]. Dos cardenales efectuaron esta investigación, tras la cual Pierre Brès, comendador de Montpellier y procurador del Hospital en la curia papal, obtuvo de Clemente VII una bula, fechada en 24 de enero, ratificando la venta. Pero en 11 de abril Amadeo de Saboya, nieto de Isabel de Villehardouin, princesa de Acaya, que reclamaba el principado, había persuadido a Clemente VII de que anulase la ratificación de la venta. Y todavía otro pretendiente, Luis de Clermont, duque de Borbón, cuya tía María de Borbón se había casado con Roberto de Anjou, príncipe de Acaya, presentó sus pretensiones sobre el principado de Acaya, pero renunció pronto a ellas [92].

Al parecer la Corona de Aragón estaba relacionada de alguna forma con los planes de Aviñón, porque en marzo o abril de 1387 Amadeo de Saboya obtuvo de Clemente VII cartas dirigidas al rey y a la reina de Aragón *pro facto Moree*. Amadeo hizo que fuesen enviadas a Aragón, donde el rey Juan pudo haber considerado la posibilidad de emprender con los Hospitalarios una acción conjunta para inten-

[89] El texto del *liber bullarum* del maestre para 1385-1386 (Malta, cod. 323, fol. 246) está publicado incorrectamente en DELAVILLE, *ob. cit.*, pág. 380; no puede fecharse con exactitud.

[90] N. VALOIS, *La France et le grand schisme d'Occident*, II, Paris, 1896, págs. 119-122, 140-142 *et passim*.

[91] Archivio Vaticano, Reg. Vat. 298, fol. 72 v-73. Las negociaciones con María de Borbón y con los navarros tuvieron lugar probablemente en 1385 ó 1386. HOPF, *ob. cit.*, II, pág. 47, afirma, sin evidencia auténtica, que a la muerte de su marido en septiembre de 1384, María se propuso *inmediatamente* vender el principado a Fernández de Heredia, el cual aceptó *inmediatamente* e hizo sus propuestas a los navarros a fines de 1384.

[92] DELAVILLE, *ob. cit.*, págs. 222-223; R. CESSI, *Amedeo di Acaia e la rivendicazione dei domini sabaudi in Oriente*, «Nuovo archivio veneto», XXXVII (1919), págs. 5-8 (corrigiendo a HOPF, *ob. cit.*, II, pág. 48).

tar proteger los ducados [93]. Tanto Juan como su esposa, Violante de Bar, habían enviado en febrero y marzo varias cartas a Fernández de Heredia en Aviñón, pidiéndole *inter alia* que ayudase a la misión aragonesa en esta ciudad de la que formaba parte García Fernández de Heredia, arzobispo de Zaragoza. Juan estaba alineando a la Corona de Aragón con el papa de Aviñón, y se encontraba en situación de presentar reclamaciones allí. El 29 de mayo Juan escribió al maestre del Hospital y al papa Clemente VII acerca de cierto negocio secreto en Aviñón y en junio y julio se habló de una visita de Fernández de Heredia a Aragón [94]. El 2 de septiembre de 1387 Juan expidió un salvoconducto para un tal Johannes Flamenck, que iba a partir en breve hacia el principado de Morea «pro aliquibus negociis» del maestre del Hospital. Después, el 14 de octubre, Juan dio otro salvoconducto a Pierre Brès, el procurador del Hospital en Aviñón, que dejaba los dominios aragoneses con ciertos objetos de valor en dirección a Francia [95].

Los proyectos de 1387 se paralizaron. Mahiot de Coquerel murió en 1386 y la jefatura de los navarros pasó a Pedro de San Superan, que concluyó un tratado con los venecianos en julio de 1387; este tratado contaba con el respaldo de los barones de la Morea y entre ellos de Adam Boulart, prior de Francia y comendador del Hospital en la Morea [96]. El 30 de septiembre de 1388, Eustace Haste, que había sido designado para suceder a Boulart, el cual había muerto, obtuvo licencia para ir a la Morea con otros dos Hospitalarios que debían residir allí. Eustace Haste estaba en Aviñón, aconsejando a Fernández de Heredia, cuando el 26 de septiembre de 1389 el maestre designó al Hospitalario Domenico de Alamania para que tomase posesión del principado de Acaya «pro adipiscenda reali et corporali possessioni principatus Achaye». Se declaró explícitamente que el principado se había comprado a Luis de Anjou. Domenico de Alamania recibió poderes para conseguir 15.000 ducados que se necesitaban «pro prosecutione et expeditione negotii presentis principatus Achaye». Otros dos Hospitalarios, Hesso Schegelholtz y Pons de Geys, fueron nom-

[93] La única evidencia es un asiento en las cuentas de Amadeo para marzo o abril de 1387 referente a un mensajero enviado a Aviñón *occaxione habendi litteras a domino nostro papa dirigendas Regi et Regine Arangonie pro facto Moree* (texto en Cessi, *ob. cit.*, pág. 46).

[94] ACA, Reg. 1751, fols. 21, 66, 69, 85; Reg. 1952, fol. 20; Reg. 2053, fol. 1-1 v.

[95] ACA, Reg. 1953, fols. 25 v, 45 v.

[96] Texto en L. de Mas-Latrie, *Documents concernant divers pays de l'Orient latin: 1382-1413*, «Bibliothèque de l'École des Chartes», LVIII (1897), págs. 92-94.

brados procuradores con poderes similares a los de Domenico de Alamania; el 3 de octubre Eustace Haste obtuvo licencia para recibir a dos «fratres servientes armorum» en el Hospital en Morea y el 8 de octubre se le concedieron 150 florines para sus misiones y gastos [97]. Es probable que este proyecto de 1389 se considerara muy seriamente, porque Eustace Haste, Hesso Schegelholtz y Domenico de Alamania habían servido todos en Grecia entre 1378 y 1381 [98].

La situación de la Morea permanecía inestable y favorecía muy poco a los Hospitalarios. En 1387 los turcos tomaron Tesalónica y después recorrieron la Morea, habiéndose aliado con el déspota Teodoro. En 1388 Nerio Acciaiuoli se apoderó de Atenas, pero cuando los venecianos compraron Argos y Nauplia a Marie d'Enghien, Teodoro tomó Argos, y comenzó una larga y confusa pugna en la que venecianos y navarros se enfrentaban a Nerio y Teodoro; en septiembre de 1389 los navarros hicieron prisionero a Nerio. Las posibilidades de que los Hospitalarios intervinieran con éxito eran escasas, sobre todo teniendo en cuenta que Amadeo de Saboya había entablado negociaciones para asegurar sus derechos sobre el principado. En 1391 los venecianos, los navarros y Nerio Acciaiuoli habían reconocido a Amadeo de una forma u otra, pero tras la muerte del conde de Saboya en 1391, dejando a un menor de edad como sucesor, Amadeo de Saboya se vio obligado a permanecer en el Piamonte; nunca llegaría a ir a Grecia [99]. De todas formas no volvió a oirse hablar de los proyectos de Fernández de Heredia sobre Grecia. El maestre tenía unos ochenta años y vivía lejos de las realidades griegas, en medio de las atracciones literarias y de las intrigas eclesiásticas de Aviñón. Los recursos de los Hospitalarios se encontraban disminuidos a causa de las disensiones motivadas por el cisma y de la acuciante necesidad de defender Rodas y Esmirna. Estaba fuera de toda cuestión el enviar a Grecia una expedición de importancia. El rey Juan de Aragón abandonó sus derechos sobre Atenas y Neopatria en 1392 y los turcos conquistaron el condado de Salona en 1394. En 1395 aún retenían los Hospitalarios su castillo de Sykaminon, cerca de Atenas [100], así como

[97] Malta, cod. 324, fols. 71 v-72 v, 141v, 160 v, 183-186. MOREL-FATIO, *ob. cit.*, pág. XVII, afirma erróneamente que Haste condujo una expedición armada a Grecia.

[98] LOENERTZ, «OCP» (1956), págs. 332-333, 337.

[99] R.-J. LOENERTZ, *Pour l'histoire du Péloponese au XIVe siècle: 1382-1404*, «Études byzantines», I (1943), págs. 167-172; SETTON, págs. 192-193.

[100] Sobre Sykaminon, véase L. LEGRAND, *Relation du pèlerinage à Jérusalem de Nicolas de Martoni, notaire italien: 1394-1395*, «Revue de l'Orient latin», III (1895), págs. 655-656.

otras plazas de la encomienda de Atenas[101]. En 1397 los Hospitalarios compraron el despotado de la Morea y ejercieron su dominio durante unos cuantos años sobre Corinto y parte de la Morea[102]. Pero Fernández de Heredia había muerto ya en 1396 y todas sus ambiciones sobre Grecia habían fracasado.

Cuando el rey Juan sucedió a su padre Pedro IV en 5 de enero de 1387, se encontraba seriamente enfermo, aunque el 5 de marzo se dijo que estaba ya convaleciente[103]. Gerau de Rodonelles, que había sido enviado por Pedro de Pau, capitán de Atenas, con cartas fechadas en la propia Atenas en 4 de noviembre de 1386, vio a Juan en Barcelona el 18 de marzo. El nuevo rey había ya vuelto a nombrar vicario general de los ducados al vizconde de Rocabertí, y en abril Rodonelles fue reenviado a Grecia con buenas palabras: los habitantes de los ducados eran súbditos de la Corona y se les enviarían tropas, y el propio Juan visitaría Atenas. Juan estaba aún ignorante de la desesperada situación de los ducados; el 17 de abril de 1387 llegó a escribir a Nerio Acciaiuoli manifestando sus intenciones de mantener la antigua tregua de 1382. Se ocupó también de otros asuntos de menor importancia referentes a los ducados, manteniendo contacto con los navarros e interesándose en los nombramientos eclesiásticos. En noviembre designó a Pedro de Vilalba para sustituir a Pedro de Pau que, según se le había informado, había muerto, pero revocó el nombramiento al oir que Pedro de Pau vivía aún. Cuando una última llamada de socorro le hizo saber que Nerio estaba a punto de tomar la Acrópolis, escribió a Pedro de Pau diciendo que no podía prestarle ayuda. Todo lo que hizo fue ofrecer el gobierno del castillo de Atenas a Helena Cantacuzena si ella lo salvaba y lo defendía[104]. En realidad Juan probablemente podía haber enviado una pequeña expedición, porque los otros asuntos que según alegaba le impedían hacerlo sólo podían ser su propia coronación y las cortes de 1388[105].

[101] El 16 de junio de 1392 se confirmaba a Ramón de Mallorca como comendador del ducado de Atenas y se le donaba el *domus* de Negroponte, donde había de recuperar los derechos y bienes del Hospital; el 18 de junio se le concedía licencia para partir de Rodas hacia Grecia (Malta, cod. 326, fol. 127-127v). En junio de 1401, al dimitir Ramón de Mallorca, Martín de Aynar se convirtió en comendador del ducado de Atenas, de Negroponte y de Carystos, y se le dio licencia para partir de Rodas a fin de gobernar su encomienda (cod. 331, fol. 159 v, 164-164 v).

[102] Loenertz (1943), págs. 186-196; (1964), págs. 422, 426-427.

[103] ACA, Reg. 2053, fol. 2 (considerado erróneamente como de 15 de marzo en Setton, pág. 178).

[104] *DOC*, docs. 602-621; Loenertz (1958), págs. 77-79.

[105] Cf. Soldevila, *ob. cit.*, II, pág. 507.

Pedro de Pau estaba aún «in civitate de Cetines» el 4 de noviembre de 1386, pero al parecer Nerio Acciaiuoli había ocupado la ciudad baja y se encontraba en ella el 15 de enero de 1387, y tras un prolongado sitio tomaba la Acrópolis el 2 de mayo de 1388. La peste había estallado en Atenas y Nerio se trasladó a Tebas casi inmediatamente. La lucha continuó en los ducados. Neopatria, bajo su capitán catalán Andreu Savall, fue sitiada por Acciaiuoli y el 3 de enero de 1390 Juan escribió a Helena Cantacuzena para que le prestase ayuda. En realidad Nerio Acciaiuoli había sido apresado por los navarros el 10 de septiembre de 1389. Los catalanes disfrutaron de un breve respiro y el 12 de abril de 1391 Juan escribió a Rocabertí pidiéndole su parecer «per tal com nos son demanades algunes provisions tocants lo fet del ducat de Athenes...»[106]. Rocabertí demostró una vez más su falta de interés por el vicariato de Grecia. De 1387 en adelante tenía ocupación en Cataluña como primer consejero del rey, y en 1392 marchó a Sicilia con el hermano de Juan, Martín, duque de Montblanc, y murió allí en aquel mismo año[107]. A principios de 1390, el joven Martín, hijo del duque de Montblanc, se había casado con María de Sicilia, y desde entonces compartió con ella el título de duque de Atenas y Neopatria. Al parecer el rey Juan había abandonado sus pretensiones de tener cualquier interés en los ducados[108]. Martín y María, actuando bajo la tutela del duque de Montblanc, emprendieron viaje a Sicilia para gobernarla como rey y reina, llegando a la isla en marzo de 1392, y en Catania el 1 de septiembre de 1392 el duque, en nombre de su hijo y de su nuera, designó vicario general de los ducados al catalán Pedro de Fenollet, vizconde de Illa y de Canet. Neopatria había caído ya en poder de Nerio Acciaiuoli a fines de 1391, pero Helena Cantacuzena retenía aún el condado de Salona. En la pri-

[106] *DOC*, docs. 600, 602, 622, 624-630.

[107] Zurita, II, 404 v; Sobrequés, *ob. cit.*, pág. 225: obsérvese que Rocabertí estaba casado con Esclaramonda de Fenollet.

[108] Pedro IV se denominó a sí mismo *dux* hasta su muerte. Juan utilizó el título por lo menos hasta el 7 de noviembre de 1387 y actuaba todavía como duque en 12 de abril de 1391 (*DOC*, docs. 616, 630 *et passim*). María contrajo matrimonio con Martín poco antes del 5 de febrero de 1392, en cuya fecha Juan escribió a su hermano Martín para felicitarle por el matrimonio de su hijo: A. Rubió i Lluch, *Documents per l'història de la cultura catalana mig-eval*, I, Barcelona, 1908, núm. 419. Loenertz (1955), pág. 153, a modo de tentativa, fecha el matrimonio en 29 de noviembre de 1381. Juan había renunciado ya a sus derechos sobre los ducados, probablemente entre el 12 de abril y el 1 de octubre de 1391, en cuya fecha un documento real se refiere a María, a quien se reconocía como reina de Sicilia desde hacía tiempo, como *ducissa* de los ducados griegos (ACA, Reg. 2026, fols. 64-64 v). El 1 de diciembre de 1391, María delegó sus poderes sobre los ducados: I. La Lumia, *Storie Siciliane*, II, Palermo, 1882, pág. 328. Tras su matrimonio, Martín y María actuaron conjuntamente como *dux et ducissa*, aunque la facción antiaragonesa de Sicilia reconocía únicamente a María (*DOC*, doc. 635; La Lumia, *ob. cit.*, II, pág. 339, n. 1; pág. 421, n. 1.

mavera de 1393 llegó a Cerdeña una nave vizcaína que volvía de los ducados griegos con la noticia de que Livadia había sido tomada por el gascón Beltranet Mota de Salahia, «un capità del ducham de Athenes» que poseía también un feudo en la Morea. Beltranet Mota había estado al servicio de Nerio Acciaiuoli, pero era también íntimo amigo del barón siciliano y pro-catalán Guglielmo Raimondo de Moncada. Probablemente fue también en 1393 cuando Martín y María hicieron un último esfuerzo para recuperar Tebas, muriendo al parecer en el asalto al castillo el caballero Guillem Torrelles. Después, en enero de 1394, el gobernante otomano Bayaceto invadió la Grecia central y se anexionó Neopatria, Livadia y el condado de Salona[109].

En Salona gobernaba aún Helena Cantacuzena. El 17 de abril de 1387 el rey Juan le había escrito informándole del nuevo nombramiento de Rocabertí y presionándole para que se realizase el viejo proyecto del matrimonio de su hija María con Bernaduc de Rocabertí, que —según escribe— iba a emprender viaje a Grecia. En 7 de noviembre Juan volvió a escribir para protestar de las noticias del compromiso de María con Mateo, hijo de Guglielmo Raimondo de Moncada, el más pro-catalán de los grandes magnates sicilianos. Guglielmo Raimondo era hijo de un antiguo vicario general de los ducados griegos. Junto con Rocabertí, había asegurado la huída de María de Sicilia de Augusta en 1382, y en 1383 había presentado a Pedro IV ciertas proposiciones referentes a los ducados griegos; desde luego los Moncada tenían intereses en Grecia. De todas formas, en 22 de abril de 1388 Juan ofreció a Helena permitirle gobernar el castillo de Atenas si podía defenderlo; en realidad Atenas debió caer antes de que llegase este mensaje. El 7 de enero de 1390 Juan escribió a Helena pidiéndole que enviase ayuda a Neopatria, y esta vez expresaba su complacencia ante el proyectado enlace con Moncada, que aún no se había efectuado. Pero a principios de 1394 Bayaceto recorrió el condado de Salona con sus dependencias de Zitounion, Lidoriki, Vidrinitza y probablemente Siderocastron; tanto Helena como su her-

[109] *DOC*, docs. 635, 637 y nota, docs. 638-639, 644, 661; Loenertz (1955), págs. 153-155, 169. Parece que Beltranet servía a los navarros. En 1390, cuando los navarros tenían prisionero a Nerio Acciaiuoli, este prometió «che io atendero a Beltraneto quello che io li o promeso» (texto en Mas-Latrie, *ob. cit.*, págs. 99-102). Probablemente Beltranet estaba ya al servicio de Nerio en 1392 o al mismo principio de 1393, cuando tomó Livadia a los turcos y era «un dels maiors capitans» de los ducados. El testamento de Nerio de 17 de septiembre de 1394 dejaba Tebas y Livadia a su hijo natural Antonio, y a Beltranet «quello che possedeva in prima nello paese nostro». Probablemente los turcos habían ocupado ya estas tierras. Tras la muerte de Nerio en 25 de septiembre de 1394, tanto Beltranet como Antonio se unieron al Déspota Teodoro para atacar Corinto (*DOC*, doc. 637 y nota, docs. 638-639; Setton, págs. 193, 197, 199 nota 77).

mosa hija María Fadrique pasaron al harén de Bayaceto, y en 1395 ambas habían muerto[110]. Sólo la isla de Egina, que Pedro IV había dispuesto en 1381 que pasase a Dulcia, esposa de Bonifacio Fadrique de Aragón, y a su hijo Juan Fadrique, permaneció en manos catalanas. En 1402 la isla había pasado al catalán Aliot de Caupena. La familia Caupena retuvo Egina hasta 1451 y sostuvo también la fortaleza de Piada, en la Argólida, hasta 1460[111].

Juan hizo mucho más por el estudio del griego en Cataluña-Aragón[112] que por la Grecia catalana. Su actitud hacia los ducados fue siempre literaria, como por ejemplo cuando dijo a los representantes de Atenas que habían venido a rendirle homenaje a Barcelona:

> Ni us pensets que tan asenyalat membre com es aqueix de la nostra corona metam en oblit, ans havem esperança en nostre senyor Deus que per avant lo irem personalment a visitar ... [113]

Juan estaba claramente influenciado por el encanto de la Grecia clásica. Tal declaración era típica en él; de la misma forma actuó en el problema de Cerdeña, que era mucho más acuciante. Así, en 18 de septiembre de 1392 anunció también su intención de ir allí en persona, hablando de su deseo de seguir el glorioso ejemplo de sus predecesores y la memoria de los hechos registrados en Suetonio, Orosio y Valerio Máximo[114]. No sólo no llegó Juan a ir a Cerdeña, sino que ni siquiera envió allí una expedición[115]. Juan abandonó también el valioso mercado catalán de las Canarias. Incluso antes de su subida al trono ignoró la política tradicional. Había rechazado mucho tiempo antes el matrimonio siciliano; renunció tanto al proceso de expansión por el Atlántico como a la hegemonía del Mediterráneo para volverse hacia las princesas francesas y los papas de Aviñón[116]. A pesar de la negligencia de Juan, la presencia aragonesa persistió en Sicilia y Cerdeña, pero muy pocos súbditos de la Corona de Aragón tenían algún auténtico interés material en los escuálidos fragmentos que quedaban

[110] *DOC*, docs. 554, 605, 615, 621, 628 y notas; cf. D. NICOL, *The Byzantine Family of Kantakouzenos (Cantacuzenus) : ca. 1100-1460*, Washington, 1968, págs. 160-163.

[111] *DOC*, docs. 483, 488, 653-655, 669, 696-698; SETTON, págs. 108, n. 27, 211-212. Sin embargo no pasa de ser una conjetura el que Aliot se casara con una hija de Juan Fadrique de Aragón: cf. LOENERTZ (1958), págs. 178, 180.

[112] A. RUBIÓ I LLUCH, *Joan I humanista i el primer període de l'humanisme català*, «Estudis universitaris catalans», X (1917-18).

[113] *DOC*, doc. 608.

[114] RUBIÓ, *Documents*, I, núm. 421.

[115] SOLDEVILA, *ob. cit.*, II, pág. 506, con referencias.

[116] M. MITJÀ, *Abandó de les illes Canàries per Joan I d'Aragó*, «Anuario de Estudios Atlánticos», VIII (1962), págs. 334-340.

de la Grecia catalana en 1387, y era natural que se abandonaran las tierras griegas. Los recursos aragoneses se habían agotado en Cerdeña y en la expedición a Sicilia dirigida por el hermano de Juan, Martín, en 1392. El propio rey Juan carecía de la energía, la habilidad y el deseo de organizar una intervención en Grecia.

En cierto sentido, Pedro IV y su hijo se mostraron sensatos al evitar interesarse seriamente en aquellos ducados distantes y aislados, que habían sido adquiridos casi por casualidad. Podían haber dilapidado recursos que se necesitaban con mucha más urgencia para defender lugares en los que la Corona tenía más auténticos intereses y problemas más serios [117]. En cualquier caso, en una época en que la entera posición cristiana en Oriente se tambaleaba ante el avance de los otomanos y en que la propia Cataluña se encontraba en decadencia, poco importaba probablemente la actitud de la Corona. El fin de los ducados no supuso que finalizasen totalmente las relaciones comerciales o diplomáticas con Grecia y con los emperadores bizantinos [118], pero el peso del comercio catalán giró hacia los puertos mamelucos de Siria y Egipto [119]. Quedaron catalanes en tierras griegas de los Balcanes. El anónimo autor del romance histórico *Història de Jacob Xalabín*, que muestra tal familiaridad con los asuntos de los Balcanes en la década del 1380 al 1390, aunque no se ocupa en absoluto de Atenas o Tebas, pudo muy bien haber sido un renegado catalán [120]. A la muerte de Martín de Sicilia en 1409 el título de Atenas y Neopatria revirtió a la Corona de Aragón. Por lo demás, el dominio catalán en los ducados siguió siendo durante el siglo xv lo que en realidad había sido entre 1379 y 1392: una cuestión de prestigio hasta cierto punto, un recuerdo propio para ser evocado en la retórica de las cortes, una frase en los títulos reales, una base diplomática para ambiciones comerciales o imperialistas [121] —pero nunca una auténtica realidad.

Versión castellana de Carmen Guzmán

Accademia Britannica. Roma

[117] Cf. SOLDEVILA, *ob. cit.*, II, págs. 507-508.

[118] *DOC*, docs. 613, 651, 656-697 *passim*; C. MARINESCO, *Du nouveau sur les relations de Manuel II Paléologue (1391-1425) avec l'Espagne*, en «Atti dello VIII Congresso internazionale di studi bizantini», I (= Studi bizantini e neoellenici», VII [1953], Roma, 1953).

[119] A las obras citadas *supra*, nota 8, añádase VICENS *et al.*, *ob. cit.*, págs. 122, 131-134; J. AINAUD, *Quatre documents sobre el commerç català amb Síria i Alexandria: 1401-1410*, «Homenaje a Jaime Vicens Vives», I (Barcelona, 1965).

[120] *Història de Jacob Xalabín*, ed. A. PACHECO, Barcelona, 1964; cf. M. DE RIQUER, *Història de la literatura catalana*, II, Barcelona, 1964, págs. 569-574. Esta obra pudo muy bien haberse redactado entre 1389 y 1404.

[121] Los detalles en SETTON, págs. 31, n. 37, 212-215, 258-260.

XII

Aldobrando Baroncelli in Greece: 1378-1382

Four letters addressed by Aldobrando Baroncelli of Florence to Lorenzo Acciaiuoli were among seven letters from the Acciaiuoli family correspondence which were published by the Florentine Carmelite Ildefonso di San Luigi in 1781 (1). These four documents which were written in Greece during 1381 and 1382 have been overlooked, despite the light they throw on Greek affairs (2). Though the printed texts may be corrupt, there is no reason to doubt the genuineness of any of these seven documents which their editor, who himself apparently worked from copies, described as follows:

> Lettere familiari di Niccola Acciaiuoli gran Siniscalco del Re, e della Regina di Napoli, e di altri suoi congiunti impiegati in quella Corte. *Da MS. presso di me, intitolato, Notizie Istor. della Città di Firenze, T. 1. da c. 14. a 22.*

Presumably Ildefonso di San Luigi's papers were at one point in his Florentine convent of San Paolino, but the documents from this house now in the Archivio di Stato at Florence do not seem to include this manuscript (3), nor is it among the materials

(1) Ildefonso di San Luigi, *Delizie degli eruditi toscani*, XIV (Florence, 1781), 235-248.

(2) C. Ugurgieri Della Berardenga, *Avventurieri alla conquista di feudi e di corone: 1356-1429* (Florence, 1963), 69-70, did cite them but without realizing their importance.

(3) Judging at least by the indices to the Corporazioni Religiose Soppresse (Inventario no. 157) and to the Spoglio delle Cartapecore (Inventario no. 51).

from San Paolino preserved in the Biblioteca Nazionale at Florence (1).

The originals of the seven letters, which almost certainly were once part of the Acciaiuoli correspondence, are apparently lost. That part of the Acciaiuoli correspondence remaining in the Ricasoli-Firidolfi family archive in Florence contained parchments, donations and wills, together with a seventeenth-century register with copies of many letters, the originals of which are not with the other Acciaiuoli documents in the Laurenziana Library at Florence; in about 1932 there were some hundred pieces relating to Niccolò Acciaiuoli and his immediate descendants (2). Buchon (3), Lampros (4), and Longnon and Topping (5) worked on and published documents from the Ricasoli archives, but none of them mentioned any of the seven missing documents, which are not now in that archive (6). A large part of the Acciaiuoli correspondence finally reached the Biblioteca Laurenziana; this series, the *Carteggio Acciaiuoli* formerly in the possession of Lord Ashburnham, contains many fourteenth-century documents, among them a letter from Aldobrando Baroncelli to Lorenzo Acciaiuoli written in 1379, but it includes none of the seven letters published in 1781 (7). Other parts of the Acciaiuoli archives

(1) It is apparently not recorded in the manuscript *Inventario dei Mss. dei Conventi Soppressi;* a volume from S. Paolino in this *fondo* (Ms. A. 3. no. 414) entitled *Discorso Della Città di Fiorenza, sua antichità ed Origine, con alcune notizie* does not contain the Baroncelli letters.

(2) É.-G. LÉONARD, *Histoire de Jeanne Ire, reine de Naples, comtesse de Provence: 1343-1382*, I-III (Monaco-Paris, 1932-1937), I, pp. xli-xliii. Although he collected the material, LÉONARD did not publish the fourth volume of his work, covering the period 1362-1382; in a letter dated 5 June 1958, he confirmed that he had found no new documents concerning Greek affairs for the years 1376-1381.

(3) Especially J. BUCHON, *Nouvelles recherches historiques sur la principauté française de Morée et ses hautes baronnies*, 2 vols. (Paris, 1843).

(4) F. GREGOROVIUS - S. LAMBROS, *Historia tes poleos Athenon kata tous mesous aionas*, III (Athens, 1906), 143-229.

(5) J. LONGNON - P. TOPPING, *Documents sur le régime des terres dans la principauté de Morée au XIVe siècle* (Paris – The Hague, 1969), docs. I-III.

(6) As Barone Luigi Ricasoli has most kindly confirmed.

(7) The Laurenziana *Carteggio* (Fondo Ashburnham 1830, *olim* 1751) has a Ms. inventory which states (pp. xxviii-xxix) that it does not contain the seven letters; they do not appear in this detailed

are now in the Archivio di Stato at Florence (1), and elsewhere (2).

The first three of the seven letters published by Ildefonso di San Luigi were addressed to Lapa Acciaiuoli:

1. Niccolò Acciaiuoli to his sister Lapa, dated Calanna, 8 September 1357, and Tropea, 14 September 1357; the letter contains no reference to Greece, and has been republished twice (3).
2. Francesco Buondelmonti to his mother, Lapa Acciaiuoli, dated Aversa, 10 December [1370] (4); one passage refers to Greece:

---

inventory of documents, nor were they found by scholars such as GREGOROVIUS, LÉONARD, and LONGNON.

(1) Corporazioni Religiose Soppresse, Convento no. 51: San Lorenzo al Galluzzo detto Certosa, sezioni 214-217 (*olim* 334-337); eg. LONGNON - TOPPING, docs. IV-VI, IX, XII. The Baroncelli letters are not in the archive of this *convento*.

(2) The *Privilegia Acciaiolae Familiae* in Athens, Gennadius Library, Ms. 95 (*olim* Phillipps Ms. 5671), does not contain the Baroncelli letters, as Mr. Francis R. Walton most kindly confirmed. The Acciaiuoli correspondence in the University of Pennsylvania Library, Mss. Lea 28 and 441 (*olim* Phillipps Ms. 21499), does not contain them either, as Dr. Rudolph Hirsch most kindly confirmed. The extensive indices under « Acciaiuoli » and « Buondelmonti » in the Poligrafo Gargani at the Biblioteca Nazionale, Florence, give no reference to the *Lettere familiari* used by Fr. Ildefonso.

(3) *Delizie*, XIV. 235-237; reprinted in L. TANFANI, *Niccola Acciaiuoli: studi storici* (Florence, 1863), 117 n. 1, and in LÉONARD, III. 614-616.

(4) *Delizie*, XIV. 238-240. The letter reports the marriage of Philip of Anjou, titular Emperor of Constantinople, to Elizabeth daughter of Stephen, brother of King Louis of Hungary: *Lo Imperadore si dice ha presa per moglie la Cugina del Re d'Ungheria, cioè Nipote a la Reina vecchia Ducana sua Matre, et già ha recercati li Napoletani suoi famigli, che l'accompagnino a Giara, non dice quando*. Papal dispensations for the marriage were issued on 8 and 13 January 1370; news of the marriage had *nuper* reached Avignon on 1 June 1371: texts in A. THEINER, *Monumenta Historica Hungariae*, II (Rome, 1860), 95-96, 107-108. The letter must date to 1370. The *Carteggio Acciaiuoli* contains three letters from Francesco Buondelmonti (Fondo Ashburnham 1830, cassetta II, nos. 182-184). The text of the first, to Giovanni Acciaiuoli from Ancona, 13 July 1360, is in V. BRANCA, « La prima diffusione del Decameron ", *Studi di filologia italiana* VIII (1950), 48. The other two were addressed to

Mess. Neri (Acciaiuoli) *si sta a Coranto* (Corinth), *nemico, secondo si dice, dell'Imperadore* (Philip of Anjou, titular Emperor of Constantinople), *et se questi volesse Coranto, non l'harebbe; hacci voluto mandare Lione, non so sel manderà. Anichino tornò a questi dì di Romania, portò lettere della Contessa* (probably Francesco's sister Maddalena Buondelmonti, wife of Leonardo Tocco, Count of Cephalonia), *et stavano bene, dice, e prova, ma ella no mi lo scrive.*

3. Leonardo Tocco, Duke of Leucadia and Count Palatine of Cephalonia, to Lapa Acciaiuoli, dated Naples, 28 May [1374]. On 19 May Leonardo reached Castellammare di Stabia near Naples from Cephalonia, where he had left his wife (Lapa's daughter Maddalena Buondelmonti) and their daughters, who were well. He had been sent from the Morea with other *signori* to offer the Principality of Achaea to Joanna of Anjou, Queen of Naples; the mission had not yet been carried out. The text has some relevance to Greek affairs (1):

Reverenda, et carissima Madre. Da poi la felice salute. Sacciate come per la gratia di Dio Noi con tutta nostra Compagnia assieme achiegamo sani, e salvi a Castellamare a' dì xix. di Maggio, dove trovammo che Madama la Reina era a Nocera, et come seppe la nostra venuta, di presente mandò a noi Mess. Andrea di Fonto con molti de' suoi cavalli, e compagnia d'altri suoi Cortigiani, e volse che noi andassimo a la sua Maestà, et così facemmo, dove da essa gratiosamente, et effettuosamente fummo veduti, e ricevuti, facendosi assai allegra della nostra venuta: Et così da tutti altri Signori semo stati honoratamente ricevuti, tanto che più non si potria dire.

A Castell'a Mare vennono a noi molti Cavalieri di Napoli a farne festa, et carezze molte; e così ne rinfrescammo alcuni giorni, et venimmo a Napoli, dove da tutti siamo honorati, et veduti con tanta festa, e carezze, che più non si potria dire.

Lapa Acciaiuoli from Aversa, 4 December, and Naples, 16 December, almost certainly in the same year.

(1) *Delizie*, XIV. 241-242; for the date and details of this embassy, A. LUTTRELL, " Vonitza in Epirus and its Lords: 1306-1377 ", *Rivista di Studi bizantini e neoellenici* XI (= ns. I) (1964), 140.

In Calavria fummo alla Roccella, et loco trovando lo Conte, e la Contessa di Catanzano con tutti i loro figli a stare per la gratia di Dio bene, salvo che Pietro di Catenzano, che ne venne a scontrare, et a riceverne: Incontronne, et con lui era Simoncino, et Andrea, et assai honorata Compagnia, et grande: Assai consolatione havemmo con Madama di Catanzano, e grande allegrezza fece di nostra venuta con farne assai carezze, et per havere manco affanno, et per più nostra sicurtà da la Roccella con tutta nostra compagnia di Cavalieri, e Gentilhomini per terra venimmo a Briatico, et loco stemmo tanto, che la Galea, et due altri nostri legni armati giunsono a Bibona, havendo per spatio di x. giorni a lo detto loco tenute carezze quanto havessimo ricevuto a li proprii lochi nostri, e più; Et così havemo trovato in ciascuno loco dello Reame, dove havemo preso terra in questo viaggio.

A la partita nostra di Cifalonia lassammo la Duchessa, e le nostre figlie (1) star bene, et ogni giorno ne aspettiamo novelle: Preghemovi, che ne scriviate novelle di vostro stato, che noi semo assai desiderosi d'udirne spesso buone novelle a consolatione di noi.

Ancora non sapemo come sarà lunga, o corta la nostra stanza, et però non ve lo scrivemo: come piacerà a Madama la Regina, così faremo, proveduto, et hordinato che essa havrà a lo suo honore, et stato, al Principato della Morea; per la qual cosa semo noi con alcuni altri Signori venuti per parte dello Principato: Altro per mò non vi scrivemo; se non che se per noi si può fare cosa che vi piacerà, scrivetenelo, che noi siamo parati a ogni vostro piacere.

Salutate per nostra parte Mess. Francesco, et Madama Margherita, et Isau, et le vostre figlie: Iddio sia in vostra guardia.

Scritta in Napoli a di xxiix. di Maggio.

Dux Lucate, et
Comes Cephal. } Palatinus.

A tergo
Magnifice Mulieri Domine Lape
de Acciarolis de Florentia
Reverende et Charissime Matris nostre.

(1) *figlie:* the Tocco sons were presumably born after May 1374 (*infra*, 287).

Aldobrando Baroncelli, the author of the other four letters which were written in 1381 and 1382, served in Greece for some years. In November-December 1379 he drew up two *quaderni* listing the Greek incomes of Angelo and Lorenzo Acciaiuoli, while from Clarenza on 15 December 1379 he sent the first of his five surviving letters to Lorenzo Acciaiuoli, in which he gave a detailed account of Greek affairs (1). The language of all these documents presents difficulties and, in the absence of the originals and of the manuscript in which they had been copied and from which they were originally published, the four letters are here republished, without alteration, in the somewhat corrupted printed version in which they survive; the punctuation, capitals and accents were clearly not to be found in the originals (2). Baroncelli's letters and his *quaderni* are extremely important for the information they provide about prices, crops, estate management, trade and other aspects of the social and agrarian history of the Morea, but since these topics have been dealt with by Longnon and Topping, no attempt is made here to assess the letters from that point of view. The letters do throw much new light on the obscure events in the Morea during 1381 and 1382. The implications of this important new information should ultimately be worked out in the full context of the complicated history of Latin Greece in the later fourteenth century. The present work aims merely to make the texts as published more readily available, and to provide limited interim editorial annotations.

* * *

The Baroncelli family was well established in Florence, and important enough to have a finely decorated chapel in the church of Santa Croce. Some of the Baroncelli were bankers at Avignon and they had close connections with the Florentine families of Buondelmonti and Acciaiuoli (3). Salvestro Baroncelli

(1) The letter and one *quaderno* were printed in GREGOROVIUS-LAMBROS, III. 95-105, 129-132; all three are given, more accurately, in LONGNON - TOPPING, docs. X-XII.

(2) Very little of the punctuation supplied in the published text of Baroncelli's letter of 1379 (*ibid.*, doc. X) exists in the original.

(3) Limited information in J. GIRARD, *Les Baroncelli d'Avignon* (Avignon, 1957), and *Dizionario biografico degli Italiani*, VI (Rome, 1964), 434-444.

was a partner in the Acciaiuoli banking company (1) and in 1341, together with Jacopo di Donato Acciaiuoli and Manente di Gherardo Buondelmonti, he was acting as Niccolò Acciaiuoli's representative at Clarenza in the Morea (2). Niccolò Acciaiuoli, who became the greatest figure in the Kingdom of Naples, had important family interests — landed, financial and commercial — both in Puglia and across the Adriatic in the Morea. Furthermore Manente Buondelmonti married Niccolò Acciaiuoli's sister Lapa, and in addition to two sons, Francesco and Esau, they had a daughter, Maddalena Buondelmonti; Maddalena married the Neapolitan Leonardo Tocco, Duke of Leucadia and Count of Cephalonia, who dominated the Adriatic islands as a kind of maritime marcher lord. It was in this Adriatic milieu between Southern Italy and Greece that Aldobrando Baroncelli found employment in the service of the Acciaiuoli and their Buondelmonti kinsmen. Although this group of Florentines had settled in the Neapolitan kingdom and married into its noble families, they remained Florentines and their interests were hard hit by the conflict which broke out between Florence and the papacy in 1376. Florentine goods and credits were seized at Avignon; the Florentines were expelled from Dubrovnik; in December 1377 the pope ordered the seizure of large quantities of Florentine cloth and merchandise in the Adriatic ports of Barletta and Manfredonia. Such moves had considerable effect, though they were often mitigated by the lenience of rulers like Queen Joanna of Naples, who published the interdict but never applied it strictly. Pope Gregory XI even relaxed his own decrees, and a papal bull of 24 January 1378 dispensed Angelo Acciaiuoli, Grand Seneschal of the Neapolitan kingdom, and all his family from the excommunications and penalties imposed on them (3).

A number of Florentines were able to circumvent the papal prohibitions by attaching themselves to the *passagium* of Hospitallers organized by Pope Gregory XI. In 1377 the Hospitallers

(1) *Cronica di Giovanni Villani*, ed. F. DRAGOMANNI, IV (Florence, 1845), 95.

(2) TANFANI, 42.

(3) Details in R. TREXLER, *Economic, Political, and Religious Effects of the Papal Interdict on Florence: 1376-1378* (Frankfurt, 1964), 78-84 *et passim;* Giovanni Baroncelli, banker and papal sergeant-at-arms, had his credits seized (*ibid.*, 40: table).

of Rhodes leased the Principality of Achaea from Joanna of Anjou, Queen of Naples and Princess of Achaea; they also acquired rights to the port of Vonitza in Epirus from Maddalena Buondelmonti who, following her husband's death, was acting on behalf of her small sons Carlo and Leonardo Tocco. Early in 1378 the Hospitallers reached Vonitza, but they were soon defeated by Ghin Boua Spata, the Albanian Lord of Arta, and their Master, Fr. Juan Fernández de Heredia, was captured and held to ransom (1). In order to sustain this *passagium* Gregory XI was compelled to grant a series of dispensations which permitted the Hospitallers to conclude the necessary commercial transactions with the Florentines, despite the interdict. The Hospitallers were, in fact, accompanied on their *passagium* by Francesco and Esau Buondelmonti, and the *regimen et expeditio* of their vessels was given to *Adebrandus* of Florence — Aldobrando Baroncelli (2). Baroncelli may himself have been involved in the campaign in Epirus, and thereafter he was concerned with the estates in the Morea which Angelo Acciaiuoli had inherited from his father Niccolò. Angelo had pawned part of his Greek lands, including Corinth, to Nerio Acciaiuoli, adoptive son of Niccolò and Lord of Corinth, while other lands were held by Lorenzo Acciaiuoli, possibly as Angelo's vassal (3).

The Hospitallers' concern was to defend the Morea, and they hired certain Navarrese mercenaries who had been stranded at Durazzo in 1376. The Navarrese, some of whom were also in the service of Nerio Acciaiuoli, attacked the Catalans of the

(1) R.-J. LOENERTZ, " Hospitaliers et Navarrais en Grèce, 1376-1383: régestes et documents ", *Orientalia Christiana Periodica* 22 (1956), 329-331, with amendments in A. LUTTRELL, " Interessi fiorentini nell'economia e nella politica dei Cavalieri Ospedalieri di Rodi nel Trecento ", *Annali della Scuola Normale Superiore di Pisa: Lettere, storia e filosofia* II ser., 28 (1959), 322-324; A. ESZER, *Das abenteuerliche Leben des Johannes Laskaris Kalopheros* (Wiesbaden, 1969), 68-72, 143-146.

(2) Archivio Vaticano, Reg. Aven. 204, f. 139v, and LUTTRELL (1959), 323-324; the papal documents were exploited independently, and with greater detail, in TREXLER, 84-86, who studies them from the Florentine viewpoint and without utilizing the works on the Greek background (LOENERTZ, LUTTRELL, etc.) cited here.

(3) In addition to LONGNON - TOPPING, 194-195, see P. TOPPING, " Le régime agraire dans le Péloponnèse latin au XIVe siècle ", *L'Hellénisme contemporain* II ser., X (1956), 293-295.

Duchy of Athens from whom, probably early in 1379, they captured Thebes (1). Baroncelli's letter of 15 December 1379 (2) shows that the Hospitallers were maintaining the machinery of government in the principality, and that Angelo and Lorenzo Acciaiuoli's Greek estates were still functioning; it contained no mention of any Navarrese operating to the south of the Gulf of Corinth. In his letter Baroncelli, assuming that Lorenzo has not received four earlier letters, gives an account of events in Greece. Baroncelli's first piece of news was that the Hospitallers Fr. Domenico de Alamania (3) and Fr. Gautier de la Bastide, Prior of Toulouse, had arrived from Rhodes; Alamania had been made *bailli* or Governor of the Morea by the council of government and had formally received the banners (4). Despite the opposition of certain members, including Baroncelli himself, who feared that taxation was forcing the peasants off the land, the council

(1) Cf. K. SETTON, in *Cambridge Medieval History*, IV part I (2nd ed.: Cambridge, 1966), 420 note; ESZER, 74, accepts the date of 6 March 1378 for the fall of Thebes. The Hospitallers' relations with the Navarrese remain obscure.

(2) Text in LONGNON - TOPPING, doc. X, where the date is established as 1379, following the Angevin indiction which began on 1 September (ie. December, III Indiction, fell in 1379).

(3) LONGNON - TOPPING misleadingly refer to him as *Dominique d'Allemagne* and as *prieur* (ESZER calls him *Dominikus von Deutschland*). In fact, he was a leading Southern Italian Hospitaller who held various preceptories, including those of Naples and San Stefano Monopoli near Bari, and who had by September 1379 become Lieutenant in Italy of the Master of Rhodes: references in A. LUTTRELL, " Intrigue, Schism, and Violence among the Hospitallers of Rhodes: 1377-1384 ", *Speculum* 41 (1966), 34-35, 41. Alamania was at Clarenza in May 1379 (Royal Malta Library, Archives of the Order of St. John, cod. 48, f. 11v), and he carried out several important missions for the Hospital in Greece (LOENERTZ, 332, 335, 337 [as *de Bolunya*], 339-340; *infra*, 286).

(4) The previous *bailli*, the Hospitaller Fr. Daniele del Carretto, died at Clarenza: *Libro de los fechos et conquistas del Principado de la Morea*, ed. A. MOREL-FATIO (Geneva, 1885), 160. Carretto's death was known in Italy to have occurred *nuper* by 29 December 1378 (Archivio Vaticano, Reg. Vat. 291, f. 91v-92). On 23 September 1380 King Pedro of Aragon addressed the Hospitaller Priors of France and Toulouse as *pro eodem ordine aut eius magistro capitanei gencium armorum campi de la Morea:* text in A. RUBIÓ I LLUCH, *Diplomatari de l'Orient català: 1301-1409* (Barcelona, 1947), doc. 425. LOENERTZ' article made no use of this letter; LONGNON - TOPPING ignore LOENERTZ' article.

decided to impose a new *cholta* of 15,000 florins (1). In addition to the financial and business details of his stewardship, Baroncelli's letter gave incidental news of various significant personalities. Busone da Fabriano, an old servant of the Acciaiuoli, who had been *bailli* in the principality in about 1360 (2), was involved in financial dealings with the new *bailli* and had become a Hospitaller (3); John Lascaris Calopheros, who was concerned in some way with the affairs of the Hospital and of the Morea, was in Rhodes (4); Maddalena Buondelmonti, regent at Cephalonia, had put her *galeotta* to sea, and her brother, Esau Buondelmonti, had arrived at Clarenza with two ressels on his way to fetch his wife (5); Fr. Domenico de Alamania would possibly send Baroncelli to Angelo and Lorenzo Acciaiuoli, because " he did not wish to trust anyone else", which may have meant that Alamania hoped to raise money from the Acciaiuoli in Italy to pay for the ransom of the Master of the Hospital and to defend the Morea (6).

(1) Note that Alamania's accounts of August 1381 showed that a *capinico* of 9000 ducats had been raised in the principality (text in LOENERTZ, 351).

(2) In addition to the references to Busone noted in LONGNON - TOPPING, 152, 196-198, 206-207, 213-214, see texts in GREGOROVIUS - LAMBROS, III. 124; LÉONARD, III. 651-652.

(3) Busone was at Rhodes as a Hospitaller on 24 February 1382 (Malta, cod. 321, f. 205).

(4) In addition to ESZER, 75-76 *et passim*, see D. JACOBY, " Jean Lascaris Calophéros, Chypre et la Morée ", *Revue des études byzantines* 26 (1968), 207 *et passim*.

(5) Isau's bride-to-be is not named, and nothing else is known of any such marriage; cf. S. CIRAC ESTOPAÑAN, *Bizancio y España: El legado de la basilissa María y de los déspotas Thomas y Esaú de Joannina*, I (Barcelona, 1943). Isau went to Epirus with the Hospitallers in 1378 (*supra*, 280); he was captured with them at Arta and became the prisoner of Thomas Preljubovich, Despot of Jannina: LAONICUS CHALCOCANDYLES, *Historiarum Demonstrationes*, I, ed. E. DARKÓ (Budapest, 1922), 197. By December 1379 he was free again.

(6) *Infra*, 286; cf. LONGNON - TOPPING, 196 n. 6. Other *addenda* to LONGNON - TOPPING: Andronico Asan Zaccaria had been *bailli* in about 1375 (*Libro de los fechos*, 156); on Janni Misito, see *infra*, 294; on Jacomo, Lord of Tzoya, see A. LUTTRELL, " The Latins of Argos and Nauplia: 1311-1394 ", *Papers of the British School at Rome* 34 (1966), 39, 44, 48-49, 53-55. Correct LUTTRELL (1959), 324, where it is wrongly assumed that the phrase *chapitano della Morea* referred to the captain of the Hospitallers.

By April 1381 the situation had changed significantly, and the Navarrese were active south of the Gulf of Corinth. With the progressive collapse of Angevin government both in Italy and in Achaea, and the consequent incursions of the militarily powerful Navarrese mercenaries, the Hospitallers, who faced serious financial difficulties, were abandoning the principality and Queen Joanna had recently appointed a new *bailli*. The Navarrese were already in the Morea, extorting money from the Hospitallers who were unable to control them. The Buondelmonti at Cephalonia and Aldobrando Baroncelli, as the agent of Angelo and Lorenzo Acciaiuoli, looked for support to Nerio Acciaiuoli, and Esau Buondelmonti travelled to see Nerio at Corinth. A year later the Hospitallers had gone and the Navarrese were in control; the Viscount of Rocaberti, who had been sent from Spain by the King of Aragon, had saved Athens from Nerio Acciaiuoli and the Navarrese, and had made a truce with both. Queen Joanna of Naples had been overthrown by Charles of Anjou-Durazzo who became king, while the claims of Jacques de Baux to the Principality of Achaea had been recognized by the Navarrese. The result was chaos in Greece. In April 1382 Baroncelli reported that Janni Misito, the Grand Marshal, was in prison. In June and July Baroncelli wrote that the Navarrese were attacking Angelo Acciaiuoli's possessions, while he himself visited Nerio, no longer the accomplice of the Navarrese, at Corinth to enlist his support for an abortive Buondelmonti scheme to attack Jacques de Baux and the Navarrese with the assistance of King Charles of Naples. In the event the Navarrese retained control of the Morea (1). Aldobrando Baroncelli, for his part, continued to serve his patrons; in 1388, for example, he was travelling from Cephalonia to Angelo Acciaiuoli in Puglia on business connected with the proposed

(1) For the state of the question, see K. SETTON, *Catalan Domination at Athens: 1311-1388* (Cambridge, Mass., 1948); additional materials, references and amendments in LOENERTZ, 337-349; ESZER, 74-83; A. LUTTRELL, "La Corona de Aragón y la Grecia catalana: 1379-1394", *Anuario de estudios medievales* VI [forthcoming]; and *infra*. The substance of the purely historical part of A. BON, *La Morée franque: recherches historiques, topographiques et archéologiques sur la principauté d'Achaïe (1205-1430)*, 2 vols. (Paris, 1969), was apparently completed in 1951; subsequent amendments are incomplete and much of the historical material requires revision.

marriage of Nerio Acciaiuoli's daughter Francesca to Angelo's son [1].

* * *

Letter I, pp. 245-247: 27 April (1381)

[1] Magnifico Domino. Dapoi la debita raccomadatione. In questo dì per un Navilio d'Otranto vi scrissi simile, per questa v'avviso chom'io imprimieri dell'une patte per Simone Rondinelli, io non ne ho potuto havere; sì che il cangio suo non riuscirà salvo: se esso mi scrivesse che io gli accattasse delle nuove, insino da mò io l'agio scritto, adesso non so che mi rispondere.

[2] Con fra Domenico parlai, dice li suoi denari non aspetta se non di Settembre, si che per mò non faria sangio, salvo se voi fossi contento d'havergli al tempo ch'io dico; di ch'io vedendo così, sì mi parto, e vado a Modone, et là per la via di Puglia, o di Napoli ve li manderò o per cangio, o in seta, o in quella maniera, che vedrò che sian più salvi.

[3] Isau si parte hoggi di quà, et va a Coranto per essere con lo Duca dell'Arcipelago, et seguire il Matrimonio, et staranno là più dì, di ch'io chora io farò a Modone, et cercherò di spacciarmi degli dinari, et poi me ne andrò per Terra a Coranto, et saremo insieme, et vedremo se Mess. Neri vorrà seguire quello dice, e così habbiamo ordinato in sembra con Isau.

[4] Mess. Neri si ha accattato il Duca mio per xxx. m. fiorini, e pagati i mezzi, et li altri mezzi per tutto Maggio, c'ha ricevuto risine ella levadia, (*così*) c'ha soldati i Navarresi, ch'erano con Giancho per viij. m. fiorini a servigio di questo Maggio insino a l'altro, cioè un Anno, et ha mandato per Turchi, che vuole fare il guasto a Setine, se non si rendono, che insino a mò non si vogliono dare.

[5] Il Paese si contenta male di Mess. Marchesano, ma pure converrà loro riceverlo da poi Madama lo comanda, ma per ancora non li hanno assignate le bandiere, et so ha presa per mogliera la figlia del Dispoto Ispada, et ha havuto di dota ducati viij. m. i quali de' dare il gran Mastro, forse per avventura dimorrà ad haverli.

[1] Text in Gregorovius - Lambros, III. 119.

[6] Mess. Marchesano ha portata la mogliera a Nepanto, e là vole, che stia.

[7] Signor mio i Navarresi dipoi mi partì hanno fatto molto più dannaggio, chen prima, ed hanno preso da lo Sprone il vino tutto, e sale la maggior parte, et habitano allo Sprone, e hanno mal conciato le case de' Villani: Ancora in Chiarenza habitano per tutto, e in casa vostra assai, e non vi hanno lassato biada, nè legname, e ancora Porti, e Tettora dirupate per havere il legname, sì che a voi ne è seguito gran danno, per avventura vie più, che non stimate, e niuno rimedio non ci si mette, se non di parole. Il Gran Commendatore fa per certo quanto può, et spetialmente di difendere le vostre.

[8] Egli è venuto hoggi un Velier di Rodi, e dice che l'altro viene hora, saranno alla prova se passeranno i Navarresi: Il Gran Commendatore dice che aspetta due Frieri, che gli portano denari, in questi paesi debbono venire alle mani de' Bonciani; sicchè io vi ricordo, che voi diciate a lo Mezza, e ancora lo scriva esso a Napoli, che se denari hanno in mano di persona, li voglia quà che li vi dia, e voi me li mandate a pagare a me.

[9] Raccomandomi sempre alla S. V. Scritta a Chiarenza a' dì xxvij. d'Aprile... Inditione...

Vostro servitore
Aldobrando.

[10] Sacciate Sig. mio, che le sei Galere, che passarono de' Genovesi per Natale erano in Levante, posono a lo Grigio, ch'è in mezzo tra Modone, e Corone, et sì v'hanno fatto grande dannaggio, hanno presi huomini, e bestiame, e biade, e vino, malamente hanno corso quello Casale: se vi pare ne fate mentione al Consolo de' Genovesi, che è a Barletta.

[11] E mi pare che i Navarresi non sieno atti a passare in Ponente, ma mi pare voglino passare inverso Drusa per guastare l'avanzo del paese: Haremo secondo io veggio di quà travagli assai dipoi che ci ha niuno altro remedio.

A tergo
Magnifico Sig. mio Lorenzo di Acciaioli
suo Domino Reverendissimo.

[**1**] Simone Rondinelli was probably kinsman to Bartolomeo Rondinelli, who was Baron of Chalandritsa in 1357 (LONGNON-TOPPING, 133 n. 3).

[2] Following their defeat in Epirus the Hospitallers needed money to ransom their Master and to defend the Morea. They borrowed at least 2000 ducats from Centurione Zaccaria, Grand Constable of Achaea, all but 180 of which had been repaid by 6 April 1382 (Malta, cod. 321, f. 219v). The accounts of 24 August 1381 mentioned 1500 ducats received from Zaccaria, various sums repaid to Nerio Acciaiuoli, and 4500 ducats received from Isabelle de Lusignan, widow of Manuel Catacuzenus (text in LOENERTZ, 350-355). A document of 6 April 1382 shows that Isabelle advanced a total of 9500 ducats: Malta, cod. 321, f. 235, published by D. ZAKYTHINOS, in *Revue des études grecques* 49 (1936), 73-75. Some time before 25 February 1382, the Hospitallers repaid Nerio, through Giovanni Corsini of Florence, a further 3000 florins; these redeemed their *baiulia duchatus athenarum* which had been pledged *(obligata)* to Nerio (Malta, cod. 321, f. 232v). Baroncelli's letter of 15 December 1379 mentioned the possibility that Fr. Domenico de Alamania would send him to Lorenzo and Angelo Acciaiuoli, possibly in an attempt to raise a loan (*supra*, 282). The present letter reinforces the possibility that the Hospital had borrowed from Lorenzo, since in April 1381 Alamania was apparently in Clarenza, where he told Baroncelli that he was not expecting his money before September, so that for the time being he would not change the money, provided that Lorenzo was content to have it at a later time. On the other hand, the accounts which were presented by Alamania, who was responsible for the Hospital's financial operations in Greece, and which were approved at Rhodes on 24 August 1381 mentioned repayments to Centurione Zaccaria, Isabelle de Lusignan, Nerio Acciaiuoli and others, but not to Lorenzo (text in LOENERTZ, 350-355). Possibly the repayment was in fact made later, in September as suggested, for on 20 September 1381 Alamania was about to leave Rhodes as captain of a galley bound for Cephalonia, with instructions to return to Rhodes after not more than eight days (Malta, cod. 321, f. 213v).

[3] Esau Buondelmonti is leaving Clarenza to join Niccolò dalle Carceri, Duke of the Archipelago, at Corinth where there will be a marriage, presumably that of Niccolò.

On 28 October 1372 the Venetians wrote to Leonardo Tocco, Count of Cephalonia, saying that they could provide galleys for the forthcoming wedding *(pro cellebrandis nuptiis et sponsalis matrimonii)* of Leonardo's *primogenita*, who had been betrothed to the *iuvenis* Niccolò dalle Carceri, only if the galleys were not needed in the Aegean (Venice, Archivio di Stato: Misti, xxxiv, f. 32). K. HOPF, *Geschichte Griechenlands vom Beginn des Mittelalters bis auf unsere Zeit*, II (Leipzig, 1868), 29, without sources, assumes that the *primogenita* was Petronilla and that the marriage took place in 1372; LUTTRELL (1964), 140, follows his assumption. Tocco certainly had a daughter by 1362 (text in BUCHON, II. 207) and more than one by 1374 (*supra*, 277 n. 1), but it is doubtful whether either can have been at all old then; in about 1377 their brother Carlo was very young and the younger brother Leonardo was still at the breast: G. SCHIRÒ, " Struttura e contenuto della cronaca dei Tocco ", *Byzantion* 32 (1962), 208. Leonardo had a daughter named Petronilla who married Niccolò Venier: text in C. SATHAS, *Documents inédits relatifs à l'histoire de la Grèce au moyen âge*, I (Paris, 1880), 34-36. Apparently Petronilla was the *primogenita* and her marriage had been postponed until 1381, when she would have been about twenty. Presumably she married Niccolò Venier after Niccolò dalle Carceri's death in 1383, but not later than 1386: texts in K. HOPF, *Chroniques gréco-romanes* (Berlin, 1873),. 183, 185. A marriage between Petronilla Tocco and Niccolò dalle Carceri, in the Acciaiuoli stronghold of Corinth and in the presence of Esau Buondelmonti, would have fitted into the general picture of an Acciaiuoli-Buondelmonti-Tocco alliance with the Navarrese against the Catalans. Some time before April 1381 Niccolò dalle Carceri had, in fact, made an alliance with the Navarrese which threatened the Catalans (texts *ibid.*, 183; RUBIÓ, doc. 457).

Some arrangement, possibly financial and perhaps connected with the projected marriage, has been made, apparently between Nerio Acciaiuoli and the Tocco-Buondelmonti family, but Baroncelli doubts whether Nerio will honour it.

[**4**] This section remains obscure. It may mean that Nerio Acciaiuoli has obtained or bought the duchy (*il Duca mio*) for 30,000 florins, having paid half and owing the rest in May. There was no Acciaiuoli duke, and since earlier in the same letter Baroncelli wrote *lo* (not *il*) *Duca* this passage, presumably corrupt,

may have read *il Ducamio*, ie. the Duchy, presumably of Athens but possibly of the Archipelago.

c'ha ricevuto risine ella levadia, (così) c'ha soldati i Navarresi: the *così* may be suppressed as being an editorial interpolation, and the passage is probably corrupt. It may mean: "He has received the places of *Risine* (?) and Levadia, and has paid the Navarrese..." Levadia was captured from the Catalans by the Navarrese between July 1380 and about February 1381 (LOENERTZ, 335).

Nerio has hired those Navarrese who serve under Juan de Urtubia (*Giancho*, or *Iancono de Vrtobia;* LOENERTZ, 352) for 8000 florins to serve a year from May (ie. from May 1381 to May 1382), and he has sent for Turkish mercenaries to destroy Athens *(Setine)* unless it surrenders. Nerio had been allied with Urtubia against the Catalans at least since 1379; the Navarrese had already taken Livadia and attacked Athens (LOENERTZ, 332, 335, 339). In April 1381 a new attack on Athens was an obvious move, but in the autumn the Viscount of Rocaberti reached the Catalan duchies from Spain and relieved Athens; subsequently he made a truce with Urtubia's Navarrese who moved south into the Morea (LOENERTZ, 341, 345-346).

[**5**] *Mess. Marchesano* was a baron of Achaea. Philip of Anjou, Prince of Achaea, shortly before his own death in November 1373, named *micer Marquesan de Flor de Napol* as *bailli* of the Morea (*Libro de los fechos*, 155: for the correct reading as *Marquesan* rather than *Ojarquesan*, see Madrid, Biblioteca Nacional, Ms. 10131, f. 263v); BON, I. 251, has "Ojarque san de Flor". In about 1377 he held in the Morea *lo castello novo de messer marchisano:* text in A. LUTTRELL, in *Byzantinische Zeitschrift* 57 (1964), 344.

Apparently *Madama*, Joanna of Anjou, Queen of Naples and Princess of Achaea, had recently appointed Marchesano *bailli* again, and he had been badly received; he had yet to be invested with the pennants (cf. *supra*, 281). Fr. Domenico de Alamania's journey from Apulia to Achaea to resign his office as *bailli*, mentioned in the document of 24 August 1381 (text in LOENERTZ, 351), presumably took place before 27 April 1381, by which time Marchesano had been nominated *bailli;* LOENERTZ, 329, places the journey "peu avant" 24 August 1381.

Baroncelli states that Marchesano has married the daughter of the *Dispoto Ispada*, who was presumably Ghin Boua Spata Despot of Arta, with 8000 florins as dowry which Spata was to receive as the ransom of the Master of the Hospital, whom he had captured in 1378 (*supra*, 280); Baroncelli thinks the ransom might not be paid for some time. The names of Ghin Boua's daughters are apparently not known with certainty, except that a daughter Eirene married Isau Buondelmonti in 1396 (CIRAC, I. 139-141, 171-172). The genealogy of the Spata family given in HOPF, *Chroniques*, 531, is altogether inaccurate. According to HOPF (*ibid.*, 182), a 16th-century compilation of Stefano Magno stated, under 1373: *Lepanto paret Despotae Artae et Ianinae "Mauritio Spata"*. The original (Venice, Biblioteca Correr, Ms. Cicogna 3531, f. 59v) reads: *Gli dispoti de romania hebe mauritio spata zoe le citade mediteranee zo ianina dita latine ioanine item Nepanto etc questo mauritio se stitulava dispoti di arta et ianina.* Ghin Boua Spata acquired Arta in 1373/4 (CIRAC, I. 139), but he was not Despot of Jannina; the previous sentence refers to events of 1379, and this text is a doubtful authority for the idea that the Spata held Lepanto (*Nepanto* or Naupactos) in 1373.

There seems to be no evidence for the story (accepted in LOENERTZ, 331), that Fr. Juan Fernández de Heredia and the Hospitallers sailed to Lepanto and captured it on their way to Vonitza early in 1378; cf. A. LUTTRELL, "Venice and the Knights Hospitallers of Rhodes in the Fourteenth Century," *Papers of the British School at Rome* 26 (1958), 207-209. Payments by the Hospitallers to Paolo Foscari, Archbishop of Patras, and to others for the defence of Lepanto, which technically formed part of the Principality of Achaea, appeared in Fr. Domenico de Alamania's accounts of 24 August 1381 (text in LOENERTZ, 352, 354-355). LOENERTZ, 335, assumes, probably correctly, that this defence occurred before September 1380.

A document, dated at Constantinople in September 1380, mentioned "the Lord of Naupactos, the Despot Boua Spata": text in F. MIKLOSICH - I. MÜLLER, *Acta et diplomata graeca medii aevii*, II (Vienna, 1862), 11-12; LOENERTZ, 335, was not necessarily correct in supposing that this was Ghin Boua Spata. Baroncelli's next paragraph states that Marchesano has taken his wife to live at Lepanto; presumably Marchesano's marriage and his acquisition of Lepanto came between mid-1380 and April 1381, when Baroncelli wrote. He certainly held Lepanto by 17 August 1386 when King Pedro of Aragon addressed a letter to *micer Marquesa senyor de loch de Neopaton* (text in Rubiò, doc. 592). According to the Tocco Chronicle (Schirò, 208) Lepanto was controlled by Ghin Boua's brother Sguros Spata, but this was presumably after 1386; in fact, a text of 1386 described Sguros merely as *Sguros Buda Spada dominus Angelicastro et Albanie;* V. Lazzarini, " L'acquisto di Lepanto: 1407 ", *Nuovo archivio veneto* VIII (1898), 269 n. 3.

This letter solves the old problem of the identity of *Myrsi Makatsanos* (Messer Marchesano), about whom Hopf and others made the most improbable suggestions. The Epirus Chronicle stated that in mid-1382 " Myrsi Makatsanos, the *gambros* (ie. son-in-law) of Spata, entered Jannina with great ceremony, and he (ie. Makatsanos) drew up a bogus treaty (which involved a dowry) with Spata in relation to Helena (sister of Thomas Preljubovic, Despot of Jannina) and so induced him (ie. Spata) to withdraw ". Whatever the implications of this text for the history of Jannina, it seems likely that after Spata had attacked Thomas in May 1379 he was glad to find an ally in Marchesano: text and references in Cirac, I. 149-156.

[**7**] Despite the efforts of the Grand Commander of the Hospital to restrain the Navarrese and to protect the Acciaiuoli estates, the Navarrese have met little opposition and have caused serious damage to the Acciaiuoli's rich *casale* at Sperone in Elis, and to their property at Clarenza; on these properties, see Longnon-Topping, 196, 235-236.

The Grand Commander, Fr. Bertrand Flote, was at Clarenza on 6 December 1380, and was appointed Papal Collector in *Romania* by Clement VII on 10 May 1381: Luttrell (1966) 40 n. 44. On 31 (*sic*) April 1381 King Pedro of Aragon addressed him as the Hospitallers' *capitaneus gentium armorum in partibus dela Morea* (text in Rubió, doc. 467).

Baroncelli makes it clear that certain of the Navarrese were in the Morea by April 1381 and that, even if they had come as a result of some form of agreement rather than as mere invaders (cf. Loenertz, 332-333, 337), they had used violence once they had come. On 24 August 1381 Fr. Domenico de Alamania had lately *(nuper)* paid to those Navarrese in the Morea *(Societati sistente in dicto principatu)* 2900 ducats promised them by Fr. Bertrand Flote and Fr. Hesso Schegelholtz and by the *homines* of the principality (text in LOENERTZ, 351). The Hospitallers' relations with the Navarrese, some of whom had been hired to serve the Hospital, certainly went back to 1378 or 1379 but their exact nature remains obscure; LOENERTZ, 331-333, is not necessarily correct in assuming that the payments accounted for in August 1381 related to services performed as early as 1378 and 1379. Once the Navarrese reached the Morea, the main body of the companies seems to have turned against the Hospitallers who apparently attempted to purchase their good behaviour. LOENERTZ, 337, does not seem justified in interpreting the text of August 1381 as showing that the Navarrese recognized Joanna of Naples as Princess of Achaea.

[**8**] A fast sailing-boat *(Velier)* from Rhodes has arrived at Clarenza, and another is expected. Fr. Bertrand Flote says he is expecting two Hospitallers (*Frieri*) with money, presumably to pay off the Navarrese. A Hospitaller galley *(.j. galia de la maxon da Ruodo armada a do per bancho charga de formaio e pan, che andava a fornir alguni suoi luogi de la Marcha)* was off Cape Malia on 21 April 1381: DANIELE DI CHINAZZO, *Cronica de la Guerra da Veniciani a Zenovesi*, ed. V. LAZZARINI (Venice, 1958), 178-179.

The Bonciani were Florentines, presumably merchants or bankers.

Lo Mezza: probably Filippo delle Mazze, an Acciaiuoli agent in Greece (LONGNON - TOPPING, 197, 207, 213-215).

[**9**] 27 April 1381. The year 1381 fits with the known activities of Fr. Domenico de Alamania, with the Navarrese still being near Athens (*supra*, 288), and possibly, though not certainly, with the Genoese attack on Grizi (*infra*, 292). Baroncelli's references to Fr. Bertrand Flote, who was dead by 9 April 1382 (LUTTRELL [1966], 40 n. 44), and to the Navarrese occupation of Androusa as being in the future (*infra*, 292) seem to rule out 1382. Furthermore Baroncelli was at Cephalonia on 24 April 1382 (*infra*, 295), and since nothing in the present letter, dated 27 April, suggests

that he had just arrived from Cephalonia, the letter of 27 April was probably not written in 1382.

[**10**] Six Genoese galleys which had been in the Levant since the previous Christmas have attacked Grizi, an Acciaiuoli *casale* on the coast between Corone and Modone (on which see LONGNON - TOPPING, 252-253; BON, I. 433-435), presumably in April since the news was included in the postscript written at Clarenza apparently on 27 April. This incident probably occurred during the war of Chioggia; see especially CHINAZZO, 162-188; RAPHAYNUS DE CARESINIS, *Chronica*, in *Rerum Italicarum Scriptores*, ns. 12 part 2 (Bologna, 1923), 52-53; *Vita Caroli Zeni*, in *ibid.*, ns. 19 part 6 (1941), 69-70. There were eight Genoese galleys at Zara in December 1380 and in April 1380 (CHINAZZO, 162, 185). The attack probably took place before the fleet which left Venice on 2 April under the command of Carlo Zeno and reached Zante on 15 April, arrived at Modon on 17 April (*ibid.*, 178). The twenty and more Genoese galleys which Zeno chased into the Adriatic in May had come from Genoa (*ibid.*, 179-180). Peace between Genoa and Venice was ratified in August 1381. There is no known reference to an attack on Grizi between 1380 and April 1381, and it could conceivably have occurred in 1382, after the end of the war; G. STELLA, *Annales Genuenses*, in L. MURATORI, *Rerum Italicarum Scriptores*, 17 (Milan, 1730), 1119, mentioned that after October 1381 four Genoese galleys were stationed in Cyprus, two in Sicily, two in *Romania* and one in the Adriatic.

[**11**] Baroncelli does not consider that the Navarrese are about to move westwards but to ravage the country towards Androusa (*Drusa;* LONGNON - TOPPING, 246) near Kalamata in the south. The Navarrese occupied Androusa before 18 January 1382: text in L. DE MAS-LATRIE, " Documents concernant divers pays de l'Orient latin: 1382-1413 ", *Bibliothèque de l'École des Chartes* 58 (1897), 82-87.

Letter II, pp. 247-248: 24 April 1382

[1] Reverendissimo Domino. Di poi la debita raccomandatione: A questi dì venendo in Cifalonia trovai Pagolo da Perugia, il quale mi diede una lettera vostra, dove mi scrivete havere ricevuto per Sandro quanto io vi mandai: di ciò mi piace, e scrivetemi

che per allhora m'avete avisato, sacciate chom'io non ho havuto niuna altra vostra lettera, ma bene saccio che sono venute a mano di Navarresi, e ancora l'hanno tanto quelle, quanto molte altre.

[2] Sig. mio per molte lettere i v'aggio avvisato dello male stato di questo Paese, e dello dannaggio hanno ricevuto le vostre cose, et simile credo Madama la Duchessa ve lo harà detto, et avisatovene sicchè però poco mi stendo a lo scrivere, perché so siate avisato di tutto; ma pure il debito mio deggio fare di ricordarlovi sempre, e così faccio, e prego la S. V. ci dobbiate provedere: se grande tempo stanno così, si possono mettere a uscita non sono cose, il perchè si debbino così abbandonare: lo vostro tutto tengono, e così di molti altri dello Paese.

[3] Mess. Giovanni Misto è ancora prigione esso, e la figlia, e hanno havuto due delle sue migliori Castella: Adesso sta a Pencholo.

[4] Ancora andando a questi dì Mess. Marotto, e Perardo a la Pesliza la Prenzessa gli mandò incontro loro uno de' suoi frati per far loro honore, di che l'hanno preso di presente, et in effetto hanno preso la Terra, e lo Castello: la Prenzessa mostra se ne voglia andare a lo Padre a Scio.

[5] Sopra li fatti di Mess. Neri già mai non fu tempo quanto mo, e sono ben fido; Madama la Duchessa ve ne harà avisato di tutto, et come savio seguirete quanto vi parrà lo meglio.

[6] Con lo Bisconte parmi s'accorderanno, e cercasi e quasi si tiene fatta, che lo figlio della Bisconte prenderà la figlia picciola di Mess. Neri, e rimarrà a lo Paese il figlio, ed esso lo governerà, cioè Mess. N.

[7] Delli danari che scrivete dello avanzo, facciovi a sapere come Madama la Duchessa prese per portarmi la seta, e la cera, la quale seta vale ducati cc. o circa: la Cera è bene da c. libre.

[8] I denari ch'erano in Cifalonia si erano ducati 67. cioè la valuta ducati 80. pagati a questi Navarresi per la Colletta di 500. ducati. Li ducati 80. haveva a mano, e dieli, perchè non corressono, e ardessino, ma pure alla fine poco varrà.

[9] Io sono venuto in Cifalonia per due cose; l'una perchè di là io non fo niente, che tutto hanno preso, e io non voglio fare spesa; la seconda per haver consiglio da Isau quello li pare ch'io faccia, Et secondo mi dice a giorno a giorno aspetta novelle

di Napoli, et saperassi in che modo rimarrà lo Paese di quà, arricordovilo sempre: Di poi haggio saputo come la Duchessa lassò a Santa Maura la seta, et la cera, terrassi quello modo che voi la harete, o denari: sempre mi raccomando a la S. V.

[10] Scritta in Cifalonia a' dì xxiiij. d'Aprile v. Inditione.

[11] Filippo delle Mazze vostro buon servitore si raccomanda alla S. V.

Vostro buon servitore
Aldebrando di Firenze

A tergo
Magnifico Domino Lorenzo de Acciaioli
Domino suo Reverendissimo.

[**2**] *la Duchessa:* Maddalena Buondelmonti.

[**3**] Janni Misito was made Grand Marshal of Achaea in 1376 (*Libro de los fechos*, 159) and held the castles of Stala, Greveni and Turcata in 1377: text in LUTTRELL, in *Byzantinische Zeitschrift* 57 (1964), 344. Misito was apparently free in November 1379 when Baroncelli recommended that Lorenzo Acciaiuoli should write to him (LONGNON - TOPPING, doc. X). By April 1382, Misito and his daughter were prisoners at *Pencholo* (unidentified), presumably of the Navarrese who seem to have taken two of his castles.

[**4**] *La Prenzessa* was Marie de Morphou, daughter of Jean de Morphou of Cyprus, Count of Roucha (Edessa); she married Hugues de Lusignan, titular Prince of Galilee, son of Marie de Bourbon and claimant to the Principality of Achaea: G. HILL, *A History of Cyprus*, II (Cambridge, 1948), 310 n. 4, 394 n. 1, with references.

It seems that the Navarrese had taken the lands and castles of *la Prenzessa*. When Marie de Bourbon made her will in 1387 and an attempt was made to discover what were the *biens mobles et heritages* in the Morea of her late son, his former confessor reported *que quant les Navarrois prinrent le chasteau de la Votisse* (Vostiza), *les mobles de madame la princesse* (Marie de Morphou?) *et du dit chastel, tant de joyaux que aultres furent portez a Modon...*: text in L. DE MAS-LATRIE, *Histoire de l'île de Chypre*, II (Paris,

1852), 409-412. LOENERTZ, 333 n. 1, suggests that this occurred in 1385/6, but Baroncelli's letter indicates 1382.

Princess Marie wanted to go to her father Jean de Morphou at Chios (*Scio*); Jean had been imprisoned on Chios in 1374; reference in HILL, II. 395, who mentions with disbelief the tale, here proved false, that Jean died suspiciously in Cyprus in about 1379.

[**5**] The nature of Lorenzo's business with Nerio Acciaiuoli, known to Maddalena Buondelmonti and mentioned again in June 1382 (*infra*, 296), is not made clear.

[**6**] Nerio Acciaiuoli had two natural daughters. Bartolomea was already married to Theodore, Despot of the Morea, by 1383 or 1384: G. DENNIS, *The Reign of Manuel II Palaeologus in Thessalonica:* 1382-1387 (Rome, 1960), 119. Francesca's marriage to Angelo Acciaiuoli's son was under discussion in May 1388 (text in GREGOROVIUS - LAMPROS, III. 119); she married Carlo Tocco some time before 1394 (text *ibid.*, III. 147-152). Whichever was *la figlia picciola*, it seems that negotiations for her to marry the son of the *Bisconte* were almost complete in April 1382. The *Bisconte* was presumably Felipe Dalmau, *visconde* of Rocaberti, who had arrived in Greece late in 1381 and who left again in about April 1382, having concluded a truce with Nerio (LOENERTZ, 341, 345). The betrothal may never even have been agreed, for in the same year one of Rocaberti's sons, Bernaduc, was in fact betrothed to marry the daughter of Helena Cantacuzena, dowager Countess of Salona: RUBIÓ, docs. 525-528.

[**8**] The Navarrese are raising a *Colletta* in the principality; this is the *cholta* or subsidy also mentioned in Baroncelli's letter of 1379 (LONGNON - TOPPING, doc. X and n. 6). The Navarrese leader Mahiot de Coquerel was already acting as *bailli* (*infra*, 297).

[**9**] Baroncelli went to Cephalonia to consult Isau Buondelmonti; news was expected from the Kingdom of Naples.

Santa Maura: castle on the Tocco's island of Leucadia.

[**10**] 24 April 1382 (cf. *supra*, 291); there seems no reason to doubt the correctness of this date.

[**11**] Filippo delle Mazze (cf. *supra*, 291).

Letter III, pp. 242-243: 15 June 1382

[1] Reverendissimo Domino. Di poi la debita raccomandatione. Sacci la V. S. chom'io vado a Coranto per parlare con Mess. Neri per lo fatto che voi sapete; et di poi tornato di là con Dio avanti verrò a la V. S. per meglio avisarvi di tutti i vostri fatti, che mi pare ch'al provederci si dia grande indugio: sopra questo non mi stendo di troppo scrivere, perchè per più altre lettere v'ho scritto come sono andati i vostri fatti di quà.

[2] Sacci la V. S. come lo Sig. Ysau havendo preso uno si chiama Petrillo Serpandi, il quale veniva da lo Imperadore se li trovò più lettere, tra le quali trovò una lettera aperta con sigillo pendente, la quale lo Imperatore mandava a la Compagnia, comandando che di presente levassero tutte le cose del Gran Siniscalco, et del Prenze, e a lor possa quelle di Cefalonia, e che prendessero tutti loro Ufficiali passati, e quelli che si trovassino, et che si facessino rendere ragione di tutto, et sopra ciò ancora n'haveva fatto Capitoli: de' quali Capitoli, e lettera Ysau ne manda la copia a Madama la Duchessa: Vedetela, e sarete poi avisato quello harete a fare: Per mò non mi stendo in più scrivere, che come vi dico, con Dio avanti, tornato da Coranto, sarete per me informato ancora di ciò che mancasse, et di quello sarà seguito: Pregovi ch'io vi sia raccomandato.

[3] Scritta in Cifalonia a' dì xv. di Giugno v. Inditione.

[4] Catanzano mi diè una vostra lettera, e quanto comandate sarà fatto.

Vostro servitore
Aldobrando Baroncelli di Firenze.

A tergo
Magnifico Viro Lorenzo de Acciaroli
suo Domino Reverendissimo.

[**1**] Baroncelli was to go from Cephalonia to Corinth to discuss certain affairs concerning Lorenzo with Nerio Acciaiuoli, and then travel to inform Lorenzo about this negotiation.

[**2**] Esau Buondelmonti, who was apparently not at that point in Cephalonia itself, had captured Petrillo Seripandi carrying a letter from the *imperadore* (Jacques de Baux, titular Emperor of Constantinople) which instructed *la compagnia* (the

Navarrese) to take everything from the Grand Seneschal (Angelo Acciaiuoli), from the *Prenze* (Hugues of Galilee), and from *quelle di Cefalonia* (the Tocco and Buondelmonti).

Jacques de Baux was probably at Taranto. By January 1382 his claims to the Principality of Achaea had been accepted by the Navarrese, whose leader Mahiot de Coquerel he had constituted as *bailli* of Achaea: LOENERTZ, 340-345. Jacques' opponents included the Acciaiuoli, Tocco and Buondelmonti, and Hugues of Galilee, another pretender to the principality whose wife was apparently in Cephalonia, or Greece, in April 1382 (*supra*, 294-295). There seems to be no clear evidence to support the affirmation in LOENERTZ, 340, that the barons (" hommes-liges ") of Achaea recognized Jacques de Baux; the agreement of 18 January 1382 involved only the Navarrese and the Venetians: text in MAS-LATRIE, in *Bibliothèque de l'École des Chartes* 58 (1897), 82-87.

Hugues de Lusignan, Prince of Galilee, was the son of Marie de Bourbon, whose second husband was Robert of Anjou, Prince of Taranto and Achaea as well as titular Emperor of Constantinople. Between 1364, when Robert died, and 1370 Marie and Hugues fought jointly in the Morea in an attempt to secure the Principality of Achaea from Robert's brother Philip (*Libro de los fechos*, 152-155).

[**3**] 15 June 1382.

Letter IV, pp. 243-245: 12 July 1382

[1] Reverendissimo Domino: Da poi la debita raccomandatione. Io haggio iscritto molte lettere a la V. S. avisandovi del male stato di questo Paese da quà, et come questi Navarresi hanno preso tutto, tanto le cose vostre, quanto d'altrui, et ancora credo sarà venuto a Napoli il Prenze di Galilea, il quale porta copia d'una lettera, mandata lo Imperatore alla Compagnia di quà, che vi levassero tutte cose: Di che a me pare ch'al tutto niente vi curiate delle vostre cose di quà, che molto leggiermente con Mons. lo Re al presente vi potete aiutare: Con poco di soccorso fosse mandato quà a Ysau, il quale have rotto con loro; e pur ch'esso habbia aiuto di Ponente di Galee, ed alcuna gente, leggiermente si ricovererà tutto lo Principato, che meglio ene

assai paese guasto, che tutto perduto: Hora sopra questo la S. V. n'è bene sì informato per più fiate, crederò ci provedrete.

[2] Sig. mio havendo i Navarresi levato tutto, venni in Cifalonia per havere consiglio dal mio Sig. Ysau di quello ch'io havessi a fare: Ho trovato lui essere in guerra, di ch'io conosca il miò essere mancamento di me partire: E considerando che di ciò voi farete contento, per sua lettera vi avviserà di tutto.

[3] A questi dì fummo a Coranto la mia moglie ed io, cioè Ventura Buondelmonti, et là ordinammo alcuna cosa, della quale Madama la Duchessa di Cifalonia, e Federigo Tiranesi di Firenze, apportatore di questa vi aviseranno di tutto.

[4] L'amico s'è recato a tutte cose ragionevoli, e così n'aggio scritta di sua mano, e mandovene la copia per lo detto Federigo, il quale v'aviserà di tutto: Parmi l'Amico al tutto ha voglia d'esser con voi quello, che dee.

[5] Tornando noi da Coranto, essendo noi in Palermo, a Ventura Buondelmonti venne certo disastro: Il perchè esso si è andato a Paradiso: Dio li perdoni: Il come non vi scrivo, che Federigo ve lo dirà a bocca.

[6] Mandovi per lo detto Federigo un sacco di seta, il quale ene a questo peso libre Lxxiij. de la Crestiere al peso di costà, et si la mando nelle mani del Nuezza a Barletta: In caso là si trovi buona vendita, la vendino, et rimettavi i denari: In caso che no, ve lo mandi a Napoli, et ne facci la vostra voluntà. Rispondetemi quando havete ricevuto i denari, o la seta.

[7] Altro per questa non ci ha di nuovo da scrivere: Imperocchè dal detto Federigo sarete informato di tutto a pieno: Sempre mi raccomando a la S. V.

[8] Scritta in Cifalonia a' dì xij, di Luglio v. Inditione 1381.

Vostro servitore
Aldobrando Baroncelli di Firenze

A tergo
Magnifico et Potenti Viro Lorenzo
de Acciaiuoli &c. suo Dom. Reverendissimo.

[9] Voi vedete la voluntà di Mess. Neri, e però se vi disponete di venire, con poco aiuto di Mons. lo Re potresti venire, et faresti i fatti vostri, et raggiunteresti il Principato: E questo mi pare non vi saria poco honore, e aspetterestine merito dal Signore.

[**1**] The Navarrese have ruined the country and taken everything, including the goods of Lorenzo Acciaiuoli; Baroncelli complains that Lorenzo has done nothing about this although he could easily secure the aid of *lo Re,* ie. Charles of Anjou-Durazzo, King of Naples. Charles, then at Naples, had been opposed by Jacques de Baux, whom he had summoned to come to Naples to explain his rebellion (LOENERTZ, 343-345). In Baroncelli's opinion, if a few troops and galleys had been sent to Cephalonia to Esau Buondelmonti, who had broken with the Navarrese, he could easily have recovered the Principality of Achaea.

It is probable that Jacques de Baux' hostility to the Tocco and Buondelmonti was expressed in the concession, made before February 1383, of the County of Cephalonia to John Lascaris Calopheros (text in RUBIÓ, doc. 541). By 22 August 1384 Louis of Anjou, the heir of Jacques de Baux who died in 1383, had confiscated from the Toccos all their islands and possessions, on account of their treason in supporting his opponent, Charles of Anjou-Durazzo: text in G. SAIGE, *Documents historiques antérieurs au quinzième siècle relatifs à la Seigneurie de Monaco et à la maison de Grimaldi,* I (Monaco, 1905), 505-510. Neither act had any practical effect.

Hugues de Lusignan, Prince of Galilee, will carry to Naples a copy of Jacques de Baux' letter to the Navarrese. Hugues and his wife were in Apulia, borrowing money for a journey to Cyprus, in 1383 (Venice, Archivio di Stato, xlvii, f. 69, wrongly given as 1393 in MAS-LATRIE, *Chypre,* II. 457).

[**2**] Baroncelli has travelled from the Morea to Cephalonia to consult with Esau whom he found at war, possibly in Epirus (cf. SCHIRÒ, 208-209).

[**3**] Baroncelli and his wife have been to Corinth on business which Maddalena Buondelmonti and the bearer, Federigo Tiranesi of Florence, will explain to Lorenzo. *Cioè* is apparently an error in transcription. Ventura Buondelmonti's activities remain obscure.

[**4**] *L'Amico:* conceivably Nerio Acciaiuoli.

300

[**5**] Ventura Buondelmonti must have died on his return from Corinth at Patras (not Palermo). P. LITTA, " Buondelmonte di Firenze ", *Famiglie celebri di Italia* (Milan, 1850), tav. VI, shows Ventura as belonging to a different branch of the Buondelmonti family from that of Maddalena, and states that he died at Patras in 1381 (" serviva ammiraglio nell'armata marittima degli imperatori d'Oriente, e morì a Patrasso nel 1381 ").

[**8**] 12 July 1382; the " 1381 " is clearly an error.

[**9**] Baroncelli again implies that Nerio Acciaiuoli is well disposed towards Lorenzo who, with some aid from King Charles, could come to the principality.

XIII

Guglielmo de Tocco, Captain of Corfu: 1330–1331

Those portions of the Angevin archives at Naples which had survived earlier disasters were destroyed in 1943, yet documents issued during the fourteenth century by the various Neapolitan branches of the Angevin dynasty can still be discovered in private archives and elsewhere.[1] Such texts are particularly important when they concern Latin Greece for which the sources are strictly limited.[2] The hitherto unknown act published here shows Angevin administrations at work both on Corfu, where the Latins had established Neapolitan institutions,[3] and at Naples, where the Angevin Princes of Achaea and Taranto kept their archives. This document throws light both on the early genealogy of the Tocco[4] and on the way in

1. Professor Antonio Allocati, who will shortly publish an inventory of the Archivio Tocco di Montemiletto now in the Archivio di Stato at Naples, most kindly facilitated the study of the document here published in many ways. See, meanwhile, A. Allocati, 'Archivi privati conservati nell'Archivio di Stato di Napoli', in Sovrintendenza Archivistica per la Campania, *Atti del Convegno per i primi trent'anni di Attività della Sovrintendenza* (Rome, 1973), 78–85. The present author intends to use other materials in this private archive to illustrate the Italian background to the Greek operations of the Tocco family.

2. See J. Longnon–P. Topping, *Documents sur le régime des terres dans la principauté de Morée au XIVe siècle* (Paris—The Hague, 1969).

3. For an introduction to Angevin administrative practice and the relevant bibliography, see A. Allocati, *Lineamenti delle istituzioni pubbliche nell'Italia meridionale*, I: *dall'età prenormanna al viceregno spagnolo* (Rome, 1968). On the Angevin administration of Corfu down to 1300, see C. Perrat-J. Longnon, *Actes relatifs à la principauté de Morée: 1289–1300* (Paris, 1967).

4. The erroneous genealogy in C. Hopf, *Chroniques gréco-romanes inédites ou peu connues* (Berlin, 1873), p. 530, is repeated in A. Bon, *La Morée franque: recherches historiques, topographiques et archéologiques sur la principauté d'Achaïe (1205–1430)*, I (Paris, 1969), p. 707.

which the family initiated the acquisition of its extensive possessions in Greece and the Ionian islands;[5] it contributes to the reconstruction of the history of the Tocco family during the decades before the period described in their family chronicle, the first folios of which are missing so that it now effectively begins around 1375.[6] In the case of Corfu in the early fourteenth century, the existing accounts are based in part on exceptionally unsatisfactory materials in the shape of confirmations of privileges granted to the Jewish community. These confirmations, which were issued around 1370 and which contained copies of earlier documents, were preserved in the archives of the Corfu synagogue. They were available to the nineteenth-century Corfiote scholar Andreas Moustoxydes in certified copies translated into what J. A. C. Buchon, to whom Moustoxydes 'communicated' his papers, described as 'detestable Italian'. Moustoxydes used these documents in a careless way, with misprints and contradictions, while Buchon's versions of what they contained vary from those of Moustoxydes;[7] any control of their content is now impossible since the archives at Corfu, including those of the Jewish community, were destroyed in 1943.[8] Reliable information such as that provided by the document of 1345 preserved in the Tocco family archives and published below is, therefore, especially valuable.

The document of 1345 was issued at Naples by Robert of Anjou, Despot of *Romania* and Prince of Achaea and Taranto, at the request of Pietro, Leonardo, Nicoletto and Lisolo, sons and heirs of Guglielmo de Tocco of Naples. Guglielmo had served

5. Cf. A. Luttrell, 'Vonitza in Epirus and its Lords: 1306–1377', *Rivista di studi bizantini e neoellenici*, XI (=n.s.I) (1965), 131–41.

6. *Cronaca dei Tocco di Cefalonia di Anonimo: Prolegomeni Testo Critico e Traduzione*, ed. G. Schirò (Rome, 1975). Schirò, pp. 10–11, states, erroneously, that Guglielmo was governor of Corfu from 1328 to 1335, and that he married Margherita Orsini, 'signora' of half of Zante. There is no good evidence for this information which is derived from the undocumented tables in Hopf, op. cit., p. 530.

7. J. Buchon, *Nouvelles recherches historiques sur la principauté française de Morée*, 2 vols. (Paris, 1843), I, pp. 407–11; A. Mustoxidi, *Delle Cose Corciresi*, I (Corfu, 1848), pp. 445–7.

8. C. Soldatos, 'La Bibliothèque Publique de Corfou', *L'Hellénisme contemporain*, II ser., I (1947), 373 and n. 3.

Philip of Anjou, Prince of Taranto, as Captain of the City and Island of Corfu from 19 March 1330 to 18 March 1331; from 19 March until 23 April 1330 he was also *Magister Massarius* of the island. His predecessor in both offices was Guido de Villaperusa, while he was succeeded as Captain by Rogerio Cappasanta of Amalfi and as *Magister Massarius* by Johannes Mansella de *Acon*. Philip of Anjou died at Naples on 26 December 1331. Philip's widow Catherine of Valois, who was titular Empress of Constantinople and became regent for their son Robert, approved the accounts for Guglielmo de Tocco's Corfiote administration on 13 June 1335 but, in view of *varia impedimenta*, she did not seal the *apodixa* or formal receipt, and Guglielmo himself died on 22 September of the same year.[9] The *quietantia* of 1335 showed that the Captain of Corfu was responsible, among other things, for paying the salaries and furnishing victuals for the garrisons of the *Castrum vetus*, of the *Castrum novum*, of the castle of Sant'Angelo, of the *Porta Ferra* of the city of Corfu, and of two mainland castles at Butrinto in Albania and at Vonitza in the gulf of Arta in Epirus. These accounts were finally approved, confirmed and sealed by Robert on 12 January 1345.

In 1294 Charles II of Anjou, King of Naples, had enfeoffed his second son Philip, Prince of Taranto, with the *insula* of Corfu and the *castrum* of Butrinto.[10] In addition, Philip subsequently became Prince of Achaea, Despot of *Romania* and titular Emperor of Constantinople. In 1322 he invested his brother, John of Gravina, with the Principality of Achaea; and in 1325 John went to Cephalonia and to the Morea, but not to Corfu.[11] According to Buchon, who based his argument on the dubious reading of a coin which he claimed was inscribed IOHS DESPOTVS and CVRFOV CIVIS, John took the title of Despot, became Lord of Corfu and sold the island in 1333: 'J'ai entre les mains un denier tournoi qui prouve que, non content du titre de prince

9. According to his epitaph, published in F. Strazzullo, *Saggi storici sul duomo di Napoli* (Naples, 1959), p. 207.

10. Text in Buchon, op. cit., II, pp. 407–9 = Perrat–Longnon, pp. 114–15; cf. D. M. Nicol, 'The Relations of Charles of Anjou with Nikephoros of Epiros', *Byzantinische Forschungen*, IV (1972), 193–4.

11. J. Longnon, *L'empire latin de Constantinople et la principauté de Morée* (Paris, 1949), pp. 313, 320–1.

d'Achaye, il avait même pris le titre de despote et cherchait à étendre sa jurisdiction sur Corfou, après l'avoir fait valoir sur Céphalonie. Ce denier, autant du moins qu'il m'est possible de le reconnaître . . .'[12] Buchon admitted that the reading of his coin was uncertain, and in any case Corfu, unlike Cephalonia, did not form part of the Principality of Achaea but was attached to the Principality of Taranto, which John of Gravina did not hold.[13] In fact Philip of Anjou, who was the Prince of Taranto, continued to act as Lord of Corfu. Moustoxydes mentioned several documents, including the concession of a fief to Guglielmo di Rinaldi degli Ugoti in '1722' [*sic*], and a text of 14 December 1370 from the Corfu synagogue which confirmed a document of '12 March 1324' in which Philip was acting as Lord of Corfu.[14] Buchon, who summarized this document, stated that it was dated in Naples on '12 March 1224' [*sic*] in the VIII Indiction, which would actually give 1325, and that it showed Philip exercising jurisdiction in Corfu with the titles of Emperor of Constantinople, Prince 'superior' of Achaea and Despot of *Romania*.[15] A text of 7 May 1326 spoke of *nonnulli homines civitatis et insule Corphiensis, vassalli domini Philippi tarentini Principis*,[16] while the accounts of Guglielmo de Tocco demonstrate that it was as Philip's representative that he was Captain of Corfu in 1330–1. It seems clear that John of Gravina was neither Lord of Corfu nor Despot of *Romania*; there is certainly no evidence that he sold Corfu in 1333.

Guglielmo de Tocco's accounts show that the castle at Vonitza was in Angevin hands during the months preceding March 1331. It has been supposed that the Angevins lost control of Vonitza to the Counts of Cephalonia either in 1314, when the port was being besieged, or shortly after, and also that it was retaken by Gautier de Brienne, titular Duke of Athens, during

12. Buchon, op. cit., I, pp. 409–10.

13. As already pointed out by Mustoxidi, op. cit., I, pp. 692–3.

14. Mustoxidi, I, p. 445 and note (e), but the dates and details are incredibly garbled and confused; it is not clear how many of Philip's acts concerning Corfu he really saw.

15. Buchon, op. cit., I, p. 408.

16. Cited in R. Caggese, *Roberto d'Angiò e i suoi tempi*, II (Florence, 1930), p. 318 n. 1. Corfu was under attack in 1328: . . . *castra civitatis Nepanti et terre Corfoy . . . per hostes regios . . . obsessa* (text of 19 June 1328 cited ibid., II, p. 319 n. 2).

the course of his campaign in Epirus which began in August 1331; this expedition most probably did use Vonitza as a base, and it is certain that Gautier subsequently became its lord.[17] Either the Angevins did not lose Vonitza in 1314 or thereafter; or it was lost but had been recovered by 1330, possibly by John of Gravina when he retook Cephalonia from its Count, Guglielmo Orsini, in 1325; or, though it seems unlikely, the place was lost soon after 18 March 1331 and then recovered almost at once by Gautier de Brienne, who could in that way have become Lord of Vonitza.

According to Buchon, a copy—communicated to him by Moustoxydes—of a confirmation made by Philip of Anjou's son Robert on 20 April 1336 showed that Guglielmo de Tocco, acting as *Capitaneus civitatis et insule Corphoi*, and 'Jean Manuel d'Aycoy' [*sic*], *Magister Massarius* of Corfu, jointly took cognizance of the concession of a fief on Corfu granted by Philip of Anjou to Johannes Cavasilla, who was described as *Miles, baro civitatis et insule Corphoi* and as *Comes Aycoy, marescallus despotatus Romanie*. Elsewhere, Buchon gives the date of Philip's concession to Johannes Cavasilla as 1330, though he wrongly states that Guglielmo de Tocco was then Captain of Corfu 'au nom de l'empereur Robert'.[18] The text given below suggests that this recognition must have taken place between 23 April 1330, when Johannes Mansella de *Acon* became *Magister Massarius*, and 18 March 1331, when Guglielmo de Tocco's Captaincy ended; Philip's original grant must, therefore, also be dated before 18 March 1331. Moustoxydes confused all this by placing the recognition of Cavasilla's privilege, and thus Guglielmo de Tocco's Captaincy, in the year 1336, when Guglielmo was already dead, and also by dating Philip's original grant to 20 December 1331, by which time Guglielmo de Tocco was no longer Captain of Corfu.[19]

17. See Luttrell, op. cit., 133–4, and K. Setton, 'The Catalans in Greece: 1311–1380', *A History of the Crusades*, III, ed. H. Hazard (Madison, Wisconsin, 1975), pp. 189–90; both accounts utilize material in the often inaccurate work of Hopf which was based on the Angevin archives destroyed in 1943.

18. Buchon, op. cit., I, p. 307 and n. 1, pp. 410–11.

19. Mustoxidi, op. cit., I, pp. 446–8, citing the 'copie presso noi esistenti dei due privilegj del 1331'. The same author stated, contradictorily and erroneously, that Philip died in 1330. Mustoxidi, I, p. 447, also mentioned a

Following Philip's death in December 1331, John of Gravina refused to do homage for the Principality of Achaea to Philip's widow Catherine, and on 17 December 1332 the principality was transferred to Philip's son Robert.[20] In the document of 1335, which was repeated in that of 1345 given below, Catherine was entitled solely as Empress of Constantinople and Princess of Taranto. From 1335 to 1338 she acted with the same two titles jointly with Robert, who was entitled Despot of *Romania* and Prince of Achaea and Taranto, but in an act of 17 July 1341 Catherine was also entitled Princess of Achaea. An act of the King of Naples, given on 27 April 1342, did not describe her as Princess of Achaea, but in the document of 12 January 1345 which is published here her son Robert again entitled her Princess both of Achaea and of Taranto.[21]

Royal University of Malta

NAPLES; ARCHIVIO DI STATO; ARCHIVIO TOCCO DI MONTEMILETTO; PERGAMENA No. 6

Original parchment, slightly damaged and worn at the folds, with a large fragment of the seal attached with red and yellow cord.

Robertus, dei gratia, Romanie Despotus, Achaye et Tarenti Princeps, Tenore presentium notum facimus, Uniuersis earum seriem inspecturis tam presentibus quam futuris, Quod domino Petro de Tocco de neapoli nostri hospitij Senescallo, Excellentie nostre nouiter exponente, tam pro se, quam nomine et pro parte Leonardi de Tocco Cambellani, Nicolecti et Lisuli fratrum suorum, filiorum et heredum ut dicunt quondam domini Guillelmi de Tocco de Neapoli, familiarium, et deuotorum nostrorum, quod dictus quondam dominus Guillelmus eorum genitor, dudum Capitaneus et Magister Massarius Ciuitatis et

letter of '11 February 1336' by which Robert instructed his officials at Corfu to assist Theodore son of Johannes Cavasilla to recover certain lands; Buchon, I, p. 411, shows that the date was actually 11 February 1356 (or maybe 1357).

20. Longnon, op. cit., pp. 322–3.

21. Texts in Buchon, op. cit., II, pp. 32–114; the document of 17 July is given as being dated to the VIII Indiction, which would place it in 1340.

Insule Corphiensis, dum olim Serenissima Principissa, domina Catherina Constantinopolitana Imperatrix, Achaye et Tarenti Principissa, mater nostra carissima, et domina reuerenda pro nobis Baliatus officio fungeretur, nobis in etate existentibus pupillari, presentatus de mandato Curie, coram Rationali Curie nostre, ad ponendum ipsi Curie de dictis Capitanie, et Magistri Massariatus officijs, finalem, et debitam rationem, et ad satisfaciendum eidem Curie, de toto eo, in quo per finalem discussionem rationis eiusdem, debitor rationabiliter appareret Rationem ipsam finaliter posuit, et discussa ratione predicta, per quondam magistrum Adam de Neapoli, Rationalem nostrum, facta fuit exinde dicto quondam domino Guillelmo, sub nomine et titulo dicte domine Matris nostre de officijs ipsis, finalis quietantie apodixa, que scripta in forma debita, secundum ordinem processus Rationis ipsius, et subscripta manu propria dicti quondam Magistri Ade, prout moris, et ordinationis erat tunc Curie memorate, propter uaria tandem impedimenta sigillo dicte domine matris nostre sigillari nequiuit, Et propterea supplicante tam pro se, quam quo supra nomine, ut prouidere illis de alicuius cautele suffragio dignaremur. Nos eius in hac parte supplicationibus iustis ut pote benignius exauditis. Archiuum nostrum Neapolis queri fecimus diligenter. In quo conperta sub nomine, et titulo dicte domine Matris nostre sine tamen illius sigillo, quadem finalis quietantie apodixa facta in forma premissa subscriptione proprie manus dicti quondam magistri Ade, nota et uera subscripta, tenoris, per omnia, et continentie subsequentis. Catherina, dei gratia, Imperatrix Constantinopolitana, et Principissa Tarenti, tenore presentis finalis quietantie apodixe, Notum facimus uniuersis tam presentibus, quam futuris, quod dominus Guillelmus de Tocco de Neapoli miles, Capitaneus et Magister Massarius Ciuitatis et Insule Corphiensis, presentatus de mandato Curie principalis, coram Rationali eiusdem Curie, ad ponendum finalem et debitam rationem, de ipsis Capitanie, et Magistri Massariatus officijs gestis per eum, ex Commissione Recolende memorie domini viri nostri, ab olim die nonodecimo mensis Martij, usque per totum vicesimumtertium mensis aprilis tertiedecime Ind., et de dicto Capitanie officio, a die vicesimo quarto prefati mensis aprilis dicte tertiedecime, usque per totum octauumdecimum mensis Martij quartedecime

Indictionum proximo preteritarum, quod tempus est menses decem, et dies vigintiquinque, quo dictum gessit Capitanei officium, et mensis unus, et dies quinque, quo dicta exercuit Capitanie et Magistri Massariatus officia, precedente Sibi in dictis officijs domino Guidone de uillaperusa et Rogerio Cappasanta de Amalfia in dicto Capitanie, ac Iohanne Mansella de acon in prefatis Magistri Massariatus officijs succedentibus. et ad satisfaciendum eidem Curie, de toto eo, in quo per finalem discussionem rationis ipsius, debitor rationabiliter appareret. Prefato[22] prius per [com . . . . ione . .][23] ipsa ponenda fideliter, ut est moris corporaliter iuramento, assignauit in positione rationis eiusdem quaternum unum Introytum et exitum pecunie, frumenti, et aliarum rerum particulariter continentem, per quem quidem quaternum docuit recepisse infra p[. . . . .]m[24] tempus de Cabellis et Iuribus alijs Ciuitatis et Insule predictarum pecunie, frumenti et aliarum [rerum][25] quantitatem subscriptam uidelicet, de Iuribus Cabellarum predictarum Ciuitatis et Insule Corphiensis yppa. Septingenta quinquagintatria et gross. quatuor, De luribus detairhiarum[26] quatuor Baiulationum dicte Insule yppa. Centum, gross. undecim, et torn. quatuor, de Iuribus Censuum gross. undecim, et Cere libr. septem. Item ex uenditione dicte Cere yppum. unum et gross. duos. Item de prouentibus acquisitis per eum yppa. nonagintaocto, et gross. quatuor. Item ponit emisse[27] pro munitione Castri Bonditie, frumenti mod. octuagintaduo, Crithomigij mod. viginti unum et med. Summa uniuersalis Introytus est in tornensibus paruis decem pro quolibet grosso, et gross. ipsis duodecim pro quolibet yppo. conputatis yppa. nongenta quinquaginta quatuor, gross. octo et torn. quatuor, frumenti mod. octuagintaduo, Crithomigij mod. vigintiunum et med., Cere libr. septem. Ostendit deinde per dictum

22. *sic*: read *Prestito.*

23. One word illegible; possibly *compromissionem.*

24. One word almost illegible; possibly *predictum.*

25. One word almost completely illegible.

26. *sic*, perhaps from *doaria* (dowry); cf. text of 1387: *Et quia ipsi Corphyenses in facto dohariorum et aliorum possent habere suas consuetudines, . . .* (*Diplomatarium Veneto-Levantinum*, ed. G. Thomas, II (Venice, 1889), p. 207). Alternatively perhaps from the Greek *hetaireia* meaning 'company', 'association', or even 'order' (as kindly suggested by Professor Peter Topping).

27. *sic*: read *emississe.*

quaternum Exitus mandata originalia, et cautelas alias in ipsius rationis positione productas, et in principali archiuo deinde assignatas se soluisse ac exhibuisse subdictis Castellanis, Comestabulis, et seruientibus subdictorum Castrorum, ac retinuisse sibi pro gagijs ei per principalem Curiam stabilitis in dictis tornen. et gross. computatis ut supra infrascriptam pecunie quantitatem, videlicet Castellano, et seruientibus Castri noui Corphoy, excomputanda in gagijs eorum temporis supradicti yppa. vigintiquinque, Castellano et seruientibus Castri ueteris Corphoy, excomputanda in gagijs eorum dicti temporis yppa. vigintiquinque, Castellano et servientibus porte ferre Ciuitatis Corphoy, excomputanda in eorum gagijs temporis supradicti, yppa. quinquagintasex, et gross. octo, Castellano et seruientibus Castri Sancti Angeli, excomputanda in eorum gagijs temporis supradicti yppa. tredecim, Castellano, Comestabulo et seruientibus Castri Botrontoy, excomputanda in gagijs eorum predicti temporis, yppa. quinquagintaocto, et gross. sex, Castellano et seruientibus Castri Bonditie excomputanda in eorum gagijs temporis supradicti yppa. Centum septuagintaquatuor, gross. tres. Et pro munitione eiusdem Castri, frumenti mod. octogintaduo, Crithomigij mod. viginti unum et med. Item ponit soluisse Iudici Mine Stefanitio, et certis alijs personis in dicto quaterno distinctis pro pretio, et integro pagamento frumenti et Crithomogij predictorum emptorum ad diuersas rationes, in dicto quaterno distinctas, yppa. nonagintanouem, gross. undecim, Domino Iohanni [. .]uasule[28] militi, pro prouisione sua per Principalem Curiam stabilita ad rationem de yppis. triginta per mensem, yppa. Trigintaquinque, Domino Iohanni apocasto pro prouisione sua yppa. tria, Siri Martutio Maczaro de Venetijs, ex extenuatione certe quantitatis pecunie, ei debite per Principalem Curiam yppa. quindecim. Item ponit soluisse pro naulo duorum lignorum armatorum pro delatione victualium delatorum ad Castrum Bonditie et Botrontoy, necnon pro deferendis certis reliquijs, et Iocalibus de dicto Castro Botrontoy yppa. sexaginta quinque, et gross. quatuor, Iudici Guillelmo de amirato de Baro, Iudici et assessori pro gagijs suis mensis unius, et dierum quinque yppa. viginti septem, gross. duos, et torn. septem, Notario Marino de Baro, actorum

28. Partially illegible, but must be Johannes *Cauasule*, on whom *supra*, p. 49.

notario pro gagijs suis in dicto quaterno distinctis, yppa. sex. Item ponit soluisse pro cartis et Cera neccessarijs in administratione dicti officij yppa. duo, et gross. sex. Item retinuit sibi dictus dominus Guillelmus pro robba una sibi per Principalem Excellentiam gratiose donata, yppa. quinquaginta. Item retinuit sibi dictus dominus Guillelmus pro gagijs suis mensis unius et dierum quinque, pro dictis Capitanie et Magistri Massariatus officijs, ad rationem de uncijs auri Centum per annum, yppa. nonaginta septem, gross. duos, et turon. septem. Item retinuit etiam dictus dominus Guillelmus sibi pro supplemento gagiorum suorum mensis unius, et dierum decem et octo, quibus tantum, dictum Capitanie gessit officium, yppa. Centumsex, et gross. octo. Item ponit uendidisse ad rationem de gross. duobus per libram Cere libr. septem. Summa totius uniuersalis Exitus est yppa. Octingenta sexaginta, gross. tres, torn, quatuor, frumenti mod. Octogintaduo, Crithomigij mod. vigintiunum, et med., Cere libr. septem. Facta igitur diligenti collatione de predicto Introytu ad ipsum Exitum Restabant liquide penes eundem dominum Guillelmum, yppa. nonaginta quatuor, et gross. quinque, que reducta ad Carolen. argenti, sunt, uncie octo, turon. quindecim, et gross. decem, quas et quos in nostra Camera exhibuit, atque soluit. Et quia de solutionibus factis predictis Castellanis, Capellanis, et seruientibus dictorum Castrorum, per dictum olim Capitaneum nulla producitur apodixa, sed reperitur per Rationes successorum eius in dicto officio, in successiuis solutionibus computata iuxta tenorem pendentium[29] datorum per eum successori suo predicto, dicte Curie reseruamus, quod si contingat imposter[30] per dictos Castellanos, Capellanos et seruientes prefatorum Castrorum, uel heredes et successores eorum, dictam pecuniam reperi, de cuius solutione ut predicitur per apodixas debitas non docet dictus Capitaneus, heredes et successores ipsius respondere exinde et satisfacere teneantur [. . . . .][31] rationis questionibus alijs, dubijs, et defectis in [. . . . .]e[32] ipsa notatis, per nos, ei gratiose remissis. Reputantes itaque predictam rationem suffi-

29. *sic*: read *precedentium*.
30. *sic*: read *impostea*.
31. Two words illegible; possibly *prout su(. .)*.
32. One word illegible; possibly *r(ation)e*.

centem ydoneam, et legalem, eundem dominum Guillelmum, heredes et successores ipsius ab omni nexu et onere quibus ipse heredes et successores sui, nobis, heredibus et successoribus nostris essent propterea obligati tacite uel expresse, Baliatus filiorum nostrorum, qua fungimur auctoritate absoluimus, liberamus, et perpetuo finaliter quietamus. Ita quod [nullo unquam] tempore ipse, heredes et successores sui affati, per nos, heredes, et successores nostros impetantur seu quomodolibet molestentur. Nobis tamen, nostrisque heredibus, et successoribus reseruamus expresse quod si processu temporis per inquisitionem factam, uel faciendam, inueniatur dictum dominum Guillelmum plus recepisse, minusque soluisse, quam quod supra distinguitur, et dictus eius quaternus continet, et declarat, ipse heredes, et successores sui affati nobis, heredibus, et successoribus nostris respondere et satisfacere teneantur, iuxta Ritum Regie Curie, qui in talibus obseruatur. In cuius rei testimonium, et predicti domini Guillelmi, heredum et successorum suorum cautelam, presentem finalis Quietantie apodixam ei fieri, et pendenti nostro sigillo iussimus comuniri. Datum Neapoli per Magistrum Adam de Neapoli, Rationalem, Consiliarium, et familiarem nostrum dilectum. Anno domini millesimo, Trecentesimo, Tricesimoquinto. Die tertiodecimo mensis Iunij tertie Indictionis, dictam finalem quietantie apodixam, benigna intpetratione,[33] ueram et congruam, ac rationabilem reputantes, illam presentium serie ratificamus, approbamus, et confirmationis nostre munimine roboramus. Volentes, et decernentes expresse de scientia certa nostra ut eadem finalis quietantie apodixa, seu ipsius apodixe scriptum sit ut premictitur prefati Magistri Ade propria manu subscriptum, non obstante quod Sigillo pendenti dicte domine matris nostre sigillatum non extitit ut prefertur, illius efficatie robur obtineat pro cautela dictorum Senescalli et fratrum, eorumque heredum, cuius efficatie et uigoris existeret si sigillatum fuisset magno sigillo pendenti prefate domine matris nostre. cuius impedimentum sigillationis ipsius, prefatis Senescallo et fratribus, et eorum heredibus, ad in cautelam, uel ad alicuius dubietatis scrupulum uel anfractum, nolumus aliquatenus imputari. In cuius rei testimonium, et prefatorum Senescalli et

33. *sic*: read *interpretatione*.

fratrum, ac eorum heredum, presentes testimoniales licteras nostras exinde fieri, et pendenti Excellentie nostre sigillo iussimus communiri. Datum Neapoli per Iudicem *americum de placza de neap*:–[34] Iurisperitum, hospitij nostri Iudicem, Consiliarium, et familiarem nostrum. Anno domini M°CCCxlv°. Die xij° Ianuarij xiij^e Ind.

Registrata:–[35]

[*on fold below*]

Federicus. Rub:– . .Unc.j

34. Written in a different hand.
35. MS: *Rgta:–*

XIV

POPES AND CRUSADES: 1362-1394

Résumé

Commencée en 1362, la mobilisation des forces disponibles pour la croisade devait déboucher sur l'expédition chypriote qui prit, puis abandonna, Alexandrie en Egypte en 1365. Dans le même temps le mouvement des croisades était en train de changer de direction. En 1366, Amédée de Savoie prit aux Turcs ottomans Gallipoli dans les Dardanelles. En 1367, le pape Urbain V retourna avec la papauté en Italie et en 1369 Jean V Paléologue fit lui-même, à Rome, sa soumission personnelle au pape. Cependant les Grecs ne reçurent qu'une faible aide matérielle de la part des Latins. Le pape Grégoire XI, élu en 1370, projeta d'organiser à Thèbes une assemblée pour la croisade qui ne se réunit jamais. Il eut à faire face à des problèmes à l'ouest, à des querelles intestines à Chypre, à l'effondrement du royaume chrétien d'Arménie Cilicienne, et à des guerres civiles aussi bien entre les Latins qu'entre les Grecs. Grégoire XI avait à peine les moyens de défendre Smyrne et, pour une aide militaire, il ne pouvait compter que sur les Hospitaliers de Rhodes sur les ressources desquels il fit réaliser, en 1373, une enquête générale. Le *passagium* projeté par les Hospitaliers fut retardé par des difficultés financières, par le retour de Grégoire XI à Rome et par les guerres de la papauté avec Florence. Les études de base sur le mouvement des croisades s'arrêtent à ce point. Le livre d'Halecki sur Jean V se termine en 1375 et son article sur le Schisme commence aux alentours de 1383. Halecki était surtout intéressé par les rapports Latino-Byzantins; de plus, les sources vaticanes sont peu abondantes pour la période qui suit le départ de Grégoire XI d'Avignon. Il existe cependant des documents qui illustrent la croisade des Hospitaliers abandonnée à son triste destin en 1378, après la mort de Grégoire XI mais avant que ne commence le Schisme. Ces faits, bien connus des historiens de la Grèce, n'ont jamais été intégrés dans une étude des croisades vues comme un mouvement continu. Le Schisme n'interrompit que partiellement la résistance latine contre les Turcs. Il n'empêcha pas les partisans des deux papes de combiner une expédition à Mahdia, en Afrique, en 1390. Il n'arrêta pas les Hospitaliers des deux obédiences de défendre Rhodes et Smyrne et, après 1394, il n'empêcha pas les Hongrois, les Bourguignons et beaucoup d'autres d'entreprendre la grande croisade de Nicopolis en 1396.

During the fourteenth century the crusade remained a papal institution. Only the pope could sanction an expedition as a crusade, whether as a limited *passagium* or *parvum passagium* or a full-scale *generale et magnum sanctum passagium,* and the pope alone could authorize the relevant indulgences and other spiritual concessions. The papacy, however, could never provide the military or naval strength on the scale necessary for a truly papal campaign so that effective action was always dependent on secular initiatives which were usually organized by Latin princes. The crusade was part of a perpetual frontier confrontation between Christians and non-Christians, a permanent activity involving the Latins of Cyprus, Rhodes and Greece, of Valencia and Castile, of Prussia and Livonia. Particular crusades were armed expeditions directed periodically from the heartlands of Western Christianity against the infidels and pagans beyond the frontiers of Christendom, while within its boundaries crusades were also launched against schismatic Greeks and heretical Latins, and even against the Latin enemies of the papacy. Behind political machinations there lurked financial calculations. Popes were sometimes reluctant to preach a crusade which would mean granting ecclesiastical tenths to lay rulers who could not be trusted to expend the monies raised on genuinely crusading activities; at other times popes were themselves tempted to proclaim a crusade in order to raise money through the sale of indulgences.

The recovery of the holy city of Jerusalem remained a theoretical objective of the crusade, and as late as 1403 the Genoese under the Marshal Boucicault and the Hospitallers of Rhodes were plundering the coasts of Syria. Increasingly, however, the crusade was becoming defensive in character and its emphasis moved northwards into the Aegean and the Balkans. During the pontificate of John XXII, who died in 1334, the accent shifted from schemes for renewed Latin attacks on the Greek empire of *Romania* in the tradition of the crusade which captured Constantinople in 1204, towards the defence of Latin trade and shipping in the Aegean against the piratical depredations of the Turks from the Emirates of Aydin and Menteshe; the culmination of this anti-Turkish campaign came in 1334 when a Latin crusade captured the harbour castle of Smyrna, which then became a papal outpost. Once the Ottoman Turks had established themselves in Europe at Gallipoli in 1354, they gradually became the major, though by no means the sole, concern of the crusade. The mounting of a crusading expedition was always conditioned by practical considerations : by the commercial interests of the great Italian republics which controlled the sea-power essential for action; by the instabilities and internal conflicts within the Byzantine state; by the Anglo-French wars and other hostilities in the West; by plague and economic recession which reduced the resources available for a crusade; and by the Italian preoccupations and expenditures of successive French popes who were committed, however reluctantly, to the return of the papal *curia* to Rome.

During the pontificate of Urban V the crusade finally changed its direction. From 1362 to 1365 the triumvirate of Pierre de Lusignan, King of Cyprus, Philippe de Mézières, his chancellor, and Pierre Thomas, papal legate, was mobilizing men, money and shipping in the West for a grand crusade. In 1365 a large fleet sailed from Rhodes to Alexandria where the great port was sacked, ruined and then abandoned in a campaign which demonstrated both the amphibious potentialities provided by Latin domination of the seas and the fundamental strategic bankruptcy of crusading leaders who had no notion how to control or retain a major Mamluk port once it had been captured, and who were forced to capitulate to the majority anxious merely to sail away with their loot. Philippe de Mézières, the unrealistic propagandist, and Pierre Thomas, the unbridled fanatic, had diverted crusading resources away from the Aegean area to a futile assault on the Mamluks at the very moment when the Ottoman Turks were consolidating their position in the Balkans. The exploits of Amadeo Count of Savoy, whose crusade recaptured Gallipoli in 1366, marked the first significant Latin opposition to the Ottoman Turks; once again an initial success could not be sustained permanently, but the principle of resistance to the Ottomans was firmly established. In 1367 Urban V took the papal court back to Italy where in 1369 the Byzantine Emperor John V Palaeologus, under pressure from his close kinsman Amadeo of Savoy, made a personal submission of faith to the pope in Rome. This incident was without any effective sequel, for popes and emperors saw their own problems clearly enough but failed to grasp the realities of each others' situations; the popes could never raise the material strength to provide the military aid promised to Byzantium, while the emperors lacked the spiritual authority to impose on their own Greek subjects the requisite submission to Rome.

Urban V returned to Avignon and died there. Gregory XI, who succeeded him in December 1370, continued the struggle with these and other Eastern problems. Pierre de Lusignan had been assassinated in 1369 and Cyprus relapsed into a quasi-anarchy compounded by Genoese intervention; the Armenian Kingdom of Cilicia was finally extinguished by the Mamluks in 1375; Rhodes and Smyrna had to be defended, as did the Latins of the Aegean and mainland Greece; the Ottomans crushed Serbian resistance on the Maritza River in September 1371; John V Palaeologus was compelled to make an accomodation with the Turks in 1373; Genoese fought Venetians, and Venetians fought Hungarians; and warfare dragged on in Italy and elsewhere in the West. Gregory made standard diplomatic moves to organize naval defence for Latin Greece, to secure Venetian, Genoese and Hungarian participation, and to assemble a congress of Christian Levantine powers at Thebes; but these proposals were uniformly abortive. By 1373 Gregory must have realized that he could expect active support only from the Hospitallers of Rhodes. The Master of Rhodes was sent to settle the crisis in Cyprus, where he died in February 1374. The defence of Smyrna was confided exclusively to the Hospital in September 1374. Two Hospitallers were sent on a papal mission to Constantinople following schemes elaborated in 1373 for a Hospitaller *passagium* against the Turks. Behind this project lay complicated preparations which included a universal inquest into the Hospital's finances and manpower, and assemblies held at Avignon in 1373 and 1374 to reform the Order. On 8 December 1375 Gregory summoned 405 *milites* of the Hospital, each to be accompanied by a *scutifer,* to serve in a *passagium* which had become the only crusading action the pope could contemplate.

*
**

This outline of papal crusading policy from 1362 to about 1375 is firmly laid down in the standard works and should arouse little controversy [1], though Gregory's policies still remain to be described in more detail. [2]. At this point, however, the narrative as at present established breaks down for a variety of reasons. Gregory was increasingly preoccupied with his return to Rome and it has often been assumed, wrongly, that crusading affairs were totally neglected in consequence. It has not usually been understood that the Hospitaller expedition of 1378 was in fact the *passagium* originally planned in 1373 [3]. The works of Oscar Halecki, which were concerned with papal-Byzantine relations rather than the crusade, left a hiatus between 1375 and 1381 [4]. It is difficult stet to contruct a continuous picture of policy since the papal archives were disrupted by the move from Avignon in 1376 and by subsequent upheavals. The calendars of papal documents produced by the Ecole Française de Rome come to a close in 1378. A number of relevant bulls of Gregory XI which do survive have been overlooked because they are in the *Registri Avenionenses* rather than the *Registri Vaticani,* while later documents have been missed because they are in the registers of Clement VII rather than those of Urban VI who was closer to Eastern affairs but some of whose registers are lacking. In addition, though a number of bulls have long been available in Rinaldi's *Annales,* there are many other documents which have been cited but are not yet published [5]. Other difficulties derive from uncertainties about the nature and purposefulness of Gregory's character and intentions. Nor is it clear which, if any, of his numerous advisers on Eastern matters really influenced his policies. Catherine of Siena repeatedly pressed for crusading action [6]; Simon Atoumanos, Latin Archbishop of Thebes, was in Avignon in 1373 [7]; Juan Fernández de Heredia, who as Master of the Hospital eventually led the *passagium* of 1378, was closely connected to Gregory throughout his pontificate [8]; and that shadowy intriguer Johannes Lascaris Calopheros was especially active in Levantine affairs [9]. Others were certainly influential as well, yet none of these personages can be shown to have determined crusading plans, though their interests and intrigues confuse the diagnosis of policies.

*
**

Despite the delays caused by Gregory's journey from Avignon to Rome, preparations for the Hospitaller *passagium* did go slowly ahead, the financial aspects causing particular difficulties. Plans to intervene in *Romania* were impeded by the revolt of the emperor's son Andronicus, while the Venetians occupied Tenedos just outside the Dardanelles in October 1376 and began a war with Genoa in 1377. Before August 1376 there was talk of a Hospitaller *passagium* to the Catalan Duchy of Athens, but even this must have been judged impractical. Once in Italy Gregory became involved with wars and difficulties there, yet on 24 September 1377 he provided Juan Fernández de Heredia to the Mastership of the Hospital, and in the same year the Hospitallers leased the Principality of Achaea for five years from Queen Joanna of Naples and acquired the port of Vonitza on the Gulf of Arta in Epirus from Maddalena Buondelmonti, widow of Leonardo Tocco Duke of Leucadia and Count of Cephalonia; intervention in the Aegean was abandoned in favour of resistance to the Turks on the eastern shores of the Adriatic. Gregory XI died on 27 March 1378 and Urban VI was elected to succeed him on 8 April. A small group of Hospitallers was already in Vonitza together with a number of Florentines who were connected to the Buondelmonti. In midsummer they were ambushed and many of them slaughtered by Ghin Boua Spata, the Albanian Lord of Arta, and the Master was taken prisoner [10]. Gregory's crusade had taken place but his death apparently contributed to its failure for, even before the election of Clement VII as a rival pope on 20 September 1378 provoked schism in the papacy, Urban VI had — or so an admittedly biased French royal envoy to the Count of Flanders alleged early in 1379 — ensured the Hospitallers' defeat by detaining their envoys in Rome and countermanding Gregory's preparations in support of their *passagium*. Urban, who probably viewed the Hospitaller expedition as an essentially French initiative, perhaps refused to pay out essential monies promised by Gregory before his death [11].

The two rival popes launched crusades against each other's supporters as, for example, when an English Urbanist army invaded Flanders. Both papacies exploited crusading theory to raise tenths, which were originally intended for the crusade but in practice had become a purely financial expedient [12], and they appointed bishops [13] and collectors [14] in *Romania,* though most of these nominations had little connection with the defence of Latin Greece. The Roman pope, who was closer to the East and to the Italians who constituted the majority of its Latin population, naturally sought more actively to profit from the established machinery of the crusade. However, as Turkish advances continued, the Christians of the East remained in need of protection and there were occasions on which both popes were marginally involved in their defence or, largely for reasons of their own prestige, gave papal authorization to resistance against the Turks. At first Urban VI did nothing for the crusade, though between 1383 and 1387 he was sending agents to Constantinople. In 1385 he received an appeal from Thessalonica to which he despatched a legate in 1386, only for the city to fall to the Turks in the following year [15]. In September 1387 Urban instructed the Archbishop of Patras to act, in conjunction with the Navarrese Companies established in Greece, against the Turks or schismatics — *infideles aut scismatici* — in the Morea, while in April 1388 he issued a bull to preach the crusade and to sell indulgences to finance the two galleys which he proposed to arm at Venice against the Turks [16]. None of these moves led to any known military action [17], and the Ottomans again defeated the Serbs at Kossovo in June 1389. Urban died on 15 October 1389 and his successor, Boniface IX, proved equally ineffective; his bulls of 1391 encouraging the Hungarians and others to resist the Turks achieved little or nothing [18].

Clement VII at Avignon had no contact with Byzantium [19], but he did support the French element on Cyprus [20]. His Hospitaller allies tried to defend the Principality of Achaea until 1381 when they returned it to Joanna of Naples. Joanna was overthrown in July 1381 by the Urbanist Charles of Durazzo, and by January 1382 Charles' supporter Jacques de Baux had been recognized as prince in Achaea by its barons and by the Navarrese [21]. Thereafter Clement was without influence in the Morea where confusion prevailed, though the Hospitallers repeatedly and unavailingly attempted to secure a variety of Latin claims as a basis for renewed intervention there [22]. Clement gave considerable assistance to the predominantly French and pro-Avignon Hospitallers, whose new statutes he had already confirmed by 9 August 1379. On 6 September he provided a new Archbishop of Smyrna, and on 19 January 1380 he allotted the tenths of Cyprus and the Latin Orient to the Hospital to finance the defence of Smyrna. In 1381 the Archbishop and Constable of Smyrna travelled to Avignon and secured new funds to pay the garrison. Meanwhile on 2 March 1381 Urban VI opened an inquiry which led to the "deposition" of the Master of Rhodes, to the election of a Neapolitan "anti-Master" and, in 1384, to an unsuccessful plot to convert both Rhodes and Cyprus. This Urbanist campaign was so ineffective that when the "anti-Master" Riccardo Caracciolo died in 1395 the Roman pope decided not to replace him [23]. The Hospital's unceasing concern for the Rhodian archipelago deepened after 1389 when the Ottoman ruler Bayezid began his rapid conquest of the Anatolian emirates and brought direct pressure against Smyrna, still technically a papal city. Clement had continuously supported the Hospitallers, and on 19 April 1391 he granted indulgences for the defence of Smyrna which brought them a considerable income [24].

Elsewhere matters touching the crusade proceeded without reference to any pope. The King of Aragon adopted a policy of *indiferencia,* refusing to recognize either papacy, so that in September 1382, for example, he ordered the Hospitallers of Aragon not to take sides in the schism and instructed his officials to prevent the Hospital exporting money [25]. In the opposite sense, the King of England, though certainly an Urbanist, positively encouraged the English Hospitallers to travel to Clementist Rhodes and to send monies there, holding the defence of a "frontier of Christianity" to be a more fundamental consideration than schism within the papacy; in 1384 the considerable if exceptional sum of 25,000 florins was sent [26]. In Lithuania the annual expeditions of the Teutonic Order were maintained, despite the union of Lithuania with Poland and the conversion of the pagan Lithuanians to Christianity in 1386, and despite Urban VI's recognition of the union on 1 April 1388 when he authorized indulgences for a Lithuanian-Polish crusade against the Tartars. French, English and other Western crusaders of both obediences continued to serve in the Teutonic campaigns, even though these could no longer be justified as wars against pagans; in about 1394 the Duke of Burgundy himself was reported to be hesitating between the crusade of Hungary and that of Prussia [27].

The popes of the schism patronized crusades they had not themselves initiated. On 29 January 1389 Boniface IX enfeoffed the Sicilian magnate Manfredi Chiaramonte with Jerba and the Kerkena islands off Tunisia which had been seized by a Siculo-Genoese expedition in 1388. Louis de Bourbon, leader of the coming Franco-Genoese attack on Mahdia in Tunisia, visited Clement VII at Avignon in 1390 and received papal crusading absolutions; but problems arose when crusaders of both obediences assembled at Genoa, so that orders were given that the schism was not to be mentioned and the departing fleet had to be blessed by representatives of the two papacies [28]. In 1394 King Sigismund of

Hungary began to organize the great crusade which fought at Nicopolis on the Danube in 1396. Appeals were made to Boniface who on 3 June 1394 proclaimed two crusades both with the usual indulgences, one against the Clementists of Naples and another against the Turks in Sigismund's territories; one bull also mentioned Athens and Achaea, for in January 1394 the Ottomans had invaded Central Greece, taking Neopatras, Salona and Livadia. Bulls of 15, 18 and 30 October nominated a new nuncio to preach this crusade against the Turks and arranged for the sale of indulgences to finance it [29]. Clement VII's successor, Benedict XIII, subsequently gave his support by granting crusading privileges to Jean de Nevers and his Avignonist companions on the forthcoming Nicopolis expedition [30].

It became a standard contemporary commonplace that an Anglo-French peace, the ending of the schism, and effective resistance to the Turks were all somehow interdependent; but there was much ambiguity, even hypocrisy, as to which of these objectives depended upon or should precede which. The concept of the crusade could be employed to justify each of these aims, though in practice it generated diplomatic posturing rather than direct military action. The appeal to Jerusalem did not persuade the English to withdraw from France, but it provided a useful excuse or cover for diplomatic manœuvres; it did not disguise the nature of quasi-piratical assaults in North Africa, though it assisted in mobilizing support for them. Most crusading schemes, genuine or otherwise, placed little emphasis on papal intervention. Philippe de Mézières' indefatigable propaganda and his literary projects for a new crusading order were realistic in that they looked to kings and magnates, to the chivalric element, to take the lead. They called for an Anglo-French entente and an armed attack on the Roman pope as essential preliminaries to the crusade proper; Jerusalem remained the ultimate worldly objective but holy wars in Spain and Africa, Byzantium and Cilicia, Egypt and Syria, were theoretically envisaged as preludes to the grand *passagium* [31]. Such arguments were not without influence, especially in France where it was claimed around 1390 that Charles VI's proposed invasion of Italy was intended not only to end the schism but also to be followed by an attack on the Turks; the king was even said to have declared his wish to engage the Ottoman sultan in single combat [32].

The crusading ideal continued to quicken the conscience of many Latin Christians, who were in any case uncomfortably aware of the approaching Turkish menace. The institution of the holy war was much abused, but successive popes gave it limited support until the moment of Gregory XI's death in 1378. Urban VI seemed to have betrayed it even before the schism began, and thereafter crusading machinery was often, though not exclusively, exploited by rival popes for reasons of politics, finance and prestige; the sale of crusading indulgences aroused particular fury among reformers such as John Wyclif [33]. The schism did not always produce clear-cut diplomatic alignments; some rulers and individuals avoided involvement or inaugurated ecclesiastical policies on their own account, and others sought to insure against all eventualities by recognizing both papacies but paying obedience and taxes to neither. The struggle against the infidel was maintained continuously in certain quarters, most notably by the Hospitallers with Clementist assistance, while princes and governments occasionally conducted major crusading campaigns but with little regard for rival popes or schismatic allegiances. The crusade was not merely a papal institution; the idea aroused such genuine devotion that it survived the absence of clear papal direction to inspire powerful impulses which ensured it a measure of continuity, though not of success.

NOTES

1. A. ATIYA, *The Crusade in the Later Middle Ages* (London, 1938); *A History of the Crusades,* ed. K. Setton, iii (Madison, Wisc., 1975); K. SETTON, *The Papacy and the Levant: 1204-1571,* i (Philadelphia, 1976). See also A. LUTTRELL, "The Crusade in the Fourteenth Century", in *Europe in the Late Middle Ages,* ed. J. Hale *et al.* (London, 1965).

2. A. LUTTRELL, "The Papal Inquest into the Hospital of 1373 and its Historical Background" (forthcoming), will provide a detailed discussion; cf. J. GLÉNISSON, "L'Enquête pontificale de 1373 sur les possessions des Hospitaliers de Saint-Jean-de-Jérusalem", *Bibliothèque de l'Ecole des Chartes,* cxxix (1971).

3. Cf. A. LUTTRELL, *The Hospitallers in Cyprus, Rhodes, Greece and the West: 1291-1440 – Collected Studies* (London, 1978), I 301-303 *et passim.* N. JORGA, *Philippe de Mézières (1327-1405) et la croisade au XIVe siècle* (Paris, 1896), 411, wrote of this *passagium*: "... inutile de dire qu'elle ne fut jamais entreprise."

4. O. HALECKI, *Un Empereur de Byzance à Rome: Vingt Ans de Travail pour l'Union des Eglises et pour la Défense de l'Empire d'Orient, 1355-1375* (Warsaw, 1930), and "Rome et Byzance au Temps du Grand Schisme d'Occident", *Collectanea Theologica* [Lwów], xviii (1937); the former is reprinted with the latter in appendix (London, 1972). Halecki scarcely used the *Registri Avenionenses* in the Vatican Archives.

5. L. BOYLE, *A Survey of the Vatican Archives and of its medieval Holdings* (Toronto, 1972). See also G. DENNIS, *The Reign of Manuel II Palaeologus in Thessalonica: 1382-1387* (Rome, 1960), 10-11; J. FAVIER, *Les Finances pontificales à l'époque du Grand Schisme d'Occident: 1378-1409* (Paris, 1966), 9-16. All relevant bulls should eventually be analysed for the precise implications, financial and otherwise, of such terms as *indulgentia* and *subsidium, scismatici* and *infideles*: cf. W. LUNT, *Papal Revenues in the Middle Ages,* 2 vols. (New York, 1934), i. 111-121; ii. 485-497, 512-520 *et passim*; J. BRUNDAGE, *Medieval Canon Law and the Crusader* (Madison, Wisc., 1969), 22-25, 144-155.

6. R. FAWTIER, *Sainte Catherine de Sienne: Essai de Critique des Sources,* 2 vols. (Paris, 1921-1930), i. 161, 168 n. 3, 184-188; ii. 179, 236-238, 257-261; *Epistolario di Santa Caterina da Siena,* i, ed. E. Dupré Theseider (Rome, 1940), *passim.*

7. G. FEDALTO, *Simone Atumano, monaco di studio, arcivescovo latino di Tebe: secolo XIV* (Brescia, 1968), 95-100.

8. Luttrell (1978), VIII, XXIII *et passim.*

9. A. Eszer, *Das abenteuerliche Leben des Johannes Laskaris Kalopheros* (Wiesbaden, 1969). This work gives a more continuous picture of Gregory XI's policy, but may have exaggerated Calopheros' role; cf. D. Jacoby's review in *Byzantinische Zeitschrift,* lxiv (1971), 378-381.

10. Luttrell (1978), I 301-303; V 207; VIII 322-324; XVIII 139; XXII 340-343; further information in the forthcoming work cited *supra* note 2. This assumes (eg. *ibid.*, XXIII 33) that Fernández de Heredia, who was in Epirus at the latest by 24 April 1378, left Italy before Gregory died on 27 March or at least without hearing of his death. The envoys' failure to return may explain why the Hospitallers delayed around the Gulf of Arta until midsummer.

11. *Eius stultitia fuit causa, quod Magister Hospitalis cum sua militia fuerunt victi et pro magna parte occisi, qui detinuit Romae Ambassiatores Hospitalis et reuocauit quidquid Papa Gregorius ordinauerat de omnium fratrum consilio, nullo penitus discrepante*: text in C. du Boulay, *Historia Universitatis Parisiensis,* iv (Paris, 1668), 520-522. N. Valois, *La France et le Grand Schisme d'Occident,* 4 vols. (Paris, 1896-1902), i. 255-257, discusses this text, apparently the only source to mention Urban's conduct.

12. Favier, 208-217.

13. G. Fedalto, *La Chiesa Latina in Oriente,* ii: *Hierarchia Latina Orientis* (Verona, 1976).

14. Lists in Favier, 718-719, 733-734; add. Halecki (1937), 481-482, 486-487, 492-493, 501, and Luttrell (1978), XXIII 40 n. 44.

15. Dennis, 132-150; cf. J. Barker, *Manuel II Palaeologus (1391-1425): a Study in Late Byzantine Statesmanship* (New Brunswick, 1969), 55/56 n. 152.

16. Halecki (1937), 488-492.

17. D. Geanakoplos, in *Crusades,* iii. 80, supposes, apparently without evidence, that the two galleys were actually sent.

18. Halecki (1937), 494-495; three bulls of 1391 are printed in A. Tăutu, *Acta Urbani P.P. VI (1378-1389), Bonifacii P.P. IX (1389-1404)* ... = *Pontificia Commissio ad Redigendum Codicem Iuris Canonici Orientalis,* III ser., xiii – I (Rome, 1970), 13-15, 59, 60.

19. Dennis, 136 n. 10.

20. Valois, ii.218-221; J. Richard, "Le Royaume de Chypre et le Grand Schisme", in his *Orient et Occident au Moyen Age: Contacts et Relations (XIIe-XVe s.)* (London, 1976).

21. A. Luttrell, "Aldobrando Baroncelli in Greece: 1378-1382", *Orientalia Christiana Periodica,* xxxvi (1970).

22. A. Luttrell, "La Corona de Aragón y la Grecia Catalana: 1379-1394", *Anuario de Estudios Medievales,* vi (1969).

23. Luttrell (1978), XXIII.

24. Valois, ii. 223-224; J. Delaville le Roulx, *Les Hospitaliers à Rhodes jusqu'à la mort de Philibert de Naillac: 1310-1421* (Paris, 1913), 225-234.

25. J. Vives, "Juan Fernández de Heredia, Gran Maestre de Rodas: vida, obras, formas dialectales", *Analecta Sacra Tarraconensia,* iii (1927), 130 n. 30.

26. C. Tipton, "The English Hospitallers during the Great Schism", *Studies in Medieval and Renaissance History,* iv (1967), 107-108 *et passim.*

27. Halecki (1937), 521-523; for Clementist crusading in Prussia, see R. Vaughan, *Philip the Bold: the Formation of the Burgundian State* (London, 1962), 60-62.

28. Setton, i. 330-333.

29. Halecki (1937), 498-502; Setton, i. 342-343. Six bulls are printed in *Monumenta Vaticana Historiam Regni Hungariae Illustrantia,* I ser., iii (Budapest, 1888), 259-260, 269-278.

30. Valois, iii.98-99.

31. Jorga, 433, 465-466, 469-471; Atiya, 136-154; A. Hamdy, "Philippe de Mézières and the New Order of the Passion", *Bulletin of the Faculty of Arts* [Alexandria], xvii-xviii (1963-1964); Philippe de Mézières, *Le Songe du Vieil Pelerin,* ed. G. Coopland, ii (Cambridge, 1969), 96-103, 429-440. The important hypo-

theses in J. PALMER, *England, France and Christendom: 1377-99* (London, 1972), 180-205, 240-244, seem to demand further investigation.

32. VALOIS, ii. 175-182, and SETTON, i. 340-341; see especially *Œuvres de Froissart,* ed. Kervyn de Lettenhove, xiv (Brussels, 1872), 279-283.

33. VALOIS, ii. 232; ATIYA, 188. Indulgences for the recovery of Jerusalem, but not for wars against infidels in general, were defended in *The Tree of Battles of Honoré Bonet,* trans. G. Coopland (Cambridge, Mass., 1949), 126-128.

XV

Gregory XI and the Turks: 1370-1378

Gregory XI was the first of the popes who was compelled to face the realities of expanding Turkish power in the Balkans, a problem which had been growing since the Ottoman occupation of Gallipoli in 1354. A small Latin force intervened indecisively against the Turks in the Dardanelles in 1359 and Gallipoli was recaptured in 1366 by Amedeo of Savoy; in 1369 the Greek Emperor John V Palaeologus even travelled to Rome to make a personal submission of faith to Pope Urban V in the hope of securing further aid for Byzantium. Yet the West was slow to realize that the defence of the Christian East, both Greek and Latin, was of greater fundamental importance than the temporary gains derived from essentially piratical assaults on Mamluk Egypt and Syria. Demetrius Cydones reported from Constantinople, probably in 1364, that even the Turks were asking derisively "whether anyone had further word of the crusade", and while the Ottomans were advancing far into Europe Urban V allowed the Latins' limited crusading resources to be diverted to a major Cypriot expedition, though he may not have known the precise objective of this armada which sailed in 1365 to sack Alexandria (1).

Gregory XI, who was elected pope on 30 December 1370, had been created a cardinal in 1348 by his uncle Pope Clement VI who had himself shown an active and effective concern for

(1) The standard treatments are *A History of the Crusades*, ed. K. SETTON, iii (Madison, Wisc., 1975), and K. SETTON, *The Papacy and the Levant: 1204-1571*, i (Philadelphia, 1976); see also A. LUTTRELL, "The Crusade in the Fourteenth Century", in *Europe in the Late Middle Ages*, ed. J. HALE *et al.* (London, 1965), and *idem*, "Popes and Crusades: 1362-1394", in *Genèse et Débuts du Grand Schisme d'Occident* (Paris, 1978). Many standard works say very little about Gregory and the crusade. Cydones' remark is cited in SETTON, i. 259.

Eastern affairs [2]. The new pope, still only forty-two years old, was in many ways a purposeful and determined man [3] but he was hampered by the multiplicity of his problems, by chronic financial difficulties and by his own ill-health. Gregory was perhaps easily enthused, enraged or depressed, but it is unlikely that he was significantly influenced by characterful personalities such as Catherine of Siena or Bridget of Sweden, both of whom urged him most forcefully to take the papal *curia* back from Avignon to Rome [4]. An experienced and subtle diplomat, the new pope had to wrestle with the problem of Italy, to which he undoubtedly gave priority; he transformed the struggle against

(2) The most detailed study of Gregory's activity is still that in O. HALECKI, *Un Empereur de Byzance à Rome – Vingt Ans de Travail pour l'Union des Églises et pour la Défense de l'Empire de l'Orient 1355-1375* (Warsaw, 1930), though his work now requires modification; see the works cited *infra*, and especially the summary of more recent researches in A. ESZER, *Das abenteuerliche Leben des Johannes Laskaris Kalopheros* (Wiesbaden, 1969). For the background, see also G. DENNIS, *The Reign of Manuel II Palaeologus in Thessalonika: 1382-1387* (Rome, 1960), 26-40 *et passim*, and J. BARKER, *Manuel II Palaeologus (1391-1425): A Study in Late Byzantine Statesmanship* (New Brunswick, New Jersey, 1969), 16-31 *et passim*. Many of the relevant bulls are calendared in *Lettres secrètes et curiales du pape Grégoire XI (1370-1378) relatives à la France*, 5 fascs., ed. L. MIROT *et al.* (Paris, 1935-1937), and *Lettres secrètes et curiales du pape Grégoire XI (1370-1378) intéressant les pays autres que la France*, 3 fascs. ed. G. MOLLAT (Paris, 1962-1965), but these works are for the most part cited here [as MIROT no. and MOLLAT no.] only when they give the actual texts. Some texts are printed in *Pontificia Commissio ad Redigendum Codicem Iuris Canonici Orientalis: Fontes*, series III, xii: *Acta Gregorii P.P. XI (1370-1378)*, ed. A. TĂUTU (Rome, 1966). Only a fraction of the documents in the papal registers is utilized below; a number were kindly indicated by Professor José Trenchs Odena.

(3) "... one of the most active and purposeful of the Avignon popes": P. PARTNER, *The Lands of St. Peter: the Papal State in the Middle Ages and the Early Renaissance* (London, 1972), 358. See also L. MIROT, *La politique pontificale et le retour du Saint-Siège à Rome en 1376* (Paris, 1899).

(4) Italian historians have probably exaggerated in their criticisms; eg. E. DUPRÈ THESEIDER, *I papi di Avignone e la questione romana* (Florence, 1939), 191-193. See G. MOLLAT, "Grégoire XI et sa légende", *Revue d'histoire ecclésiastique*, xlix (1954); B. GUILLEMAIN, *La cour pontificale d'Avignon, 1309-1376: étude d'une société* (Paris, 1962), 144-149.

the Milanese and the Florentines into separate crusades and his persistence finally secured the papacy's return to Rome, whatever the expenditure involved and however unfortunate the ensuing schism in the Roman church. Gregory also bore, though with less determination and even more unsatisfactory results, the ultimate Latin responsibility for resisting the mounting Turkish threat to the whole of Eastern Christendom, but there he never backed his diplomatic activities with the funds which were essential to success.

The traditional type of crusade had been discredited once again by the evident futility of the grandiose attack on Alexandria which had exploited genuine crusading idealism for short-term material motives; it had become clear that the Latins had no hope of holding such a city even if they could capture and pillage it (5). Men and money, together with the peaceful conditions on which they depended, were lacking in the West while in the East rivalries and struggles — Cypriots against Genoese, Genoese against Venetians, Venetians against Hungarians — hampered Latin resistance to the Turks. When the Ottomans crushed Serbian resistance at Cernomen near Adrianople on 26 September 1371, Gregory was threatened with the total collapse of the whole Christian East. Thessaly, Macedonia and Albania lay open to Turkish incursions, and John V Palaeologus, who in 1369 had submitted to the pope without receiving any effective assistance in return, was forced to make an agreement with the Ottomans in 1373. Pope and emperor saw their own problems clearly enough but failed to grasp the realities of each other's situations. The one could never mobilize the material strength to provide the military aid promised to Byzantium; the other lacked the spiritual authority to impose on his own Greek subjects their submission to Rome. There were, furthermore, countless complications in Hungary and throughout the Balkans. The enfeebled Catalans of Athens and Thebes were being attacked by Latins as well as by Turks. Pierre de Lusignan, the crusader King of Cyprus, had been assassinated in 1369 and his kingdom

(5) P. EDBURY, "The Crusading Policy of King Peter I of Cyprus: 1359-1369", in *The Eastern Mediterranean Lands in the Period of the Crusades*, ed. P. HOLT (London, 1977).

came under heavy pressure from the Genoese, while the Christians of Cilician Armenia were left defenceless to suffer their final disaster when they were overrun by the Mamluks in 1375. Smyrna had to be garrisoned and defended, and the Hospitallers were in difficulties at Rhodes. All these Eastern problems figured prominently in the registers of Gregory XI, whose library at Avignon, incidentally, contained at least fifteen crusading treatises (6).

During 1371 and 1372 Gregory XI explored a somewhat bewildering variety of policies. Following the restoration of Latin trade and peace with Egypt in 1370, it became possible to concentrate Western attention upon the Aegean and the Balkans. On 7 July 1371 the pope wrote to the Doge of Genoa concerning a forthcoming naval expedition or *passagium* (7). In August he addressed various powers urging them to support this Genoese expedition which was due to sail eastwards in March 1372, but after receiving news of the Turkish victory at Cernomen and also of the increasing preoccupations of the Genoese with their interests in Cyprus the pope sought help from Hungary and Venice. During 1372 Gregory realized that even wider resistance to the Ottomans was essential. On 13 November 1372 he sent bulls to almost all the Eastern Christian rulers, including John V Palaeologus, the Hospitallers of Rhodes and the petty Latin states of the Morea and the Aegean, summoning them to a congress to be held in October 1373 at Thebes, the chief city of the Catalan duchies, in order to form a grand anti-Turkish league. These appeals did not take account of religious or political rivalries between Christian powers, but they emphasized the danger to the Catalans and they pointed to the need for a concerted attempt by the Latins of the Levant to organize their own defence. The congress never met (8). The notion of an

(6) Details in F. EHRLE, *Historia Bibliothecae Romanorum Pontificum tum Bonifatianae tum Avenionensis*, i (Vatican, 1890), 500-501, 504-505, 546, 557-558. Gregory was also active in support of the Asiatic missions: details and references in J. RICHARD, *La Papauté et les Missions d'Orient au moyen âge: XIIIe-XVe siècles* (Rome, 1977), 130-135 *et passim*.

(7) Archivio Segreto Vaticano, Reg. Vat. 263, f. 77v-78.

(8) Details in HALECKI, 250-262; texts of 13 November 1372 in TĂUTU, 93-96. Some authors assume that the congress took place, but

intervention to defend the Catalan duchies did not die out altogether and as late as 10 August 1376 the Master of the Hospital at Rhodes referred to the difficulties preventing the *passagium ad partes ducatus Athenarum* (9), but Gregory soon turned to alternative proposals. On 20 November 1372 he called on the faithful to attack the Turks in defence of *Romania* and of other Eastern regions, offering plenary indulgences to those who died in the attempt (10), and on 10 February 1373 came orders for a papal inquest into the European commanderies of the Hospitallers of Rhodes (11).

Gregory had already called for a survey of the Hospital's resources in June 1372, and by the following February he must have been convinced that there was little chance of finding any source of military power apart from that of the Hospitallers, yet he had not abandoned all expectation of other support; in March 1373 and thereafter he was encouraging crusading preparations in Hungary and was still hoping for naval contingents from Venice and Genoa. Gregory's difficulties at this moment exemplified his long-term problems. On 18 December 1372 he refused to dispense the Hungarian clergy for one year from the payment of an ecclesiastical tenth, this being the king's condition for a crusade. Gregory stated that the money was needed in Italy, and he maintained that the defence of the Latin East depended on the defeat of the Visconti at Milan who were paralyzing

---

there is no evidence that it did so and HALECKI shows that it almost certainly did not; see also R.-J. LOENERTZ, "Athènes et Néopatras: régestes et documents pour servir à l'histoire ecclésiastique des duchés catalans, 1311-1395", *Archivum Fratrum Praedicatorum*, xxviii (1958), 66.

(9) Text in S. PAULI, *Codice Diplomatico del Sacro Militare Ordine Gerosolimitano, oggi di Malta*, ii (Lucca, 1737), 99-101.

(10) Reg. Vat. 264, f. 77v-78.

(11) On the Hospital, see J. DELAVILLE LE ROULX, *Les Hospitaliers à Rhodes jusqu'à la mort de Philibert de Naillac: 1310-1421* (Paris, 1913), and A. LUTTRELL, *The Hospitallers in Cyprus, Rhodes, Greece and the West: 1291-1440 – Collected Studies* (London, 1978). Limited use of the papal registers for Gregory's pontificate was made in J. BOSIO, *Dell'Istoria della Sacra Religione et Illustrissima Militia di San Giovanni Gierosolimitano*, ii (2nd ed: Rome, 1629), 110-129, but BOSIO made a number of errors and his treatment of the years 1376 to 1378 is seriously inaccurate.

the church's activity. The Hungarian king gave way. On 23 March 1373 the pope preached a crusade and granted indulgences, but he still insisted on receiving the tenth. He did not trust the king with the money and suspected that it would be used to attack Christian schismatics in the Balkans rather than to fight the Turks in defence of Christendom as a whole; the Hungarians did in fact attack the Venetians early in 1373 (12).

One problem which Gregory shared with the Hospitallers was that of the papal city of Smyrna. The papacy and the Hospital had both played a leading part in its recapture in 1344 and in its subsequent defence. When Pietro Raccanelli of Genoa was appointed captain of Smyrna for ten years on 12 May 1363, the annual 6000 florins for the wages of the captain and garrison were to be provided half by the Hospital and half by the papacy which was to pay 3000 florins out of the papal incomes from Cyprus (13). On 7 March 1371, following Raccanelli's resignation, Gregory instructed the Master at Rhodes to ensure that Raccanelli presented proper accounts and to install as his successor for ten years the Genoese Ottobono Cattaneo who was an inhabitant of Rhodes (14). Bulls of 16 February and 15 August 1372 demonstrated Gregory's determination to secure payment of the annual 3000 florins due from Cyprus (15). In January 1373 the pope was again worried by the continued non-payment of the monies which were supposed to be contributed by the Cypriot clergy, and also by threats from Smyrna that the garrison would

(12) Details in HALECKI, 265-279, 289-291.

(13) Reg. Vat. 245, f. 189-191v; cf. SETTON, i (1976), 247. For earlier arrangements of 1359 see partial texts *ibid.*, i. 234-235. In 1365 the Hospital was due to pay Raccanelli 15,000 florins in connection with Smyrna: Valletta, National Library of Malta, Archives of the Order of St. John of Jerusalem, cod. 319, f. 265v-267v, 312-312v (1/2 July 1365). The final 6000 of the 15,000 florins were paid in 1368: cod. 16 no. 46. All the documents of 1365 refer to this as a loan to Raccanelli (*ad ipsius preces promisimus mutuare* ... and ... *mutuo tradere debebamus*), but such formulae could have disguised some other arrangement. DELAVILLE, 144-145, speaks of a "rembourse" to Raccanelli of 15,000 florins "que celui-ci avait avancés".

(14) Reg. Vat. 263, f. 300-300v; Reg. Vat. 274, f. 17-20. HALECKI, 250, wrongly states that the Master was to "choose" a successor.

(15) Reg. Vat. 264, f. 201 (16 February 1372), f. 203v-204v (15 August 1372); Reg. Vat. 268, f. 310v-311v (15 August 1372).

abandon the city unless they were paid the 5000 florins or more still owed them by Raccanelli (16). By March 1373 the pope had news of forthcoming Turkish attacks on Smyrna, and by June he had heard that the unpaid mercenaries might surrender the city in return for huge bribes. In June 1374, following further complaints from the garrison, a new set of papal threats sought to secure payment from Raccanelli, from Cattaneo and from the Cypriot collectors and clergy. With the merchant-captains of Smyrna clearly operating a lucrative racket, Gregory finally altered papal policy. On 21 September 1374, further alarmed by reports of John V's entente of 1373 with the Turks, he revoked Cattaneo's command and confided Smyrna for five years to the direct care of the Hospitallers who were to receive 3000 florins per annum from papal incomes in Cyprus. The Master of the Hospital, then at Avignon, was ordered to travel to Rhodes within three months to carry out these instructions (17).

The Hospitallers also figured, at least on the diplomatic side, in Gregory's Cypriot problems. The Hospital was traditionally involved in the politics of Cyprus, drawing considerable sums from its sugar plantations there. The Order had collaborated in the Cypriot campaigns in Cilician Armenia and in the sack of Alexandria in 1365, but after the assassination of King Pierre de Lusignan in 1369 the affairs of Cyprus fell into confusion as the Genoese mercantile community seized the opportunity to interfere in local quarrels and thus establish a clear predominance there (18). On 28 April 1371 Gregory ordered the Hospitaller Fr. Bertrand Flote to travel to Cyprus to act as protector to the young King Pierre II (19), and on 4 June he instructed the

(16) Reg. Vat. 269, f. 5, 5v, 258 (10, 20, 29 January 1373).

(17) The Smyrna affair can be followed in great detail in the innumerable papal bulls (some utilized in HALECKI, 264, 300-301, and SETTON, i [1976], 328) dating from 26 February 1373 to 19 October 1374, especially Reg. Vat. 266, f. 22v-27v, 51-52, 55, 64-65, 68; Reg. Vat. 269, f. 27v-28, 37v-38, 42, 73v-74, 262v-263, 270-270v, 315-316; Reg. Vat. 270, f. 33v, 37v-38, 63v. Damiano Cattaneo commanded the Genoese fleet which attacked Cyprus in 1373. Gregory knew of the Byzantine-Turkish entente by September 1374: DENNIS, 35.

(18) G. HILL, *A History of Cyprus*, ii (Cambridge, 1948), 308-378, provides an outline of these events.

(19) Archivio Segreto Vaticano, Reg. Aven. 182, f. 501; there is no evidence that Flote actually went to Cyprus, as HILL, ii. 378, perhaps implies.

Master to go there as papal nuncio as soon as possible ([20]). On 8 February 1373 the pope wrote ordering the Master to remain in the East, partly because of trouble in Cyprus ([21]). At that point Gregory had not, however, heard that a Genoese fleet was invading the island. The Cypriots were compelled to abandon Antalya on the Anatolian mainland to the Turkish Emir of Tekke who took oaths of vassalage to the King of Cyprus on 14 May ([22]). On 10 June the pope instructed the Master at Rhodes not to give any assistance to the Genoese in Cyprus ([23]), and in that same month the Marshal of the Hospital, Fr. Pons de Tournon, went there to mediate but he soon returned to Rhodes when his mission failed. In January 1374 the Master, Fr. Raymond Bérenger, himself sailed to Cyprus only to die there, reportedly of vexation at his lack of diplomatic success, on 16 February. That the Hospitallers were fundamentally in fear of the triumphant Genoese became clear in April 1374 when the Marshal of the Hospital refused to shelter Pierre II's uncle, Jacques de Lusignan Constable of Cyprus, who had sought refuge at Rhodes and whom the Hospitallers allowed to be taken to Genoa where he was imprisoned ([24]).

In pursuing his inquiry into the Hospitallers' commanderies Gregory evidently had in mind not only the general situation in the East but also the state of the Hospital in the West ([25]). On 17 June 1372, some eight months before he ordered the inquest into the commanderies, he had instructed the Master on

([20]) Reg. Vat. 263, f. 187-187v; BOSIO, ii. 111, stated, without evidence, that the Master went.

([21]) Reg. Vat. 269, f. 8v.

([22]) HILL, ii. 388-389. On 22 January 1372 Gregory had requested the Hospitallers and other powers to assist the Armenians: texts in TĂUTU, 41-46.

([23]) Text in PAULI, ii. 406-407.

([24]) Details, from the chroniclers, in HILL, ii. 389-390, 402-403, 410-411; the Marshal is named in Reg. Aven. 193, f. 406-406v (2 September 1374).

([25]) DELAVILLE, 166-169, described a supposed Chapter-General of 1370 and deduced from its decisions (which actually date to 1373) that the Hospital was "en plein crise". There is peripheral evidence of anarchy from marginal priories such as Portugal and Bohemia (*ibid.*, 167, 170-173, 376-379), but such evidence is available at almost any point in the fourteenth century.

pain of excommunication to summon a *capitulum generale* or assembly of Hospitallers to meet somewhere near Avignon on 1 May 1373. His bull of 17 June contained rhetorical exhortations cast in biblical language; there was to be a *reformacio* of the brethren, who were accused of inactivity, negligence, nepotism and other corruptions, and were reminded of their duty to fight the holy war in the East. Gregory asked for details of the number of commanderies and the number and age of the Hospital's *sacerdotes, milites* and *oblati*. On 21 June 1372 a bull was sent to the Master stating that, for reasons of economy, only four brethren were to be sent from Rhodes to represent the Convent at the assembly (26). It was on 8 February 1373 that the pope ordered the Master not to come to the assembly himself on account of his age and also of the need both to face the Turks and to deal with troubles in Cyprus (27). By 10 June Gregory had received Fr. Raymond Bérenger's reply; he proposed to resign the Mastership, a notion firmly rejected by the pope (28). Meanwhile Gregory, having apparently received no answers to the questions he had posed the Hospitallers in June 1372, had initiated the papal inquest through his bulls of 10 February 1373 in which he confided the inquisition to the bishops, whereas in the preceding June he had called on the Hospitallers themselves to collect and present the information required (29). At some point the pope had, furthermore, postponed the Hospitaller assembly until 1 September 1373 (30).

A number of experts in Levantine affairs were available at Avignon to advise on policy. The former supporters of the anti-Mamluk crusade were less strongly represented. The Master at Rhodes clearly had little direct contact or influence with the new

(26) Reg. Vat. 268, f. 39-39v, 41v-42. Gregory was sending the Augustinian Pierre de *Ungula* to the Master on 26 August 1372: f. 174-174v.

(27) Reg. Vat. 269, f. 8v.

(28) Text in PAULI, ii. 407-408.

(29) Text and discussion in J. GLÉNISSON, "L'Enquête pontificale de 1373 sur les possessions des Hospitaliers de Saint-Jean-de-Jérusalem", *Bibliothèque de l'École des Chartes*, cxxix (1971). On 17 February 1373 Gregory summoned Fr. Bartolomeo Benini, Admiral of the Hospital, to give advice concerning the assembly: Reg. Vat. 269, f. 259v.

(30) Text of 12 May 1373 in Reg. Vat. 269, f. 44v.

pope, while the two heroes of the Cypriot crusade of 1365, Pierre Thomas and Pierre de Lusignan, were dead. Amedeo Count of Savoy, the reconqueror of Gallipoli, was occupied in the Italian wars. Philippe de Mézières, Chancellor of Cyprus and the most persistent of contemporary crusading enthusiasts, reached Avignon from Venice in February 1372 and stayed there for some months but by March 1373 he had moved to Paris, thus losing much of the influence he might have had in the determination of crusading policy had he remained in Avignon (31). A principal agent of the pope in Levantine matters was the Greek John Lascaris Calopheros, a convert to the Roman faith and a former protégé of Pierre I of Cyprus; he had participated in various crusading expeditions and had interests in Cyprus and the Morea. He appeared at Avignon early in 1373 and his role in Gregory's crusading projects was certainly both extensive and important, though probably not decisive in the evolution of policies (32). Other personalities may also have influenced papal decisions. These included the Florentine Giovanni Corsini, a Rhodian landholder whose brother was a cardinal (33), and Simon Atoumanos, Archbishop of Thebes, who may have been connected with the summonses of November 1372 to a congress at Thebes. Simon Atoumanos was definitely at Avignon in January 1373, and in July 1374 the pope exhorted him to accompany the mission of

(31) N. JORGA, *Philippe de Mézières (1327-1405) et la croisade au XIVe siècle* (Paris, 1896), 404-409, but it is not at all clear exactly when Mézières left Avignon; he was apparently near to the King of France in March 1373: text in HALECKI, 387.

(32) It cannot be shown, though HALECKI presumes it, that Calopheros initiated or dominated Gregory's Eastern policy. He was in close touch with the Hospitallers: details and texts in ESZER, 51-59, 127-146, 168-183. See also D. JACOBY, "Jean Lascaris Calophéros, Chypre et la Morée", *Revue des Études Byzantines*, xxvi (1968), and R.-J. LOENERTZ, "Pour la biographie de Jean Lascaris Calophéros", *ibid.*, xxviii (1978). JACOBY plays down the importance of Calopheros, which he considers is exaggerated by ESZER: see his important review of ESZER in *Byzantinische Zeitschrift*, lxiv (1971), 378-381. Calopheros' problematical involvement in the *passagium* to Greece in 1377 and 1378 is a different matter: see ESZER, 68-80.

(33) Details and text in HALECKI, 289-292, 390-391; LUTTRELL, see note 11 (1978), VIII 324-325. Corsini was a *civis* of Venice, but not a Venetian.

Hospitallers and theologians soon to leave for Constantinople (34). Catherine of Siena was pressing in 1372 for the prosecution of the crusade, a matter to which she continued to attach much importance (35); when Gregory summoned a *passagium* or expedition of Hospitallers in December 1375 she was quick to refer to the matter, about which she wrote again in 1377 (36). Many of these personages knew each other well (37), and some of them probably discussed crusading affairs among themselves at Avignon during 1372 and 1373. His cardinals and advisers included others whose opinion also carried weight with Gregory, yet in the last resort it was the pope himself who determined the formulation of policy (38).

In Hospitaller affairs a feature of the new papacy was the return to Avignon of Fr. Juan Fernández de Heredia who had already succeeded in establishing himself inside the papal palace in the brief period during the conclave before Gregory's election in December 1370 (39). This Aragonese Hospitaller at once requested the new pope to provide him to the Southern French Priory of Saint Gilles, but on 18 February 1371 Gregory merely wrote requesting the Master to give Fernández de Heredia two or three commanderies near Avignon, both in recognition of his past services in defence of the city and also to enable him to live

(34) Details in G. FEDALTO, *Simone Atumano, monaco di studio, arcivescovo latino di Tebe: secolo XIV* (Brescia, 1968), 95-100; *infra*, n. 67. Gregory was sending Atoumanos to Venice on 17 December 1372, and he summoned him to Avignon on 9 December 1373: texts in TĂUTU, 98, 181-182.

(35) This point is emphasized in R. FAWTIER, *Sainte Catherine de Sienne: essai de critique des sources*, 2 vols. (Paris, 1921-1930), i. 161, 168 note 3, 187-188; ii. 257-261 *et passim*.

(36) See Appendix *infra*, 415-417.

(37) Cf. ESZER, 110-117.

(38) The documents, in any case, do not allow an insight into the workings of the pope's inner councils. To distinguish with certainty between makers of policy, competent agents and self-interested intriguers is not possible; only the pope himself can be seen to be continuously and ubiquitously involved.

(39) Archivio Segreto Vaticano, Introitus et Exitus, 335, f. 76v: *Item pro una clauj necessaria pro porta Camere dominj Castellanj Emposte infra dictum Palacium in qua dormiebat tempore conclauj.*

decently at Avignon where the pope wished him to stay (40). By 24 August 1372 Fernández de Heredia had become Prior of Catalunya (41), probably through papal influence. Between 1371 and 1376 he was active at Avignon though not continually in residence there; he seems to have been far away, with the King of Castile, at the moment when the inquest into the Hospital was launched in February 1373 (42). On 12 May 1373 the pope summoned him to be present at the assembly in September and to send ahead his advice about how it should be managed (43); papal bulls of 9 August called on King Pedro of Aragon not to obstruct Fernández de Heredia's attendance, and on Cardinal Guy de Boulogne to urge him to come (44). Fernández de Heredia was at the assembly in Avignon by September 1373 (45) and by this time he was certainly beginning to play a leading part in the Hospitallers' crusading plans; by August 1374 he had also been re-appointed Captain-General of Avignon (46) and he again

(40) Reg. Vat. 263, f. 259. This bull does not really demonstrate that Fernández de Heredia was again active in defence of Avignon in February 1371: correct LUTTRELL (1978), XIX 312.

(41) Malta, cod. 322, f. 302-302v.

(42) He was in or around Avignon from January to about April 1371 when he went to Paris: Barcelona, Archivo de la Corona de Aragón, Reg. 1737, f. 5v, 7v-8, 24-24v, 38, 50, 68. Thereafter his movements are not known. From December 1371 to March 1372 he was in Avignon: Barcelona, Reg. 1738, f. 73-73v, 75, 81-81v, 82v, 84v. He was assumed to be at Avignon on 8 March: text in J. VINCKE, *Documenta selecta mutuas civitatis Arago-Cathalaunicae et Ecclesiae relationes illustrantia* (Barcelona, 1936), 484-485. He was at Avignon in October, and about to leave on 30 October: Barcelona, Reg. 1739, f. 4v; Reg. 1236, f. 18-18v, 32-32v. He was in Barcelona on 6 and 22 December, but by January 1373 he had left: Barcelona, Reg. 1550, f. 45v-50; Reg. 1450, f. 54v-63; Reg. 1735, f. 130v. In February and March he was apparently in Castile for on 3 March King Pedro wrote to him acknowledging a message from Enrique of Castile and requesting Fernández de Heredia to continue his dealings with the Castilians: text in J. MA. MADURELL I MARIMON, "Les noces de l'infant Joan amb Matha d'Armanyac", *Estudis Universitaris Catalans*, xix (1934), 49.

(43) Reg. Vat. 269, f. 44v; the summons was repeated on 28 July (f. 68v).

(44) Text in VINCKE, 496.

(45) The assembly opened on 1 September: Malta, cod. 320, f. 42.

(46) Archivio Segreto Vaticano, Collectorie 265, f. 238, 277. On 5

became active in its defence (47). This astute politician, like so many others at the papal *curia*, had multiple allegiances and interests: in his career at Avignon, in his Hospitaller priories, in his family and its estates, in Aragonese politics, and in his literary activities. However, once associated with the organization and financing of the Hospitaller *passagium*, a man of such ambition naturally acquired a vested interest in its success so that, without his necessarily having been in any way involved in the initiation of the scheme, he may gradually have come to devote himself to it as the path to the promotion to the Mastership which he did eventually secure (48).

During 1373 Gregory continued negotiations concerning a variety of Eastern projects. The proposed continental crusade in the Balkans had run into difficulties over the pope's mistrust of the Hungarians who declared war on the Venetians, so that by 22 March 1373 papal policy had returned to the notion of a Christian naval league (49). The Hospital was scheduled to provide a land force. On 29 June, in view of the coming assembly, Gregory requested the Venetians and Genoese to suggest a point where the Hospitallers could not only make a landing but also hold whatever territory they might acquire (50), and on the same day he was sending John Lascaris Calopheros with crusading information to the Master and Convent at Rhodes (51).

August 1375 he was appointed Captain-General in the Comtat Venaissin: text in MIROT, no. 1657.

(47) Details in Collectorie 265, f. 167, 188v, 189, 234v-235, 277, 294v-305 (August 1374 – July 1376); see also GUILLEMAIN, 622-624; LUTTRELL (1978), XIX 312.

(48) On Fernández de Heredia, see LUTTRELL see note 11 (1978), *passim*. Though he was close to the pope and was involved in the organization of the *passagium*, it cannot be shown that he initiated it or determined its final objective, as so often claimed (e.g. in DELAVILLE, 189, 201). Nor can it be shown that he initiated the Hospitaller *negotium Achaye* of 1356-1357: LUTTRELL (1978), XX 402, XXI 237-238.

(49) Details in HALECKI, 265-275.

(50) Reg. Vat. 269, f. 59v: *intendimusque diuino suffragante auxilio ex ipsis fratribus qui multi sunt per orbem illum numerum qui commode mitti poterit ad partes ultramarinas ad eas defendendum ...* The request was repeated on 24 August: f. 74-74v. See also texts in ESZER, 168, 169-170.

(51) Text in ESZER, 168-169.

By 30 August the Genoese had offered to provide two galleys out of the twelve it was hoped to raise, and they had sent advice about the Hospitallers' best line of action (52). By the time that the Hospitaller assembly met in Avignon the results of some of the episcopal inquests must actually have reached the papal *curia* (53). The Master, forbidden to come himself, had appointed Fr. Robert de Juilly, Prior of France, to act as his Lieutenant at the Assembly, but he fell ill, and on 13 September Gregory empowered the brethren gathered at Avignon to choose an alternative Lieutenant (54); eventually Fr. Juan Fernández de Heredia was nominated to preside in the name of the Master and Convent (55).

The *congregatio* or *assembleya* which met during September, October and November was convened at the pope's command. It was decided to effect various reforms but there was little in these decisions to reflect either a disastrous crisis in the West or any immediate intention of launching a crusade in the East (56). The financial question remained fundamental. It was agreed, entirely unrealistically, to raise 40,000 florins annually for three years to be sent to Rhodes for the sustenance of the island, together with a further 80,000 florins to be collected each year for three years for a *passagium* against the Turks. Of the annual 80,000 florins, 30,000 were to come from the Hospitallers' ordinary taxes or *responsiones*, 20,000 from a special imposition or *taille* of one-third of the *responsiones*, 10,000 from the *spolia* of deceased brethren, 10,000 from arrears of *responsiones*, and 10,000 from debts owed by laymen and from the incomes of vacant priories and commanderies. These monies were to be collected by Fr. Juan Fernández de Heredia, who was appointed to manage them by papal authority, and they were to be sent to Avignon

(52) Text in HALECKI, 388-389.

(53) Only a few inquests were complete by September: DELAVILLE, 170 note 2, some of whose dates are however inaccurate.

(54) Reg. Aven. 191, f. 386v-387.

(55) Malta, cod. 320, f. 2; cod. 347, f. 51-51v; it is not clear how this nomination was made.

(56) These decisions are published from Reg. Vat. 270, f. 14-15v, and Reg. Vat. 244 G, f. 16, 17 (with inexplicable omissions), in MIROT, no. 3283; DELAVILLE, 166-169, wrongly dates them to 1370.

and Venice through the Florentine bankers, the Alberti Antichi; the funds for the projected *passagium* were to be held separately on deposit, 50,000 florins at Avignon and 30,000 at Venice (57). Apparently no precise decision concerning Hospitaller crusading activities was recorded, but on 2 December 1373 Gregory, at the request of the Master and Convent, empowered his own apostolic *camera* to proceed against Hospitallers who refused to pay their *responsiones* (58). On 7 December the pope also appealed to various Western rulers to return possessions usurped from the Hospital since the assembly had complained that otherwise it could not find the monies required (59). On 13 January 1374 envoys sent by the Master from Rhodes met Fr. Juan Fernández de Heredia and other brethren at Avignon and further financial arrangements were agreed; the Hospitallers were to make up any deficiency in the annual 80,000 florins out of their own incomes, and two cardinals were appointed to ensure that the monies were not spent improperly (60).

Fr. Raymond Bérenger died in Cyprus on 16 February 1374 and the Convent at Rhodes rapidly elected Fr. Robert de Juilly, who was then in France, to succeed him (61). Another assembly of Hospitallers met at Avignon to advance preparations under the new Master who was there from 18 August to about 13 October (62). On 21 September the pope entrusted the defence of Smyrna wholly to the Hospital, while arrangements were made for Juilly's own journey to Rhodes and for the financing of the coming Hospitaller *passagium* (63); on 10 October Juilly created

(57) Details from Malta, cod. 23 no. 4; cod. 320, f. 2-3, 11v, 41v; Reg. Aven. 197, f. 40-40v, 111-111v.

(58) Reg. Aven. 191, f. 374-374v.

(59) Reg. Vat. 269, f. 240-240v.

(60) Reg. Aven. 197, f. 111-111v; Reg. Aven. 201, f. 6v-7.

(61) Juilly was elected by the brethren at Rhodes: Paris, Bibliothèque Nationale, Ms. franç. 17,255, f. 77. He was acting as Master, at Paris, by 8 June 1374: Paris, Archives Nationales, MM 29, f. 121.

(62) Malta, cod. 320, f. 1-45v.

(63) *Supra*, p. 397; financial details in Malta, cod. 23 no. 4; cod. 320, f. 2-3, 11v, 41v. It was reported from Avignon on 14 December 1374 that the pope's decision to return to Italy was *firmissimus* and that the Master of the Hospital was to provide ten galleys to be armed in Aragon which would accompany the pope and then sail to Rhodes: text

Fr. Juan Fernández de Heredia the Master's Lieutenant in the West (64). The monies already collected for the *passagium* were evidently a temptation and on 30 September 1374 the pope, acting in the light of a reported dearth of victuals at Rhodes, had empowered Fernández de Heredia to lend the Convent 20,000 out of the 50,000 florins due to come to him at Avignon each year for three years to finance the *passagium*, but on the strict condition that the money was repaid within two years. However, probably because these prospective incomes were never fully paid in, the Master eventually borrowed money from the Alberti Antichi, and papal bulls of 13 and 25 January 1375 again insisted that the monies for the *passagium* be carefully preserved at Avignon and Venice under the supervision of two cardinals, and that they should not, as certain Hospitallers wished, be sent to Rhodes (65).

Crusading business had dragged slowly on with a succession

---

in A. SEGRE, "I Dispacci di Cristoforo da Piacenza procuratore mantovano alla corte pontificia: 1371-1383", *Archivio Storico Italiano*, 5 ser., xliii (1909), 63-67. Juilly himself had already left for Rhodes, apparently before 15 October, and Gregory wrote to Genoa on 15 and 16 October 1374 that Juilly was coming there for talks which apparently concerned Cyprus: Reg. Vat. 270, f. 68-68v, 150v, 215v-216. Juilly left Avignon between 13 and 16 October and was in Genoa at least from 9-14 November: Malta, cod. 320, f. 45v, 51v, 55.

(64) A brief document of 10 October 1374 was copied into the Master's register and then cancelled: Malta, cod. 320, f. 44. It was replaced by a fuller text of the same day conceding Fernández de Heredia wider powers to negotiate with the pope and other rulers: copy of 1393 in Malta, cod. 23 no. 3. DELAVILLE, 184, citing Malta, cod. 320, f. 49, incorrectly implies that Fernández de Heredia was appointed Captain of the *passagium* by Juilly on 20 October 1374; correct this ambiguity which is also repeated in LUTTRELL see note 11, (1978), I 301.

(65) Bulls of 30 September 1374 in Reg. Aven. 193, f. 502, and also in Reg. Aven. 197, f. 38, where it was subsequently crossed out, and others of 13 and 25 January 1375 in Reg. Aven. 197, f. 111-111v, 40-40v. On 1 September 1374 the pope instructed Fernández de Heredia to pay the Master, then at Avignon, 40,000 florins due yearly for three years, to the Master and Convent *pro eorum prouisionę* and to secure a receipt: Reg. Aven. 193, f. 502. These monies were not, apparently, part of the 80,000 florins supposedly being raised for a *passagium*. 24,500 florins were borrowed from the Alberti Antichi in 1374: Malta, cod. 16 no. 52.

of letters, missions and negotiations in which Giovanni Corsini and John Lascaris Calopheros were involved. On 21 June 1373 the pope had written to John V that he was assembling a fleet to rescue Constantinople and Thessalonika which were reported to be almost surrounded by Turks (66). As early as February 1374 Gregory planned to send an embassy to Constantinople to discuss the proposed *passagium*. In April the Venetians gave an evasive reply to various questions on this topic, including the query about where the Hospitallers' forces should best intervene; on that point they wrote *quod multa sunt loca ad hoc apta in partibus Constantinopolis sive Romanie* (67). The news of the entente between the Greek emperor and the Turks may have delayed matters, and Gregory's mission of two theologians and two Hospitallers, Fr. Hesso Schegelholtz and Fr. Bertrand Flote, did not leave for Constantinople until October 1374 (68). The background to these negotiations was not promising. During 1373, in his concern to deal with his own rebellious son Andronicus, the Emperor John V made arrangements with Murad which had the effect of allowing a considerable Turkish army into Europe, and by July 1374 news had reached Venice that John V and Murad had agreed to arm a fleet (69). In December 1374 the Venetians

(66) Texts in MOLLAT, nos. 1933-1934.

(67) Text of 4 April 1374 in HALECKI, 390-391; this shows that in February Gregory also intended to send Giovanni Corsini and the Archbishops of Patras and Thebes to Constantinople.

(68) It was the Hospital, not the papacy, which disbursed at least 6677 florins for the expenses of the Hospitallers and theologians on this mission: Malta, cod. 16 no. 52. On 1 September 1374 Gregory instructed Fernández de Heredia to pay these expenses: Reg. Aven. 193, f. 496v. On 21 September Gregory instructed the Master and Convent to provide the mission with further funds at Constantinople: Reg. Vat. 170, f. 58-58v. The theologians were the Franciscan Bartolomeo Cherrazio and the Dominican Tommaso de Bozolasco: further details in HALECKI, 292-297. The 1374 mission was accompanied by a papal inquiry into the documents connected with Clement VI's negotiations with the Greeks: text of 19 March 1374 in HALECKI, 389. The accounts of Gregory's Eastern policies after 1375 in HALECKI, 289-324, and ESZER, 132-146, are to some extent incomplete, partly because interest turned to Gregory's Italian projects, partly because of losses among the papal registers for Gregory's final years.

(69) I. BELDICEANU-STEINHERR, "La conquête d'Andrinople par

decided to renew their important commercial treaties with Byzantium, but the negotiations they initiated during 1375 failed completely [70]. In the autumn of 1375 the papal mission returned with news which was extremely serious but which offered some hope of future action. It was reported that John V had promised, presumably under pressure from the Hospitaller embassy, to hand over Thessalonika and one "other" city to the pope; the two cities were to be defended by the Hospitallers who were to reside in them, and in response Gregory ordered a *passagium* against the Turks which would be designed to liberate "parts of Greece" [71]. Whose proposal this was, in what way theological questions were involved, whether the "other" city was Gallipoli, how many Hospitallers would have been available to garrison the two cities, where the *passagium* was at that point designed to intervene, and whether the Venetians had been consulted or had agreed was not reported. Gregory certainly renewed his diplomatic efforts. On 27 October 1375 he was sending Fr. Hesso Schegelholtz to Hungary in an attempt to reactivate the land crusade which Louis of Hungary had abandoned [72]. On the same day he wrote to Queen Jeanne of Naples calling on her to supply shipping. Gregory announced that Constantinople was already tributary to the Turks, that it was in great danger

---

les Turcs: la pénétration turque en Thrace et la valeur des chroniques ottomanes", *Travaux et mémoires: Centre de Recherche d'Histoire et Civilisation byzantines*, i (1965), 452-455.

(70) J. CHRYSOSTOMIDES, "Studies on the Chronicle of Caroldo with Special Reference to the History of Byzantium from 1370 to 1377", *OCP*, xxxv (1969), 148-150.

(71) ... *ordinatur pasagium contra Turchos pro liberatione partium Grecie et Imperator Constantinopolitanus promitit dare domino pape civitatem Salonichi et quandam alliam quas tenebunt fratres Jerosolimitani et in eis residebunt*: despatch sent from Avignon to Mantua on 22 November 1375 by Cristoforo da Piacenza: text in SEGRE, 80-82. Though not corroborated by any other document this proposal may be accepted as fitting reasonably well in the known pattern of events, but whether it was a sincere or realistic proposal may be doubted. This very significant offer by John V, which throws important light on the situation, has not previously been noted in this context.

(72) Text in O. RINALDI, *Annales Ecclesiastici*, vii (Lucca, 1752), 264.

of falling, and that the Ottomans would then take the rest of the Christian East and threaten the Principality of Achaea and even the Kingdom of Naples. It was essential to assist the Greeks withtout delay by preventing the passage of the Turks from *Turchia* into *Romania* and *Bulgaria.* If sufficient support were to reach the Greeks they would recognize papal supremacy, and Gregory planned to send Hospitallers "in good number" and "several" galleys, some of them promised by various powers and some to be hired by the pope himself (73). An intervention in the Dardanelles may have been envisaged, and in December 1375 a papal bull spoke of the *passagium generale faciendum contra Turchos* (74). Yet another Hospitaller assembly met at Avignon under Fr. Juan Fernández de Heredia probably in November (75). Fr. Bertrand Flote and the Priors of France, Champagne and Saint Gilles were there, and it was decided to call for 500 *milites* each with a *scutifer* for a *passagium* which had by then been postponed until the spring of 1377. On 8 December 1375 the pope issued bulls to the European priors instructing them each to hold chapters which were to designate a total of 405 *milites* to participate in the coming expedition (76), even though the inquests of 1373 had made it fully evident that such large numbers of Hospitaller *milites* did not exist (77). Nothing was done during

(73) Text in F. CERASOLI, "Gregorio XI e Giovanna I Regina di Napoli: documenti inediti dell'Archivio Vaticano", *Archivio Storico per le Province Napoletane,* xxv (1900), 6-8. Bartolomeo Cherrazio, one of the two theologians on the Constantinople mission, was being sent to Naples: see also HALECKI, 317-318.

(74) MOLLAT, no. 3622. Though SETTON, i. 328 n. 9, suggests that this was probably a device to collect money, a *passagium* of a sort did eventually take place.

(75) The summonses *pro certis arduis negotiis* were dated 15 October 1375: Reg. Vat. 277, f. 64-64v.

(76) Reg. Vat. 267, f. 46v-48: text in PAULI, ii. 97-98, with complete statistics in Mcllat, nos. 3634-3635. DELAVILLE, 188-191, and HALECKI, 316-317, give incomplete figures. HALECKI's work closes before the Hospitaller *passagium* of 1378 of which he takes no account. Bosio, ii. 120-121, misdated the assembly to 1376 and wrongly stated that the *passagium* was to go to Rhodes. 500 knights was apparently the number it was proposed to send to *Romania* in 1369/70: text now lost but referred to in HALECKI, 214, 357.

(77) The paucity of *milites* and the Hospital's poverty are shown

1376, all efforts being directed towards the pope's return to Italy.

The situation in the East went from bad to worse during 1376. In May or June a Venetian embassy, which was accompanied by a fleet, secured from John V an agreement by which Venice was to occupy the island of Tenedos just outside the Dardanelles. Meanwhile the emperor's son Andronicus escaped from captivity and led a revolt which had Genoese and Turkish support, and the emperor himself was imprisoned. Andronicus proposed to award Tenedos to the Genoese, and the Ottomans were allowed to reoccupy Gallipoli; the Venetians therefore themselves occupied Tenedos in October 1376 after which the conflict between Venice and Genoa escalated progressively until armed hostilities began in mid-1377. It was possibly at this point that the Ottomans captured Adrianople which seems to have fallen to other non-Ottoman Turkish leaders some years earlier in about 1369 ([78]).

On the financial side, it must have been amply clear to the pope by August 1376 that the funds available were insufficient. Gregory's war with Florence and the papal interdict of March 1376 hit all Florentine merchants and meant that the papacy ceased to use the Alberti Antichi as its bankers, even though the Alberti's possessions at Avignon were not apparently seized, possibly in order to limit the repercussions in the papacy's financial department ([79]). What happened to any Hospitaller monies deposited with the Alberti Antichi was not recorded in the papal or other documents; probably the Hospitallers had little or noth-

---

clearly in the 1373 inquests, many of which are in the course of publication by Mlle. Anne-Marie Legras at the Institut de Recherche et d'Histoire des Textes at Paris.

([78]) DENNIS, 37-40; BELDICEANU-STEINHERR, 454-458; BARKER, 24-32, 458-461; CHRYSOSTOMIDES, 151-159. The precise date on which the Turks occupied Gallipoli is uncertain. If the Turks recovered it in 1369, that would make it less likely that it was the "other" city offered by John V to the Hospital in 1375.

([79]) Y. RENOUARD, *Les relations des Papes d'Avignon et des compagnies commerciales et bancaires de 1316 à 1378* (Paris, 1941), 288-295, 334-338 *et passim*; R. TREXLER, *The Spiritual Power: Republican Florence under Interdict* (Leiden, 1974), 44-45, 50 n. 33, 53-54.

ing to deposit and they had in fact borrowed money from the Alberti Antichi (80). In any case further efforts had to be made to raise funds. On 10 August 1376 the Master at Rhodes authorized the alienation of lands in the West (81). On 13 February 1377 the pope sought once again to compel certain Hospitallers to pay the taxes which had been agreed on 13 January 1374 (82). In March Gregory confirmed Juilly's bull of August 1376 and, in bulls which still spoke of 500 *fratres milites* each with a *scutifer*, he gave papal authorization for the sale or mortgaging of Hospitaller lands in Italy up to 60,000 florins (83), in Germany and Bohemia up to 60,000 florins, in Spain and Portugal up to 60,000 florins, and in France up to 30,000 florins (84), making a theoretical total of at least 210,000 florins (85).

None of Gregory's bulls gave any precise indication of the destination of the *passagium* but it must have been aimed at defending Greece or some other part of the Balkans against Ottoman incursions. Cyprus was in turmoil but it was not in danger from the infidel; Cilician Armenia had already been overrun by the Mamluks in 1375; Smyrna was important, but the problem there was the comparatively minor, though always difficult, one of finding 6000 florins a year to pay the garrison; and as for Rhodes itself, special measures had been taken to prevent the *passagium* funds being employed there. The preparations made all pointed to an intervention in the Aegean or the Balkans. The mission of 1374 had gone to Constantinople, in November 1375 there was talk of liberating certain *partes Grecie* and of acquiring Thessalonika, and in August 1376 the Master at Rhodes spoke of an expedition to the Duchy of Athens (86), but it soon became evident that the deposition of the Emperor John V and hostilities between Venice and Genoa would rule out effective crusading

(80) Malta, cod. 16 no. 52, which also shows that during 1374/5 3064 florins of "other expenses" were paid to the Alberti Antichi.

(81) Text in PAULI, ii. 99-101.

(82) Reg. Aven. 201, f. 6v-7.

(83) Texts of 1 and 7 March 1377 in PAULI, ii. 98-101.

(84) Reg. Aven. 201, f. 62-62v, 189-189v (1 March 1377).

(85) There is no known evidence in the archives that such alienations were actually made.

(86) Text of 10 August 1376 in PAULI, ii. 99-101.

action in the Dardanelles or in the Aegean. In October 1375, after his return from Constantinople, Fr. Hesso Schegelholtz had been sent to Hungary to discuss the defence of Bulgaria and *Romania*, but at that time Gregory and the Hospital were quarrelling with the Hungarian king who refused to recognize the newly-nominated Hospitaller Prior of Hungary (87). Eventually the Hospitallers' expedition merely sailed to Vonitza in Epirus on the Balkan shore of the Adriatic.

The *passagium* had been postponed for a time while Gregory XI left Avignon for Italy; Fr. Juan Fernández de Heredia served as Admiral of the papal fleet and entered Rome with the pope in January 1377. Preparations for the expedition continued, slowly as ever, with the financial measures of February and March. Fr. Robert de Juilly died at Rhodes on 29 July 1377 and on 24 September Gregory, who had previously reserved the election to himself, exercized his papal powers in providing Fernández de Heredia to the vacant Mastership. The pope was risking resistance, which did in fact materialize from the French Hospitallers at Rhodes, presumably in the hope that the promotion of his own favourite would ensure the continuation of papal crusading schemes. During 1377 the Hospitallers were making arrangements with Queen Jeanne of Naples to lease from her the Principality of Achaea which they then administered for some five years; they also secured a lease on the town of Vonitza in the Gulf of Arta from Maddalena Buondelmonti of Florence who was the widow of Leonardo Tocco, Duke of Leucadia and Count of Cephalonia. Finance and provisions for the *passagium* came from a group of Florentines who had to be exempted from the restrictions of the papal interdict upon them and who possibly conditioned the choice of objective so that the expedition appeared to be designed merely to defend the Tocco possessions against the Albanians in Epirus. In 1378 the new Master sailed to Vonitza with a small group of Hospitallers and certain Florentines who were related or connected to Maddalena Buondelmonti.

(87) Details in DELAVILLE, 196-198. There is no hint that Gregory also wanted the Hospital's monies, though the suspicion would have been a natural one. On 24 September 1373, at the very moment the Hospitaller assembly was opening, the pope gave instructions that his jewels be pawned to raise 50,000 florins: text in MIROT, no. 1393.

Gregory XI died in March 1378 and his successor, Pope Urban VI, apparently abandoned the Hospitallers' expedition to its disastrous conclusion. On 23 August 1378, somewhere between Vonitza and Arta and while still at the very gateway into Greece, Fr. Juan Fernández de Heredia, presumably short of men, money and supplies, was defeated and captured by the Albanian Lord of Arta, Ghin Boua Spata, and subsequently he had to be ransomed from his fellow-Christian captors (88).

Gregory XI had clung to two objectives: his major concern was the re-establishment of the papal *curia* at Rome while the other, the defence of the Christian East, was never allotted the resources necessary for effective action. In both tasks the pope was hampered by profound economic and spiritual crises within Western Christian society, by armed conflict and dissension throughout Europe and by the papacy's own shortage of money. On 18 May 1375 Gregory wrote in rhetorical style to the King of France emphasizing that peace had to be established in the West before an effective *passagium* could be planned (89), and there was certainly truth in that. The pope's determination to take the papacy back to Italy involved wars against Milan and

(88) The events of 1377-1378 remain obscure. Details and references in LUTTRELL see note 11, (1978), I 302-303, V 207-208, VIII 322-324; ESZER, 66-78, 145-146; and TREXLER, 88-90. See also A. LUTTRELL, "La Corona de Aragón y la Grecia catalana: 1379-1394", *Anuario de Estudios Medievales*, vi (1969); "Aldobrando Baroncelli in Greece: 1378-1382", *OCP*, xxxvi (1970). For Albanian attacks on the Tocco which are difficult to date, see *Cronaca dei Tocco di Cefalonia di Anonimo*: *Prolegomeni, Testo Critico e Traduzione*, ed. G. SCHIRÒ (Rome, 1975), 14-16, 25-34, 223-229. The date of the ambush at Arta is in Arles, Bibliothèque Communale, GG 76, f. 311. The expedition followed an abortive Latin attack on Durazzo, but the Navarrese leader Louis d'Évreux seems not to have died in Albania, as generally supposed. He made a will while ill at Trani on 1 August 1376: text in E. ROGADEO, "Il primo matrimonio di Giovanna duchessa di Durazzo", *Rassegna Pugliese*, xix (1902), 185-187. The *Chronicon Siculum incerti authoris*, ed. J. DE BLASIIS (Naples, 1887), 29, states that he died in Trani in August 1376. The "Aliud Diarium" in the same *Chronicon* said that he died on 26 August while taking "many Gascons and Navarrese" to *Romania*: *ibid.*, 124. *I Diurnali del Duca di Monteleone*, ed. M. MANFREDI, in L. Muratori, *Rerum Italicarum Scriptores*, xxi part 5 (revised: Bologna, 1958), 19, states that news of Louis' death at Gravina reached Queen Giovanna on 19 October 1376.

(89) Text in MIROT, no. 1898.

Florence and led to crippling papal expenditures, to the uneasy reoccupation of Rome, and to the ultimate disaster of the schism in the Latin church. In financial terms Western policies took absolute precedence. Apart from a few thousand florins a year which went to subsidize the garrison at Smyrna, Gregory spent little or nothing for the East. Yet in the five years before the return of the *curia* to Italy the pope expended on his Italian wars an average of 194,000 florins a year, or 42 percent of an average annual income of 466,000 florins (90). The conflict with Milan was in itself a decisive obstacle to crusading action (91).

In the East the proposed congress at Thebes proved abortive; the Christian kingdom of Cilician Armenia collapsed; Venetian and Genoese hostility degenerated into a major naval war; there was no real understanding with the Greeks, who allied with the Turks; and the Turks continued to consolidate their conquests in the Balkans. Only the Hospitallers seemed to offer any reliable prospect of money and manpower, however limited. To them the pope entrusted the papal city of Smyrna, and on them he had to rely for a military *passagium*. Gregory did at least succeed in turning the Hospital's attention away from its traditional spheres of action in Mamluk Egypt and Syria or in the Turkish emirates of the Anatolian seaboard towards the more urgent and fundamental problem of defending Greece and the Balkans against the major long-term threat from the Ottomans. Gregory floundered from one combination of alliances to another. The inquest into the Hospital and the assembly of 1373 were followed by the Hospitaller mission to Constantinople of 1374; by the summonses to action of 1375 which took no account of the findings of the pope's own inquiry; and, following delays occasioned by the pope's return to Rome in 1376 and 1377, by the Hospitallers' *passagium* of 1378. Gregory's insistence on this unrealistic programme led him to impose the organizer of this expedition upon the Hospital as its Master, and the long-planned crusade which followed was ignominiously ambushed by Christian opponents; in the East, as in the West, the best intentions produced the worst results.

(90) RENOUARD, 32 (Table B); these are, of course, crude figures.

(91) On 30 April 1375 a leading figure at Avignon was reported as saying *Malledicantur isti de Mediolano. Nisi esset guerra ita, dominus papa habet multa et magnas intentiones in terris Soldanj et in multis alijs locis ibidem astantibus*: text in SEGRE, 74-75.

Appendix

ST. CATHERINE AND THE HOSPITALLERS

One of St. Catherine's major concerns during Gregory XI's pontificate was the writing of letters urging the pope and other individuals to prosecute the holy war. For Catherine the crusade involved not only the recovery of Jerusalem, the possibility of securing individual salvation through martyrdom and the opportunity of saving infidel souls, but also the bringing of peace to the Latin West by removing the mercenary companies, such as that of John Hawkwood then active in Tuscany, and by uniting the warring kingdoms in a joint attack on the infidels; it was also connected with the return of the papacy from Avignon to Rome (92).

The practical effect of Catherine's crusading letters cannot be measured. When Gregory mobilized the Hospitallers for their *passagium*, Catherine was informed of events. In a letter *A Conte di monna Agnola ed a' compagni in Firenze* she incited this unidentified personage and his companions, presumably Florentines or at least Tuscans, to participate in the Hospitallers' expedition — *Il santo padre manda e' frieri* — which Catherine saw as merely the preliminary to a major crusade, a *passagium generale* (93). This letter could have been written as early as Gregory XI's bulls of December 1375 promulgating the *passagium* (94), but a date in 1377 when the expedition was actually due to depart seems more likely, especially in view of the fact that a number of Florentines did take part in this minor crusade; in fact Vonitza, to which the Hospital acquired a title in 1377, was held by the Florentine Maddalena Buondelmonti.

(92) *Epistolario di Santa Caterina da Siena*, i, ed. E. Dupré Theseider (Rome, 1940); cf. P. Rousset, "Sainte Catherine de Sienne et le Problème de la Croisade", *Schweizerische Zeitschrift für Geschichte*, xxv (1975). Catherine urged even the nun Domitilla to go on a crusade: Fawtier, i. 54.

(93) Text in *Epistolario*, i. 190-194.

(94) Dupré Theseider, in *Epistolario*, i. 190, dates the letter "1375 fine" for that reason.

Catherine also wrote a lengthy letter full of exhortations to martyrdom addressed:

> A misser Nicolo priore dela prouincia di thoscano, essendo ito a Vinegia per dare ordine al passagio sopra gli infideli, il quale doueano comminciare (95).

This letter must have been written to the Hospitaller Prior of Pisa who went to Venice, apparently in April 1377, in order to secure galleys for the *passagium*; on 19 April the Venetians refused his request.

> Quod Respondeatur Isti priori pisarum, cum Illis verbis que videbuntur, quod semper fuimus et essemus dispositi, deo teste, liberaliter complacere, Sancte Matri ecclesie et ordini suo, sancti Johannis Jerosolimitani, in omnibus nobis possibilibus, sed ad presens propter multas galeas. et Nauigia, que habemus extra, in diuersis partibus, non possumus sibi complacere, super requisitis per eum, quare placeat eidem, Nos exinde habere rationabiliter excusatos. de parte – 61 (96).

Niccolò seems to have taken notice of Catherine's exhortations, for he was at Vonitza on 24 April 1378 when he appeared as *nicolaccius de ystorchiis de floren' pisarum prior* (97). This crusader was presumably Fr. Niccolò de Strozzi who had been Commander of Padua in November 1373 when he was at the Hospitaller assembly in Avignon (98). On 11 March 1374 the pope was sending

(95) Letter XLVI of the 1500 edition; the rubric is that of the mss., according to Fawtier, ii. 179.

(96) Venice, Archivio di Stato, Misti del Senato, xxxvi, f. 5v. Immediately following is a slightly different version of this same reply which postponed a final decision and which received 21 votes with three abstentions. On the background, see LUTTRELL, see note 11, (1978) V 207-208 *et passim*.

(97) Malta, cod. 48, f. 168v-169 (contemporary copy).

(98) Malta, cod. 347, f. 51-51v. F. BURLAMACCHI, *Epistole della serafica vergine S. Caterina de Siena*, ii (Milan, 1843), 13, identified him with the Hospitaller who seized Alberese and Talamone from Siena in 1376 and April 1377, but that seems almost impossible. On that unnamed *friere di San Giovanni*, see *Chronache Senesi*, ed. A. LISINI and F. IACOMETTI, in *Rerum Italicarum Scriptores*, ns. xv part vi (Bologna, 1932-1937), 661-662, 667. P. LITTA, *Famiglie Celebri Italiane*, vi (Milan, 1819), Strozzi di Firenze VI, gives Niccolò as the son of Paolo Strozzi, who was at Rhodes in 1365, who was Commander of Ferrara and Prior of Pisa, and who fought in the East. The source of this information is as yet unknown. There is no evidence that Niccolò's connections involved financial dealings between the Hospital and the Strozzi bankers.

him to the Master at Rhodes (99). The Prior of Pisa may well have died in Epirus during 1378, for he is not heard of again. On 1 May 1380 Fr. Bartolomeo Castellani was acting for the Master as his lieutenant in the Priory of Pisa (100), and by February 1382 there was a new Prior of Pisa (101). Fr. Niccolò had faithfully followed the injunctions of Catherine's letter, which must be dated around April 1377 (102).

University of Malta
Msida-Malta

(99) Reg. Aven. 193, f. 280v. On 4 March Gregory requested the Master to provide Strozzi to an office or post in the Hospital: Reg. Vat. 270, f. 18v.

(100) *Le carte strozziane del R. Archivio di Stato in Firenze: Inventario*, I ser., ii (Florence, 1891), 823.

(101) Malta, cod. 321, f. 191-191v.

(102) FAWTIER, ii. 179, proposed "début de 1377".

XVI

THE CRUSADE IN THE FOURTEENTH CENTURY[1]

The crusade was essentially a Latin movement, and the crusaders' ideal of a holy war remained foreign to other Christians. During the crusading period the Latins, responding to social, economic and demographic forces within the West, invaded the eastern Mediterranean and established colonial bridgeheads in Syria, Greece and elsewhere. This heroic phase of a perennial conflict of East and West which had its roots deep in antiquity was no straightforward confrontation of Christendom and Islam, since the Latins, while reacting in a crude militaristic way against Muslim expansion around the Mediterranean, also attacked Orthodox Greek and other Christians. Oriental Christians, such as the Nestorians and Maronites, were tolerated by their Muslim rulers for, despite Islam's origin as a militant religion, its holy war or *jihad* demanded the enlargement of its domain rather than the forcible conversion of all unbelievers. The Muslims, ignorant of and uninterested in the Latins, saw little difference between the crusaders and their

[1] The standard work is A. Atiya, *The Crusade in the Later Middle Ages* (London, 1938) [cited as Atiya]; but see the extensive criticisms of F. Pall in *Revue historique du Sud-est européen*, xix (1942), 527–83. The pioneer works, J. Delaville le Roulx, *La France en Orient au XIV*^e *siècle*, 2 vols. (Paris, 1886) and N. Iorga, *Philippe de Mézières (1327–1405) et la croisade au XIV*^e *siècle* (Paris, 1896), remain important. S. Runciman, *A History of the Crusades*, iii (Cambridge, 1954), 427–64, covers the period as an 'epilogue'. *A History of the Crusades*, ed. K. Setton, i–ii (Philadelphia, 1955–62), is especially valuable on the Oriental background, necessarily neglected here; vol. iii should eventually constitute the standard work and bibliography for the fourteenth century. Meanwhile, H. Mayer, *Bibliographie zur Geschichte der Kreuzzüge* (Hanover, 1960) and the many recent works cited below provide further references. *The Cambridge Medieval History, iv: The Byzantine Empire,* 2nd. ed. (Cambridge, announced for 1965), appeared too late to be of use here.

other enemies, whether Christian or not.[1] Far more dangerous to Islam were the Mongols, whose defeat by the Egyptian Mamluks in 1260 was a decisive event which perhaps saved both the Muslim and Christian West from the Asiatic barbarians. Subsequently the Mongols were converted to Islam and in 1291 the Mamluks finally completed the reconquest of Syria, where the Latins had long been clinging defensively to a coastal strip originally secured during a period of Muslim disunity. Thereafter Christendom was expanding only in north-east Europe and, marginally, in Spain. In certain ways Latin Europe was entering a period of economic and spiritual stagnation. The crusade was no longer a movement of populations or of colonial conquests but a largely defensive struggle against Islam.

In the fourteenth century the Latins were beginning to identify Christendom with Europe and to distinguish Christians outside Europe as belonging to *la crestienté d'outremer.*[2] Some people, particularly readers of William of Tyre's popular crusading history which opened with Heraclius' seventh-century wars in the holy land, perhaps thought in terms of an East-West duel. Generally, however, the crusade was viewed not as a continuous struggle between civilizations or continents but as a particular event or expedition with a religious character, a *sanctum passagium*, a *negotium crucis* or an *armata christiana.* The crusader was *cruce signatus*, a *peregrinus* who fought as an *athleta Christi* and a *fidelis pugil ecclesie*; men spoke of the *recuperatio terre sancte* and Guillaume Adam wrote a *De modo sarracenos extirpandi.*

The crusading ideal reflected basic impulses to wage holy war against the infidel and to defend or conquer territory; it involved especially the recovery of the holy places in Syria. The mechanism of the crusade survived, and its symbol, the cross, retained a potential vitality. The age of children's and shepherds' crusades, disorganized collective migrations, anti-Jewish riots and other irrational symptoms of social unrest associated with crusading fanaticism was not altogether past. As late as

[1] C. Cahen, 'L'Islam et la Croisade', *Relazioni del X Congresso internazionale di scienze storiche* [cited as *Relazioni*], iii (Florence, 1955); F. Gabrieli, 'The Arabic Historiography of the Crusades', in *Historians of the Middle East*, ed. B. Lewis-P. Holt (London, 1962).

[2] D. Hay, *Europe: the Emergence of an Idea* (Edinburgh, 1957), 50–1, 56–68, 73–6, gives examples.

1344 the Latins' capture of Smyrna aroused considerable popular ferment, with reports of visions and miracles and with enthusiastic bands setting out from Italy for Jerusalem.[1] But the fall in 1291 of Acre, the last major Latin outpost in Syria, seemed a divine judgment upon the Latins. After decades of failure that mystical exultation which infused the earliest crusades with the character of a spontaneous mass movement had largely evaporated, and crusading preachers and tax-collectors met increasingly widespread disinterest and hostility. The emergence of more sophisticated forms of urban society in the West had reduced many of the pressures which had originally stimulated Latin aggression and the development of the crusading mystique. Living standards had improved and men had less reason to leave their lands, businesses and womenfolk to embark on increasingly hopeless ventures; in particular, they feared the sea.[2]

The growth of the pilgrimage habit which took people peacefully to Rome, Santiago, Canterbury and other centres, as well as to the holy places, diluted popular warlike zeal; so did pacifist notions that the conversion of infidels was preferable to their destruction. The importance of studying languages like Greek, Arabic, Hebrew and Mongolian was realized during the thirteenth century. The friars made converts in many parts of India, China, central Asia, eastern Europe, Spain and North Africa, but the results were largely disappointing and the missionary movement gradually lost strength. The last Latin archbishop of Pekin was murdered somewhere in China in 1362, and after the Ming dynasty replaced the Mongol khanate in 1368 foreign cults there were suppressed. The Dominican William of Tripoli in his *De statu sarracenorum* strongly disapproved of the use of force and genuinely tried to understand Muslim viewpoints. The great Mallorcan philosopher Ramón Llull, who himself preached and disputed in Tunisia, encouraged the use of the sword—even against the Christian Greeks—for the recovery of Jerusalem, but he also advocated missionary work to convert infidels 'through the way of love'. Though it was accepted that Christianity and Islam had much

[1] P. Alphandéry-A. Dupront, *La Chrétienté et l'Idée de Croisade*, ii (Paris, 1959), 258–70, *et passim*.

[2] P. Throop, *Criticism of the Crusade: a Study of Public Opinion and Crusade Propaganda* (Amsterdam, 1940); S. Runciman, 'The Decline of the Crusading Idea', *Relazioni*, iii (1955).

in common, most missionaries failed to understand Islam and made little attempt to advance arguments likely to impress anyone not already converted; many were concerned chiefly to achieve martyrdom. Thus Llull's treatise on the Trinity was being debated, peaceably but without effect, at Fez in 1344; in the following year a Franciscan provoked his own death by crying out against Islam—in French—during the sultan's Friday prayer in a Cairo mosque. The study and translation of Muslim writings commonly led to the dissemination of crude and nasty-minded anti-Muslim propaganda concentrated on such themes as Mohammed's alleged sexual immoralities and perversions, rather than to a better understanding of the foe. In reality much of this Latin writing was aimed at preventing the Christian minorities under Muslim rule from passing to Islam, while the conversion of schismatic Greek and Armenian Christians was commonly regarded as more important than their defence against the infidels.[1]

The crusading theorists, anxious to exclude a rabble of undisciplined peasantry, made their appeal to the princes who could provide the efficient fighting forces essential to military success. The holy war was part of the chivalric ideal, and it was the feudal class in society which preserved the spirit of aggression and continued to form the backbone of the great crusading expeditions. Knights like Chaucer's pilgrim or magnates such as Henry Bolingbroke still regarded the crusade, whether in Prussia, Spain or the Levant, as a normal opportunity for travel and adventure.[2] Such crusading could cover a variety of activities. For example, when Henry of Grosmont, earl of Derby, and Richard, earl of Arundel, appeared as crusaders at the siege of Algeçiras in 1344 their real purpose was to conduct diplomatic negotiations; and they were accompanied by Derby's sister with whom Arundel was having an affair.[3] Crusading enthusiasm was kept alive through the foundation of chivalric orders, as also by treatises on knighthood, chronicles

[1] In addition to Throop, see N. Daniel, *Islam and the West: the Making of an Image* (Edinburgh, 1960); R. Southern, *Western Views of Islam in the Middle Ages* (Cambridge, Mass., 1962); R. Sugranyes de Franch, 'Els projectes de creuada en la doctrina missional de Ramon Llull', *Estudios lulianos*, iv (1960).

[2] M. Bowden, *A Commentary on the General Prologue to the Canterbury Tales* (New York, 1957), 44–73; lists of crusaders in Atiya, 517–28.

[3] *The Complete Peerage*, i (London, 1910), 243; material kindly made available in K. Fowler, *Henry of Grosmont, First Duke of Lancaster, 1310–1361* (unpublished Ph.D. thesis: University of Leeds, 1961), 153–63, 588–9.

and historical romances of the kind Peter IV of Aragon recommended knights to read at table or when unable to sleep.[1] There was even a propaganda piece at a royal banquet at Paris in 1378 in which the towers of Jerusalem were defended by turbaned Saracens reciting prayers in Arabic and attacked by crusaders in moving boats who fell off scaling-ladders to provide comic relief; apparently the same properties were later used for the Fall of Troy.[2]

The essential manpower, money and enthusiasm came above all, as they always had, from the Frankish heartlands. Levantine rulers, Greek, Armenian and Latin, journeyed to Dijon, Paris and London seeking assistance; the great crusading enthusiasts, like the Gascon Pierre Thomas and his biographer the Picard Philippe de Mézières, were French-speaking, as were many of the Hospitallers who held Rhodes. In northern and western Europe, where exaggerated chivalric sentiments of courage and honour were manifested in duels and tournaments, the holy war was something more than a pious dream and could arouse genuine fervour among men who had no personal stake in the crusade. Like that of the universal church, the crusading ideal was changing and waning, yet it was still a deeply ingrained habit of thought which had real meaning in many spheres of life.[3]

Though the church by itself could achieve little, the direction of the crusading forces traditionally lay with the papacy, especially as the German emperors played little or no part. The popes conceded the indulgences and spiritual rewards, authorized the collection or appropriation of ecclesiastical revenues, appointed the leader and performed other acts canonically and juridically necessary to qualify a war as a crusade.[4] These powers allowed the pope to try to control the direction of the crusade. In 1309, for example, Clement V withheld money and crusading indulgences from a campaign in Granada because he was organizing an expedition to the Levant.[5] The fiscal and administrative machinery, the prestige

[1] *Tractats de Cavalleria*, ed. P. Bohigas (Barcelona, 1947), 142, *et passim*.
[2] L. Loomis, 'Secular Dramatics in the Royal Palace, Paris, 1378 . . .', *Speculum*, xxxiii (1958).
[3] J. Huizinga, *The Waning of the Middle Ages* (London, 1924), 74–94.
[4] M. Villey, 'L'idée de la Croisade chez les juristes du moyen-âge', *Relazioni*, iii (1955).
[5] V. Salavert, *Cerdeña y la Expansión mediterránea de la Corona de Aragón*, ii (Madrid, 1956), docs. 323, 332, 340, 345.

and leadership of the papacy were bound up with the holy war, but the persistent preaching of crusades against schismatics, heretics and other Christian enemies of the church, or merely to raise taxation, produced an increasingly bitter literature of criticism, much of it in the vernacular. 'His every enemy was Christian', wrote Dante condemning Boniface VIII, while a fiasco such as Bishop Dispenser's political crusade of 1383 appalled John Wyclif and many others. Following its attempt to control Italy by imposing Angevin rule at Naples, the papacy fell under French influence and from 1309 was established at Avignon. French policy was often determined by men devoid of chivalric ideals such as the chauvinistic lawyers Pierre Dubois and Guillaume de Nogaret, who conceived of the crusade as a political expression of the lay state and hoped to use it as a cover for French dynastic ambitions against the Greeks in *Romania* and as an excuse for royal taxation of the clergy. The French popes did attempt to prevent the many and various wars which attracted and absorbed the chivalric impulses, the desire for plunder and the economic resources essential for an effective crusade, but they expended much of their own wealth and energies on the struggle for control in Italy. The slow emergence of lay states and their mutual rivalries in the West militated against success, as did economic and demographic decline, recurrent plague and social conflict. In the end the crusade seemed possible only in the intervals of the Anglo-French war.

The fall of Acre in 1291 closed a stage but was scarcely a turning point. The holy war preserved the pattern, set long before, of a slow monotonous struggle interrupted by major expeditions, truces and defeats. During the thirteenth century the crusade acquired the character of a steady defensive retreat in which a dwindling band of Latin *colons* and their half-caste mercenaries, aided by the knights of the military orders from the West, sought to hold the great stone strongholds of the desert with thoroughly inadequate resources. As the Frankish nobility of *outremer* retired to Cyprus the wealth of Syria gradually passed to the Italian merchants, whose willingness to bargain with rather than fight against the infidel became an established characteristic of crusading affairs. The Latins relied on their control of the sea for essential reinforcements, but the occasional expeditions which princes or great nobles brought from Europe were often of a pilgrim rather than a crusading nature; they secured only temporary relief for the enfeebled Frankish kingdom. After 1291 the Latins withdrew to Cyprus, placing the sea between themselves and the Mamluks, and only occasionally employed their naval superiority in crusading assaults on Egypt and Syria; the Armenian Christians resisted doggedly in the mountains of Cilicia.

One chance of recovering Syria lay in the Mongols. The appearance of these nomadic hordes early in the thirteenth century enormously enlarged the known world and placed the crusade in a new and larger context, for the Mongol empire stretched from China to the Mediterranean and the Ukraine. Despite the Mongols' gradual conversion to Islam, Latin merchants and missionaries travelled along the caravan routes of central Asia and China throughout the fourteenth century, and both Christians and Mongols proposed grandiose alliances against the Mamluks. In 1307, for example, Mongol envoys at the papal curia offered over 100,000 horse for a joint campaign. The Mongols, however, were unreliable and destructive. They disrupted the course of eastern European history and it was probably fortunate for Christendom that they impinged on the Mediterranean world only for brief periods.[1]

The contemporary Tunisian politician Ibn Khaldun condemned the Bedouins of the desert as landlubbers, while in Egypt the Mamluks, cavalrymen who despised navies, lacked the naval spirit and strength to make much impact at sea. Real changes in the balance of Mediterranean power during the fourteenth century came with the emergence of a new barbarian force, the Turks, who steadily advanced overland against weakening Byzantine resistance and harassed the Latins in the Aegean. The Latins diverted crusading resources to defend the Balkans but their interventions were chiefly maritime in nature; not until 1396 did they assemble a substantial land force to oppose the Ottomans, who crushed it at Nicopolis on the Danube. Elsewhere the Muslims, having lost their predominance at sea centuries earlier, lay behind a frontier running along the Mediterranean roughly from Gibraltar to the Bosphorus.

[1] G. Soranzo, *Il papato, l'Europa cristiana e i tartari* (Milan, 1930), 352, *et passim*; cf. L. Olschki, *Marco Polo's Asia* (Cambridge, 1960).

THE CRUSADE IN THE FOURTEENTH CENTURY

Though the Moors and the Turks had considerable fleets, the Latins mainly controlled the sea, its islands and its trade. They could launch surprise amphibious attacks on the Muslim coasts but faced the problems of finance and shipping involved in raising and concentrating men and supplies at the end of long lines of communication. Whether directed against the Moors of Spain and the Mahgrib, towards the recovery of the holy places in Syria or to the defence of *Romania*, the crusade was staged primarily within a Mediterranean arena, even if the vital aggressive impulses behind it often stemmed from beyond its peripheries, from the continental hinterlands of the Franks and Turks. The Latins had little choice but to attack across the Mediterranean; yet their assaults on its southern coastline failed and even in the Aegean, where they had colonial and commercial positions to sustain, they had only very limited success. Fundamentally this was the result of growing contradictions between the enthusiasms and aims of the northern crusaders and the interests of the maritime powers on which they depended for transportation and supplies. Because the Mediterranean Latins were reluctant to launch attacks on their Muslim neighbours for ideological reasons alone, and were apt to obstruct the crusade or to abuse it as a cloak for their own commercial or dynastic ambitions, the crusaders could never fully exploit Latin naval superiority. In the resulting stalemate significant gains were only made overland, by the Christians in Spain, by the Muslims in Armenia, Anatolia and the Balkans.

The Mediterranean world, though vast in terms of the weeks needed to traverse it, possessed certain unities. By the fourteenth century the development of the compass and other aids to navigation had made even winter sea-voyages much easier. The Mediterranean joined rather than divided the peoples of its islands and ports, its coastal plains and mountain slopes, who shared the heritage of Rome and whose culture was urban rather than nomadic. The encyclopaedic scholar-statesman Ibn Khaldun, with his subtle geohistorical and sociological insights, understood much of this. He knew regions like Egypt and Spain where there were important religious minorities, and he realized that economic, social and other common factors tended to outweigh religious divergences. Following the great commercial revolution of previous centuries the Mediterranean constituted an economic unit. Its trade was controlled by the

Latins who carried cloth, timber and metals to Muslim ports such as Tunis, Alexandria or Caffa in the Crimea, and returned with precious Oriental stuffs and spices. Grain was shipped enormous distances and an extensive interior commerce in such commodities as wines, fish and honey continued to flourish despite economic fluctuations and major crises like the Black Death. The great merchant powers, Genoa and Venice, the smaller maritime republics like Pisa and Dubrovnik, and such powerful trading towns as Naples, Barcelona and Palermo, customarily opposed breaking the truces with the Muslims from which they profited so highly, though, when their shipping was attacked or their lucrative Black Sea trade endangered, Genoa and Venice prepared reluctantly to fight.[1]

Since most of the Asian and all the African caravan routes towards Europe terminated in Muslim ports, schemes for economic warfare, involving a police-force of galleys, trade with Asia through Christian Cilicia, and the production of commodities such as cotton in Christian lands, were generally accepted as desirable. In practice, however, papal prohibitions against trading with the infidels in iron, wood and other raw materials they badly needed, and in slaves—Tartars, Bulgars, Turks and Greeks who often became Mamluk soldiers—proved largely ineffective and were gradually relaxed. When the Hospitallers attempted to interfere with the Genoese slavers in 1311 the Genoese, who specialized in the Egyptian slave trade, actually bribed the Turks to attack Rhodes.[2] A blockade which could only be enforced by those who stood to lose by it had little chance of success.

The crusaders realized that the key to their fundamental objective in Syria lay in Egypt, which they twice invaded, unsuccessfully, during the thirteenth century. The Mamluks constituted an alien ruling class, a military oligarchy of slave origins which controlled an efficient army and an excellent bureaucracy and could tax the wealth of the corn-producing

[1] Ibn Khaldûn, *The Muqaddimah: an Introduction to History*, trans. F. Rosenthal, 3 vols. (London, 1958). Cf. F. Braudel, *La Méditerranée et le monde méditerranéen à l'époque de Philippe II* (Paris, 1949); M. Mollat *et al.*, 'L'économie européenne aux deux derniers siècles du moyen-âge', *Relazioni*, iii (1955); J. Heers, *L'Occident aux XIVe et XVe siècles: aspects économiques et sociaux* (Paris, 1963).

[2] J. Delaville le Roulx, *Les Hospitaliers à Rhodes jusqu'à la mort de Philibert de Naillac, 1310–1421* (Paris, 1913), 10–11.

Nile valley and the luxury trade from India through the Red Sea to the Mediterranean. After inflicting their first great defeat on the Mongols in 1260, the Mamluks made their state the focus of orthodox Muslim religion and culture, for the Mongols had destroyed the religious pre-eminence of Baghdad. The aggressive Sultan Baybars and his successors attacked both the Il-khanid Mongols whose power was centred in Persia, and their Latin and Armenian allies. The Mamluks sought support from Byzantium, the Seljuks of Rum in Anatolia, the Mongols of the Golden Horde on the Volga, and certain Latin rulers such as Manfred of Sicily. They extended their power to the Sudan, expelled the Latins from Syria and ravaged Armenian Cilicia, but an attack on Cyprus in 1271 failed. The Latins' chances of success were slight, and the twenty-five galleys sent from Cyprus to assault Alexandria in 1292 only provoked the Sultan Al-Ashraf Khalil—shouting 'Cyprus, Cyprus, Cyprus'—to order a hundred galleys to be built for a counter-attack. Renewed Mongol attacks in Syria in the following decades impeded those plans but the Latins neglected various opportunities of co-operating with the Mongols, who were reported to be willing to grant them Jerusalem.[1] The Latins still dreamed of reconquering Syria themselves. They had faced the strategic problems involved long before 1291. Considerations as to numbers of men and ships, advice about the climate and the local inhabitants, the arguments for a blockade of Egypt, and the idea of uniting the military orders were all advanced in manuals which were originally commissioned at the Council of Lyons in 1274 from such experts in Eastern affairs as the Dominican William of Tripoli and the Franciscan Fidenzio of Padua. After 1291 the masters of the military orders, the king of Naples, an Armenian prince, the Venetian Marino Sanudo, and others drew up reports.[2] These were essentially variations on the earlier proposals and they provided information to a wide public; the papal library alone contained over twenty manuals of this sort in about 1375.[3]

Despite this theorizing, it fell chiefly to the feeble Latin

[1] G. Hill, *A History of Cyprus*, ii (Cambridge, 1948), 167, 204–5, *et passim*.

[2] In addition to Throop and Atiya, see J. Verbruggen, *De Krijgskunst in West-Europa in de Middeleeuwen: IXe tot begin XIVe eeuw* (Brussels, 1954), 465–88 (French summary: 575–7).

[3] G. Golubovich, *Biblioteca bio-bibliografica della Terra Santa e dell'Oriente francescano*, i (Quaracchi, 1906), 410–12.

powers in the East to assist the Armenians in Cilicia, where the Mamluks steadily advanced overland in a protracted war of ambushes, sieges and truces. In Cyprus the Lusignan kings and their nobility retained both their titular claims in the kingdom of Jerusalem and the old weaknesses of the Latins of *outremer*; closely inter-married, given over to feuds and frivolous luxuries, they had become partly Oriental and preferred trade and intrigue to warfare which might bring complete disaster.[1]

In 1291 the military orders retreated to Cyprus with their numbers sadly reduced and their prestige low. In 1309 the Teutonic Knights, who had contracted out of the Mediterranean struggle, established their headquarters at Marienburg, utilizing in crusades against the pagan Lithuanians and in their colonization of Prussia the experience and techniques acquired in Syria.[2] The Templars, after the protracted *affaire* in which the gravest and not altogether unjustified suspicions were cast on their morality and crusading enthusiasm, were suppressed in 1312 and their lands transferred to the more active Hospitallers. Between 1300 and 1304 Guillaume de Villaret, master of the Hospital, twice took aid to the Armenians.[3] But neither Cilicia nor Cyprus offered a satisfactory base and from 1306 to 1310 the Hospitallers were conquering Rhodes from the Greeks, assisted in 1309 by a meagre force assembled by Pope Clement V for a crusade. The Hospitallers fortified Rhodes and organized themselves there as an independent state, while they incorporated the Templars' possessions into the European estates from which they drew their incomes. Clement V tried to involve them in a 'crusade' against the Catalans at Athens. The Hospitallers sought instead to implicate Catalan and Aragonese strength in the Levant by fostering Jaume II of Aragon's marriage to Marie de Lusignan in 1315; the Cypriot princess, however, died childless and the project foundered.[4] Catalunya-Aragon lacked the resources to sustain effective military action in the East, but the Aragonese crown advanced Catalan commercial interests in Syria, Egypt and Tunis by diplomatic means, and sought prestige through special agreements negotiated in Cairo for the release of Christian prisoners,

[1] Cf. S. Runciman, *The Families of Outremer* (London, 1960).
[2] F. Carsten, *The Origins of Prussia* (Oxford, 1954), 5–9, 52–72, *et passim.*
[3] H. Finke, *Acta Aragonensia*, iii (Berlin, 1922), 146.
[4] A. Luttrell, 'The Aragonese Crown and the Knights Hospitallers of Rhodes: 1291–1350', *English Historical Review*, lxxvi (1961).

for pilgrims to visit Syria and for Aragonese protection of the holy places.[1]

The dispute among the experts as to whether an overland advance from Cilicia into Syria was preferable to an amphibious assault on Egypt was largely academic, for the essential Western aid, the money, fleets and armies, the unity of purpose, the gifted leadership and careful preparations called for by the theorists were not forthcoming. Edward I's French and Scottish wars, for example, resulted in shipping vital to the crusade being transferred from the Mediterranean to the Channel. In crusading affairs the papacy was traditionally tied to France, and the French crown tried to exploit both the vulnerable situation of the Avignonese popes and the genuine crusading enthusiasm of a small group of French nobles so as to secure the maximum financial advantage for the minimum of crusading activity. Clement V granted huge sums, but the next pope, John XXII, who himself subordinated the holy war to his German and Italian quarrels and ambitions, proved reluctant to concede further tenths. A small Franco-papal fleet was made ready to blockade Egypt, only to be handed over to the king of Naples and destroyed by the Genoese in 1320. In general the pope and cardinals opposed expenditures on small and insufficiently prepared campaigns which, even if initially successful, could never achieve lasting results in Egypt or Syria. They favoured sending military and financial aid to Cilicia, where the Mamluks captured Laiazzo in 1322, but in 1323 the Armenians themselves advised against a minor expedition which would only provoke renewed Mamluk attacks.[2]

In 1331 Philip VI of France promised a crusade for 1334 and John XXII finally granted the tenths. Philip took the cross in 1333 as a diplomatic expedient and four French galleys did join the Christian fleet which defeated the Turks on the Aegean in 1334, but the crusade proper was postponed. By September 1335 John XXII's successor Benedict XII and his cardinals realized that the king's objectives were primarily financial, and when they probed his delegates as to Philip's real intentions the marshal of France lost his temper and replied with *verba*

[1] F. Giunta, *Aragonesi e Catalani nel Mediterraneo*, ii (Palermo, 1959), 7–18, *et passim*; P. Vilar, *La Catalogne dans l'Espagne moderne*, i (Paris, 1962), 366–499, *et passim*.

[2] G. Tabacco, *La casa di Francia nell'azione politica di Papa Giovanni XXII* (Rome, 1953), *passim*.

inordinata et indecencia. Meanwhile Armenian appeals for help in 1335 met no effective response and in January 1336, when the preaching of the crusade in Cyprus was reported to be dangerously provocative, Benedict ordered its suspension until an expedition was ready in the West. Philip had prepared men and ships in Languedoc but they were destined for the English war, and in March 1336 Benedict postponed the crusade indefinitely on the grounds that Anglo-French and other hostilities were imminent and that he feared the consequences of an unsuccessful crusade. Soon after, Philip moved his fleet to the Channel and, though Benedict refused to grant tenths to finance the Anglo-French war, Philip spent on it the crusading monies already raised and tried to get more.[1] Benedict's moves were largely forced upon him, but papal insistence on unity and peace as an essential prerequisite to a crusade tended to become an excuse for permanent, and apparently miserly, inactivity. When Benedict refused in 1336 to help finance an expedition which the Venetians and Hospitallers proposed to organize, crusading activity ceased almost totally.[2] Furthermore, he allowed the Hospitallers' incomes, which should have been devoted to crusading purposes, to be used instead to build up an enormous credit with the pope's own hard-pressed Florentine bankers.[3] Benedict's treasure was expended by his successor Clement VI, who demonstrated what papal enthusiasm could accomplish when the campaign he initiated captured Smyrna from the Turks in 1344.

The Armenian Christians suffered from Mongol and Turkish as well as Mamluk attacks. They were hampered by their strife with the rulers of Cyprus and by endless doctrinal disputes with the Roman church. The Hospitallers and others provided some assistance, and John XXII sent money through the Bardi, his Florentine bankers. Yet, of 30,000 florins he promised in 1324, less than 17,000 florins reached Cyprus; some 2,600 of these

[1] G. Daumet, 'Benoît XII et la croisade', in his *Benoît XII (1334–1342): lettres closes, patentes et curiales se rapportant à la France*, introduction (Paris, 1920), xliv–lix; Hill, ii, 299, n. 1. There is much disagreement about these problems; J. Viard, 'Les projets de croisade de Philippe VI de Valois', *Bibliothèque de l'Ecole des Chartres*, xcvii (1936), seems unsatisfactory, cf. E. Lunt, *Financial Relations of the Papacy with England: 1337–1534* (Cambridge, Mass., 1962), 88–94, 525–31.

[2] A. Luttrell, 'Venice and the Knights Hospitallers of Rhodes in the Fourteenth Century', *Papers of the British School at Rome*, xxvi (1958), 203.

[3] A. Luttrell, 'Interessi fiorentini nell'economia e nella politica dei Cavalieri Ospedalieri di Rodi nel Trecento', *Annali della Scuola Normale Superiore di Pisa: lettere, storia e filosofia*, ser. II, xxviii (1959), 317–20.

were expended on arms, provisions and ship-building in Cyprus, and the Armenians actually received less than 11,000 florins.[1] In 1335 the pilgrim Jacopo da Verona, reporting atrocity stories heard from Armenian refugees he met in Cyprus, denounced the rich Cypriots who prospered from their trade in Cilicia and Syria, careless of the fate of the Armenian Christians and the holy places.[2] Soon after, Clement VI, faced with the Anglo-French war, abandoned the papacy's traditional reliance on the French as the major instrument of the crusade. Instead he utilized Italian strength, and Italian interests diverted crusading activity away from Cilicia towards Smyrna and the Aegean. Hospitaller and Cypriot forces brought temporary relief to the Armenians in 1347, but after 1351 they received little help until Pierre I de Lusignan, king of Cyprus, garrisoned the Cilician port of Gorighos in 1359 and captured Adalia from the Turkish emir of Tekke in 1361.

The crusade against the Mamluks had deteriorated into sporadic piracy when Pierre I, convinced of his divine mission to recover his ancestors' kingdom of Jerusalem, organized the only major crusading expedition of the period generated by a Levantine power and dominated by a leader of real prestige. Between 1362 and 1365 Pierre, accompanied by his chancellor Philippe de Mézières and the papal legate Pierre Thomas, made an extensive tour of Europe where their essentially Frankish, chivalric fanaticism succeeded in raising money, ships and men and in turning the Latins' resources away from the defence of the Aegean back towards an old-style crusade. In September 1365 some 165 ships assembled at Rhodes, and the Turkish emirs from the nearby coasts hastened to offer tribute. The objective, a well-kept secret, was the immensely wealthy port of Alexandria which, as expected, was inadequately defended. A landing was effected after some hard fighting and, though some of the barons were reluctant to assault the city, a few crusaders got into the town through a water conduit; others soon scaled the walls, the gates were opened, and there was little further resistance. Colossal pillage and massacre followed. The king, the legate and the chancellor wanted to hold Alexandria, probably hoping to blockade Egypt and thus

[1] Hill, ii, 275–8, *et passim*; J. Richard, *Chypre sous les Lusignans: Documents chypriotes des Archives du Vatican (XIVe et XVe siècles)* (Paris, 1962), 36–49.
[2] *Liber peregrinationis di Jacopo da Verona*, ed. U. Monneret de Villard (Rome, 1950), 17–18.

drastically reduce the sultan's revenues. But the crusaders were dangerously short of men and horses. The majority, including the king's two brothers and the admiral of the Hospital, were half-hearted and anxious to secure their enormous plunder and, as the Egyptian army approached, they forced Pierre to sail away. Hopes of further success were deliberately ruined during 1366 by the Venetians who deterred prospective reinforcements, which included Amedeo of Savoy and Bertrand du Guesclin, by falsely announcing the conclusion of peace; they also negotiated with the Mamluks in order to safeguard their own Egyptian commerce. The crusade lost all impetus. In 1367 Pierre I sacked Tripoli and other places in Syria, but after his assassination in 1369 peace with the Mamluks was concluded in 1370.[1]

In Cilicia the situation remained desperate. Pierre I's death left the Christians without effective leadership; in 1373 the Genoese secured control of Famagusta in Cyprus; and in 1375 the Armenian kingdom collapsed and King Leo VI was incarcerated in Cairo. In Egypt the Mamluks took revenge upon their Christian subjects, taxing them heavily to pay for the crusaders' unrestrained vandalism. The Copts, who were often rich merchants or bureaucrats and had long been accused of aiding the Latins and committing outrages such as destroying mosques with naptha, suffered particularly. The Christians' morale fell, and many went over to Islam.[2]

There was never another grand assault on Egypt or Syria. The truce suited the Mamluks who faced political problems, drought, plague and economic decline in Egypt.[3] They profited greatly from the organized groups of pilgrims who flocked guidebook in hand to Jerusalem and Cairo[4] and from taxation of the Latin merchants who flourished at Beirut and Alexandria. Latin piracy and the more carefully regulated *guerra di corsa*, an economic activity with its own rules,[5] were directed against Christians as well as Muslims, and for long provoked the Mamluks to little more than the frequent seizure of Christian

[1] Atiya, 301–78; Hill, ii, 299–416; J. Gay, *Le pape Clément VI et les affaires d'Orient, 1342–1352* (Paris, 1904), 20, 133–50; J. Smet, *The Life of Saint Peter Thomas by Philippe de Mézières* (Rome, 1954), 96–141.

[2] M. Perlmann, 'Notes on anti-Christian Propaganda in the Mamluk Empire', *Bulletin of the School of Oriental and African Studies*, x (1940–2).

[3] D. Ayalon, *Gunpowder and Firearms in the Mamluk Kingdom* (London, 1956), 103–6, *et passim*.

[4] H. Prescott, *Jerusalem Journey* (London, 1954).

[5] Mollat *et al.*, in *Relazioni*, iii (1955), 760–1.

merchants and their goods. In 1403 the Genoese under the French marshal Boucicault pillaged a number of ports on the Cilician and Syrian coasts, but their scheme to attack Alexandria was betrayed by the Venetians and foiled by adverse winds; the campaign ended in a major sea battle with the Venetians off Modon.[1] Emmanuele Piloti, a Cretan merchant long resident in Egypt, judged that Boucicault could have surprised and captured Alexandria. He also stated that the Mamluks were seriously short of wood for ship-building, and that the Hospitallers stopped their Rhodian subjects carrying Dalmatian and Cilician timber to Egypt;[2] yet in 1366, even before they had completed their conquests in Cilicia with its rich forests, the Egyptians were able to procure enough wood from Syria to build well over 100 ships.[3] By 1426 their fleet was strong enough to reduce Cyprus and its king to tributary status, and Mamluk progress was only halted by the successful defence of Rhodes in 1444.

At the western end of the Mediterranean the *reconquista*, both a colonizing movement and a holy war, traditionally absorbed Spanish crusading vigour and enthusiasm. Ramón Llull, Philippe de Mézières and others considered it part of the crusade: the Christians would advance by way of Granada and Africa to the holy places.[4] After the great conquests of the thirteenth century there was a pause in the *reconquista*. The Moors rallied in their mountain kingdom of Granada. The Christians fought each other and settled the extensive lands already won in Valencia and Andalucia, a process sometimes involving bitter strife with the conquered population, for anti-Muslim attitudes and prejudices could be hard to unlearn.[5] Catalan mercantile interests, especially those of Barcelona, were concentrated on the continuous struggle to control Mallorca, Sardinia and Sicily, and thus to secure the routes to their Levantine and African markets. The Aragonese crown engaged only intermittently in border warfare with the Moors on the Valencian frontier, representing it as a crusade in order to

[1] Delaville, *La France en Orient*, i, 436–46.

[2] *Traité d'Emmanuel Piloti sur le passage en Terre Sainte (1420)*, ed. P.-H. Dopp (Louvain-Paris, 1958), 156–7, 201, *et passim*.

[3] Atiya, 372, 375, n. 1.

[4] Ibid., pp. 80–1, 147.

[5] R. Burns, 'Social Riots on the Christian-Moslem Frontier (Thirteenth-Century Valencia)', *American Historical Review*, lxvi (1961).

persuade reluctant popes to grant ecclesiastical revenues. When Alfonso IV of Aragon genuinely tried to launch a crusade in Granada between 1328 and 1331, the jealous Castilians obstructed him. Castile, the dominant partner, profited from the combined operations in the campaign which ended in Castile acquiring Algeçiras in 1344. The Moorish fleet, mainly supplied by the African states, won a great battle against the Castilians in 1340, and only Genoese assistance later enabled the Castilian, Portuguese and Catalan galleys to cut off reinforcements for Algeçiras by blockading the Straits of Gibraltar.[1] Thereafter the crusading element was seldom dominant in Spanish affairs, and both Castilians and Aragonese allied with the Moors; in 1386 even the duke of Lancaster was accused of plotting to partition Castile with Mohammed V of Granada.[2]

In North Africa Catalan, Genoese and other trading interests dictated a largely peaceful approach, exemplified in a curious and lasting Sicilian-Tunisian feudal condominium over the island of Pantelleria. Piratical Christian attacks, such as the Genoese sacking of Tripoli in 1355, the combined Pisan, Genoese and Sicilian occupation of the island of Gerba in 1388, and the Valencian and Mallorcan expedition of 1399 to Bona, were matched by well-organized Muslim razzias on Malta, Sicily and places farther afield; a truce, an exchange of prisoners and the resumption of commerce normally followed fairly quickly on such incidents.[3] Though the Latins usually defeated them at sea, the Berbers had a considerable navy and in 1377, for example, the pope was alarmed by their attacks around Narbonne and by the presence of a dozen Berber galleys off Gaeta.[4] In 1390 the Genoese, anxious to crush these corsairs, enlisted the crusading enthusiasm of a body of French and some English knights under the duke of Bourbon and

[1] See F. Soldevila, *Història de Catalunya*, i (revised: Barcelona, 1962); J. Robson, 'The Catalan Fleet and Moorish Sea-power, 1337–1344', *English Historical Review*, lxxiv (1959).

[2] P. Russell, *English Intervention in Spain and Portugal in the time of Edward III and Richard II* (Oxford, 1955), 33, n. 1, 36, 444. On the crusade and *reconquista* in Spain see also J. Goñi Gaztambide, *Historia de la bula de la Cruzada en España* (Vitoria, 1958).

[3] R. Brunschvig, *La Berbérie orientale sous les Hafsides: des origines à la fin du XVe siècle*, 2 vols., (Paris, 1940–7) i, 110–225; F. Giunta, 'Sicilia e Tunisi nei secoli XIV e XV', in his *Medioevo mediterraneo: saggi storici* (Palermo, 1954), 151–66.

[4] *Lettres secrètes et curiales du Pape Grégoire XI (1370–1378)*, fasc. iii, ed. L. Mirot *et al.* (Paris, 1942), no. 2053; cf. Brunschvig, i, 195–7.

transported them to attack the Tunisian port of Mahdiya. But the crusaders were short of horses and when they proved unable to capture the town or to deal with the skirmishing and guerrilla tactics of the armies of Tunis and Bugia, the Genoese merely extorted from the Berbers a truce favourable to themselves and another old-style crusade had failed.[1] Yet Latin Christendom was ready to penetrate with vigour into areas beyond the shores of the familiar Mediterranean world. There were contacts with the Christians of Ethiopia and even suggestions that the Latins should maintain a fleet in the Red Sea or Persian Gulf to cut off Egyptian trade with India. Men knew that caravans crossed the African desert to Timbuctu to bring back gold and slaves from the Niger, and Mansa Musa's empire of Mali appeared on a Mallorcan *mappamundi* as early as 1339.[2] Genuine crusading sentiments, as well as gold and slaves, motivated Portuguese expansion along the African coastline which began with the capture of Ceuta in 1415 and ultimately led to a new Christian confrontation with Islam in the Indian Ocean.

The most important aspect of the fourteenth-century crusade was not the recovery of the holy places but the defence of *Romania*, the Greek empire dismembered by the crusaders in 1204 and restored in an enfeebled form in 1261. The Latin idea of an aggressive holy war was altogether alien to the Greeks,[3] but as Byzantine power declined they became seriously dependent on Latin support, especially from the Genoese. The Mongol invasions and the consequent breakup of the Seljuk empire of Rum produced an unsettled situation in Anatolia, where late in the thirteenth century a number of semi-nomadic Turkish emirates began to emerge. To some extent their success depended on enthusiasm for the holy war, and especially on the *ghazi* warriors. 'A *ghazi*', wrote the Turkish poet Ahmedi towards 1410, 'is the instrument of the religion of Allah, a servant of God who purifies the earth from the filth of polytheism; the *ghazi* is the sword of God, he is the protector and the refuge of the believers. If he becomes a martyr in the ways of God, do not believe that he has died; he lives in beatitude with Allah, he has eternal life.' The Muslims regarded the

[1] Atiya, 398–434.

[2] Ibid., 63, 65, 121, 277; R. Mauny, *Tableau géographique de l'Ouest africain au moyen âge* (Dakar, 1961).

[3] P. Lemerle, 'Byzance et la Croisade', *Relazioni*, iii (1955).

Christian Trinity as polytheistic. However, it was mainly for loot and pay that the Turks, and many Greeks as well, followed the opportunist Anatolian emirs who fought both for and against the Christians, often as mercenaries. The emirs, who needed lands and booty for their followers, finally dominated the whole of western Anatolia including Bithynia, the province facing Constantinople.[1]

Latins and Greeks distrusted one another profoundly. In 1282 Michael VIII Palaeologus and the Sicilian Vespers upset Charles of Anjou's schemes for conquest in Byzantium,[2] but in 1301 Charles de Valois, brother of Philip IV of France, married Catherine de Courtenay, heiress of the titular Latin emperors of Constantinople, and revived the traditional plans for a dynastic crusade in *Romania*, justified by Greek treachery and schism and as a necessary prelude to the recovery of Jerusalem. The Greeks of Asia Minor were so hard pressed by the Turks that in 1308 some were even prepared to submit to Charles de Valois but, even with papal and Venetian support, he could never gather the requisite force. The Angevin rulers of Naples and Taranto had claims and ambitions in Epirus and Albania. Effective power in the Morea was divided between the representatives of the Angevin princes of Taranto and Achaea, who normally resided in Italy, and the intensely chivalric feudal barons in their great castles. In 1311, however, the tough Catalan mercenaries, who in 1303 had fought the Turks in Anatolia with notable success but were later betrayed by their Greek employers, slaughtered large numbers of the Frankish nobility of Achaea at Cephissus near Thebes; they then set up an independent régime around Thebes and Athens and, while the Valois and others schemed to use them as crusaders, the popes complicated attempts to resist the Turks by excommunicating the Catalans and encouraging attacks upon them.[3]

Wars, Turkish raids and the slave trade progressively reduced the population and prosperity of Greece and the Aegean islands,

[1] These subjects are controversial: P. Wittek, *The Rise of the Ottoman Empire* (London, 1938); G. Georgiades Arnakis, *The Early Osmanlis . . . 1282–1337* (Athens, 1947) [in Greek with English summary]; G. Ostrogorsky, *History of the Byzantine State* (Oxford, 1956); P. Lemerle, *L'émirat d'Aydin, Byzance et l'Occident* (Paris, 1957).

[2] D. Geanakoplos, *Emperor Michael Palaeologus and the West, 1258–1282* (Cambridge, Mass., 1959).

[3] R. Burns, 'The Catalan Company and the European Powers, 1305–1311', *Speculum*, xxix (1954); K. Setton, *Catalan Domination of Athens, 1311–1388* (Cambridge, Mass., 1948).

yet their fertile lands and pleasant climate continued to attract astute traders and landless cadets. As in Syria and Cyprus a mercantile Mediterranean element replaced the Frankish aristocracy. Italians in particular came as Angevin officials, as ecclesiastical benefice-holders and as adventurers hoping to secure estates and rents through purchase, marriage, princely favour or conquest. The Morea, like the rest of *Romania*, was an under-developed area suitable for colonial exploitation; it exported grain, wines, honey and other primary products, and absorbed Western manufactures, chiefly cloth.[1] The Latin colonists were prepared to defend their domains but, hopelessly divided among themselves and often under attack from the Byzantine enclave around Mistra in the south-east Morea, they lacked the strength to combat the Turkish razzias effectively. The Venetians profited from their carefully regulated trade in the Morea and in their own colonial territories throughout *Romania*, but were always reluctant to assume expensive military and administrative responsibilities. They occupied only the strategic ports of call at Coron and Modon in the southern Morea and islands such as Crete and Negroponte (Euboea) which protected the shipping lanes to Trebizond and the Crimea, great markets both for the products and slaves of the Black Sea area and, especially after the fall of Acre in 1291, for luxury silks and spices from India, China and Persia. Venetian rivalry with Genoa for the control of these vital routes was intense. The Genoese had an autonomous colony at Pera on the Golden Horn opposite Constantinople, where they were uneasily allied to the emperor; they had fewer outposts to defend and exercised less control over their citizens' Levantine affairs. The Venetians' crusading policies were usually more clear cut. After 1302 they hoped to oust the Genoese by supporting Valois schemes for conquest at Constantinople; then, realizing that these projects were impracticable, they sought to safeguard their commerce through a rapprochement with Byzantium.[2]

[1] B. Krekić, *Dubrovnik (Raguse) et le Levant au moyen âge* (Paris, 1961), 158, *et passim*; P. Topping, 'Le régime agraire dans le Péloponnèse au XIV siècle', *L'hellénisme contemporain*, ser. II, x (1956).

[2] F. Thiriet, *La Romanie vénitienne au moyen âge: le développement et l'exploitation du domaine colonial vénitien (XIIe–XIVe siècles)* (Paris, 1959), 155–66, *et passim*; P. Argenti, *The Occupation of Chios by the Genoese and their Administration of the Island, 1346–1566*, 3 vols. (Cambridge, 1958); G. Pistarino, 'Nella *Romania* genovese tra i Grechi e i Turchi: l'isola di Chio', *Rivista storica italiana*, lxxiii (1961).

More dangerous to the Latins than the Turks advancing overland in Anatolia were the coastal emirates whose raiders took to the sea, recruiting renegade Greek sailors and plundering the Aegean for slaves and spoil. In 1304 they raided the island of Chios and thereafter the Greeks largely relied on the Genoese under Benedetto Zaccaria to defend Smyrna and Chios. After 1310 the Hospitallers, having conquered Rhodes from the Greeks, gained a series of naval victories against the Turks; the most notable was won with Genoese support off Chios in 1319. Turkish aggression was forced northwards away from the emirate of Mentesche on the coast opposite Rhodes, towards the area around Smyrna and the territories of the emirate of Aydin in central Ionia. In 1327 the Venetians, sensing a new threat, tried to bring Andronicus III Palaeologus, the Genoese Martino Zaccaria of Chios and the Hospitallers into a coalition to defend Smyrna. Instead Andronicus seized Chios and imprisoned Zaccaria in 1329, while the port at Smyrna fell to the great Turkish warrior Umur, who in 1334 became emir of Aydin. For some twenty years, sometimes in alliance with the Greeks or Catalans, more often at their expense, Umur conducted an amazing series of razzias in Thrace, Thessaly, Bulgaria and other parts, and became a major menace to Christian shipping in the Aegean, attacking Monemvasia, Naxos, Negroponte and other places. In 1332 the Venetians succeeded in forming a union against Umur in which they considered including the Turkish Karaman emir at Konya. An insurrection in Crete delayed operations during 1333; then in 1334 galleys sent by Venice, the Hospitallers, the pope and the kings of France and Cyprus assembled. They won a considerable naval victory, but dispersed without inflicting permanent damage on Umur whose raids continued.

Following the inactivity of Benedict XII's pontificate the enthusiastic Clement VI gathered a force from Venice, Genoa, Rhodes and Cyprus. In 1344 it surprised and captured Smyrna, the principal centre of Turkish piracy, and burnt much of Umur's fleet in the most positive and lasting Christian success of the century. Clement also launched a predominantly French crusading expedition but the response was undistinguished and the best available leader, Humbert du Viennois, was inept; he reached Smyrna in 1346, fought an indecisive engagement, opened truce negotiations and sailed away. Smyrna had been captured by those Levantine powers it particularly threatened, but none of them wanted the onerous responsibilities of its defence. In 1346 the Genoese betrayed the alliance and established themselves permanently on Chios which controlled the rich mines of nearby Phocaea, the principal source of the alum essential to Europe's textile industry. The Venetians quarrelled with the Hospitallers, who were left to defend Smyrna with papal assistance. In 1347 the Hospitallers defeated the Turks at sea off Imbros but only Clement's determination prevented their concluding a truce with the Turks at Smyrna. Umur's death in 1348 brought little immediate advantage to the Latins, for they faced a general economic and financial crisis and a catastrophic plague, the Black Death. The Venetians bargained hard for a new league which would protect their interests at the general expense but, after its renewal in 1350, they refused to pay their quarter share of the 12,000 florins needed to maintain 120 mercenaries at Smyrna. Meanwhile the Genoese gained control of access to the Black Sea and threatened Venice's hitherto prosperous commerce in *Romania*. In 1351 Venice went to war with Genoa on this issue, allying with the Turks, disrupting the whole Mediterranean and bringing the crusade to a standstill.[1]

A series of leagues designed to serve Genoese and Venetian interests and dependent on their seapower could not ensure continuous operations against the Turks. Papal intervention was limited by its expense. John XXII's four galleys each cost 600 florins monthly in 1334, and Clement VI's crusading expenditure of over 110,000 florins between 1345 and 1348 was exceptionally heavy. Subsequent popes, spending much more heavily on their Italian wars, regarded even 3,000 florins yearly for Smyrna as a burden.[2] From Avignon the Turks seemed remote. Influential cardinals like the great pope-maker Talleyrand were actively involved in preaching and organizing crusades, but few had experience of the East. Often cautious and reactionary, the cardinals could invoke bureaucratic curial procedures to obstruct or delay action.[3] The popes were

[1] Lemerle, *Aydin*, 19–238; Thiriet, 165–9; Luttrell, 'Venice', 203–5.

[2] Y. Renouard, *Les relations des papes d'Avignon et des compagnies commerciales et bancaires de 1316 à 1378* (Paris, 1941), 32 (tableaux A, C), 166–9, 249, 327–30, *et passim.*

[3] B. Guillemain, *La cour pontificale d'Avignon, 1309–1376* (Paris, 1962), 140, 222, 247–50, *et passim*; Atiya, 118, 306.

subject to countless pressures and Innocent VI, in particular, was changeable and easily influenced. He tried to end the Venetian war with Genoa, and he later resuscitated the Aegean league which defeated the Turks off Megara in about 1359.[1] When the ravages of the Catalans, Greeks and Turks threatened to produce a revolt at Corinth, the city and its defence were entrusted in 1358 to the Florentine Niccolò Acciaiuoli. Yet in 1359 Innocent declined Acciaiuoli's offer to arm a crusading fleet on the grounds that policy had already been decided by a committee of cardinals and could not be changed.[2] And by empowering the papal captain of Smyrna, the Florentine Hospitaller Niccolò Benedetti, to trade at Alexandria in order to pay for the garrison and fortifications, Innocent was financing one struggle at the expense of another. A more serious example of confused policy-making was the replacement of the Venetian archbishop of Crete Orso Delfini as papal legate commanding the successful Aegean league by a fanatical Carmelite, Pierre Thomas. The new legate reached Constantinople with a small force in 1359 and destroyed the Ottoman Turks' fort at Lampsacus in the Dardanelles, but his intransigent attitude towards all schismatics, coupled with the inadequacy of Latin military assistance, destroyed the slender possibilities of cementing an ecclesiastical union with the Greeks. Pierre Thomas then went to Cyprus, and the defence of *Romania* was neglected while he diverted papal, Hospitaller and Cypriot forces to Armenia in 1361, and later to Alexandria.[3]

With Smyrna captured and Umur dead the aggressive warrior elements of Anatolia, held in check on the Aegean by the Latins, gravitated away from Ionia towards Thrace. For centuries western Anatolia had been a bulwark of Byzantine power, but after their restoration in 1261 the Palaeologi had caused widespread discontent there through heavy taxation and their brutal persecution of the supporters of the former Lascarid régime at Nicaea. The frontier defences crumbled as Turkish raids and infiltration interrupted communications and aggravated economic decay. The Palaeologi, distracted by their

[1] Luttrell, 'Venice', 205–6. Cf. F. Giunta, 'Sulla politica orientale di Innocenzio VI', *Miscellanea in onore di Roberto Cessi*, i (Rome, 1958).

[2] J. Buchon, *Nouvelles recherches sur la principauté française de Morée*, ii (Paris, 1843), 135–6, 143–60.

[3] Smet, 84–97, 201–12 (on Smyrna, 206); Luttrell, 'Venice', 206.

Balkan problems, failed to react with sufficient vigour and in 1301 Osman, the founder of the Ottoman dynasty, won a notable victory near Nicaea. Osman and his son Orhan were petty raiders, chiefs of one of the many tribal units which had reasserted their identity after the Mongol conquests had released them from Seljuk domination. While a number of stronger Turkish emirates emerged in central and south-west Anatolia the Ottomans, a weaker group, were pushed to the fringe of the old Seljuk territories. This situation, however, enabled the Ottomans to canalize warlike enthusiasm against the Greeks and their wealth, first in Bithynia itself and subsequently in the Balkans.

In Bithynia the Ottomans captured Brusa in 1326, Nicaea in 1331 and Nicodemia in 1337. They overran the countryside, starved the cities into surrender and divided the great estates among their semi-nomadic followers who needed the pasturage and rendered cavalry service in return. The Anatolian peasants had to pay tribute but their desperate condition improved under Ottoman protection. The Ottomans' lack of religious or racial fanaticism facilitated the process of assimilation between Greeks and Turks. The Christians were treated with toleration and their collaboration sought; some Greeks learnt Turkish, some became Muslims. The Turks themselves were often unorthodox, and their culture derived from Persia rather than from the Mamluk-dominated Arab world. There was little co-operation between Mamluks and Turks in attacks on the Cilician Christians, though after the Latin sack of Alexandria in 1365 the Egyptians did propose a joint blockade and invasion of Cyprus and Rhodes. None the less Islam constituted an element of cohesion in building up support for the Ottomans and, to a limited extent, it inspired *ghazi* and dervish enthusiasm on the frontier, even if a greater incentive there was the pay and plunder provided by enterprising leaders such as Umur and Orhan, for whom war was an economic rather than a spiritual necessity. The first four Ottoman leaders, capable and determined men who enjoyed long reigns and kept power firmly in the hands of the dynasty, slowly created an Anatolian hegemony. They partially subdued the neighbouring emirates, gradually attracting supporters away from the older tribal groupings and absorbing them into the wider and more profitable sphere of Ottoman allegiance, a process which depended above all on success against the Christians.

The Ottomans profited from John V Palaeologus' struggle with his father-in-law John Cantacuzenus. Cantacuzenus tried to use the Latins against the Turks and the Turks against the Serbs, and he married his daughter to the Ottoman Orhan. So there had long been Turks serving in the Balkans when, following an earthquake in 1354, the Ottomans occupied Gallipoli and installed themselves permanently across the Dardanelles. The Latins were slow to act upon the need to co-operate with the Palaeologi. In 1353 Innocent VI replied to an appeal from the Greeks still resisting at Philadelphia in Anatolia that the price of Latin assistance was complete submission in matters of faith. Then Stephen Dushan, who had extended Serbian power into Albania, Epirus and Thessaly and threatened Byzantium with extinction, proposed an ecclesiastical and political union with the Latins whose seapower he needed; but his death in 1355 deprived Innocent of the champion he hoped might defend *Romania* against the Turks.

In 1355 John V, threatened by Turks and Serbs, revived the old project for the union of the Greek and Roman churches but, partly because Innocent could provide no significant military aid in return, the proposals lapsed. In 1360, when the papal legate abandoned both the Greeks and the Latins in *Romania*, the Latin naval league collapsed at once and all the available crusading forces were subsequently employed against the Mamluks; by 1361 Demotica and Adrianople in Thrace were in Ottoman hands. Genoa and Venice gave the Greeks some support and Amedeo of Savoy sailed to recapture Gallipoli in 1366, but John V, who even visited the pope at Rome in 1369, sought in vain for substantial Western help. Most Greeks were reluctant to accept the Roman church; many preferred co-existence with the Turks. The Balkans in general, hopelessly divided in race, politics and religion, provided only fragmentary opposition to the disciplined Ottoman troops. After crushing Serbian resistance at Cernomen in 1371 the Turks penetrated the valleys and plains of Macedonia and Albania and reached the Adriatic, devastating the crops and country. They were quite unable to settle or administer so much territory at once, but Ottoman successes made it increasingly easy to secure service from the Balkan and Anatolian nobles and their followers. There was probably a majority of Christian troops in many Ottoman armies.

In 1372 Pope Gregory XI, despairing of the West, encouraged the Levantine Latins to act in union and summoned them to an abortive conference at Thebes. Abandoning the insistence on ecclesiastical union, he also planned to send a small expedition of Hospitallers, the most he could hope to raise, to assist the Greeks in the Aegean or in the Dardanelles, where the Latins had conspicuously failed to use their seapower to obstruct Turkish communications. Then in 1373 John V, desperately poor, isolated in the face of a revolt by his son Andronicus and disillusioned with the Latins, became a tributary of the Ottoman Murad. This situation was not novel, but the pattern of affairs in which one or more of the Palaeologi were usually allied with the Ottomans against their own kinsmen, with Venice and Genoa taking opposite sides, now assumed permanent shape. In 1376 Andronicus allied with Murad and the Genoese, and handed back Gallipoli to the Turks; the Venetians occupied the island of Tenedos to counter the threat to the Dardanelles, and war with Genoa followed. In this strife the religious issue counted for little.[1]

Financial difficulties and the papacy's return to Rome in 1377 delayed the Hospitallers' expedition, and it was eventually diverted to protect the Latins in Greece. In 1377 the Hospitallers leased the principality of Achaea for five years from Joanna of Anjou, queen of Naples, and acquired the port of Vonitza in Epirus which was being attacked by the Albanian despot of Arta, Ghin Boua Spata. Early in 1378 a small force of Hospitallers under their master, Juan Fernández de Heredia, reached Vonitza. Then Gregory died and Urban VI, his successor, apparently failed to dispatch reinforcements.[2] Later in 1378 the Albanians, who probably had Turkish support, ambushed and defeated the Hospitallers near Arta. Soon after Latin Greece was thrown into confusion. The Acciaiuoli at Corinth were attacking the Catalans, and Thebes was captured by bands of Navarrese mercenaries who then invaded the Morea and set up a principality there. The Hospitallers eventually evacuated mainland Greece altogether in 1381.[3]

[1] In addition to Wittek and Georgiades Arnakis, see Smet, 64–80, 193–212; G. Dennis, *The Reign of Manuel II Palaeologus in Thessalonika: 1382–1387* (Rome 1960), 26–40, 52–6.

[2] Luttrell, 'Venice', 206–9; 'Interessi', 322–4; on Urban VI, C. du Boulay, *Historia universitatis parisiensis*, iv (Paris, 1668), 521.

[3] R.-J. Loenertz, 'Hospitaliers et Navarrais en Grèce, 1376–1383: régestes et documents', *Orientalia Christiana Periodica*, xxii (1956).

After the schism in 1378 the Avignonese pope, Clement VII, sought prestige by assisting the Hospitallers, most of whom supported him, in the defence of Rhodes and Smyrna. The Roman popes made contacts with the Palaeologi. Both sets of popes authorized crusades, some of them against their rival's supporters, but neither initiated any positive crusading action.[1] The Greeks' fate again depended largely upon Venice. Venetian traffic in *Romania* had been dwindling for several decades and had become less important than that in Egypt and Syria, partly because the breakup of the Mongol empire disrupted the caravan routes across Asia to the Black Sea. However, the Venetians were concerned to preserve their access to the products of the Black Sea area. They tried to slow down the Turks' advances while making trade agreements with them; in 1385 they refused to help the Greeks defend Thessalonika, but on other occasions they provided discreet assistance, as at Constantinople in 1395. Ottoman successes also compelled the Venetians to occupy certain strategic positions: Corfu, the key to their Adriatic lifeline; Argos and Nauplia in the Morea; and, in 1395, Athens.[2]

As the conflict became increasingly continental its Mediterranean aspects grew marginal and only the mountains held up the Turks. The Greeks, mingling defiance with appeasement, lost Serres in 1383 and Thessalonika in 1387. More important, the Serbs were defeated and Balkan resistance broken at Kossovo in 1389; Bulgaria was conquered by 1393; Constantinople besieged in 1394; the Morea ravaged in 1395. Then, with the Greeks in despair and the Latins in schism, the threat to Hungary and the lands across the Danube produced a reaction. Sigismund of Hungary with his vassal princes from Wallachia and Transylvania collected a great army. It included Germans and other northerners, but the union of the Polish and Lithuanian ruling houses in 1386 involved the Poles in struggles to the east and prevented the realization of the much-discussed Polish campaign against the Turks. A lull in the Anglo-French wars allowed the departure under Jean de Nevers, son of the duke of Burgundy, of a large chivalric Franco-Burgundian

[1] O. Halecki, 'Rome et Byzance au temps du Grand Schisme d'Occident', *Collectanea Theologica* (Lwow), xviii (1937); Dennis, 132–50.

[2] Thiriet, 353–63; Dennis, 123–7, *et passim*. Cf. F. Thiriet, 'Quelques observations sur le trafic des galées vénitiennes . . .', *Studi in onore di Amintore Fanfani*, iii (Milan, 1962), 502–3, 505–16.

contingent, genuine crusaders some of whom had fought at Mahdiya in 1390. No English participation was organized although both popes gave their blessing. Venetian, Genoese and Hospitaller forces arrived by sea and sailed up the Danube to Nicopolis where a horde of crusaders converged, slaughtering many Bulgarian Christians. Delayed by their lack of siege-engines, they indulged in demoralizing debauchery while Bayezid, the Ottoman leader, hurried up with his army and his Serbian vassals. There were probably some 20,000 men on either side. The French magnates were arrogant and over-confident, and their chivalric jealousies and quarrels led them to ignore Sigismund's more mature judgment. Without any proper plan of battle, they charged wildly at the auxiliary troops in the Turkish van and, when they had to dismount to uproot rows of pointed stakes, Sigismund's vassals fled at the sight of their riderless horses. The Turks' losses were heavy, but the superior disciplined mobility and the effectiveness of their archers allowed the regular Turkish cavalry to cut down the exhausted and largely horseless crusaders. The Christians suffered a colossal defeat.[1]

The news of Nicopolis provoked incredulity and dismay in the West. Many blamed the Hungarians, while Philippe de Mézières diagnosed a profound moral malaise in Christian society and called for a new crusade. The Franco-Burgundian nobility had been crushed and cruelly humiliated; it never again launched a major crusade. The Latins, however, could not altogether ignore the perilous situation of Constantinople. Isolationist Venice negotiated with Bayezid, but reluctantly sent aid to Constantinople to prevent the Turks acquiring control of the Straits and a stranglehold over Venetian grain supplies from the Black Sea. The Morea was ravaged again in 1397; then the Hospitallers occupied Corinth and defended the isthmus for seven years, probably saving the Morea from Turkish occupation. In 1399 the French marshal Boucicault, a veteran of Nicopolis, conducted a minor crusade designed to protect the interests of Genoa, then under French control. With an entourage of experienced warriors and with Venetian and Hospitaller assistance, he evaded twenty-seven Turkish ships

[1] Atiya, 435–62, and A. Atiya, *The Crusade of Nicopolis* (London, 1934); these works require considerable modification as, e.g., in C. Tipton, 'The English at Nicopolis', *Speculum*, xxxvii (1962).

and relieved Constantinople. Boucicault pillaged a number of villages on the Turkish coast and then, leaving a small Latin garrison at Constantinople, he returned to France to seek further help. The Emperor Manuel accompanied him and toured the courts of Europe, but with little result.[1]

While the Ottomans consolidated their territorial gains in the Balkans and Anatolia, Byzantium survived largely because the Turks lacked the naval strength to blockade Constantinople and the artillery to capture it.[2] But the overgrown Ottoman state was vulnerable in Asia. There the Turco-Mongol conqueror Timur, after defeating the Mamluks in Syria in 1400, won a decisive victory over the Ottomans near Ankara in 1402. Then, having captured Smyrna from the Hospitallers, he withdrew from the western fringes of the enormous Asiatic world and died in China in 1405. The Ottoman state was dismembered and almost destroyed. The Turks remained in Europe, but there followed some twenty years of comparative peace in the Levant. Constantinople was safe after seven years of siege, and in 1403 Christian truces with the Mamluks and Turks marked the end of an epoch.[3] The Latins had at last made good use of their seapower. Their support for the Greeks, though scanty, was extremely important in the crucial years between Nicopolis and Ankara.

Too often the Latins lost battles. The Mamluk state was efficiently organized for war by a military oligarchy. Standing armies and better tactics, weapon-drill and discipline, not numerical advantage, ensured Mamluk and Ottoman superiority. The Latins, like the Muslims, produced numerous treatises on the arts of war. They knew, in theory, the importance of bringing the enemy to battle and destroying him, and of tactical points such as sending out scouts and regrouping after a cavalry charge. Yet even when seapower and surprise brought initial successes the crusaders seldom ventured inland, and lack of stamina, of resources and of proper planning usually meant that advantages gained were soon lost. Pierre I of Cyprus raised

[1] R.-J. Loenertz, 'Pour l'histoire du Péloponnèse au XIVe siècle, 1382–1404', *Revue des études byzantines*, i (1943), 186–96; Delaville, *La France en Orient*, i, 337–83; Thiriet, 362–7.

[2] Atiya, 466.

[3] P. Wittek, 'De la défaite d'Ankara à la prise de Constantinople', *Revue des études islamiques*, xii (1938), 6–25. 1403 also saw an Aragonese-Sicilian truce with the Berber states (Brunschvig, i, 223–5).

a powerful force and successfully concealed its objective during the lengthy preparations necessary; he captured Alexandria but could not hold it. The Latins had shallow-draught barges which landed cavalry directly on to the beach, but horses were expensive and difficult to transport and, as at Mahdiya in 1390, their shortage could be crippling. In a fortified position the defenders still enjoyed the advantage. The Muslims employed naptha against wooden siege-engines, and although artillery came into use among the Latins, Moors, Berbers and Mamluks—but not the Ottomans—during the fourteenth century, only in the western Mediterranean did it play even a minor and indecisive part in Christian-Muslim conflicts. The Latins in their heavy armour suffered from heat, thirst and exhaustion, while bad wine and disease undermined their morale. The Muslims, lightly armed and extremely mobile, often avoided battle with the heavy Latin ironclad shock-troops, preferring to wear them down with guerrilla and skirmishing tactics. Experience and determination could overcome such manœuvres, as Ferdinand of Castile, victor at Antequera in 1410, showed in Spain where there was permanent contact with the Moors.[1] The Hospitallers provided a small but experienced standing army, available for crusading expeditions and often invaluable in covering a rearguard action. Western princes, however, tended to cut off their supplies, and the Hospitallers could seldom afford a proper navy, but at Rhodes they provided a secure base for crusading operations; they defended the Morea for seven critical years and held Smyrna until 1402. By contrast, the average crusader's excessive desire for personal glory or salvation repeatedly militated against success; at Nicopolis it was disastrous.

In 1365 Philippe de Mézières had to restrain Pierre Thomas from leaping into the water and singlehandedly precipitating a premature attack on Alexandria. Yet this spirit was the essence of the crusade. On the next day Pierre Thomas, as papal legate, stood high on a galley holding aloft a cross and blessed the crusaders: 'Chosen knights of Christ, be comforted in the Lord and His Holy Cross; fight manfully in God's war, fearing not your enemy and hoping for victory from God, for today the

[1] Atiya, 18–21, 482, *et passim*; Verbruggen, 575–7, *et passim*; Ayalon, 1–44, 141–2, *et passim*; Brunschvig, ii, 75–98; G. Scanlon, *A Muslim Manual of War* (Cairo, 1961), 4–21, *et passim*; I. MacDonald, *Don Fernando de Antequera* (Oxford, 1948), 33–51, *et passim*.

gates of Paradise are open.'[1] This concept of holy war could be exploited or perverted by colonialists, merchants, and freebooters, kings, popes and republics only because it retained some meaning in the Latin conscience. Men, though not necessarily less religious, were turning away from the church and its institutions, including the crusade, yet traditional ideals survived alongside growing pacifist and anti-crusade sentiment. For many the failure of the *gesta Dei per Francos* was explicable only in terms of a divine judgment upon their sins; and their sins included greed, jealousy, disunity and a stupid lack of planning. Until the schism the popes tried to encourage the crusade but, like the secular princes, they gave precedence to their problems in the West. The crusade could never become a coherent foreign policy for Christendom, the successful defence of which necessitated something more permanent than an irregular series of chivalric expeditions with varied objectives. Once resistance against the Turks had become the first essential, Tunis, Egypt and even Armenia were false objectives, and Jerusalem a mere distraction. The crusade lost almost all its appeal as a popular movement, and during the fourteenth century came to depend, except where Latin lands or interests were directly threatened, on small groups and individuals: a pope; the duke of Burgundy; the Hospitallers; or bodies of French nobles. The crusade's betrayal by those whose economic position it threatened seemed inevitable. Emmanuele Piloti, the Cretan merchant in Egypt, saw that materialist urban patriciates rather than chivalric princes were predominant in the Mediterranean world and, convinced of the immutable nature of the trade between the Orient and the Mediterranean and of the Christians' dependence upon it, he realized that a blockade was unenforceable. In his crusading treatise he argued that the conflict between crusading and commercial objectives could only be resolved by harnessing the Latins' seapower and their desire for gain to a crusade in which the great commercial powers would seize control of Egypt and its wealth, and of the holy places as well.

By 1402 the crusade had failed to recover Jerusalem, to succour the Eastern Christians, or to defend the Balkans, though Cyprus, the Aegean islands, parts of Greece, and Constantinople

[1] Smet, 103, 131.

were still in Christian hands. Eastern Europe protected itself more successfully during the fifteenth century than the West had the Balkans in the fourteenth. For many crusaders the holy war came to involve the defence of their homelands, and John Hunyadi in Hungary and Serbia, Skanderbeg in Albania and other great patriots fought to save Europe from the Turks. Western European forces occasionally participated, as in the Varna crusade of 1444; the Hospitallers repulsed Mamluk and Ottoman attacks on Rhodes; the Council of Florence sought theological agreement between Latins and Greeks; and, after the fall of Constantinople in 1453, Pius II and other popes belatedly projected crusading expeditions.[1]

The papacy also encouraged the renewed, oceanic expansion of Christendom, in which financial, nautical and colonial techniques largely developed in the Levant were transferred by Italian merchants and sailors to the Atlantic world. Following the discovery of the first Atlantic islands before 1339 by Lanzarotto Malocello, an Italian galley-captain in Portuguese service, a series of Mallorcan, Catalan, Castilian and Portuguese expeditions, some with genuine missionary aims, set out for the Canaries. The Portugese advance along the African coast, inaugurated in 1415 with the capture of Ceuta from the Moors, soon received official papal patronage as an extension of the *reconquista*. The chivalric Portuguese leaders' crusading sentiments were partly sincere. They really hoped to find a Christian ally, perhaps even a black Prester John, in Africa or Asia; they were not totally cynical in claiming that by securing gold and slaves from West Africa, for centuries a Muslim zone of influence, they were impoverishing Islam and that in enslaving the natives they were making new Christians.[2] The completion of the *reconquista* in Spain by the capture of Granada in 1492 coincided with the opening of a new field for the *conquistadores* in America. In 1513 the Portuguese Albuquerque, having destroyed the Mamluk fleet in the Indian Ocean, considered that it would be easy to land a force in the Red Sea, capture Mohammed's body at Medina,

[1] O. Halecki, 'The Defence of Europe in the Renaissance Period', *Didascaliae: Studies in Honor of Anselm M. Albareda* (New York, 1961).

[2] J. Vincke, 'Die Evangelisation der Kanarischen Inseln im 14. Jahrhundert im Geiste Raimund Lulls', *Estudios lulianos*, iv (1960); G. Pistarino, 'I Portoghesi verso l'*Asia* del Prete Gianni', *Studi medievali* (Spoleto), III ser., ii (1961), 113–37, *et passim*; P. Russell, *Prince Henry the Navigator* [=*Diamante*, xi (1960)]; R. Mauny, *Navigations médiévales sur les côtes sahariennes antérieures à la découverte portugaise (1434)* (Lisbon, 1960, 53–70).

and exchange it for the temple at Jerusalem.[1] Christendom had outflanked Islam on the oceans, while on land the Christians of eastern Europe, who had sheltered the West from the barbarians for so long, gradually halted the Turks. The objectives of the holy war had always changed as circumstances altered and, although enthusiasm for the crusade progressively declined, its ideals survived the disaster at Nicopolis in 1396 just as they had the fall of Acre in 1291.

[1] *The Commentaries of the Great Afonso Dalboquerque*, trans. W. Birch, iv (London, 1884), 37.

ADDENDA ET CORRIGENDA

Study I

P.254 (and XIV p.581): For "1391" read "1390": Malta, cod. 11 no. 11. On the defence of Smyrna, see the forthcoming monograph: A. Luttrell, Timur in Anatolia: July 1402 to March 1403 (provisional title).

P.266 n.91: See also A.Forey, "The Military Orders in the Crusading Proposals of the Late-Thirteenth and Early-Fourteenth Centuries," Traditio XXXVI (1980).

Studies II-V

These items should eventually be revised to create a more coherent account of Hospitaller historiography. Note that the Hospital's surviving Syrian parchments seem to have disappeared in 1291 and to have reached Malta only in the eighteenth century: R.Hiestand, Papsturkunden für Templer und Johanniter (Göttingen, 1972).

Study II

Pp.149-150: On Caorsin, see K.Setton, The Papacy and the Levant, 1204-1571, II (Philadelphia, 1978), 346-363, 392-394.

Study III

Pp.68-69: See also K.Shimizu, "Un curioso dialogo sull'Ordine dei Cavalieri di Malta nel Cinquecento," in Studies in Socio-Cultural Aspects of the Mediterranean Islands (Tokyo, 1979).

Study VIII

Pp.41 & 46: The Enghiens claimed only Athens, not Neopatras which the Catalans did not conquer in 1311 but took from the Greeks in 1318/9.

Pp.52 & 54: D.Jacoby, "Quelques considérations sur les versions de la Chronique de Morée," Journal des Savants (1968), reprinted in Société et démographie à Byzance et en Romanie latine (London, 1975), 167 n.164, points out that since the lands of Jacques de Veligourt were in Elis, they cannot be identified with the three fiefs in the region of Argos and Corinth. He observes that di raggione must mean "by right", and adds that there is no evidence that Renaud de Veligourt, Rinaldo de Valgonato and Rinaldo delle Porte were the same person.

Pp.53-55: D.Jacoby, La féodalité en Grèce médiévale: les "Assises de Romanie" - sources, application et diffusion (Paris/The Hague, 1971), 215 n.3, 218 n.2, argues for the readings di possiesses (possessions) at p.53 (last line); Porico or Aporico Catello at p.54 (line 6); che la eredita at p.54 (line 10); and possesso e uno corpo at p.55 (line 8).

Study IX

In addition to M.Balard, La Romanie génoise: XIIe - début du XVe siècle, 2 vols. (Rome/Genoa, 1978), see M. Balard, "A propos de la Bataille du Bosphore: l'expédition génoise de Paganino Doria à Constantinople (1351-1352)," Travaux et Mémoires IV (1970); M. Costa, "Sulla Battaglia del Bosforo: 1352," Studi Veneziani XIV (1972); G.Meloni, "Sull'alleanza veneto-aragonese all'epoca di Pietro il Cerimonioso," in his Medioevo: Età Moderna (Padua, 1972); C.Kyrris, "John Cantacuzenus, the Genoese, the Venetians, and the Catalans: 1348-1354," Byzantion IV (1972).

Study XI

P.219: Nerio Acciaiuoli was Niccolò's adoptive son..

P.220 n.1: See also K.Setton, Los Catalanes en Grecia (Barcelona, 1975).

P.234: Albertí was apparently the son of Ramón, not Galcerán de Vilanova.

P.243: For "Urban VII" read "Urban VI".

Study XIV

P.576: For "1334" read "1344".

P.578: Line 28 should commence: "difficult to construct".

P.581: See Addenda to I p.254.

Study XV

P.413 n.88: Add A.Luttrell, "Appunti sulle Compagnie Navarresi in Grecia: 1376-1404," Rivista Internazionale di Studi Bizantini e Slavi (forthcoming).

P.416: Read "prouincia di thoscana, essendo esso ito a ..."

INDEX

The Index lists most personal and many place names in their simplest form, omitting place names of very general interest such as "Venice","Rhodes","Achaia" and so forth. The initial table of contents provides a broad indication of topics covered; thus the names of slaves at Rhodes are not indexed but can be found in Item VI, while Catalan merchants' names are in Item XI. All Hospitaller brethren (Fr. for *Frater*) and possessions (*Langues*, Priories, Preceptories and *Casales*) are listed. An asterisk indicates a note in the *Corrigenda et Addenda*.

WESTFIELD
UNIV.
LONDON
COLLEGE